Beyond the Surface

*Navigating Challenges & Finding Fulfillment
In Modern Muslim Marriages*

Qasim Rafique
Scottish Relationship Coach

Copyright © 2025 by Qasim Rafique

The right of Qasim Rafique to be identified as the author of this work has been asserted in accordance with the Copyright, Designs and Patents Act of 1988.

All rights reserved. No part of this publication may be reproduced, stored in a retrieval system, or transmitted, in any form or by any means, electronic, mechanical, digital, photocopying, recording or otherwise, nor translated into a machine language, without the written permission of the Qasim Rafique.

Published by IDIFY Publishing
www.idifyconsulting.com

Cover Design: Gould Studio
hello@gouldstudio.com

Book Design: Megan McCullough

ISBN: 979-8-9852918-5-8 Hardcover
ISBN: 979-8-9852918-3-4 Paperback
ISBN: 979-8-9852918-4-1 Digital

First Printing May 2025
Printed in the United States of America

Visit website at:
www.QasimRafique.com

Social Media:
Instagram: @Qasim_Rafique_Scottish
www.facebook.com/QasimRafiqueRelationshipExpert
www.facebook.com/Qasim.Rafique.Scotland

Email:
BeyondTheSurfaceQR@gmail.com

About the Author

Qasim Rafique was born in the quiet valleys of Wales and raised in the rugged beauty of Scotland—two landscapes that shaped his inner resilience and sharpened his sense of justice. He was educated at Kelvinside Academy, a historic boys' school founded in 1878, where he was shaped by tradition, excellence, and discipline— though emotional depth, like in many such institutions, remained quietly in the background. But Qasim was never built for surface living. Even as a boy, he was drawn to a deeper calling—the need to serve, to protect, to make sense of human pain in a world that often silences it.

He began his journey in the Strathclyde Police Force, wearing the badge with pride and purpose. But beneath the uniform, questions burned. The questions no academy, no badge, no protocol could answer: *Why do people break? Why do they betray? Why do some wounds never heal?*

Then came the rupture that changed everything.

His mother—a deeply soulful and vibrant woman, whose quiet strength and nurturing heart left an indelible mark on everyone she touched—was only 43 when she returned to her Lord after a sudden heart condition back in 2001. That moment, raw and devastating, shattered his world. Her death wasn't just a personal tragedy—it was an emotional earthquake that split his identity in two: the man he was, and the man he was called to become.

Grief didn't take him to a therapist's office. It took him to the Himalayas.

In 2008, Qasim joined a British expedition on Mount Everest. He wasn't chasing adrenaline. He was searching for meaning—something beyond the ache, beyond the badge, beyond the anger he didn't yet know he carried. The team raised powerful awareness and funds for the British Heart Foundation, which he did in honor of his mother—but Qasim came back with more than fundraising stats. He came back *transformed*. Something cracked open on that mountain—something spiritual, something ancestral, something real.

Something in him had shifted forever. The police force—once a symbol of order and justice—began to feel like the wrong battlefield. He realized that the real wars were being fought behind closed doors, in homes, in hearts, in conversations never had. And so, with quiet conviction, he changed course—not to escape pain, but to walk straight into it, to understand it, to meet it in others.

He began with the body—the vessel that carries trauma, stress, heartbreak, and suppressed emotion. He studied naturopathic nutrition at the College of Naturopathic Medicine (CNM) in Edinburgh, Scotland, seeking to understand how what we consume affects not just our health, but also our mood, our energy, and even our relationships. However, he soon discovered that nutrition science alone couldn't heal the deeper wounds people carried.

He wanted to go further. Deeper. Into the invisible forces that drive human behavior—into the messy, beautiful, sometimes brutal world of love, loss, and emotional survival.

Today, Qasim is a certified practitioner in Cognitive Behavioral Therapy (CBT), Neuro-Linguistic Programming (NLP), and hypnotherapy. He is also an internationally certified relationship and life coach, specializing in one of the most excruciating human experiences: infidelity recovery. This is not just his profession—it is his life's work.

Beyond his therapeutic and coaching roles, Qasim also serves as a consultant in **Human Trafficking Prevention** and **Human Rights**, where he brings his trauma-informed lens to global issues of injustice, exploitation, and systemic harm. His work in this space reflects the same unwavering commitment to protecting human dignity, healing deep wounds, and giving voice to the silenced.

He has completed specialized courses and undergone extensive training with elite organizations, including the globally renowned Gottman Institute in Seattle and has spent years immersed in the trenches of human pain: betrayal, childhood trauma, communication breakdowns, failed marriages, emotional abandonment, broken attachment systems, father wounds, mother wounds, and the silent grief of men who were never taught to feel.

Qasim's work is gritty, grounded, and deeply spiritual. He doesn't offer fairy tales or surface-level advice. He walks people through their darkness—and then helps them find the light. His clients range from young couples wrestling with the hopes and fears of lifelong commitment to divorcees trying to rebuild their lives from the ashes of heartbreak.

He is an accomplished author and a prominent voice on social media, known for blending clinical insight with compassion, and raw truth with practical wisdom. His content doesn't coddle—it awakens. Through his words, his coaching, and his lived experience, he has become a powerful guide for men and women seeking real, lasting change in their relationships and within themselves.

Drawing from years of coaching, therapeutic training, Islamic spirituality, and his own scars, Qasim offers more than strategies—he offers soul medicine. His mission is simple but radical: to help people love with integrity, heal with honesty, and live with courage.

Connect with Qasim:

Instagram: @Qasim_Rafique_Scottish

Website: www.QasimRafique.com

Email: BeyondTheSurfaceQR@gmail.com

Author's Note to Readers

All views expressed in this book are based on the author's personal experiences, observations, and extensive knowledge gained through working with individuals and couples. In addition to these personal insights, the book draws heavily on the expertise of renowned relationship scientists and professionals in the field of relationships. It also integrates faith-based principles derived from the Qur'an and Sunnah, offering a comprehensive and balanced approach.

While the author has made every effort to seek out correct Islamic sources and scholarly opinions, he does not claim to be a qualified Islamic scholar. Readers are encouraged to seek further clarification from trusted scholars and to approach any religious matters mentioned in the book through a scholastic lens. The author has worked tirelessly to ensure fairness, balance, and accuracy throughout the text, aiming to honor both the spiritual and relational dimensions of the topics discussed.

Some AI tools were utilized to assist in sourcing information and references from articles and scientific journals, enhancing the depth and breadth of the content. Any names and identifying details used in illustrative case examples have been changed to protect privacy.

The material is thoughtfully designed to assist and support readers in their journey toward building healthier relationships. However, it is important to note that while the insights provided are grounded in both scientific research and faith-based wisdom, they are not guaranteed to yield the same results for every reader. This book is intended to serve as a valuable tool for fostering a healthy marriage but should not be relied upon as the sole solution for achieving that goal, nor does it substitute for therapy.

Dedication

This book is dedicated to my beloved wife Yasmin, whose quiet strength and unwavering presence anchor my soul; to my children, whose laughter lights the corridors of my heart and reminds me daily of life's sacred purpose; and to my late mother, Asphia (may Allah envelop her in mercy), whose past prayers still shield me and whose wisdom echoes in every decision I make.

To those navigating heartache, uncertainty, or the long, silent nights of self-doubt—this is for you. To the ones rebuilding after betrayal, to the men and women searching for belonging, love, or healing—this book was born from the same soil of pain and transformation that you now walk upon. I have been where you are: shattered, questioning, searching. But I promise you, there is light beyond the wreckage.

I write these pages not as one who has mastered life, but as one who has wrestled with it—bled, healed, and risen with scars that now speak louder than shame. If this book holds any worth, let it be this: that in your darkest hour, you remember you are not alone. You are not broken beyond repair. You are not abandoned.

This book is a prayer in ink. A map drawn in tears and tawbah (repentance). A quiet whisper to every soul that has ever felt forgotten: you are seen. You are loved. And your story is not over.

With all that I am,
Qasim Rafique

Qasim Rafique
Scottish Relationship Coach

Contents

About the Author..iii
Dedication..ix
Foreword...1
Introduction..3

Foundations of Muslim Marriages

Chapter One: The Muslim Marriage Dilemma......................................7
Chapter Two: Lessons Learned, Lives Transformed.............................13
Chapter Three: Faith in the Face of Challenges...................................15
Chapter Four: Modern Courtship: The Good, Bad, and Ugly.............19
Chapter Five: Spotting Red Flags in Courtship...................................25
Chapter Six: Essential Questions During Courting.............................29
Chapter Seven: Lavish Weddings, Heavy Mahr: The Cost of Tradition..43

Building Strong Marital Foundations

Chapter Eight: Beyond the Honeymoon Phase...................................47
Chapter Nine: The Layers of Love..51
Chapter Ten: "You Complete Me" – Myth or Reality?........................53
Chapter Eleven: Growing Through Love..57
Chapter Twelve: Purposeful Conversations...61

Challenges in Marriage

Chapter Thirteen: Surviving Toxic In-Law Drama 65

Chapter Fourteen: Addicted to Pain: Breaking Free from Trauma Bonds ... 71

Chapter Fifteen: Outsmarting the Narcissist's Game 77

Chapter Sixteen: Parental Alienation: A Child's Heartbreak 109

Chapter Seventeen: Pornography: The Hidden Wound That Bleeds Marriages Dry 115

Chapter Eighteen: Ashes of Us: How Infidelity Burns What We Built .. 121

Chapter Nineteen: More Than Flirting: The Hidden Wounds of Emotional Affairs 127

Chapter Twenty: Two Hearts, One Trust: The Guardianship of Love ... 133

Chapter Twenty-One: The Polygyny Puzzle: Navigating the Complexities in Modern Times 139

Mental and Emotional Health in Marriage

Chapter Twenty-Two: The Silent Struggles: Vaginismus and Erectile Dysfunction 149

Chapter Twenty-Three: Mental Health and Marriage 157

Chapter Twenty-Four: Healing After Abuse 167

Chapter Twenty-Five: Culture vs. Islam 175

Chapter Twenty-Six: The Emasculation Epidemic 183

Chapter Twenty-Seven: The Missing Links Between Intimacy and Connection 193

Chapter Twenty-Eight: The Sleep Connection in Marriage 203

Psychological Insights and Practical Tools

Chapter Twenty-Nine: Mastering Conflict Management 211

Chapter Thirty: Attachment Styles in Love 221

Chapter Thirty-One: Hormones and Their Hidden Impact 227

Chapter Thirty-Two: The Art of Marriage Communication 241

Chapter Thirty-Three: Childhood Trauma's Grip on Marriage 251

Strengthening and Affair-Proofing Marriage

Chapter Thirty-Four: Affair-Proofing Your Marriage 259

Chapter Thirty-Five: Infidelity Recovery: Healing Together 269

Contemporary Issues in Relationships

Chapter Thirty-Six: Cracking Relationship Slang 277

Chapter Thirty-Seven: Dating Apps: Modern Love or Social Chaos? .. 283

Chapter Thirty-Eight: Your Phone vs. Your Marriage 297

Chapter Thirty-Nine: Modern Masculinity Redefined 307

Chapter Forty: The Gift and the Grief of Feminism 319

Emotional and Spiritual Dimensions of Marriage

Chapter Forty-One: Mother Wound - Father Wound 331

Chapter Forty-Two: Emotional Intelligence 339

Chapter Forty-Three: Emotional Incest (Parental Enmeshment) 351

Chapter Forty-Four: Athkar: Protecting Marriage Through
   Remembrance 359

Conclusion

Chapter Forty-Five: Conclusion: A Heartfelt Reflection on Love,
    Resilience, and Growth 375

Bibliography 379

Foreword

So often we hear terrifying statistics about the divorce rate. The argument we often hear is that people have simply lost their sense of commitment and sanctity for marriage. There is a popular notion that "if they wanted to, they would." But, I would argue that this notion is not exactly accurate. I would argue that most people would do better–if they had the proper tools and capacity. And so I would argue, it is more accurate to say: "If they could, they would."

Now, don't get me wrong. I don't mean that people have no power over the choices they make in life and in relationships. I mean something more nuanced. Each and every one of us is a product of our past, our childhood programming, our trauma wounds, and the survival strategies we developed along the way.

We each carry a box of "tools" into every relationship. These tools are meant to help us regulate our emotions and communicate our needs in a healthy way. But for many people, that box is empty. For others, that box is full of outdated and, in many cases, harmful programmed strategies. Many of these strategies were passed on from generation to generation in a toxic cycle of trauma. Many people enter relationships full of shame and core beliefs of unworthiness. Some enter with abandonment wounds, while others carry a fear of engulfment.

So many people misunderstand why they get "triggered" in intimate relationships. Triggers are nothing but pointers to our unhealed wounds and programmed coping strategies. Triggers can actually help us recognize our dysfunctional "tool kit". But most people deflect blame onto their partners.

And so, relationships often fail–not because people don't want it to work–but because the programming and the tools they bring into the relationship do not serve them.

Beyond the Surface is a book that provides those healthy tools. It delves deep into the most pressing issues facing modern Muslim marriages and provides practical steps towards healthier and more fulfilling relationships. Qasim provides a roadmap to understand and heal the deep rooted causes of marital breakdown.

This is a book that is desperately needed today.

Yasmin Mogahed

Introduction

> *"Life can only be understood backwards;
> but it must be lived forwards."*
> -Søren Kierkegaard 1843

There are mottos you forget. And then there are mottos that get carved into your soul.

At Kelvinside Academy—a private school founded in 1878—amid the grey, windswept days of 1980s Glasgow, Scotland, I first encountered the phrase that would not only shape my life, but quietly haunt my soul.

ΑΙΕΝ ΑΡΙΣΤΕΥΕΙΝ — Aien Aristeuein.
"Ever to Excel."

An ancient Greek ideal, lifted from Homer's *Iliad*, it wasn't just printed above the school crest. It became a whisper in my conscience, a kind of silent dare: Don't settle. Don't shrink. Don't die with your potential still caged inside you.

Even as a wee boy—in my school uniform, shorts and knee-high socks, blazer, tie, and cap, with a brown leather satchel strapped to my back—I sensed it was more than just a slogan. It was a summons. And somehow, with God's mercy, I've carried that ancient echo in my heart across every battlefield of my life.

But here's the thing no school motto will prepare you for: excellence doesn't come wrapped in applause. It comes soaked in grief, blood, loneliness, and soul-deep wrestling.

In 2001, I lost my mother—my rock, my mirror, my heart. She was only 43. May Allah (God) have endless mercy on her soul. I was barely in my

20s. A young father, a young husband, a young son—suddenly motherless. No script. No manual. Just grief like a hurricane, and me, a kite with a torn string, flying ragged through a world that suddenly felt unsafe.

They don't tell you that death rearranges you. It doesn't just take someone you love; it forces you to meet the versions of yourself that only grief can introduce. I met my despair. I met my rage. I met my helplessness. And I met the boy inside me who still wanted his mother to say, "I'm proud of you."

But even that loss, even that breaking, planted a seed.

By 2016, after walking through hells of my own making and others', I published my first book: *7 Life Lessons on the Myths of Marriage*. It wasn't born from a place of success, but from the wreckage—**divorce, debt, failure, humiliation, confusion, and the desperate need to make sense of why things kept falling apart**. It was less a triumph and more a survival cry. And a turning point.

Because "ever to excel" isn't about perfect outcomes—it's about refusing to numb yourself and call it peace.

I was the eldest child. The family empath. I had a radar for pain, a sixth sense for disappointment in the room. From an early age, I carried an invisible burden: *keep the peace, hold the family together, never fall apart, be okay so everyone else can be okay.*

But I wasn't okay.

My father was a man torn between two unforgiving worlds: the rigid, stoic masculinity of the 1970s—where emotions were buried, not spoken—and the weight of traditional Pakistani culture, where honor came before healing, and silence often masked suffering. He wasn't taught how to feel—only how to survive.

He had moved to the UK in the 1970s, bringing with him all he knew: a deeply embedded Pakistani culture riddled with unspoken generational trauma. What he carried across continents wasn't just heritage—it was heartbreak handed down from father to son, wrapped in expectations, patriarchal pride, and emotional suppression disguised as strength.

He worked very hard. He sacrificed. But emotionally, he was often an empty chair. Present, but unreachable. Loving, but distant. I grew up hungry—for affection, for connection, for a father I could feel.

My mother? She was warmth, presence, poetry. But even her love couldn't protect me from the subtle wounds of inconsistency and the emotional abandonment that shaped my attachment patterns. I became the classic anxious-avoidant. The one who wants closeness but flinches when it arrives. Who craves love but doesn't trust it. Who yearns for security but sabotages it.

And yet—through the chaos, faith was the thread that never snapped.

In the blackest nights of my soul, when I didn't recognize myself anymore, it was only Allah who saw me. Only dhikr that anchored me. Only sujood that reminded me I still had worth, even when the world said otherwise. Faith didn't save me from the darkness. It walked me through it. Step by trembling step.

Years later, those broken pieces—those heartbreaks, divorces, disillusions—became a map. Not just to my own healing, but to the healing of others. I started seeing the patterns. The emotional blueprints. The traumas people were dragging into marriage like unspoken ghosts. That's when I realized: *This is why I was made to feel it all. So I could help others name what they never had the words for.*

That's how *Beyond the Surface* was born—not as a book, but as a **lifeline**. A mirror. A balm. A reckoning. Eight years in the making. Not because I lacked the words, but because I needed the wounds to mature into wisdom.

We're living in a time where marriage is under siege.

Not from one enemy—but from a thousand little cracks:

- The dopamine high of Instagram and the soul-deadening lows of pornography.
- The normalized betrayal of emotional affairs and digital flirtations.
- The slow death of intimacy under the glare of glowing screens.
- Fatherlessness. Narcissism. Phone addiction. Trauma bonding. Broken men. Numb women. And children caught in the crossfire.

We're not just fighting for love—we're fighting for the very definition of what love means.

Sex has been monetized. Commitment has been mocked. Trust has been shattered. The sacred has been made shallow. And many Muslims—despite our beautiful tradition—are drowning in silence, shame, and confusion.

I've sat with them. The betrayed wives, the heartbroken husbands, the confused singles, the angry sons, the shut-down daughters. I've looked into their eyes and seen the same pain I once carried.

This book is for them.
For you.
For the part of you that is still searching for something real. For the part that wants to believe that healing is possible. That marriage can still be sacred. That men and women were not created to be rivals—but divine counterparts in a journey of growth.

Beyond the Surface is not neat. It's not always pretty. It's messy, raw, honest—and **unapologetically human**. It digs beneath the curated highlight reels and explores the quiet desperation so many of us live with but never say out loud.

If there's one truth I've learned, it's this:

Excellence doesn't mean perfection. It means refusing to give up on becoming whole.

And if I can pass anything on from this journey, it's this:

Pain is not the end of your story.
Faith is still your superpower.
And **"Ever to Excel"**—with Allah as your support—means you rise again. Every. Single. Time.

Chapter One

The Muslim Marriage Dilemma

In every generation, the path to marriage has presented its own unique set of challenges—but today's landscape feels particularly complex. For many Muslims, finding a suitable spouse has become a deeply emotional and often frustrating journey, marked by confusion, cultural tensions, and spiritual longing. Whether you're a young adult navigating the pressures of compatibility and timing, a divorcee seeking a second chance, or someone simply trying to make sense of the process, the struggle is increasingly real and widespread.

This isn't just a crisis of logistics—it's a reflection of deeper societal shifts: the rise of individualism, changing gender dynamics, globalised expectations, and the erosion of traditional support systems. What once was a communal and spiritually guided process has, in many cases, become a solitary pursuit filled with uncertainty and noise. And while Muslims are not alone in facing these difficulties, the intersection of faith, family, and modernity adds a unique layer of complexity.

Understanding this dilemma requires more than just listing statistics or anecdotes. It calls for a compassionate and honest look at the emotional, psychological, spiritual, and cultural factors shaping the modern Muslim experience of courtship and marriage. Only by acknowledging these layered realities can we begin to heal what feels fractured—and chart a path forward that honors both our values and our humanity.

10 Raw, Present-Day Reasons Why Many Muslims Struggle to Get Married – and Why Their Relationships Keep Crashing

1. **Emotional Intensity Too Soon:** Many people mistake emotional hunger for emotional connection. They dive in too deep, too fast—pouring their heart out, fantasizing about the future, and building castles on unstable foundations. What they call "connection" is often just desperation in disguise. Without pacing, discernment, and structure, intensity becomes volatility. Emotional maturity means slowing down, checking your blind spots, and letting time reveal what chemistry can't.

2. **Lingering Attachments to the Past:** You can't build a future while secretly grieving the past. Whether it's an ex, a situationship that never turned official, or a ghost of what could've been, unhealed emotions contaminate new beginnings. Many bring emotional residue into new relationships—comparing, overprotecting, or projecting. Until you confront your past with honesty, clarity, and closure, it will haunt your present and sabotage your future.

3. **Fear of Being Alone:** Too many enter marriage looking for a savior, not a partner. They're not seeking love—they're seeking escape. Escape from family pressure, loneliness, heartbreak, self-doubt. But marriage built on avoidance becomes a trap. The inability to sit with one's own solitude often results in clinging to the wrong person. You must learn to be whole on your own before inviting someone else into your life.

4. **Unrealistic or Rigid Standards:** Many people claim they want a "good" spouse—but their definition of "good" is often based on status, aesthetics, or cultural checklists. They overlook spiritual compatibility, emotional presence, and shared values in favor of superficial traits. Worse still, they expect a spouse to be flawless while ignoring their own need for growth. A spouse isn't a trophy—it's a test of your own character. If your standards are stricter than your own self-work, something's off.

5. **Fast-Tracked Intimacy Without Foundation:** Whether it's late-night emotional oversharing or crossing physical boundaries too

soon, many relationships collapse under the weight of premature closeness. That deep conversation you had at 2AM may feel like a connection—but without spiritual clarity or commitment, it's just emotional vulnerability without a container. Attachment without alignment is a ticking time bomb. When the high fades, you're left with confusion, guilt, and no road map for what's next.

6. **Confusing Chemistry with Compatibility:** What feels electric isn't always safe. That "spark" you feel may not be divine guidance—it might be your trauma getting excited. People chase chemistry like it's proof of destiny, but relationships don't survive on dopamine. Compatibility is boring to some because it doesn't set your heart on fire—it sets your life on solid ground. Lasting love is found not in adrenaline, but in trust, values, and the hard conversations you don't avoid.

7. **Ignoring or Rationalizing Red Flags:** You saw it. You felt it. That spiritual mismatch, the anger under the surface, the subtle manipulation. But you told yourself, "Maybe they'll change." Or "Everyone has flaws." Or "At least they pray." Love is not blind—denial is. Many people ignore their gut to avoid being alone, only to end up lonelier inside the wrong relationship. The signs are often there—we just don't want to see them.

8. **Lack of Tawakkul (Trust in Allah) and Sabr (Patience):** Courtship can be frustrating. Delays feel personal. Every "no" feels like a rejection of your worth. But what we call delays, Allah calls protection. Tawakkul isn't passive—it's choosing peace while actively doing the work. Many panic when things don't move quickly, forcing what was never meant to be. But sacred love is slow. It requires surrender, not desperation. Sabr is not suffering in silence—it's strategic endurance with your eyes on Allah's wisdom.

9. **Parental Pressure and Cultural Mismatch:** Some people carry the weight of entire families on their shoulders. They're torn between obedience and authenticity. Pressured to marry someone from "back home" or of a certain caste or class, they feel suffocated by expectations that don't reflect their values or reality. Others internalize guilt for disappointing parents or rejecting culturally-ideal proposals. The result? Stuck in limbo, confused about whose happiness they're really chasing.

10. Emotional Unavailability and Lack of Self-Work: Marriage is a mirror. If you haven't faced your fears, healed your wounds, or built emotional muscles, marriage will expose all of it. Many walk into relationships wearing masks—trying to perform love instead of embodying it. They don't know how to apologize, listen deeply, self-regulate, or sit with their own discomfort. That's not just a skill gap—it's a self-work gap. Without internal clarity, they carry unresolved baggage into every relationship they touch.

The Silent Crisis of Modern Marriages

There is a crisis unfolding in our homes, behind wedding photos, Instagram smiles, and polite masjid conversations. It's silent, not because it's small—but because it's hidden. Marriages are breaking not just from incompatibility, but from a deeper, darker place: emotional neglect, unhealed trauma, and a collective loss of what it truly means to commit, to grow, to love through difficulty.

This is not just about "not finding the right one." Many do find someone. They say *Bismillah*, sign the contract, celebrate with flowers and fanfare. But what they weren't prepared for—what no one taught them—is that marriage will demand every part of you: your ego, your childhood wounds, your unspoken fears, your patience, your humility, your capacity to forgive, and your willingness to *truly* see someone else in all their imperfection—and still stay, still fight for the bond.

Our parents and grandparents, for all their generational flaws, had something we often lack: *grit*. They knew marriage wasn't always happiness—it was *work*. It was a divine test. They didn't glamorize love; they grounded it. They didn't run at the first sign of discomfort—they dug their heels into *sabr* and *tawakkul*. Not because they were naïve, but because they saw marriage as a spiritual contract, not just an emotional experience. A sacred trust (*amanah*), not a lifestyle upgrade.

But let's not romanticize the past either. Too many women suffered in silence. Too many men were emotionally disconnected. Too many children grew up in homes full of quiet resentment. So let's be honest: the answer is not to replicate the old ways blindly. Endurance *without healing* is just prolonged dysfunction. Islam never asked us to suffer quietly in toxic relationships. It does not sanctify abuse, manipulation, or spiritual gaslighting in the name of patience.

What Islam *does* teach is responsibility. *Accountability.* Mercy. Growth. And we now have access to tools our ancestors didn't—trauma therapy, couples counseling, somatic healing, attachment work, nervous system regulation, communication coaching. These aren't Western fads—they're *mercy in action.* They're tools of repair. And choosing to use them is not weakness—it's wisdom. It's a sign that you value your marriage enough to fight for it *properly.*

But here's the truth: many don't want to do the work. It's easier to blame your spouse than look in the mirror. It's easier to scroll than to sit in silence and feel the emptiness in your heart. It's easier to shut down than to unpack your triggers and face the parts of yourself you've buried since childhood. We've been conditioned to expect instant happiness—and when it doesn't come, we swipe left, shut down, or check out.

We need to understand this: **conflict is not a sign your marriage is broken. Disconnection is.** And that disconnection doesn't start in the bedroom or the dinner table—it starts inside of you. When you're emotionally unavailable, when your nervous system is hijacked by old trauma, when you don't know how to regulate anger, ask for affection, or offer empathy—you will sabotage even the most promising relationship.

And still—there's hope.

Power couples are not made from perfect compatibility. They're forged in *intentional struggle.* They cry together. They argue, then repair. They attend therapy. They fast, they pray, they get triggered and then *own it.* They break generational patterns. They reparent themselves. They stop blaming. They start building. They know that intimacy is not just physical—it's *emotional labor.* And they do it.

These couples don't measure success by how conflict-free their marriage is, but by how deeply they return to one another after conflict. They choose growth over comfort. Accountability over pride. *Du'a over despair.* They fall, and they get back up—together.

And that's the real crisis: not that people are struggling in marriage—but that many don't know how to struggle *well.* They think love should feel good all the time. They think challenges mean failure. But the truth is, love gets *real* when it gets hard. That's where the sacred starts. That's where Allah watches closely.

So, here's the call: stop romanticizing the surface. Stop seeking perfection. Stop delaying your healing. Marriage isn't supposed to fix you. It reveals you—and then invites you to grow.

This is where you go beyond the surface—where you face yourself with courage, learn the tools, and commit to the self-work it takes to build something real. Because beyond is where the sacred begins. That's where Allah watches closely.

Not everyone is ready for that. But the ones who are? They're the ones who rewrite the story—for themselves, their children, and the ummah.

Chapter Two

Lessons Learned, Lives Transformed

Marriage. A word that stirs hope, mystery, and at times, heartbreak. It's a sacred journey that many enter with dreams, but few truly prepare for. While opinions on marriage abound—advice columns, viral posts, cultural customs—what's often missing is the raw truth: marriage is not just a destination, but a lifelong process of growth, self-awareness, and service.

For me, the deepest truths about marriage didn't come from books or sermons. They came from breaking points. From divorces that shattered the illusion that love alone is enough. From moments when I had no choice but to ask myself, "What is it in me that keeps showing up in these patterns?"

Yes—I've been divorced more than once. And with every heartbreak, the mirror became clearer. The pain wasn't just about loss; it was a signal, a call to uncover wounds I had carried for years. I realized that before I could hope to build a healthy marriage, I had to build a healthy self.

It was this inner reckoning that opened the door to healing. I didn't want to stay bitter. I wanted to get better.

In our communities—especially in older generations—there's often a culture of silence around divorce, shame around emotional struggles, and an over-glorification of endurance in toxic situations. But healing doesn't happen through suppression. Growth doesn't happen through suffering alone. My journey taught me that while patience (sabr) and trust in Allah (tawakkul) are foundational, they must be coupled with action, insight, and deep inner work.

That's why I began exploring modern healing modalities—couples coaching, trauma therapy, inner child work, and emotional intelligence. Not as replacements for faith, but as tools to help uncover what's blocking us from living its principles in our relationships. Faith without self-awareness can become a shell. But faith paired with reflection and strategy? That becomes a transformation.

I began to see marriage not just as a union of two people—but as a mirror of our inner world. Conflict in marriage is rarely just about the other person. It's often about what we bring into the relationship: our unresolved grief, unmet needs, past hurts, and unspoken fears.

In my work, I've sat with hundreds of men and women—some in love, some on the verge of walking away—each carrying silent battles that were never taught how to be named. I saw myself in them. I saw versions of my younger self—insecure, reactive, hopeful, sometimes afraid to trust again.

But I also saw what healing looked like.

The couple who came in distant and left holding hands again. The father who realized his anger masked grief from childhood. The woman who learned to set boundaries after years of overextending herself. The divorced sister who finally stopped blaming herself and began rebuilding from within.

These stories aren't just stories. They are maps.

And so, this book became my offering—part memoir, part guide, part call to action. It's an invitation to rethink what we've been told about marriage. To embrace both tradition and transformation. To build homes rooted in faith and emotional intelligence. To stop waiting for the "perfect person" and start becoming the healed version of ourselves who can recognize, nurture, and sustain love when it arrives.

Because love isn't just found. It's built—intentionally, patiently, with God at the center and with healing as the foundation.

If you've been divorced, like me—know that you're not broken. You're awakening.

If you've been hurt—know that healing is not only possible, but sacred.

And if you're still searching—know that every step you take to understand yourself better is a step closer to the love you're seeking.

May this journey, and this book, be a companion to your growth, and a reminder that your past does not define you—your choices do.

Chapter Three

Faith in the Face of Challenges

The challenges that show up in marriage are rarely born within the marriage itself. They often begin long before two people exchange vows—long before the sacred words of *ijab* (offer) and *qabul* (acceptance) are even spoken. They're rooted in personal histories, emotional wounds, cultural expectations, and deeply held beliefs that shape how we perceive love, commitment, and vulnerability.

Imagine your mind as a landscape: some areas fertile and ready to grow, others hardened and weathered by past disappointments. When two people enter a marriage, they bring with them not just love and dreams—but also fears, unresolved trauma, generational patterns, and silent hopes. Some enter marriage open-hearted, ready to build and grow. Others come guarded, shaped by environments where trust, tenderness, or even faith were strained or missing. This inner terrain determines how we give and receive love—and how we weather conflict.

So where does hope begin?

It begins with *you*—with the courage to look inward. Faith is not just about rituals or outward identity; it's about transformation. Allah tells us, **"Indeed, Allah will not change the condition of a people until they change what is in themselves."** (Qur'an 13:11)

We often approach marriage hoping it will fix what's broken inside us—fill our emotional voids, soothe our past wounds, or make us feel complete. But marriage was never meant to be a bandage for our inner turmoil. It was meant to be a partnership—a space where healing can happen, but only when both hearts are committed to growth.

We live in a time where commitment is often feared, and instant gratification is glorified. Many seek emotional highs without enduring the low valleys that come with real intimacy. But Islamic marriage is different. It's a sacred contract with Allah at the center. It demands effort, patience (*sabr*), and reliance (*tawakkul*)—not just on our spouse, but on Allah Himself.

The Qur'an grounds us in purpose:

> **"And I did not create jinn and mankind except to worship Me."**
> (Adh-Dhariyat 51:56)

This verse reminds us: your existence is not random. It's intentional. And marriage, in the Islamic worldview, is a means of fulfilling your greater purpose—through love, companionship, and mutual support in worship.

A healthy marriage isn't just about compatibility. It's about *spiritual alignment*. A marriage rooted in mercy (*rahmah*), compassion (*mawaddah*), and faith is a form of worship in itself. But when we lose sight of this, marriage can instead become a battleground for ego, resentment, and spiritual disconnection.

"When a person marries, he has fulfilled half of his religion, so let him fear Allah regarding the remaining half" as the Prophet (ﷺ) is reported to have said. But how many of us are actively nurturing that half? How many are truly working to align their marriages with the deeper spiritual blueprint Allah has given us?

It took me years—and more than one divorce—to internalize these truths. My mistakes forced me to stop blaming others and start confronting myself. I had to go deeper. I had to face the uncomfortable truth that I was carrying wounds I had never named, expectations I had never questioned, and beliefs I had never aligned with revelation.

Through this book, I hope to pass on not just *information* but *transformation*. We'll explore not only Islamic teachings but also tools rooted in psychology, trauma healing, emotional intelligence, and self-reflection.

And let me say this clearly: **faith in marriage does not mean enduring abuse or toxicity** in the name of *sabr* (patience). Our tradition calls for dignity, justice, and emotional safety. The Prophet (ﷺ) never sanctioned emotional harm as a condition for spiritual growth. While older generations may have normalized "putting up with it," you are not meant to suffer in silence. You're meant to work, with your spouse, to co-create a better relationship—through communication, humility, shared growth, and yes, modern resources like couples coaching, therapy, trauma recovery, and honest dialogue.

True tawakkul (trust in Allah) isn't passive. It's active. It's the farmer who plants seeds, waters them daily, and *then* relies on Allah for the harvest.

As you begin—or renew—your journey through marriage, remember: the path ahead isn't about perfection. It's about sincerity. It's about being willing to evolve, to unlearn what no longer serves you, and to keep returning to Allah together, again and again.

So, let's go deeper. Let's move beyond the surface. Not just for your marriage—but for your soul.

Chapter Four

Modern Courtship: The Good, Bad, and Ugly

Over the years, I've noticed a recurring pattern in the Muslim community during the courtship stage, a phase I've come to call "The Good, the Bad, and the Ugly." Inspired by an old classic Western movie I watched in my youth featuring the legendary Clint Eastwood, this observation captures three distinct groups that many Muslims tend to fall into during courtship. These approaches significantly shape the peace, security, and blessings that couples experience in their future marriages.

The Three Types of Courtship Approaches

Group One: Keeping It Real

There's something deeply grounding about the kind of person who walks into the courtship process with clarity, boundaries, and sincerity. These individuals aren't looking for fireworks or fleeting chemistry. They're looking for something that can weather storms—something that doesn't just make sense in the moment but will still make sense a decade down the line. They don't chase after romance as the world defines it. They chase after peace, stability, shared values, and spiritual alignment.

People in this group move with intention. They're not aimlessly dating or collecting emotional scars. They understand the gravity of choosing a life partner—not just for themselves, but for their future children, for the legacy they hope to build, and for their own growth as a human being. When they engage in conversations, they're not wasting time with rehearsed charm or shallow talk. They do their due diligence. They ask the important questions—the kind that expose not just compatibility, but character. Questions about faith, family dynamics, emotional history, conflict resolution, goals, mental health, and inner wounds. They don't shy away from hard topics, because they know marriage isn't built on comfort—it's built on courage, curiosity, and alignment.

They keep faith-based principles at the forefront. They respect boundaries—both physical and emotional—not out of fear, but out of reverence for the process. Their interactions are marked by decorum and dignity. They don't blur lines to "test chemistry" or bend rules to impress. They honor the sacredness of this stage, trusting that when a relationship is built on the right foundation, it will flourish naturally.

They're not in a hurry. They know rushing leads to blindness. They take their time because they value what they're building. They know how easily infatuation can cloud discernment. So they protect their heart—not out of fear, but out of self-respect. They're cautious, but not closed off. Open, but not naive.

What sets them apart isn't perfection—it's perspective. They understand that every person has flaws. They're not chasing an ideal partner who doesn't exist. They're searching for someone who is self-aware, accountable, and committed to growth. Someone who can admit when they're wrong, apologise when needed, and come back to the table when things feel distant.

They invite their families and mentors into the process—not because they can't think for themselves, but because they value insight over isolation. They know that love is often blind, and wisdom is found in the eyes of those who've walked before them. They don't view this as interference—they see it as protection.

People in this group don't confuse lust for love, or closeness for compatibility. They guard their energy. They keep their interactions clean. They maintain boundaries that others might scoff at—but those boundaries are what protect their dignity, their mental health, and their future. They don't confuse romantic intensity with emotional safety. They know that real love doesn't have to burn. It can feel like a steady warmth—reliable, honest, and kind.

When this group finds someone, they don't expect perfection. They expect presence. They're willing to work, to compromise, to forgive, and to start again. They don't give up when things get hard, but they also don't romanticize struggle. They're building something slow, strong, and real. Not a highlight reel, but a life.

This is the kind of courtship that feels different. It's quieter, maybe even less exciting to the outside world. But it's rooted. It's intentional. It's the kind of beginning that often leads to marriages where both people feel seen, safe, and supported—not because they never face storms, but because they've chosen someone who knows how to hold an umbrella when it rains.

This is the good. The sacred. The steady. And it's still possible.

Group Two: From Emotional Entanglement to Sacred Awakening

Group Two doesn't start out on the wrong foot. In fact, they begin much like those in Group One—with good intentions, a desire to find a meaningful connection, and the hope of building something real. But unlike the first group, their journey isn't defined by clarity—it's defined by ambiguity. And in that grey area, where boundaries are blurred and intentions are unspoken, emotional chaos begins to brew.

Their connection often begins innocently enough: friendly conversations after events, shared memes, late-night check-ins that feel thoughtful but harmless. They tell themselves, *we're just getting to know each other*. But something subtle starts to shift. The messages become longer, the replies quicker. Inside jokes are born, hearts race at notifications, and suddenly, their emotional investment has outpaced any serious conversations about compatibility, family, or long-term vision.

They don't mean for it to become *that kind* of relationship. But without clear boundaries, emotional intimacy grows quietly like ivy—wrapping itself around the heart until it's hard to distinguish between curiosity and attachment, attention and affection, excitement and dependency. The soul begins to hunger for that daily emotional hit—the "good morning" messages, the compliments, the feeling of being wanted. And in that hunger, lines get crossed.

What starts as flirtatious banter and harmless emojis can evolve into innuendo. The phone becomes a portal to emotional indulgence—calls stretch into the night, photos become less modest, curiosity becomes physical. Sometimes it ends at French kissing, other times foreplay, and in more painful stories—it goes further. And when it does, the heart breaks. Not because love was lost, but because sacred limits were.

What makes Group Two's story so quietly devastating is not that they were reckless—it's that they were *unaware*. They didn't wake up one day and choose to compromise their values. They got swept away by the tide of unchecked emotions, casual digital closeness, and the illusion that *this* wasn't like all the other stories. That *they* would stay in control. That *this* was different.

But it never is.

And when reality hits—whether through guilt, heartbreak, or the sudden collapse of an unsanctioned bond—they're left carrying the weight of regret. A gnawing feeling of having lost something they didn't even know they were giving away. Their dignity. Their innocence. Their connection with Allah. The grief is real, and it is heavy.

But this is not where their story ends.

Because Group Two is also the group that often finds the most profound clarity. They hit rock bottom—and then begin the climb. They look in the mirror and don't like what they see. So they start again. With trembling hearts and tearful duas, they turn back to the One who never stopped waiting for them. They delete numbers, end conversations, and place their hearts back in the care of the One who created it. They begin again—this time with intention, with tawbah (repentance), with boundaries, and with a yearning to do it differently.

They seek mentors. They have hard conversations with themselves and with those they trust. They finally ask the questions they avoided before: *What do I really want in a spouse? What kind of life do I want to build? What kind of person do I need to become to deserve that?* These questions burn—but they also illuminate.

Group Two's strength lies not in perfection, but in redemption. They become wiser, more cautious, more honest with themselves. And their past—once a source of shame—becomes a reason for deep humility and empathy. They learn to draw firmer lines. They begin to value silence over unnecessary talk, presence over attention, and substance over sweetness.

They no longer chase the highs of romantic fantasy. They seek peace. They seek alignment. They seek someone who will walk with them to Jannah— not someone who entertains their loneliness in the dunya. And through their struggle, they grow.

Their story is proof that even when we fall, we can rise higher than before. That hearts can heal, that taqwa can be rebuilt, and that Allah's mercy reaches further than any mistake we've made.

Group Two may have started their journey with confusion—but they often end it with clarity, courage, and the kind of spiritual maturity that only comes from confronting one's shadows.

They remind us all: you are not the sum of your past. You are the story of what you choose next.

Group Three: The Collapse of Boundaries and the Crisis of the Soul

Group Three is not confused. They're not emotionally overwhelmed like Group Two. They've made a different kind of decision—one that bypasses inner alignment and heads straight toward reckless abandon. It's not just a stumble. It's a sprint away from sacred values, dressed up as modern courtship.

At first glance, it looks like they're searching for love like everyone else. But dig deeper, and you'll find something far more troubling: a slow erosion of self-worth disguised as freedom, a hollow chase for connection masked as confidence. This group doesn't just blur boundaries—they erase them. What begins as intrigue quickly devolves into late-night hookups, emotionally volatile attachments, and a pattern of using people and being used. The term "getting to know someone" becomes a euphemism for sex without commitment, and heartbreak becomes routine—almost expected.

They aren't necessarily bad people. Many are deeply wounded. What drives them isn't always lust—it's loneliness. Emptiness. A desperate craving to feel loved, seen, held. But without healing, they fall into toxic cycles of self-sabotage. Childhood neglect, emotional abandonment, covert incest, parental betrayal—these invisible scars become the lenses through which they search for "the one." And each failed attempt buries them deeper.

The problem is not that they've made mistakes—we all do. The problem is the *normalization* of those mistakes. The complete numbing to the spiritual consequences. The casual justifications: *"Everyone's doing it." "We're not ready for marriage yet." "We'll make tawbah later."*

Later never comes.

In this group, relationships become transactional. Use them. Lose them. Ghost them. Repeat. Sexual encounters are chalked up as "practice." The body count rises. The soul gets quieter. The nafs gets louder. And slowly, the heart begins to harden. What once would have triggered guilt now brings nothing but exhaustion. They don't realize it, but they're spiritually hemorrhaging.

Some even go as far as manipulating religion to soothe their guilt. They still fast. Pray when it's convenient. Attend Friday khutbahs with bodies washed but hearts stained. They live dual lives—one online, polished and filtered for the community; another offline, drowning in secrecy, deception, and self-loathing. It's a spiritual schizophrenia.

And when they do get married—if they do—it's often a disaster waiting to happen. Marriages born from emotional chaos or sexual chemistry rarely withstand the weight of real-life responsibilities. When the thrill fades, what remains is mistrust, resentment, or trauma that has no language and no container. Some find themselves divorced within months. Others stay, hollowed out, emotionally numb, or living parallel lives under one roof.

But the most tragic casualty isn't the breakup. It's the loss of *self*. The person they once hoped to become—the one who prayed for a peaceful, loving home, the one who had dreams of raising children in a righteous environment—that person gets buried under the wreckage of past choices and shame.

Yet even here—in the depths of spiritual confusion and moral collapse—there is hope. But only *if* there is honesty.

If someone in Group Three has the courage to *pause*, to stop running, to sit in their own silence, and face the person in the mirror—they can start again. If they can cry to Allah with sincerity, not performance, if they can walk into therapy not with pride but with humility, if they can admit: *"I've made a mess of things. I want to change."*—then transformation becomes possible.

But it will cost them. It will cost their ego. Their denial. Their addiction to temporary highs. They will have to mourn the old version of themselves to create space for a better one. They'll need spiritual mentorship, trauma-informed guidance, and a total recalibration of their definition of love, masculinity, femininity, and partnership.

This group is proof that freedom without submission leads to chaos. That sexuality without sacredness breeds shame. That love without boundaries becomes poison. And that real healing can't begin until the illusion is shattered.

The only way out is *in*. Into the pain. Into the shadow. Into accountability. And then into the arms of the One who never left.

Chapter Five

Spotting Red Flags in Courtship

A Wake-Up Call for the Heart

Courtship is meant to be a sacred bridge—not a battlefield. It is the space between intention and union, where two souls explore whether they can walk the same path with dignity, trust, and divine purpose. But in this vulnerable phase, hearts are easily swayed, illusions are easily sold, and patterns—often inherited or normalized—can sabotage a future before it even begins.

The red flags that show up in courtship are rarely just about the other person. They're mirrors of emotional immaturity, spiritual misalignment, and inner wounds that are still bleeding. And ignoring them isn't an act of hope—it's self-betrayal.

Here's a clearer, bolder, and more compassionate guide to the warning signs you must never brush aside.

> **Lack of Respect:** When someone dismisses your thoughts, mocks your boundaries, or talks down to you, it's not just a bad habit—it's a flashing signal that they may not honor your dignity long-term. Disrespect grows into contempt, and contempt kills love.
>
> **Dishonesty:** Whether it's half-truths, selective omission, or straight-up lies—dishonesty creates rot at the root. If someone is evasive early on, know that deception doesn't suddenly vanish after marriage. It festers.
>
> **Emotional, Verbal, or Physical Abuse:** Abuse doesn't start with bruises—it starts with manipulation, threats, control, or belittling.

If you're left feeling small, scared, or broken, don't wait for clarity. That *is* the clarity.

Controlling Behavior: From micromanaging your dress to dictating who you speak to, control masquerades as "care." But true love liberates. It doesn't imprison.

Excessive Flattery & Love Bombing: Too much too soon—grand promises, over-the-top compliments, rushed declarations of love—are often manipulative tactics to bypass healthy boundaries and build false emotional intimacy.

Lack of Communication: If someone shuts down, withdraws, or avoids difficult conversations, they're showing you they aren't emotionally available. Marriage *requires* honest dialogue—not silent treatment.

Gaslighting: When you're made to doubt your memory, feelings, or perception—it's not miscommunication. It's manipulation designed to disarm and destabilize you.

Addiction (Pornography, Substances, etc.): Unaddressed addiction is not a flaw; it's a bondage. It will shape how love is expressed, how conflict is handled, and how intimacy is built—or broken. A person must be in active healing before they're ready to commit.

Unresolved Trauma or Mental Health Struggles (Ignored): Everyone has wounds. But if they deny, suppress, or dump those wounds on you without any effort to heal—run. You're not a rehab center for someone else's emotional negligence.

Isolation Attempts: If someone tries to separate you from your support system—family, friends, mentors—they're not building intimacy. They're building a trap.

Stonewalling: Repeatedly refusing to talk, ghosting during conflict, or walking away instead of working through tension is emotional abandonment. It kills connection over time.

Criticism Disguised as "Advice": If they constantly "correct" you under the guise of love, watch how you begin to shrink around them. A healthy partner uplifts—you should never feel like you're being chipped away.

Irresponsibility: Frequent job-hopping, living in denial of financial obligations, or never following through on commitments are all signs of emotional immaturity.

Financial Irresponsibility: Money matters. A lack of planning, reckless spending, or secrecy around finances can erode a marriage's foundation, even if the love is real.

Unwillingness to Grow or Change: Stagnation is death to a relationship. If they don't self-reflect, seek growth, or take feedback seriously, they'll become a weight—not a partner.

Quick Escalation: Pressuring for marriage after a few meetings, pushing for physical intimacy early, or demanding exclusivity too fast? That's infatuation, not discernment.

Pattern of Infidelity or Boundary Violations: Multiple "talking stages" that ended messily? Cheating pasts with no remorse? A track record tells you what a future with them might look like.

Sexual Innuendo or Pressure: Making suggestive jokes, pushing boundaries, or using "connection" as a cover for sexual advances shows they're prioritizing lust over loyalty.

Religious Disregard: If someone mocks your modesty, skips prayers without concern, or shows no effort toward spiritual growth—it's not just "a personal journey." It reflects the values they'll bring into your home.

Lack of Effort: If you're doing all the emotional labor, initiating every conversation, or carrying the relationship—ask yourself what you're really signing up for.

Incompatibility in Core Life Goals: Love isn't enough. If your visions for faith, family, lifestyle, or purpose don't align, one of you will eventually be asked to sacrifice too much.

Refusal to Apologize or Own Mistakes: No one's perfect. But someone who never says "I was wrong" or always plays the victim is not safe for long-term partnership.

You Feel More Anxious Than Safe Around Them: Your nervous system knows what your heart wants to deny. If being with them creates more fear, doubt, or insecurity than peace—trust that feeling.

Final Reflection

Red flags aren't always red at first. They often show up as beige—barely noticeable until you're already emotionally attached. That's why you must stay grounded, not just in your heart, but in your values.

You deserve a partner who respects your boundaries, protects your dignity, and honors your soul. Don't settle for someone who awakens your insecurities. Wait for the one who awakens your du'as.

Chapter Six

Essential Questions During Courting

The path to a deep and lasting connection is built on understanding, which begins with asking the right questions. Courting is more than just exploration—it's a time to uncover each other's values, dreams, and personalities. The purpose of these questions is not only to gain answers but to spark conversations that go beyond the surface, fostering mutual understanding, trust, and shared spiritual aspirations. Here are 100 carefully selected questions, designed to help guide you toward a meaningful and fulfilling relationship, from both psychological and faith-based perspectives.

100 Essential Questions During Courting:

Faith and Spirituality

1. How do you prioritize your relationship with Allah in your daily life, and what practices help you maintain that connection?

   This question encourages a discussion about their spiritual habits, such as prayer, dhikr, and acts of worship, and how these influence their daily decisions and actions.

2. What does being a practicing Muslim mean to you, and how do you live that identity in various areas of your life (family, work, community)?

   Explores their interpretation of practicing Islam and how it shapes their interactions and roles in different aspects of life.

3. How do you approach balancing personal ambitions and responsibilities while fulfilling Islamic obligations and values?

   Prompts a conversation about time management, setting priorities, and integrating faith with worldly pursuits.

4. What role do you see prayer (salah) and Qur'an recitation playing in our home, and how can we make worship a shared experience?

   Encourages reflection on fostering a spiritually uplifting home environment and building a foundation of shared worship and connection to Allah.

5. How do you handle situations where your Islamic values or beliefs are challenged, either socially or personally?

   Explores their resilience and problem-solving skills when dealing with challenges to their faith or values, such as peer pressure or workplace ethics.

6. What are some Islamic principles or teachings you hold most dear, and how would you want to integrate them into our marriage?

   Reveals their core values, such as patience, gratitude, or honesty, and their vision for embedding these in a marital relationship.

7. How do you view the concept of tawakkul (trust in Allah) when it comes to handling life's challenges and making important decisions?

   Highlights their reliance on Allah and their decision-making process, including balancing faith with practical efforts.

8. What does Islamic leadership and responsibility in a marriage mean to you, and how do you envision fulfilling your role in this context?

   Encourages discussion about roles in your marriage, leadership qualities, and how Islamic teachings shape their understanding of responsibility.

9. How would you like to approach raising children in Islam, and what values or practices would you prioritize in their upbringing?

   Prompts a conversation about shared parenting goals, including Islamic education, moral upbringing, and creating a spiritually nurturing home for children.

10. What steps do you take to ensure your faith continues to grow, and how can we inspire and remind each other to stay consistent on this journey?

    Focuses on their spiritual growth strategies, such as attending classes, seeking knowledge, or volunteering, and their vision for mutual encouragement in a marriage.

Finances

1. What is your view on combining finances in marriage versus keeping them separate, and why?

    This question explores their comfort level and philosophy on financial transparency and autonomy.

2. How do you approach unexpected financial expenses or emergencies?

    Reveals their preparedness and attitude toward financial planning and handling stress.

3. What is your attitude toward charity and financial contributions to the community or family?

    Provides insight into their values and priorities when it comes to generosity and social responsibility.

4. How do you prioritize spending on personal versus family needs?

    Clarifies their decision-making process and approach to balancing individual desires with collective goals.

5. What are your thoughts on investing, and how much risk are you comfortable with?

    Uncovers their financial strategy and whether they lean toward growth or stability.

6. How do you plan for long-term financial security, such as retirement or children's education?

    Shows their foresight and sense of responsibility toward future family needs.

7. How would you handle financial disagreements or conflicts in our marriage?

    Explores their conflict-resolution style and ability to compromise when financial priorities clash.

8. What does financial independence mean to you, and how would it play into our partnership?

    Examines their expectations for self-sufficiency and its role in a collaborative financial plan.

9. Do you see us maintaining a specific lifestyle, and how would we plan financially for it?

    Explores alignment of lifestyle goals and how they translate into practical financial planning.

10. What is your approach to financial education and staying informed about money matters?

    Highlights their willingness to adapt, learn, and grow financially as a couple.

Communication

1. How do you prefer to communicate your needs or concerns within a relationship?

    This question helps uncover the person's preferred communication style (e.g., direct, indirect) and fosters understanding of how to address sensitive topics respectfully.

2. What are your expectations for resolving misunderstandings?

    Clarifies their approach to conflict resolution, whether they lean towards immediate resolution, taking time to process, or seeking external advice when necessary.

3. How do you perceive the role of non-verbal communication in understanding each other?

    Prompts reflection on body language, facial expressions, and tone, which are crucial in interpreting emotions and intentions beyond words.

4. What do you think is the most important quality of good communication in marriage?

   Encourages them to articulate values like empathy, clarity, or active listening, setting the foundation for mutual understanding.

5. How do you handle being misunderstood, and what helps you feel heard?

   Explores their emotional response to miscommunication and identifies effective ways to affirm and validate their feelings.

6. What is your approach to giving and receiving constructive feedback?

   Reveals their attitude toward self-improvement and mutual growth, and their ability to handle critique in a constructive manner.

7. How do you ensure that difficult conversations remain respectful and productive?

   This question assesses their ability to manage emotions, avoid escalation, and maintain a solutions-oriented perspective during tough discussions.

8. How do you differentiate between venting and problem-solving in communication?

   Encourages clarity on when they need emotional support versus practical solutions, fostering understanding of emotional boundaries.

9. What role does humor or lightheartedness play in communication for you?

   Invites insights into their ability to use humor as a tool for connection, easing tension, and maintaining positivity.

10. How do you envision maintaining communication if physical distance separates us temporarily?

    Focuses on their commitment to maintaining connection through proactive communication methods, demonstrating adaptability and effort.

Family

1. How do you define the balance between prioritizing our relationship and our respective families?

   Examines their views on setting boundaries and fostering harmony between families and marriage.

2. How do you navigate cultural or religious differences between families?

   Reveals their problem-solving skills and respect for diversity within family dynamics.

3. What role do you see extended family playing in our children's lives?

   Offers insight into their vision for family involvement and intergenerational connections.

4. How would you handle a family conflict that involves one of us?

   Explores their approach to protecting the relationship while addressing family challenges.

5. What is your approach to family gatherings and maintaining family connections?

   Uncovers their value for traditions, togetherness, and efforts to sustain familial bonds.

6. How do you perceive gender roles within a family structure?

   Clarifies their expectations for responsibilities and equality within family dynamics.

7. What role did faith play in your family growing up, and how does that influence you now?

   Provides a deeper understanding of their upbringing and its impact on their values.

8. How do you think our respective family dynamics could complement or challenge each other?

   Explores compatibility and potential areas for growth when families merge.

9. What boundaries would you like to establish with extended family?

   Highlights their perspective on creating healthy and respectful family interactions.

10. What do you think are the most important values to instill in a family?

    Encourages a meaningful discussion on shared principles for family life.

Personal Growth

1. What are some personal habits or routines that are essential to your well-being?

   Highlights their self-care strategies and personal priorities.

2. How do you evaluate and set personal goals?

   Explores their drive for self-improvement and approach to achieving success.

3. What books, courses, or experiences have shaped your personal growth?

   Provides a glimpse into their learning style and openness to new perspectives.

4. How do you approach self-reflection and accountability?

   Reveals their maturity and capacity for self-awareness.

5. How do you handle failure or setbacks, and what do you learn from them?

   Examines their resilience and ability to grow through challenges.

6. What role does faith play in guiding your personal growth journey?

   Explores how their spirituality influences their goals and character development.

7. How do you recharge and find motivation during tough times?

   Reveals their coping mechanisms and ability to maintain focus.

8. What qualities in yourself do you most want to improve, and how are you working on them?

   Encourages vulnerability and a proactive mindset toward self-development.

9. How do you celebrate milestones or achievements, both big and small?

   Explores their values around gratitude and recognizing progress.

10. How can I encourage your growth while maintaining space for my own?

    Facilitates a discussion on mutual support and individuality in the relationship.

Relationships and Expectations

1. How do you define the concept of partnership in marriage?

   Explores their views on teamwork, collaboration, and mutual respect.

2. What are some qualities you value most in a life partner?

   Highlights their priorities and vision for a compatible relationship.

3. How do you envision the division of household responsibilities?

   Encourages practical dialogue on roles and expectations.

4. How do you expect us to handle individual and joint decision-making?

   Clarifies their approach to balance and shared authority in marriage.

5. What does mutual respect look like to you in a marriage?

   Reveals their foundational values for a healthy relationship.

6. How do you handle differences in opinion while maintaining unity?

   Explores their capacity for compromise and conflict resolution.

7. What are some traditions or habits you'd like to create as a couple?

   Encourages creativity in building shared experiences.

8. What does a fulfilling marital relationship mean to you?

   Facilitates a discussion on emotional and practical fulfillment.

9. What is your perspective on nurturing emotional intimacy over time?

    Examines their understanding of deepening the connection in marriage.

10. What boundaries would you like to establish to protect our relationship?

    Promotes proactive thinking about safeguarding the partnership.

Past Relationships

1. What aspects of past relationships taught you the most about yourself?

   Explores self-awareness and lessons learned from previous experiences.

2. How do you ensure that past experiences don't negatively impact a new relationship?

   Reveals their ability to compartmentalize, grow, and move forward.

3. What lessons from previous relationships have shaped your expectations for marriage?

   Uncovers how past experiences influence their current views and priorities.

4. How do you view closure from past relationships in the context of moving forward?

   Clarifies their emotional readiness and capacity for commitment.

5. What are your thoughts on forgiveness and letting go of past grievances?

   Explores their ability to forgive and approach a new relationship with a clean slate.

6. How do you handle trust-building in a new relationship after betrayal or heartbreak?

   Reveals their strategies for rebuilding trust and fostering security.

7. How much do you think sharing about past relationships is important in marriage?

   Prompts a discussion on boundaries and transparency.

8. What role does self-awareness play in healing from past relationships?

   Highlights their willingness to reflect and grow emotionally.

9. What do you believe is the best way to handle lingering feelings or attachments?

   Encourages honesty about emotional baggage and closure processes.

10. How can we ensure our relationship remains unaffected by past baggage?

    Facilitates dialogue on mutual accountability and emotional maturity.

Health and Wellness

1. What role does physical health play in your life, and how do you maintain it?

   Explores their dedication to fitness, nutrition, and overall well-being.

2. What are your thoughts on mental health and seeking help when necessary?

   Reveals their perspective on addressing emotional and psychological challenges.

3. How do you approach maintaining a balanced lifestyle amid busy schedules?

   Provides insight into their time management and stress-relief strategies.

4. How do you address and overcome unhealthy habits?

   Encourages self-reflection on personal growth and discipline.

5. What are your thoughts on the role of spirituality in overall health?

   Explores how their faith integrates with their physical and mental well-being.

6. How do you prioritize rest and relaxation in your daily routine?

   Highlights their understanding of the importance of downtime for balance.

7. What are your views on maintaining privacy around health-related issues?

   Prompts a conversation about boundaries and mutual respect.

8. How do you see us supporting each other's health and wellness goals?

   Encourages collaboration and accountability in maintaining a healthy lifestyle.

9. What are your thoughts on diet and its importance in our daily lives?

    Reveals preferences and priorities in terms of food choices and routines.

10. How do you navigate challenges that may impact your health, and what support would you need?

    Explores resilience and communication around physical and emotional well-being.

Future Goals

1. How do you envision our life together in 5, 10, or 20 years?

    Encourages long-term planning and compatibility in life vision.

2. What are some personal or professional milestones you hope to achieve?

    Explores their ambitions and how they plan to pursue them.

3. What are your priorities for family life and how do they align with your goals?

    Facilitates a discussion on balancing personal ambitions with family responsibilities.

4. How do you define success in terms of career, family, and personal fulfillment?

    Reveals their values and broader aspirations.

5. What steps do you believe are necessary to achieve financial stability and growth?

    Encourages practical thinking about shared economic goals.

6. How do you balance living in the moment with planning for the future?

    Explores their approach to mindfulness and long-term vision.

7. What role does continuous learning or self-improvement play in your future plans?

    Highlights their dedication to growth and adaptability.

8. What are your thoughts on retirement and planning for later stages of life?

    Facilitates a forward-thinking discussion about life beyond work.

9. How do you envision balancing personal goals with shared goals as a couple?

   Encourages dialogue on partnership and mutual support in achieving dreams.

10. What legacy would you like to leave behind, and how can we work toward it together?

    Prompts deep reflection on purpose and shared contributions.

Trust and Loyalty

1. What does trust mean to you, and how do you foster it in a relationship?

   Explores their core understanding of trust and its importance in marriage.

2. How do you rebuild trust if it has been damaged?

   Reveals their willingness and strategies for repairing emotional bonds.

3. What boundaries are essential to maintaining trust in a relationship?

   Highlights their perspective on healthy boundaries and respect.

4. What role does loyalty play in strengthening a marital relationship?

   Encourages discussion about commitment and long-term dedication.

5. How do you differentiate between transparency and oversharing?

   Explores their views on honesty and maintaining individuality.

6. What is your approach to addressing insecurities or suspicions in a relationship?

   Reveals their ability to communicate and resolve trust issues constructively.

7. How do you handle situations where trust is tested by external influences?

   Encourages reflection on handling peer pressure or societal expectations.

8. What is your perspective on forgiving breaches of trust, and under what conditions?

   Explores their capacity for forgiveness and reconciliation.

9. How do you ensure trust remains strong during challenging times?

   Facilitates dialogue on proactive trust-building practices.

10. What steps can we take together to nurture loyalty and deepen our bond?

    Encourages collaborative thinking about sustaining a strong, trust-based relationship.

Courting, like any meaningful journey, requires both preparation and self-reflection. These 100 questions are not set in stone; they're meant to be a flexible guide, adaptable to whatever situations arise. Their purpose is to encourage meaningful and thoughtful conversations that help uncover compatibility and shared values.

These 10 categories of questions are more than just conversation starters—they're a guided path into the deeper layers of a relationship. They help uncover the areas that exist beyond the surface—the emotional, psychological, spiritual, and practical dimensions that are often overlooked but essential for lasting connection.

By engaging with these questions, couples take a step toward building a relationship rooted in mutual understanding, emotional honesty, and shared purpose. Let these questions be your invitation to explore with sincerity, to ask bravely, and to listen with the intention to grow. May they guide you toward a love built not just on attraction or potential, but on true companionship, sacred connection, and a vision that aligns with Allah's pleasure.

Chapter Seven

Lavish Weddings, Heavy Mahr: The Cost of Tradition

How Extravagance is Eclipsing the Sacredness of Marriage

In the sacred tradition of Islam, marriage was never meant to be a performance. It was a divine union—simple, soulful, and rooted in love, mercy, and mutual respect. It was meant to connect two hearts in the name of Allah, build families, preserve chastity, and strengthen the foundation of society.

But somewhere along the way, we lost our way.

Today, the path to marriage has become a treacherous climb for many young Muslims—not because they lack desire or sincerity, but because the system has become rigged with unrealistic expectations, cultural theatrics, and crippling financial burdens.

What was once a blessed act of simplicity has been hijacked by extravagance.

Weddings, now, are no longer sacred ceremonies—they are spectacles. Glorified productions drenched in vanity and pressure. It's not uncommon to hear of weddings costing $50,000… $100,000… or more. One night of glitz, lights, and filtered images that evaporate by morning—while the weight of debt, stress, and comparison quietly settles in.

Families that once gave with barakah are now burdened with expectations. Young men feel unworthy unless they can "perform" like a millionaire groom.

Young women are evaluated not by their piety or compassion, but by how glamorous their event will be. Parents compete. Communities whisper. Social media records. And in all of this noise… the *niyyah*(intention) is lost.

And then there's the Mahr.

A divine gift—a sacred right of the bride that was meant to honor her, uplift her, and symbolize commitment—has now become a tool for status, bargaining, or even revenge. What was once given with love is now negotiated with pride. Some families demand Mahr figures that are completely disconnected from reality—tens of thousands in gold, cars, or assets, turning this spiritual obligation into a financial chokehold.

And let's be honest—this isn't empowerment. It's a distortion.

Excessive Mahr and extravagant weddings are not signs of strong families. They are signs of misplaced priorities. While elders boast about the spectacle, many young people quietly retreat into fear—unsure if they'll ever be able to marry without being shamed, indebted, or disrespected.

And what's the result?

Delayed marriages. Broken engagements. Secret relationships. Zina. Debt. Depression. Disconnection between generations. A growing number of men avoiding marriage altogether. A rising number of women being unfairly blamed for asking "too much." And a slow, silent erosion of the very institution Allah elevated with His words:

> *"And of His signs is that He created for you from yourselves mates that you may find tranquility in them. And He placed between you affection and mercy…" (Surah Ar-Rum 30:21)*

Let us be clear: Islam never discouraged celebration. Joy is part of our deen. A bride deserves to be honored. A groom deserves to feel respected. Mahr is her right. Beauty is not haram. But **excess** is.

When our marriages are born in pressure, pride, and performative showmanship, we set the stage for discontent, entitlement, and comparison. When they're rooted in simplicity, sincerity, and barakah—we give them the space to flourish.

The Prophet (ﷺ), whose life was the model of balance and compassion, said:

> *"The best marriage is the one with the least burden and expense."*
> *(Sunan Ibn Majah)*

Let that be our compass.

Imagine what could happen if we stripped away the ego and returned to the heart. If we let love speak louder than luxury. If we empowered couples to start their lives with dignity, not debt. If we honored the command of Allah above the customs of men.

Marriage was never meant to be locked behind the gates of class and currency. It was meant to be an act of worship, not war. A bond of peace, not pressure. A start to something sacred—not the end of your savings.

Let's choose differently. For our sons. For our daughters. For the *ummah*. Let's restore marriage to its rightful place: a union of barakah, not a performance of burden.

Chapter Eight

Beyond the Honeymoon Phase

The early days of marriage often feel like a dream. Everything is new—every glance, every touch, every shared moment crackles with excitement. You feel chosen, seen, and cherished. This is what many call the honeymoon phase, a season where love feels effortless, and the world seems to pause just for the two of you.

But what happens when the glow fades?

When the rush settles and the rhythm of everyday life takes over, something deeper begins to unfold. The real marriage begins—not the picture-perfect version we grew up fantasizing about, but the raw, unfiltered reality. This is the part no one posts about on social media. It's where real growth starts, but only if we're brave enough to lean into it.

Before marriage, it's easy to believe you know your partner. You see their smile, you hear their laughter, and you imagine your future together. But what you don't always see are the silent fears they carry, the unhealed wounds from childhood, the shadows they try to hide even from themselves. And you bring your own baggage too—expectations, insecurities, ideals shaped by movies, culture, and sometimes, unresolved pain.

Many couples mistake infatuation for love. They ride the high of romance, believing it will last forever. But infatuation is a firework—bright and thrilling but short-lived. Love, on the other hand, is the quiet flame you build together, brick by brick, in the slow hours of ordinary days.

When the honeymoon ends, you start to see clearly. And sometimes, that clarity is uncomfortable. The same quirks that once seemed charming now test your patience. The dreams you assumed were shared may turn out to be different. It's in these moments—when reality disrupts fantasy—that couples face a choice: drift apart in disillusionment or lean in with intention.

True love doesn't ask for perfection. It demands presence. It asks: can you still hold your partner close when they disappoint you? Can you still choose them when it's inconvenient, when it's hard, when it's not romantic? That's the grit of real love—not the butterflies, but the decision to stay and build, even when the initial excitement wanes.

Marriage was never meant to be a performance. You don't need to keep up appearances, to pretend you're always in sync. In fact, one of the greatest tragedies is when partners feel the need to act like everything is fine while emotionally drifting apart inside. You don't grow closer by hiding your mess—you grow by facing it together.

But let's be honest: many of us enter marriage without knowing how to do this. We expect love to come naturally, not realizing that lasting love is learned. It's learned through awkward conversations, late-night arguments, silent apologies, and showing up even when you're tired or annoyed. It's in how you handle disappointment. How you forgive. How you stay soft even when you're tempted to go cold.

There's a tenderness that grows after the honeymoon—one that's quieter but more powerful. It's in the knowing glance across a crowded room. The way you reach for each other's hand in silence. The small sacrifices you make daily, not for praise but because you care. It's in the patience you learn when your partner is struggling, the forgiveness you offer when they fall short, and the grace you extend when you yourself are the one needing mercy.

This is the sacred middle ground between fairy tale and failure—the real marriage. It's not about keeping the spark alive by doing extravagant things. It's about keeping the heart open, especially when things get mundane, tense, or uncertain.

So if you find yourself wondering what's wrong because the butterflies are gone, know this: nothing is wrong. What's happening is that your love is maturing. You're stepping out of the storybook and into the sacred reality of partnership—a space where you're not just lovers, but mirrors, witnesses, teammates, and spiritual companions.

The honeymoon doesn't have to die. It transforms. It deepens. But only if you allow it. Only if you let go of fantasy, embrace imperfection, and choose each other—not for who you were in the beginning, but for who you are now, and who you're both becoming.

Because marriage isn't made in the glow. It's made in the shadows. In the choices. In the quiet. In the moments that no one sees.

And that's where the real beauty lives.

Chapter Nine

The Layers of Love

Love is an intricate melody that echoes throughout time,
its depth and intricacies known only through personal experience.

Love: The Untamed Flame Beneath the Surface

Love is not a soft whisper or a sweet phrase etched on a Valentine's card. It is an untamed flame, a melody that echoes through the chambers of time—ancient, primal, sacred. It sings in our bones before we even know its name. We chase it, we long for it, we write poems about it, cry over it, pray for it, and sometimes we destroy ourselves in our desperate attempt to feel it. Love is not something we understand through books or advice columns. It is known through bruises on the heart, through aching hope, through surrender and survival.

In the early days of marriage, love often shows up dressed in euphoria—bright, intoxicating, and blinding. We see only what we want to see. Every glance is magical, every conversation feels like poetry. We mistake butterflies for foundations, thinking the thrill will last forever. But love, real love, doesn't reveal itself in those soft-focus days. No. Real love emerges when the masks come off, when the dishes pile up, when the silence stretches long and the temptation to run feels easier than the effort to stay.

Because love isn't just found in candlelit dinners and perfectly curated Instagram moments. It's found in holding your partner's hand when they're breaking down. In staying up late to talk through the same issue—again. In forgiveness. In holding back hurtful words. In choosing the relationship even when everything in you is screaming to win the argument. Love is sacrifice without bitterness, presence without condition.

The world has fed us lies—movies, songs, and social media—all painting love as an endless dopamine high. But real love is more earth than sky. It's rooted. Heavy with responsibility. Messy. It demands the excavation of your soul. It forces you to confront your shadows, your childhood wounds, your pride, your ego. And it calls you to soften—to be brave enough to break open and let someone else truly see you.

And that is terrifying.

Because love demands that you risk rejection. That you let someone walk through the corridors of your soul, past the locked doors and shameful corners, and trust that they won't run. Love means vulnerability. And vulnerability is not weakness—it is the highest form of courage.

What they don't tell you is that love will exhaust you. It will test your patience, your will, your sense of self. But if you endure—if you hold on with mercy, with grace, with prayer and perseverance—then love will grow. Not like wildfire, but like roots. Quiet, steady, anchoring you to one another in ways you never thought possible.

And yet, love is not blind acceptance. It is not martyrdom. It is not about staying silent in the face of abuse, or shrinking to keep peace. Love holds a mirror. Love speaks truth. Love demands growth. And sometimes, love walks away to protect what's sacred. True love doesn't call you to destroy yourself. It calls you to rise.

In marriage, love is both sanctuary and furnace. It shelters you, but it also refines you. It strips you bare until only the truest parts of you remain. And when two people are willing to walk that fire together, with humility and faith, something beautiful is born—not perfection, but partnership. A companionship forged not in fantasy, but in faith and raw, radical commitment.

So no, love is not a feeling. Love is a choice made in the small, quiet moments no one sees. It is a verb. A discipline. A path. And when it is built on a foundation of sincerity, compassion, and spiritual alignment, it becomes not just a part of your life—it becomes the force that transforms it.

Let the world have its shallow stories.

Let us build something eternal.

Chapter Ten

"You Complete Me" – Myth or Reality?

We've all heard it—the phrase whispered in movies, etched on cards, passed through lips trembling with affection: "You complete me." It's poetic. Romantic. Even intoxicating. But is it true?

In a world consumed by soulmates, fairy tales, and curated images of perfect love, many enter marriage believing their spouse will somehow fill the emptiness within, silence the echoes of childhood wounds, and make everything whole. But here's the uncomfortable truth: **no one can complete you**. Not fully. Not forever. Not even your spouse.

The Prophet Muhammad (ﷺ), in a profound narration reported by Anas (RA), said:

> "**Whomever Allah blesses with a righteous wife, He has helped him with half of his religion, so let him fear Allah regarding the other half.**" (*Al-Haakim*)

This isn't a casual statement—it's a spiritual blueprint. Marriage isn't meant to fix you. It's meant to fortify you. It is half your deen not because your spouse replaces your missing half, but because the institution of marriage *demands* you rise to the challenge of completing the rest. It offers support, intimacy, and companionship—but the remaining half? That's **your responsibility**.

What many don't realize is that entering marriage with a void and expecting someone else to fill it is a recipe for resentment. You begin to blame them for not healing wounds they never inflicted. You silently hold them accountable for a loneliness that has always lived inside you. And you may love them, yes—but with expectation rather than intention. With desperation rather than devotion.

The truth is, **your wholeness is your work.**
Your healing.
Your journey back to Allah.
Your relationship with your past.
Your reconciliation with your pain.
No man, no woman—no matter how righteous—can do this work for you.

Marriage, when healthy, is not a merging of two halves into one. It's two whole souls walking side by side—**not to complete each other, but to reflect, support, challenge, and elevate**. A good spouse is not your other half—they're your mirror. They reveal parts of you that were hidden, dormant, or wounded. They amplify your strengths, and expose your flaws. And it's in that tension—between love and growth—that marriage becomes the refining fire Allah intended it to be.

This is why Allah calls spouses *"garments"* for one another:

> **"They are your garments, and you are their garments."** (*Qur'an 2:187*)

Garments don't complete you. They cover, protect, warm, and beautify you. They preserve your dignity and shield you from harm. In this metaphor, your spouse isn't your savior—they are your sanctuary.

But even a garment, no matter how soft, cannot heal the wounds you refuse to touch.

If you've been walking through life hoping that marriage will fix what's broken inside you—pause. Reflect. Heal. Ask yourself the hard questions. Why do I feel incomplete? Where did that belief begin? What am I really seeking in a spouse—companionship or escape?

The most powerful relationships are born not from neediness, but from **intention**. From people who have fallen, broken, wept—and still choose to rise, to love, to give. Whole people don't demand completeness from others; they share their fullness with grace. And when two people do that for each other, something sacred happens. They don't complete each other—they **magnify** one another.

So yes, seek a righteous spouse. Yearn for love. Long for companionship. But remember this: **no human being was created to complete you.** You were created whole, by a Perfect Creator, with everything you need to return to Him. Marriage is a means, not the mission. Your spouse is a blessing, not your purpose. The only One who truly completes you is the One who created you.

And maybe that's the real love story. Not one where you finally find someone to complete you—but one where you finally meet someone who inspires you to complete yourself.

Together.

In faith.
In healing.
In sincerity.

And with Allah always at the center.

Chapter Eleven

Growing Through Love

Love Isn't Enough: The Illusion Before the Storm

Love has a way of dressing itself in magic.

It makes everything feel brighter, softer, more beautiful. Before marriage, love can feel like a high—so potent, so addictive—that you forget you're only seeing part of the person standing before you. You project your dreams, your fantasies, your unmet needs onto them. You fall in love not just with who they are, but with who you *hope* they'll be. You convince yourself that love alone will carry you through the storms. That your chemistry will override any incompatibility. That your passion will somehow be enough to sustain a lifetime.

But that illusion eventually breaks.

Marriage doesn't just reveal the other person. It reveals *you*. And it does so in ways that nothing else can. Suddenly, the things you overlooked—their habits, their wounds, their silences, their flaws—begin to speak louder. And the parts of yourself you never had to confront—the anger, the fear, the insecurity, the ego—start rising to the surface.

This is when the real work begins. And this is where so many couples unravel.

Not because they don't love each other. But because they never prepared for what love would *ask* of them.

They thought love meant ease, but love demands endurance.
They thought love meant comfort, but love requires confrontation—with self, with ego, with pain.
They thought love meant romance, but real love often shows up as patience in silence, forgiveness in frustration, loyalty in exhaustion, and gentleness when it's least deserved.

Many couples enter marriage under false pretenses. They mistake attraction for alignment. They confuse excitement with compatibility. They bypass the hard conversations—about values, wounds, faith, family, money, purpose—because they don't want to ruin the "vibe." They assume that what feels good *must* be right.

But feeling good isn't enough. Not when real life hits. Not when trauma resurfaces. Not when your spouse fails to meet your emotional needs. Not when conflict keeps circling back because both of you are still carrying unhealed versions of yourselves into every argument.

And so, it begins: the slow erosion.

Resentment builds where unmet needs go unspoken.
Disconnection grows in the absence of vulnerability.
Shame festers where honesty is replaced with performance.

Many couples silently suffer in the space between expectation and reality. They look at their spouse and wonder, "Why don't you make me feel the way you used to?" forgetting that no one can sustain that high forever—not even themselves. They cling to a dream while starving in reality.

And here's the truth: **Love alone doesn't save a marriage.**

It never has.

What saves it is faith. Commitment. Radical self-awareness. The willingness to do the hard inner work, even when your partner isn't. The ability to sit with your pain without always needing someone else to rescue you from it. The humility to apologize. The maturity to hold space for someone else's humanity without making it about your own.

A couple that survives the storms isn't the one that had the best start. It's the one that kept showing up. They chose to keep learning from each other, over and over again. That understood love isn't a finished product—it's a practice. And that practice is often mundane, uncomfortable, and sacred all at once.

From an Islamic perspective, marriage isn't built on butterflies. It's built on responsibility, mercy, and intention. A righteous spouse isn't someone who completes you—they *walk beside you* as you both strive to complete yourselves through Allah. They are not your solution, your savior, or your source of happiness. They are a companion on the path—a path that sometimes gets lonely, even when you're walking together.

If you expect marriage to heal your past, you'll resent your spouse for not being your therapist.
If you expect your spouse to never trigger your pain, you'll miss the fact that they were sent to help you confront it.
If you believe that real love doesn't hurt, you'll keep running from the kind of love that could actually transform you.

The love that lasts isn't perfect. It's raw. It's bruised. It's forged in the fire of disappointment and forgiveness. It survives because both people choose—again and again—to nurture the flame when it's barely flickering.

So let go of the fantasy.

Don't seek someone to complete you.
Seek someone to build with.
Someone who sees your mess and still chooses you.
Someone who reminds you of Allah when you forget yourself.
Someone who doesn't worship your perfection—but holds space for your imperfection.
Someone who doesn't promise to fix your heart—but stands beside you while you fix it together.

That is love.

Not the one that sweeps you off your feet. But the one that holds your hand when you fall.

Chapter Twelve

Purposeful Conversations

At the beginning of marriage, communication often comes effortlessly. Newlyweds, wrapped in the joy and excitement of a fresh chapter, seem inseparable—both physically and emotionally. When not in each other's presence, their thoughts are constantly with one another, and they stay in touch with frequent calls, messages, and shared moments. This phase is often described as the "honeymoon period," when love is uncomplicated and everything feels easy. There is a longing to be close, a yearning that seems to grow with each separation. This stage, full of tenderness and connection, is beautiful—yet fleeting.

Many couples, caught up in the bliss of the early days, make the mistake of assuming this easy communication and closeness will last forever. Unfortunately, as time goes on, the simplicity of this natural bond can fade, and with it, the ease of communication. The soft, gentle exchanges that marked the early stages of marriage become harder to maintain. Arguments may be avoided early on due to both partners' eagerness to please and accommodate each other. This mutual desire to avoid conflict works for a while, but eventually, the pressures of daily life—compromises, unmet needs, unaddressed frustrations—can take their toll, and communication becomes strained.

When tension builds, it often results in misunderstandings and, eventually, disagreements. So, what should a couple do when communication starts to falter? First, they must recognize that ups and downs are completely natural. Every relationship, whether with family, friends, or a spouse, goes through phases of harmony and discord. Think back to the times when you had difficult conversations with parents or siblings—those moments didn't end the relationship, right? The same applies to marriage. The intensity of marital relationships, due to the constant proximity and emotional intimacy, can make conflicts feel more personal and amplified. It's not that conflict is inherently damaging; it's how we handle it that makes all the difference.

Healthy communication in marriage requires patience, maturity, and a willingness to work through differences. When we live in close quarters with someone, it's inevitable that small irritations will arise. Life's stresses—work, finances, family obligations—add further strain. The key is not to avoid conflict but to manage it skillfully. It's crucial to recognize that we will never see the world exactly as our spouse does, and that's okay. In fact, it's this diversity of perspectives that enriches life. If everyone thought the same way, life would lose its vibrancy.

How we communicate with our spouse influences the growth and health of the relationship. Often, it's not just the words we say, but the tone in which they are delivered that shapes the conversation. When we are first married, we tend to be on our best behavior, striving to show politeness and kindness. Over time, however, we become more relaxed, and this can have two effects: we might unintentionally become less courteous with our spouse, assuming they'll always understand us, or we might take this closeness as an opportunity to deepen our bond, knowing that we can drop our guards and be truly ourselves.

The key lies in how we use this relaxation to either build or harm our relationship. Too often, we say things without fully considering how our spouse will perceive them. How many times have you spoken without thinking, only for your spouse to react in a way that seems disproportionate to what you intended? We all do this from time to time, but it's important to pause before speaking and consider not only what we want to say, but also how it might be received. Our spouse is a trust from Allah, and how we treat them through our words and actions will be accounted for on the Day of Judgment. This understanding brings a level of responsibility and care into our communication.

A crucial aspect of communication is the timing of the conversation. Understanding your spouse's mood and circumstances can make all the difference in how a conversation unfolds. We all have moments when we're feeling tired, stressed, or overwhelmed. Being sensitive to these moments allows us to approach difficult conversations at a time when both parties are more likely to be receptive. For instance, if your spouse has just come home from a long day at work, they may not be in the best frame of mind for a serious discussion. Instead, it might be more effective to wait for a time when both of you are calm and focused.

Timing isn't just about waiting for the right moment; it's also about making space for open dialogue. Sometimes, it's best to ask your spouse to set aside time for a deeper conversation, free from distractions. This ensures that both of you are in a good mental and emotional state to address important issues. This consideration builds a foundation of respect, showing that you value your spouse's thoughts and feelings.

Another essential aspect of communication is tone. How we articulate our words can make or break the conversation. A condescending or dismissive tone can erode trust and confidence, leaving the other person feeling unappreciated. In marriage, it's essential to remember that criticism should always come from a place of love and care. The Arabic word *naseehah*, which means sincere advice or counsel, teaches us to speak with kindness, even when offering constructive feedback. Unfortunately, many well-meaning pieces of advice lose their impact when delivered in a harsh tone. It's important to be mindful of how we speak to our spouse, especially during times of disagreement.

Equally important is knowing when an apology is necessary. Sometimes, no matter how hard we try, communication fails. In these moments, a sincere apology is the bridge that restores harmony. However, an apology must be genuine and specific. It's not enough to simply say "I'm sorry"—we must understand what caused the hurt and express our regret for it. An empty apology does more harm than good. In addition, an apology should not be used as a way to justify actions or deflect responsibility. It should be an opportunity to close the chapter of conflict and move forward with a renewed commitment to each other.

Once an apology is made, it should be followed by meaningful actions. Saying sorry is important, but proving it through our behavior reinforces our commitment to not REPEAT the same mistakes. There is nothing more painful than being hurt by the same person in the same way, over and over again. Taking ownership of our actions and striving to do better is the key to maintaining trust and respect in the marriage.

Peace in marriage doesn't come automatically—it requires conscious effort. One of the best ways to cultivate peace is through effective communication. Marriage is not simply about coexistence; it's about building a life together, one where both partners feel heard, valued, and loved. When we communicate well, we foster understanding and empathy, which are the foundations of a strong and healthy relationship.

One common issue in marriage is the difference in communication styles between men and women. Women, in general, tend to be more verbal and emotionally expressive, while men often approach communication with a more logical and solution-oriented mindset. This difference can lead to misunderstandings, especially when women seek emotional support through conversation, but men feel compelled to offer solutions. These differences don't have to lead to conflict, but they do require understanding. For men, sometimes the best way to support their wives is simply to listen, to be present, and to offer comfort, rather than solutions. For women, recognizing that their husbands might feel frustrated when they can't "fix" the problem can lead to more harmonious interactions.

Communication is an ongoing process in marriage, and it takes conscious effort to keep it strong. It may start easy, but as life's complexities accumulate, the work of maintaining it becomes essential. If couples do not invest in this fundamental aspect of their relationship, they may find themselves drifting apart, unable to bridge the growing distance. Marriage requires continuous effort to communicate effectively, with consideration for timing, tone, and empathy, so that both partners feel connected and understood. By nurturing these skills, couples can maintain a relationship built on mutual respect, love, and trust—an enduring bond that withstands the challenges of life.

Chapter Thirteen

Surviving Toxic In-Law Drama

Navigating relationships with in-laws is often one of the most delicate aspects of marriage. While familial bonds can provide support and joy, they can also introduce significant challenges—especially when those relationships become toxic. The impact of a toxic in-law on a marriage can be profound, creating rifts not only between partners but also within the wider family circle. The emotional distress that results from toxic in-law dynamics can affect the overall health and stability of a marriage, causing stress and tension that might feel difficult to manage.

In this chapter, we'll explore the common toxic traits and behaviors that in-laws may exhibit, offering insights on how to navigate and ultimately protect your marriage from the impact of these dynamics. Understanding these behaviors is crucial for preserving emotional well-being, maintaining a strong marital bond, and keeping your home a place of peace.

Recognizing Toxic In-Law Behaviors

Toxic in-law dynamics can strain even the strongest of marriages. Below are 16 behaviors often seen in problematic in-law relationships.

1. **Lack of Boundaries:** Toxic in-laws may ignore healthy boundaries—dropping by unannounced, expecting immediate responses, or interfering in private matters. This creates ongoing stress and erodes a couple's sense of independence.

2. **Superficial Kindness:** They may act friendly in public but behave coldly or critically behind closed doors. This two-faced dynamic causes emotional discomfort and fosters mistrust.

3. **Gossip and Disrespect:** Spreading rumors or criticizing one partner behind their back can erode trust and sow division within the family, especially if it pits relatives against each other.

4. **Overstepping in Decision-Making:** Interference in choices like parenting, finances, or holiday plans can make a couple feel disempowered. It undermines their ability to make decisions as a unit.

5. **Controlling the Relationship:** Some in-laws try to dictate how the couple should live, where they should go, or how they should interact. This excessive influence can fracture a marriage's unity.

6. **The Silent Treatment:** Using silence or emotional withdrawal as punishment can be a passive-aggressive tactic that creates distance and emotional hurt.

7. **Constant Criticism:** Frequent negative feedback—no matter what is done—can wear down a person's confidence, making them feel inadequate and demoralized.

8. **Blame Shifting:** Assigning blame unfairly or scapegoating one spouse for problems in the extended family creates tension and resentment.

9. **Ongoing Disapproval:** Some in-laws never fully accept the marriage, expressing disappointment or hostility. This creates an undercurrent of emotional distress.

10. **False Displays of Affection:** When in-laws pretend to be kind or loving for appearances while withholding genuine care or interest, it creates confusion and emotional distance.

11. **Unwanted Advice:** Constantly offering opinions or telling the couple how to manage their home or children, even when not asked, can be invasive and demoralizing.

12. **Financial Interference:** In-laws who meddle in financial decisions, suggest purchases, or criticize spending habits may create conflict between spouses.

13. **Emotional Blackmail:** Using guilt, obligation, or emotional manipulation to get their way can destabilize the marital bond and cause emotional fatigue.

14. **Sabotaging Special Occasions:** Intentionally creating conflict around birthdays, holidays, or events can damage family unity and cause long-term resentment.

15. **Competitive Behavior:** When in-laws treat the daughter-in-law or son-in-law as a rival, it creates tension and shifts the relationship from familial support to emotional combat.

16. **Religious Abuse:** In some cases, religious teachings may be used manipulatively to control or guilt-trip one spouse—often under the guise of "piety." Misusing faith to assert dominance, shame, or silence a partner can be a subtle yet deeply harmful form of abuse.

Understanding these behaviors doesn't mean rejecting in-laws altogether. Rather, it equips couples to set healthy boundaries and protect their relationship. Where possible, seeking help from a qualified counselor or mediator can support healing and long-term family balance.

Shielding Against Toxic In-Laws

Managing toxic in-laws requires effort, patience, and a unified approach between you and your spouse. Here are some strategies for surviving and thriving amidst the challenges posed by toxic family dynamics.

1. **Recognize and Validate Emotions**: The first step is acknowledging the emotional toll toxic in-laws can have on your relationship. It's important to create a safe space for you and your spouse to talk about your feelings, fostering mutual empathy and understanding.

2. **Open Communication**: Honest and transparent communication is essential. Sharing how the toxic behavior of the in-laws affects both of you strengthens your emotional connection and helps build a resilient bond between you and your spouse.

3. **Establish Unified Boundaries**: Setting clear and mutually agreed-upon boundaries is crucial for managing toxic in-laws. By reinforcing these boundaries, you demonstrate a united front that prioritizes your relationship and well-being.

4. **Prioritize Your Relationship**: Devote time and energy to nurturing your marriage. A strong and secure relationship acts as a shield against external pressures, including interference from toxic family members.

5. **Unified Response**: When dealing with toxic in-laws, presenting a united front is key. Avoid situations where one partner contradicts the other, as this can create division. A cohesive response shows strength and support for each other.

6. **Practice Empathy and Understanding**: Develop a deeper understanding of your spouse's emotional needs. Listen attentively, share concerns, and provide emotional support. This practice strengthens your bond and enhances your ability to deal with external challenges.

7. **Limit Exposure to Toxicity**: Minimize interactions with toxic in-laws where possible. Protect your time together as a couple by avoiding situations that might trigger conflict or distress.

8. **Seek Counseling**: If the situation becomes overwhelming, seeking individual or couples counseling can provide invaluable emotional support. A professional can help you manage the emotional strain of dealing with toxic in-laws.

9. **Professional Mediation:** In some cases, involving a neutral third party—such as a qualified mediator or therapist—can help resolve conflicts constructively and foster greater understanding among all parties involved. For Muslim families, this process can be further strengthened by consulting a person of Islamic knowledge, such as a trusted imam or scholar, who can offer guidance rooted in Shari'ah and prophetic wisdom. Their involvement not only brings spiritual clarity but also ensures that reconciliation efforts align with Islamic values, fostering peace with both emotional insight and religious grounding.

10. **Assertive Communication Training**: Learning how to communicate assertively allows you and your spouse to express needs, set boundaries, and address concerns respectfully without escalating conflict.

11. **Self-Care Practices**: Practice self-care as a couple. Engage in activities that promote emotional and physical well-being, helping you both stay grounded and resilient amid challenges.

12. **Legal Guidance**: If legal matters or persistent harassment arise, it's wise to consult a legal professional to ensure you understand your rights and protect your marriage from further harm.

Conclusion

In-law relationships are a complex yet essential aspect of family life. Recognizing toxic behaviors and taking proactive steps to protect your marriage is crucial for maintaining peace and harmony in your family. By establishing healthy boundaries, practicing open communication, and seeking support when necessary, you can navigate the challenges posed by toxic in-laws and preserve the emotional well-being of your marriage. Remember, prioritizing your spouse, nurturing your relationship, and protecting your family's happiness will help ensure a balanced, harmonious family dynamic, even in the face of adversity.

Chapter Fourteen

Addicted to Pain: Breaking Free from Trauma Bonds

Navigating the Deep Emotional Attachment to an Abusive Figure

Trauma bonding represents a profound and complex attachment that can develop between a victim and an abuser, marked by an intense emotional link that persists despite consistent mistreatment and harm. This powerful bond is not constrained by age, gender, or background; it can affect anyone who finds themselves in a relationship defined by cycles of betrayal, emotional manipulation, and control. In this chapter, we'll explore the mechanisms behind trauma bonding, its psychological roots, and strategies for breaking free from this painful attachment.

Trauma bonding develops when someone becomes emotionally reliant on their abuser. This dependency often forms through a pattern of "hot and cold" behavior—periods of affection, followed by neglect or cruelty. These unpredictable shifts reinforce the bond, as the victim, craving the abuser's positive attention, often overlooks the repeated harm inflicted upon them. To break free from trauma bonding, it's essential to understand the underlying dynamics of the relationship and take practical steps toward empowerment and independence.

Understanding the Roots of Trauma Bonding

At its core, trauma bonding is an emotional entanglement shaped by several factors. One major factor is the unconscious attempt to reconcile past wounds within a current abusive relationship. Individuals who carry unresolved trauma, especially from childhood, may be more vulnerable to trauma bonding. They might unknowingly gravitate toward relationships that mirror their past experiences, hoping—albeit unconsciously—to resolve old conflicts or receive the validation and love they missed in earlier years. This desire to "fix" the painful past can make leaving the relationship especially challenging, as they feel that staying offers a chance for healing or redemption, despite the harm inflicted.

Other contributing factors can include intermittent reinforcement (the cycle of cruelty and affection that creates emotional confusion), low self-worth, dependency rooted in fear or survival, and distorted beliefs about love and loyalty. Together, these dynamics form a powerful bond that isn't rooted in safety or mutual respect, but in unresolved pain and emotional survival mechanisms.

Steps Towards Liberating Yourself from Trauma Bonding

Breaking free from trauma bonding requires both insight into the abusive patterns and determination to prioritize your well-being. The following steps provide a roadmap for reclaiming your independence and emotional health:

1. **Recognize the Abuse**: The first and most critical step in freeing yourself from trauma bonding is to acknowledge the abuse. Understand that no one deserves to be treated with disrespect or cruelty. This recognition is empowering because it affirms your right to dignity, which is essential for taking the next steps. Remember, the abuser's behavior is not a reflection of your worth.

2. **Seek Support**: Reaching out to friends, family, or a therapist can provide crucial emotional support and perspective. A trained therapist or support group can help you identify patterns in your relationship and empower you to make decisions that honor your well-being. Having a support system strengthens your resolve and lessens feelings of isolation.

3. **Create Boundaries**: Establish clear, firm boundaries with the abuser. This may mean limiting or entirely cutting off contact if possible. Boundaries act as a form of self-protection, reinforcing your right to a life free of manipulation and control. Boundaries also communicate self-respect and begin the process of emotionally separating from the abuser.

4. **Practice Self-Care**: Trauma bonding drains emotional and physical energy. Prioritize activities that replenish and rejuvenate you—exercise, meditation, prayer, athkar (remembrance), pursuing a hobby, or spending time with loved ones. Self-care not only builds resilience but also fosters a sense of self-worth and well-being, both of which are vital for moving forward.

5. **Educate Yourself**: Learning about trauma bonding and abusive relationship dynamics is empowering. Books like *Why Does He Do That?* by Lundy Bancroft or *The Verbally Abusive Relationship* by Patricia Evans provide insight into abusive behavior, helping you recognize manipulation tactics and understand the psychological hold these relationships create.

6. **Join Support Groups**: Support groups or online forums where others share similar experiences can be a lifeline. These communities provide validation, practical advice, and solidarity, helping you feel understood and supported in your journey. Knowing you're not alone in your experience can give you the strength to make difficult decisions.

7. **Safety Planning**: If the situation escalates or becomes unsafe, having a clear safety plan is essential. This may involve planning for financial independence, having an emergency contact list, and securing a safe place to stay if needed. Prioritizing your safety—emotionally, physically, and financially—is paramount as you navigate the process of breaking free.

8. **Therapeutic Techniques**: Therapeutic approaches like Cognitive Behavioral Therapy (CBT), Eye Movement Desensitization and Reprocessing (EMDR), or Dialectical Behavior Therapy (DBT) are valuable tools in trauma recovery. These methods help process painful memories, develop healthy coping mechanisms, and reduce anxiety, making it easier to rebuild your life and sense of self outside of the abusive relationship.

9. **Practice Assertiveness and Self-Assertion**: Assertiveness training empowers you to set boundaries, communicate effectively, and stand up for your needs. Learning to express yourself confidently and without fear of retribution helps break the cycle of self-doubt and manipulation, paving the way for healthier relationships in the future.

10. **Empowerment through Independence**: One of the most effective ways to break the trauma bond is to build your independence. Pursue activities that strengthen your sense of self, such as further education, career development, or financial independence. Cultivating autonomy and self-sufficiency boosts self-esteem and diminishes the power the abuser holds over you.

Expert Perspectives on Trauma Bonding

Trauma bonding is a perilous emotional state with profound implications for mental and emotional health. Dr. Judith Herman, an esteemed trauma expert and author of *Trauma and Recovery*, explains that trauma bonding often serves as a coping mechanism for those with unresolved childhood trauma. People may unconsciously seek out familiar patterns of abuse in adult relationships as they attempt to heal past wounds, perpetuating the cycle of trauma. Similarly, Dr. Bessel van der Kolk, a leading expert in trauma and author of *The Body Keeps the Score*, explains that trauma can create powerful emotional bonds between victims and their abusers. These bonds often form as a result of repeated cycles of harm and reconciliation, where the victim becomes psychologically entangled with the abusive partner. Over time, this pattern can lead to deep emotional dependency, even when the relationship is clearly harmful. The abuser's intermittent kindness strengthens this bond, making it exceedingly difficult to escape.

Dr. Patricia Evans, a well-known expert on verbal and emotional abuse, emphasizes that breaking free from abusive dynamics requires a deep understanding of how abuse operates. She advocates for survivors to seek professional guidance, as therapy and support can play a vital role in the healing process. Recognizing the psychological patterns at play is a critical first step toward reclaiming one's sense of self and building healthier relationships.

Conclusion

Trauma bonding is a complicated and often invisible trap, creating emotional dependencies that can be difficult to untangle. Recognizing the patterns of trauma bonding, building supportive connections, and prioritizing self-care are crucial steps in liberating oneself from this painful attachment. Though breaking free can be a challenging journey, it is a deeply empowering and transformative process that opens the door to healthier, more fulfilling relationships. Remember, each step toward healing brings you closer to reclaiming your autonomy, dignity, and well-being. Through understanding, support, and professional guidance, it is possible to overcome trauma bonding and move forward into a life defined by respect, self-worth, and inner peace.

Chapter Fifteen

Outsmarting the Narcissist's Game

Navigating Relationships with Narcissistic Individuals

Imagine being swept off your feet by someone who seems **perfect** – attentive, charming, and enamored with you. Yet months later, you find yourself walking on eggshells, doubting your own memories, and feeling isolated from friends and family. *How did the fairytale transform into a nightmare?* This chapter explores that journey and, more importantly, how to navigate and break free from it. We will delve into the psychology of Narcissistic Personality Disorder, understand the telltale cycles of a narcissistic relationship, learn to recognize manipulation, and discover how to reclaim your power and heal. Throughout, we'll include expert insights, real-life examples, and even some exercises to help you reflect and recover. The tone is empowering and supportive—you are not alone, and with knowledge and courage, you can emerge stronger.

Understanding Narcissism in Depth

One classic depiction of Narcissus from Greek mythology powerfully symbolizes the dangers of *self-obsession*. Narcissistic Personality Disorder (NPD) is characterized by an extreme focus on oneself, an inflated sense of importance, and a lack of empathy for others. Not all narcissists look or act the same, however. Psychologists have identified several types of narcissism, each with distinct traits. Understanding these types can help you recognize how different narcissists behave in relationships. Below, we break down four common subtypes—**grandiose, vulnerable, malignant, and communal** narcissism—with descriptions and examples of how they might manifest in real life.

Grandiose Narcissism (Overt)

This is the "classic" narcissist most people imagine. Grandiose narcissists are overtly arrogant, entitled, and charmingly self-absorbed. They boast about their achievements, crave admiration, and often lack any true empathy. In relationships, a grandiose narcissist may shower you with attention at first but will expect constant praise in return. Conversations tend to be one-sided—they can talk for hours about themselves and show little genuine interest in your thoughts or feelings. **Case Example:** Ahmed, a charismatic entrepreneur, impressed everyone in the community with his success and eloquence. His marriage to Fatima began with much joy, but over time, his need for admiration became evident. He often dismissed Fatima's achievements, interrupted her frequently, and grew irritable when conversations weren't centered around him. Gradually, Fatima realized that Ahmed viewed her more as an audience than a partner.

Vulnerable Narcissism (Covert)

Also known as covert narcissism, this type presents almost as the mirror opposite of the grandiose kind on the surface. Vulnerable narcissists may appear shy, sensitive, or insecure—but underneath lies the same sense of entitlement and lack of empathy. They often have a victim mentality, feeling that they are unappreciated geniuses or that life has given them less than they deserve. In relationships, a vulnerable narcissist is prone to passive-aggression and resentment. They might not brag openly, but they seethe when not given special treatment. They are extremely sensitive to criticism, perceiving even mild feedback as a personal attack. Covert narcissists might use guilt trips or play the martyr to get attention. **Case Example:** Aisha's husband, Bilal, initially appeared humble and devout. He often lamented that his colleagues didn't recognize his talents, claiming he "always finishes last" because of his integrity. Aisha empathized and offered support. However, when Aisha received a promotion at work, Bilal became sullen for days, accusing her of neglecting his struggles. He frequently resorted to the silent treatment instead of expressing his feelings, leaving Aisha anxious about her perceived shortcomings. Bilal's hypersensitivity and concealed grandiosity—believing he was special yet unacknowledged—gradually diminished Aisha's joy in her own accomplishments.

Malignant Narcissism

Malignant narcissists are the most toxic and dangerous subtype. This form of narcissism blends the self-centeredness of NPD with features of aggression, paranoia, or even sociopathy. In addition to feeling superior, malignant narcissists derive pleasure from exploiting and hurting others. They are often cruel, manipulative, and vengeful, seeing the people in their lives as tools to be used or obstacles to bulldoze. A relationship with a malignant narcissist can feel like a constant battle; you may feel afraid of their rage or retaliation if you challenge them. These individuals show Machiavellian traits—they will lie, scheme, and violate boundaries without remorse. **Case Example:** Khadija noticed early on that her husband, Omar, had a troubling side—he was often rude to service staff and showed little compassion for others' hardships. During their courtship, however, he never directed this behavior toward her. After marriage, Omar's charm diminished. He isolated Khadija from her family and friends, took control of all financial matters, and would erupt in anger over minor issues. When Khadija expressed a desire to leave, Omar threatened to tarnish her reputation within their community and harm her belongings. This pattern of fear-based control is characteristic of a malignant narcissist, who often leaves their partners feeling betrayed, fearful, manipulated, and devastated.

Communal Narcissism

At first glance, a communal narcissist might not seem narcissistic at all. These individuals cast themselves as do-gooders and altruists. They often loudly champion causes, present themselves as empathic and generous, and seek recognition as a "hero" or "saint" in their community. The key, however, is that their charitable acts are ultimately self-serving—they crave the validation and praise that comes with being seen as a good person. In private relationships, communal narcissists still display entitlement and lack of empathy. They might talk about compassion and kindness for the less fortunate, yet dismiss or ignore the emotional needs of their own partner or family. This duality can be very confusing for those close to them. **Case**

Example: Ibrahim was widely admired in his community for his charitable endeavors— organizing fundraisers, leading community service projects, and frequently sharing his philanthropic activities on social media. His wife, Layla, initially felt fortunate to be married to someone so devoted to helping others. However, at home, Ibrahim was emotionally distant and dismissive. When Layla fell ill, he chastised her for "inconveniencing" him and emphasized the importance of his volunteer work over her well-being. Ibrahim's public persona as a benevolent leader bolstered his ego, while privately he exhibited entitlement and a lack of empathy, typical traits of communal narcissism. Loved ones of communal narcissists often feel invisible and confused, wondering how the same person who is #SavingTheWorld on Instagram can be so neglectful and self-centered behind closed doors.

Expert Insight: According to Dr. Ramani Durvasula, a leading expert on narcissism, these types often exist on a spectrum rather than as completely separate categories. Many narcissistic individuals have overlapping traits (for instance, grandiose and malignant traits together). But whatever the type, the impact on those close to them is consistently damaging. The key is not the label, but recognizing the patterns of behavior—the constant need for admiration, the lack of true empathy, the entitlement, and the manipulative or abusive tactics that we will explore next.

The Narcissistic Relationship Cycle

One of the most bewildering experiences in a relationship with someone who has NPD is the roller coaster of emotions they put you through. Narcissistic relationships commonly follow a cycle of abuse with distinct stages. Understanding this cycle can validate that what you went through is real and predictably manipulated—not your imagination. It also reveals how this cycle forges an addictive trauma bond that keeps you attached to the narcissist despite the pain. Below are the typical stages of the narcissistic relationship cycle: Idealization, Devaluation, Discard, and Hoovering, and how each stage unfolds.

1. **Idealization (Love Bombing):** In the beginning, the narcissist is often intensely charming and attentive. This phase, sometimes called love bombing, feels like a fairy tale. You are idealized—put on a pedestal as the perfect partner. The narcissist showers you with praise, affection, gifts, and grand gestures. They insist you're soulmates, that your connection is special and "meant to be." You

might get constant texts and calls, extravagant dates, and rapid declarations of love or commitment. This overwhelm of positive attention is deliberate: by creating a whirlwind romance, the narcissist secures your trust and devotion early. **Case Example:** In the first month of their acquaintance, Bilal sent Aisha flowers daily and expressed that he had never met anyone like her. He was attentive to her every word and quickly discussed the prospect of marriage. Aisha was captivated by the intensity, unaware that this behavior, known as "love bombing," was fostering emotional dependence.

2. **Devaluation:** Once you are emotionally invested, the narcissist's bright demeanor darkens. The very qualities that they once praised in you might now be criticized or belittled. Devaluation can be sudden or gradual, overt or insidious. You'll notice coldness, criticism, and manipulation replacing the earlier adoration. They might start picking fights, making sarcastic comments, or sabotaging your successes. At this stage, victims often feel confusion and self-doubt—what did I do wrong? You try desperately to get back to the "honeymoon" phase, often blaming yourself for the change. The narcissist may gaslight you (denying things they said or did), compare you negatively to others, or withhold affection to punish you. This push-pull dynamic keeps you unstable and focused on regaining their approval. **Case Example:** After three blissful months of marriage, Bilal's behavior toward Aisha shifted. He began rolling his eyes at her opinions and dismissing her feelings by saying, "You're too sensitive; I was just joking," after making hurtful remarks. At times, he would withdraw for days without explanation. Aisha found herself walking on eggshells, anxiously trying to "fix" whatever mysterious mistake had caused his change in mood.

3. **Discard:** In many cases, the relationship cycle reaches a breaking point where the narcissist discards their partner—temporarily or permanently. In this stage, the narcissist may abruptly end the relationship or distance themselves, acting as if you no longer exist or are no longer of use to them. The discard can be emotionally brutal. Some narcissists humiliate their partners on the way out, blaming them entirely for the failed relationship. Others ghost or leave without closure. You might discover they've been lining up a new source of "supply" (another person to feed their ego) even before the relationship fully ends. The discard phase leaves you

heartbroken, confused, and traumatized. Importantly, it often isn't truly final—because of the next stage. **Case Example:** After a minor disagreement, Bilal told Aisha, "I can't do this anymore. You're a burden," and abruptly left. Aisha was devastated—within weeks, she saw on social media that Bilal was already in a new relationship. He acted as if their intense bond never existed, blaming her for "pushing him away." This kind of callous discard is a hallmark of narcissistic abuse, reflecting how narcissists often view partners as disposable once their needs are no longer being met.

4. **Hoovering:** Named after the Hoover vacuum, this stage describes the narcissist's attempt to suck you back in after a discard. Often when you begin to move on or when their new source of attention falls through, the narcissist returns with apologies, promises, or dramatic gestures to win you back. They may suddenly say they "have changed" or that they realize you are the love of their life. Hoovering is manipulative—it's not genuine remorse, but a tactic to regain control and the "supply" you provide. They are adept at telling you exactly what you want to hear. If you go back, the cycle will repeat, usually with even more intensity in the devaluation next time. **Case Example:** Two months after their separation, Bilal began reaching out to Aisha again, saying, "I can't stop thinking about you. I know I made mistakes. Please, let's meet for coffee." He sent old photos from their happier times and even appeared at her door with tears in his eyes. This classic hoovering tactic left Aisha in turmoil—part of her longed to believe in the rekindling of their past affection. Narcissists are adept at hoovering, using affectionate gestures to lure former partners back, only to resume their manipulative behavior once they regain control.

Trauma Bonding

As painful as the idealization—devaluation—discard cycle is, many survivors describe feeling addicted to the relationship. This is not because they enjoy the abuse, but because the cycle creates a trauma bond. A trauma bond as discussed in the previous chapter, is a deep emotional attachment that forms through repeated patterns of reward and punishment. The brain becomes conditioned to seek the brief highs of affection amidst long periods of despair. In narcissistic abuse, the intermittent reinforcement—occasional love bombing or apologies amid lots of abuse—literally changes your stress response. You might find yourself obsessing over how to get the good times back, much like an addiction. Intermittent kindness can actually strengthen attachment more than constant kindness. Over time, you may feel you need the narcissist, losing sight of your independent identity. As one source explains, "Trauma bonding occurs as a result of the intermittent reinforcement of 'reward and punishment' that occurs as part of the abuse cycle." This makes leaving extremely difficult, and victims often describe feeling "empty" or in withdrawal when attempting to separate. Recognizing the trauma bond for what it is—a physiological and psychological response to abuse—is crucial. It reminds you that love is not what's binding you; rather, it's the manipulation and chemical highs and lows orchestrated by the abuser. In the next sections, we will discuss how to identify the manipulative tactics that fuel this cycle and, later, how to break the cycle and heal from the trauma bond.

Recognizing Manipulative Tactics

Narcissists deploy a variety of manipulative tactics to maintain control in relationships. These tactics can distort your reality, wear down your self-esteem, and keep you off-balance and dependent. By learning to recognize these behaviors, you can better assert your boundaries and avoid getting drawn deeper into the narcissist's web. Below are some of the most common manipulation tactics used by individuals with narcissistic tendencies, along with explanations and examples:

- **Gaslighting:** Perhaps the most infamous narcissistic tactic, gaslighting involves **making you question your own reality or sanity**. The term comes from the classic film *Gaslight*, in which a husband manipulates small elements of the environment and insists his wife is mistaken or imagining things. In practice, a gaslighting narcissist will deny that things you know happened ever occurred, downplay your feelings, or outright lie about past events. They might say, "That never happened, you're crazy," or "You're remembering it wrong." Over time, this can make you genuinely doubt your memory and judgment. For example, if you confront a narcissistic partner about hurtful comments they made, they may reply, "I have no idea what you're talking about. You're so sensitive—it wasn't a big deal." By doing this, they invalidate your experience and make you wonder if you're overreacting or even losing grip on reality. **Your Response:** If you notice this pattern, remind yourself: *you are not crazy*. Keeping a journal of incidents can help affirm the truth. Gaslighting is emotional abuse, pure and simple, intended to make you feel confused and dependent on the abuser's version of reality.

- **Blame-Shifting and DARVO:** Narcissists hate taking responsibility for their misdeeds. Instead, they are experts at flipping the script and blaming *you* for exactly what they did. This is known as blame-shifting. One common form is encapsulated in the acronym **DARVO** – *Deny, Attack, Reverse Victim and Offender*. First, they deny any wrongdoing; then they attack you for bringing it up; finally, they portray themselves as the *true victim* and you as the offender. For instance, you might find yourself apologizing to them after you confronted *their* bad behavior! A concrete example: suppose you catch a narcissistic partner in a lie. A blame-shifting response might be, "If you weren't always nagging me, I wouldn't have to hide things! This is really your fault." They turn the discussion into an indictment of *your* behavior. In doing so, they avoid accountability and often guilt you into backing down. **Your Response:** Recognize this for what it is. Healthy individuals address complaints; narcissists deflect and project. Don't get derailed defending yourself against absurd accusations. Bring focus back to the original issue, or disengage from the conversation if it's going nowhere productive.

- **Silent Treatment:** This is a passive-aggressive weapon in the narcissist's arsenal. Instead of communicating openly, a narcissist might punish you by withdrawing all communication and affection—effectively freezing you out. The silent treatment leaves you anxiously guessing what's wrong and often begging to get back into the narcissist's good graces. It's a form of **emotional coercion**: the narcissist is attempting to make you so uncomfortable that you concede to their demands or forgive their bad behavior just to end the silence. For example, after a minor disagreement, your partner might ignore your texts and calls for days. When you finally reach them, they act cold and say, "You should know why I'm not talking to you." This tactic is extremely painful because humans are wired to crave social connection— being suddenly treated as invisible by someone you love triggers panic and self-blame. **Your Response:** While it's natural to feel upset, try not to *chase* or excessively apologize just to end the silence if you did nothing wrong. Calmly let them know that stonewalling is not an acceptable way to handle conflict. In a healthy relationship, both parties communicate even when upset. Prolonged silent treatment is emotional abuse, and you have the right to distance yourself from it. If they continue the pattern, recognize this as a serious red flag.

- **Triangulation:** This occurs when the narcissist **involves a third person** in your two-person relationship conflicts to manipulate you. The third party could be a friend, relative, ex-partner, or even a therapist or counselor. Narcissistic triangulation is used to create jealousy, insecurity, or a sense of competition. For instance, a narcissist might tell you *"My ex never complained about this— maybe I made a mistake leaving them,"* or they might share private details of your arguments with a mutual friend to sway that friend to their side. By pitting people against each other, the narcissist keeps the attention off their own behavior and maintains control. In a family scenario, a narcissistic parent might compare siblings: "Why can't you be more like your brother?" In a romantic setting, they might flirt with someone else or constantly mention how others admire them, to make you feel insecure. **Your Response:** Triangulation is meant to provoke you. Recognize what's happening and refuse to play the game. Don't let a narcissist isolate you from allies or dictate whom you can talk to. If they are involving outsiders inappropriately, assert that your issues need to be resolved between the two of you. Often, discussing and clarifying things directly with the third party (when appropriate) in a calm way can defuse the narcissist's attempt to control the narrative. Boundaries are crucial here: *"I won't discuss our private matters with X. If you have concerns, talk to me directly."* Knowledge is power—understanding triangulation helps you not internalize the implied message that you're *less than* someone else.

- **Boundary Violations:** People with narcissistic traits typically have little respect for others' boundaries. Boundaries are the rules or limits that you set for how others can treat you and what behavior you will accept. Narcissists often steamroll these limits. This can take many forms: showing up uninvited or at inappropriate times, going through your personal belongings or phone, pushing for rapid intimacy (emotional or physical) before you're ready, or refusing to take "no" for an answer. In a relationship, boundary violations might look like your partner demanding access to all your accounts and passwords, or conversely, insisting on privacy for themselves while prying into your life. They may make major decisions that affect you both without consulting you (like making large purchases or plans)—a sign of both entitlement and lack of empathy. Why do they do this? Boundaries are a way we carve out our own identity and self-respect; narcissists want complete control and see your independence as a threat. By violating boundaries, they assert dominance and keep you disempowered. **Your Response:** First, get clear on what your boundaries are—emotionally, physically, financially, digitally, etc. Communicate them clearly when they come up (e.g., "I'm not comfortable with you reading my journal. Please stop."). A healthy partner will apologize and respect your limit; a narcissist will likely dismiss or ignore it, or turn it into an argument about trust ("Why, what are you hiding?"). Stand firm. You do *not* have to justify reasonable boundaries. Consistently reinforcing your limits, and walking away from those who won't respect them, is key to protecting yourself. Remember that a partner who will not respect your "no" is signaling that they don't see you as an equal individual—a serious sign of toxicity.

These tactics—gaslighting, blame-shifting, silent treatment, triangulation, and trampling boundaries—are designed to confuse and control you. When you're in the fog of these manipulations, you may feel like you're constantly on trial, constantly trying to prove yourself, or losing grip on what's real. It's not uncommon to experience cognitive dissonance (feeling torn between the narcissist's version of events and your own) and even to start adopting some of the narcissist's distorted perspectives about yourself. By naming these behaviors, you reclaim some power. You can say, *"This is gaslighting, and it's not okay,"* or *"I see this triangulation for what it is."* Identifying manipulation is the first step toward resisting it. In the next section, we'll look at the toll that enduring these tactics can take on your mental and emotional health.

Psychological and Emotional Impact

Being in a relationship with a narcissist is more than just "difficult"—it can be deeply traumatic. The constant manipulation, criticism, and emotional chaos leave lasting scars. Survivors of narcissistic relationships often describe it as a kind of slow erosion of their former self. If you've been through this, you might recognize many of the following long-term effects. Understanding these common impacts can validate your experience and highlight why healing is so important. Here are some of the psychological and emotional consequences of narcissistic abuse:

- **Emotional Exhaustion and Hypervigilance:** Life with a narcissist is **draining**. You may have spent so much energy trying to keep the peace, avoid triggering their anger, or decipher their shifting moods that you ended up chronically exhausted. Many survivors live in a state of **hypervigilance**— constantly on edge, anticipating the next attack or drama. Your nervous system has essentially been on "high alert" for a prolonged period, which is physically and mentally wearing. This can lead to sleep disturbances, difficulty concentrating, and a feeling of being *"burnt out"*. You might feel older than your years or as if you're running on fumes, because the relationship never allowed you true rest or safety.

- **Self-Doubt and Low Self-Esteem:** A heartbreaking effect of narcissistic abuse is the collapse of your self-confidence. Over time, the constant criticism, gaslighting, and blame can make you doubt your own worth and abilities. You start believing the negative things the narcissist said about you: *"I'm not good enough. I'm too sensitive. I can't do anything right."* The victim's sense of self is slowly worn down. One article on narcissistic abuse notes that the victim may begin to feel *"worthless and flawed"* after enduring constant belittlement. You may become indecisive, always second-guessing yourself, because the narcissist trained you to think you're always wrong. Additionally, you might fear making even small mistakes, since you were harshly punished for them in the past. This loss of self-esteem doesn't magically return after the relationship ends; it's something you need to actively rebuild (as we'll discuss in the Healing section).

- **Anxiety and PTSD Symptoms:** It is very common for survivors to experience **anxiety disorders** or symptoms of post-traumatic stress after a narcissistic relationship. The unpredictable and threatening environment keeps your body flooded with stress hormones. You might experience panic attacks, a constant feeling of dread, or obsessive thoughts about what happened. Many survivors have triggers—maybe a tone of voice, a phrase, or seeing something that reminds you of your ex—that cause your body to react as if you're in danger *again*. This is essentially a trauma response. In fact, enduring narcissistic abuse over a long period can lead to Complex PTSD (C-PTSD), a condition resulting from *chronic* trauma rather than a one-time event. Signs of C-PTSD can include intrusive memories or flashbacks of the abuse, nightmares, hypervigilance, and avoidance of anything that reminds you of the trauma. You might also feel emotionally numb at times, or conversely, have intense emotional reactions that feel out of control. Research has shown that prolonged emotional abuse can indeed result in PTSD-like symptoms. If you're feeling jumpy, anxious, or constantly fearful even after leaving the relationship, know that this is a normal response to abnormal stress. It doesn't mean you're "weak"—it means your mind and body have been through war and are still in defense mode.

- **Depression and Despair:** Living with someone who invalidates or abuses you can also lead to depression. You might feel hopeless, like nothing you do will ever make things better (a sense of learned helplessness). Many people in narcissistic relationships become isolated—the narcissist may have driven away your friends or family, or you felt too ashamed to tell others what was happening—and this isolation worsens depression. There's also a mourning of the relationship itself: you lose the *illusion* of the person you thought you were with. As one survivor put it, "I was grieving the person I thought he was, and the future I thought we would have." Depression may come with fatigue, changes in appetite, and a loss of interest in activities you once enjoyed. In severe cases, survivors might experience **suicidal thoughts** because the situation feels so bleak. If you feel this way, please seek professional help immediately—there are therapists and support groups who understand narcissistic abuse and can help guide you out of that darkness. Remember, *depression lies*. It tells you that you're trapped and worthless, but in truth, there is a path forward, and these feelings can heal with time and support.

- **Complex PTSD and Long-Term Trauma:** C-PTSD deserves special mention. While not yet formally recognized in the DSM (Diagnostic Manual) that many therapists use, C-PTSD is recognized in the World Health Organization's ICD and by many trauma specialists. C-PTSD results from long-term trauma where escape was difficult, such as years of emotional abuse by a narcissistic partner. Along with PTSD symptoms like flashbacks and hypervigilance, C-PTSD often includes deep changes in one's belief about oneself and others. People with C-PTSD from narcissistic abuse may struggle with: **self-concept** (e.g., "I feel permanently damaged, ashamed, or like I don't know who I am anymore"), **emotional regulation** (e.g., sudden crying spells, intense anger, or complete numbness), and **relationship difficulties** (e.g., difficulty trusting anyone, or conversely falling into another abusive relationship because it feels familiar). One description of C-PTSD notes that survivors often have *"difficulty maintaining a positive outlook, problems regulating anxiety, poor self-worth, feelings of guilt and shame, and difficulty maintaining relationships"*. Does that sound familiar? It's essentially a summary of what narcissistic abuse can do to a person. The emotional wounds are deep, but with proper trauma-informed therapy, individuals absolutely can recover and even experience personal growth. Many survivors later say that while they wouldn't wish the experience on anyone, the recovery process led them to discover an inner strength and wisdom they didn't know they had.

It's important to remember that *not everyone will experience all of these symptoms*, and the intensity can vary. Factors like the duration of the relationship, the narcissist's level of abusiveness, your own support system, and prior life experiences all play a role in how it affects you. However, if you are reading this chapter because you suspect you're in such a relationship (or are recovering from one), know that any mix of these feelings—exhaustion, self-doubt, anxiety, depression—is a **valid response** to what you've been through. In fact, a combination of low self-esteem, high anxiety, and lingering trauma is sometimes informally called "narcissistic abuse syndrome"—not an official diagnosis, but a recognition that this form of abuse has a recognizable pattern of effects.

Case Example: Many survivors liken life with a narcissist to being on a roller coaster they never agreed to ride. "One day he adored me and I felt on top of the world; the next day I was the villain and everything was my fault." says Amina, 32, who spent five years with a narcissistic husband. "By the end, I genuinely felt like a shell of myself. I would burst into tears for no reason and thought I was going crazy. It took me a long time after leaving to realize that these were trauma symptoms—that he wasn't in my life anymore, but the imprint of his abuse was still in my mind." This reflection is a testament to how psychological abuse can linger. The good news is, with time and the right strategies, you can undo much of this damage. The human mind and heart are remarkably resilient. In the next section, we will discuss how to begin breaking free from a narcissist's grip, followed by concrete steps for healing and recovering your sense of self.

Breaking Free and Reclaiming Power

If you are entangled with a narcissist—whether it's a romantic partner/spouse, a family member, or even a close friend—reaching the point of deciding to **break free** is an act of immense courage. Narcissists condition those around them to feel helpless and dependent, so choosing to leave or significantly distance yourself means overcoming powerful psychological bonds (and sometimes external obstacles like shared finances or children). It's often said that *"Leaving a narcissist is one of the toughest things you'll ever do."*

But many have done it, and you can too. This section offers a step-by-step guide to help you disengage from a narcissistic relationship and begin reclaiming your power and autonomy. The focus is on **practical strategies**: setting boundaries, recognizing and resisting manipulation, seeking support, and taking legal or safety measures if necessary. Each person's situation is unique, so not every step may apply directly to you, but these guidelines provide a roadmap toward freedom.

1. **Acknowledge the Reality of the Abuse:** The first step is often the hardest: fully **recognizing and accepting** that you are in a toxic, abusive relationship and that you *deserve better*. Denial can be strong—you might find yourself minimizing their behavior ("It's not *that* bad, they're good when they want to be") or taking on blame ("Maybe if I change, it'll stop"). Breaking free requires firmly telling yourself the truth: *It's not your fault, and you cannot change them.* A narcissist's behavior stems from their personality disorder, not from anything you did. Coming to terms with this may involve educating yourself (as you're doing now), talking to a trusted therapist or friend who can validate your experiences, and perhaps keeping a written list of the abusive incidents to remind yourself "this really happened" when doubt creeps in. Think of this step as building your resolve. Many survivors describe a pivotal moment of clarity where the mask truly fell off and they knew they had to get out. If you're not fully there yet, continue to gently remind yourself of the realities—reread journal entries, articles, or lists of what you've endured. **Affirmation:** *I see things as they are. I am in an abusive situation that is damaging me, and I choose to prioritize my well-being.*

2. **Set Firm Boundaries—Up to and Including No Contact:** Once you decide you need distance (temporary or permanent) from the

narcissist, boundaries are your best friend. Narcissists notoriously trample boundaries, so you will likely need to enforce them in a clear and possibly strict way. The ultimate boundary in many cases is **No Contact**: cutting off all communication and interaction with the person. This can be incredibly difficult but is often the most effective way to stop the cycle of abuse and begin healing. If you don't share children or other unavoidable connections, strongly consider a period of no contact. This means blocking their phone number, emails, social media, and avoiding places you might run into them. As Dr. Stephanie Sarkis advises, *"Go no-contact—absolutely no-contact"* if at all possible. The reason is simple: you cannot "win" an argument or negotiate a healthy breakup with a narcissist; they will use any avenue of access to try to pull you back in or punish you. By cutting contact, you deprive them of opportunities to manipulate you (like hoovering).

If you *must* remain in some contact (e.g., co-parenting, or a family member at gatherings), set **specific limits**. This is often called the *Gray Rock* method for minimal contact: keep interactions business-like, unemotional, and brief. Do not delve into personal topics or show any vulnerability they can latch onto. For example, communicate about child logistics via email or a shared co-parenting app only, and do not respond to personal provocations in their messages. If it's a family situation, you might limit conversations to polite small talk and disengage if they try to start drama. Boundary scripts can help: *"I'm not willing to discuss this. Let's stick to [the necessary topic]."* or *"If you continue to shout at me, I'm leaving."* Decide ahead of time what you will do if (when) they violate the boundary—and then **follow through consistently**. Every time you hold a boundary, you reclaim a piece of your autonomy that the narcissist used to control.

3. **Create a Support Network and Tell Safe People:** Breaking free is exceedingly hard to do alone. Reach out to those you trust—a friend, family member, counselor, or support group. **Isolation** is the narcissist's ally; connection is yours. If you have been isolated, it might feel scary or embarrassing to open up about what has been happening. You might fear not being believed or worry about being judged. Try to identify at least one person who has shown concern or whom you sense will be empathetic. Often, people around you have noticed that something was wrong and will be relieved that you're reaching out. Share as much as you feel comfortable—you

don't have to have all the answers or a complete plan. Even saying, "I've been living in a really unhealthy situation and I think I need to get out," is a huge step.

Consider professional support as well: a therapist who understands trauma or narcissistic abuse can provide guidance and emotional help. There are also support groups (in-person or online forums) for survivors of narcissistic relationships where people *get it* and can share what helped them. Knowing that you're not alone and that others have successfully escaped and rebuilt their lives is incredibly empowering. **Important:** If you fear the narcissist's retaliation, choose carefully who you confide in—someone who won't inadvertently tip off the abuser. In some cases, especially with malignant narcissists, you may need to line up very concrete support: a place to stay, someone to accompany you when moving out, or even contacting a domestic violence advocate (narcissistic abuse is a form of domestic abuse, after all). There are free hotlines and resources that can help you craft a safe exit plan if you're in danger. Lean on expertise that's available. You deserve a team in your corner.

4. **Plan Your Exit (Logistics and Safety):** This step is about the practical aspects of disengaging—particularly crucial if you live together, are married, or have intertwined finances/assets. It's not as simple as "just leave" when your lives are legally or financially entangled, or when the narcissist might retaliate. Planning ahead can make your exit smoother and safer. Consider the following elements in your plan:

    - **Living Arrangements:** Decide where you will go when you leave. Can you stay with a friend or family member for a while? Do you need to save money for an apartment? In some cases, a local shelter or domestic violence safe house might be a temporary option if you have nowhere else to go and you fear harm. Don't let pride stop you from using resources—there are many organizations that exist to help people in your situation. If the narcissist is the one leaving (like you ask them to move out of your place), have a friend with you for support when you tell them and perhaps change the locks if possible.

    - **Money and Documents:** Narcissists often financially entrap their victims. If you have shared accounts, consider opening a new bank account in your name only, at a different bank, to start saving money that the narcissist cannot access or see. Make sure you have copies of important documents (ID, passports, financial records, marriage license, insurance, etc.). It may be wise to store digital copies in a secure cloud account or with a trusted person. If you suspect the narcissist might react by draining accounts or running up debt, consult a legal advisor about how to protect your assets (for example, you might be able to put a freeze on credit or notify banks of the situation).

- **Children and Custody:** If you have children together, this complicates things. It's often helpful to consult a family law attorney or mediator *before* you separate to understand your rights. Narcissistic parents can use children as pawns to hurt you, so it's critical to establish a formal custody arrangement. Dr. Sarkis recommends getting a detailed **"parenting plan"** in place with clear boundaries about time-sharing and communication. For instance, the plan might stipulate that all communication about the kids be via text/email (so it's documented) and only about logistical matters. It can also define pick-up/ drop-off logistics (maybe at a neutral location) to minimize contact. This legal structure provides an external reinforcement of boundaries, which is useful since a narcissist won't respect boundaries out of goodwill.

- **Safety and Timing:** If your narcissist has shown any violent or stalking behavior, your safety during and after leaving is a top priority. Choose a time to leave or have them leave when you have a back-up present or they are not home. Some survivors have moved out their belongings while the narcissist was away and informed them later, to avoid a potentially dangerous confrontation. It might feel cowardly, but it's strategic. *Your safety matters more than their feelings.* If you have to have a break-up conversation, do it in public or have someone waiting nearby. In extreme cases, law enforcement can stand by during a domestic situation to keep the peace while one person moves out belongings. Also, consider changing passwords on all your devices and accounts (narcissists might try to hack or surveil you), and updating security measures at home (locks, maybe a security camera).

- **Legal Measures:** If the narcissist threatens you, stalks you, or refuses to let go, you might need to pursue a restraining order (order of protection). Document every incident of harassment, threats, or violence with as much evidence as possible (screenshots, witnesses, dates, times). Laws vary by location, but generally, courts do take stalking and domestic abuse seriously, and a restraining order can legally prohibit them from contacting or approaching you. While a paper alone doesn't physically stop someone, it provides grounds for police to intervene and arrest if the narcissist violates it. The very existence of it also often deters further abuse, since narcissists hate facing real consequences. Don't hesitate to involve law enforcement if you feel endangered.

5. **Resist Hoovering and Manipulation Attempts:** Once you initiate distance or leave, expect the narcissist to attempt to pull you back in—especially if *they* didn't initiate the break. This is where all the earlier tactics might come back with a vengeance. You might get tearful apologies, sudden promises to go to therapy or change, gifts, love letters, or dramatic declarations ("I can't live without you!"). Alternatively, if sweet-talk doesn't work, they may switch to anger and threats ("You'll regret this," or begin spreading rumors about you). It's important to anticipate this so you're not caught off guard. Develop a mantra or reminder for yourself about *why* you left and why you must stay away. Some survivors keep a list on their phone of all the terrible incidents or a letter to self to read when they feel tempted to respond to a hoover. **Remember:** Narcissists are experts at targeting your soft spots. They know you want to hear that they're sorry and that you mean the world to them. But as one psychologist notes, *"They tell you exactly what you need to hear, and once you are sucked back in, things are back to the way they were—except maybe worse."* The cycle will start again. Every time you consider relenting, picture that cycle and how hard it was to get out.

If you've gone no contact, maintain it strictly. Do not respond, no matter how compelling the bait. Over time, they usually give up when they realize they can't reach you (or they shift to a new target, as painful as that is to consider). If you must have contact (because of children or other reasons), keep enforcing those boundaries. Respond only to necessary communications, and ignore any personal jabs or sidetracks. If they call, let it go to voicemail and respond with a brief text if needed (this also creates a written record of exchanges). Some survivors find it useful to have a friend filter messages—e.g., the narcissist emails you, you have a rule that auto-forwards it to a friend who checks if there's anything truly important, and you don't even read the unnecessary nastiness. Find a system that reduces your exposure to their attempts to hook you.

6. **Take Legal and Financial Steps to Solidify Your Independence:** This step may happen concurrently with some of the above, but it is worth highlighting. Once you're out or on your way out, **finalize the separation.** This could mean filing for divorce, legally separating finances, removing their name from leases, titles, etc., or vice versa. The cleaner the break, the less opportunity they have to entangle you again. Follow through with court proceedings and lean on your attorney to handle communications with them whenever possible. Narcissists often try to use the legal system to continue the battle (for example, dragging out a divorce to keep you engaged). As exhausting as it is, try to be *strategic*: document everything, meet your legal obligations, but avoid direct fights. Let lawyers and judges see their unreasonable behavior. Your job is to focus on *your* life.

By executing these steps, you are **reclaiming power** on multiple levels. You're saying: *I will not be controlled anymore.* Every boundary enforced, every support person rallied, every ignored message is you taking back control of *your life*. It can be scary—narcissists condition you to fear what will happen when you defy them. But countless survivors will attest that the freedom on the other side is worth the effort.

Case Study – Escaping a Narcissistic Spouse:

Amina had been married to Yusuf for 12 years, and they had two children together. Yusuf was a covert narcissist who emotionally abused Amina, constantly gaslighting her into believing she was an unfit mother. He would belittle her, twist conversations to make her doubt herself, and occasionally grab her in anger. Amina's breaking point came when, in a fit of rage, Yusuf pushed their 10-year-old son for "disrespecting" him.

Determined to protect herself and her children, Amina sought guidance from an Islamic counselor and a trusted lawyer. Over the next three months, she quietly saved money in a separate account, gathered important documents, and made arrangements to stay with her parents after leaving.

One day, while Yusuf was at work, Amina and her brother packed the essentials for her and the children and left. She left a brief note and, later that day, her lawyer served Yusuf with a temporary separation order while she filed for Faskh (Islamic annulment) at her local Shariah council and Islamic center that handles Islamic divorces. As expected, Yusuf flooded her phone with alternating messages of guilt-tripping, threats, and false promises of change. However, Amina had already changed her number and communicated only through her lawyer.

At first, the anxiety was overwhelming—would he retaliate? Would her community judge her? But her careful preparation paid off. The legal protections kept him at a distance, and with the emotional support of her family and therapist, she remained steadfast in her decision. In the following weeks, Yusuf attempted to manipulate her through their children, but the court implemented a structured visitation schedule, ensuring clear boundaries.

Looking back, Amina reflects, *"The moment I walked out was the moment I truly started breathing again. It felt like I had been suffocating for years, and I had finally found my air."*

Her journey highlights the importance of strategic planning, emotional support, and firm legal boundaries in breaking free from long-term narcissistic abuse within an Islamic marriage.

Every step you take away from the narcissist—physically, emotionally, legally—is a step toward *regaining yourself*. It may help to keep in mind: the chaos and confusion they bring to your life is *not normal and not acceptable*. You are not just "leaving a person," you are leaving chaos, pain, and fear. In doing so, you make room for stability, joy, and peace. In the next section, we will focus on what happens after you've left—the healing and recovery journey to rebuild your self-esteem, overcome that trauma bond, and embrace life on *your* terms again.

Healing and Recovery

Breaking free from a narcissistic relationship is a significant victory, but it's also the beginning of a new chapter—the chapter of healing. After enduring trauma and manipulation, you may feel like you have to rebuild yourself from the ground up. The good news is, with time and deliberate effort, survivors *do* heal and often come out the other side stronger, wiser, and more self-aware than before. This section provides a structured roadmap for regaining your emotional well-being and independence. Healing is not linear—there will be ups and downs—but each small step you take will contribute to your recovery. We'll cover strategies for rebuilding self-esteem, breaking those lingering trauma bonds, and learning to trust and care for yourself again. We'll also include some interactive exercises (like journaling prompts and mindfulness practices) to help you actively engage in the healing process. Think of this as a **toolkit** for becoming whole again.

Stage 1: Establish Safety and Stability

In the immediate aftermath of leaving (or while you are in the process of leaving), your first healing priority is to establish a sense of safety—both externally and internally. Externally, this means ensuring the narcissist is not harassing you (using those no-contact and legal measures discussed earlier) so that your environment is as calm and trigger-free as possible. Internally, "safety" means calming your nervous system, which has been in fight-or-flight mode. Focus on *basic self-care*: regular meals, rest, sleep, and routines that give structure to your day. It may sound trivial, but eating healthy food and getting enough sleep can significantly improve your ability to cope with emotional distress. Many survivors initially struggle with sleep due to anxiety or nightmares. Establishing a soothing bedtime routine and incorporating Islamic practices into your nightly routine can significantly enhance relaxation and signal to your body that it's time to rest. Performing **wudu** (ablution) before bed not only cleanses the body but also prepares the mind for sleep. Engaging in **dhikr** (remembrance of Allah) by reciting phrases like *SubhanAllah* (Glory be to Allah), *Alhamdulillah* (All praise is due to Allah), and *Allahu Akbar* (Allah is the Greatest) can calm the mind and heart. Reciting specific verses from the Qur'an, such as **Ayat al-Kursi** (Surah Al-Baqarah 2:255) and the last two verses of Surah Al-Baqarah, is believed to offer protection throughout the night. Additionally, reading **Surah Al-Mulk** (Chapter 67) before sleeping is a recommended practice. These spiritual activities, combined with creating a calming environment—such as dimming lights and ensuring a clean, comfortable sleeping space—can promote a restful night's sleep. Other techniques, such as drinking calming tea, guided meditation, and grounding exercises (such as deep breathing or the 5-4-3-2-1 technique to manage panic attacks), can also help signal to your body that it's okay to relax now. The goal of this stage is to come down from survival mode. You might still feel on edge, but you're beginning to remember what *peace* feels like, even if just in moments. Therapy often begins in this stage too—a trauma-informed therapist can provide a safe space to start unpacking what happened and validating your feelings.

Stage 2: Rebuilding Self-Esteem and Identity

Narcissistic abuse often shatters your self-esteem and sense of identity. Now it's time to reclaim *who you are*. Start by reminding yourself of the person you were before the narcissist (if this was a very long relationship or it happened early in life, think of times you felt confident or *most yourself*). It can help to engage in activities you used to enjoy that might have fallen by the wayside. If you stopped engaging in activities such as attending weekly Islamic study circles, organizing community events, participating in interfaith work, going to the gym, or spending time with friends and family due to discouragement or mockery from an abuser, rekindling these passions can be a vital step toward reclaiming your identity. These pursuits are not merely hobbies; they are integral expressions of who you are. Additionally, exploring new activities can foster personal growth and reinforce your capabilities.

Challenging negative self-talk is crucial in this stage. You likely have an "inner critic" that echoes the narcissist's put-downs. Work on replacing those thoughts with compassionate ones. For example, if you catch yourself thinking, "I'm so stupid, I'll never do anything right," pause and reframe: "I'm not stupid. I had a very tough experience and I'm doing my best. I am learning and growing each day." It might feel false at first, but keep at it—you are effectively reprogramming the brainwashing you underwent. Many survivors find **affirmations** helpful: write down positive statements about yourself and read them daily, even if you don't fully believe them yet. You could also list your strengths and achievements, no matter how small, to start rebuilding pride in yourself.

Social reconnection is part of this too. As your confidence grows, you might reach out more to friends or join groups or classes to meet new people as mentioned above. Positive social experiences will remind you that you are likable and valued by others (something the narcissist likely tried to undermine). Be cautious but open in trusting people again—not everyone is like your abuser. It's okay to take it slow; trust in yourself to discern character over time.

Stage 3: Overcoming Trauma Bonds and Emotional Dependency

Even after leaving, you might find that you *miss* the narcissist or feel oddly drawn to them. You might obsess over the good moments or feel guilty, lonely, or empty. This is the trauma bond talking. Breaking it requires conscious effort.

Cold turkey no-contact is one method—much like quitting an addiction, you don't "have just a little" of the drug without risking relapse. Stay away from their social media, avoid news about them, and resist asking mutual acquaintances about them. Instead, refocus that mental energy on *you*. When thoughts of them arise, have a plan: perhaps you immediately journal those feelings (to get them out of your head), or you call a friend, or you engage in a distracting activity (go for a run, pray, play a game, watch a favorite show). Each time you redirect your attention, the bond weakens a little more.

Another powerful tool to overcome the emotional attachment is to **write down why you left and what you will not miss**. Dr. Sarkis recommends writing down the incidents that hurt your self-esteem or sanity. Create a list of "Reasons I Left" or "What I Don't Want to Re-live." Be specific: *"I left because I refuse to be lied to and then be told I'm crazy (gaslighting on June 5th when he denied texting his ex). I left because I deserve to be spoken to with respect, not called names like I was a child. I left because my children were witnessing constant fights and I want better for them."* Keep this list handy. When nostalgia or doubt creeps in ("Maybe it really *was* my fault? Maybe it could be good again?"), read the list. It's like splashing cold water on your face—a reality check. Over time, your brain will integrate these truths and the emotional pull will lessen.

Therapeutic exercises can also help sever the bond. One common one is writing an unsent "letter" to the narcissist expressing all the pain and anger—say everything you never got to say or that they refused to hear. Pour it out, then destroy the letter in a symbolic letting go (safely burn it, shred it, etc.). Another is a visualization: imagine yourself tied to the person with ropes or chains (representing the trauma bond), then visualize cutting those ties—sometimes people picture giving the chains back to the abuser or them falling away. These mental exercises, while seemingly abstract, can give your psyche permission to release the attachment.

Stage 4: Learning Self-Compassion and Mindfulness

As you heal, you'll likely confront waves of different emotions: grief, anger, shame, relief, sadness, even joy. Practicing **self-compassion** is vital. This means treating yourself with the same kindness and understanding you would offer a dear friend who had been hurt. You might say to yourself, "It's understandable that I feel angry today; anyone who went through what I did would feel this way," instead of beating yourself up for not being "over it" yet. Recognize that healing takes time, and there's no set schedule. Be patient with emotional setbacks. If you find yourself ruminating or having a tough day, instead of saying "What's wrong with me?," try "What do I need right now to comfort myself?" It could be a walk, a nap, a call to someone supportive, or simply allowing yourself to cry and release the feelings.

Mindfulness practices can greatly assist in this stage and beyond. Mindfulness is about staying present and observing your thoughts and feelings without judgment. This can help you not get too carried away by anxiety about the future or pain from the past. Techniques include:

- **Meditation:** Even 10 minutes a day of sitting quietly and focusing on your breath can train your brain to find a calm center. When thoughts about the trauma arise, you gently bring your focus back to breathing. Over time, this can reduce stress and increase emotional regulation.

- **Deep Breathing and Body Scans:** When you feel panic or anger surging, slow, deep belly breaths can signal your nervous system to calm down. A simple exercise: inhale for a count of 4, hold for 4, exhale for 6 or 8, and repeat. A body scan involves mentally checking in with each part of your body and noticing sensations, which can ground you in the present moment.

- **Yoga or Tai Chi:** These movement-based mindfulness practices help reconnect you with your body in a positive way. Narcissistic abuse can make you feel disconnected from or even disgusted with your body (especially if there was sexual abuse or body-shaming). Gentle yoga or tai chi can help release tension and trauma stored physically, and rebuild a sense of peace in your own skin.

- **Journaling (Mindfulness style)**: Each day, or a few times a week, write down your current feelings and thoughts without filtering. This "brain dump" can be very cathartic. It's a way of saying, *I acknowledge these thoughts, but they are not permanent and I release them onto the page.* Some days you might uncover deep insights; other days it's just venting—both are beneficial.

Stage 5: Cognitive Healing–Reframing and Education

Another aspect of recovery is making sense of what happened and reframing your story. You've likely spent a long time focused on the narcissist—their motives, their issues—now it's time to focus on *your narrative*. Many survivors benefit from understanding concepts like trauma bonding, codependency, or the narcissistic cycle (some of which we've covered). This educational piece helps shift any residual blame off of you and onto the dysfunction of the abuse dynamic. It can be empowering to intellectually grasp that *anyone* can fall prey to a narcissist's charm and intermittent reinforcement—it wasn't because you were "weak" or "naive"; it's because you're human and have normal needs for love and validation that were exploited.

In therapy (or through self-help workbooks), you might identify any underlying beliefs or patterns in yourself that made you vulnerable to staying too long. This is not victim-blaming, but rather self-growth. For example, you might realize, "I have a tendency to people-please and avoid conflict, which made it easier for them to walk over me." Or "I lacked healthy boundaries because I thought I had to sacrifice myself for love." These reflections can be painful but ultimately liberating, as they highlight areas to work on so that future relationships are healthier. Maybe you'll work on assertiveness skills, or addressing childhood wounds that predisposed you to accept poor treatment. This is your journey of **self-discovery**, and it can be incredibly rewarding. Many say this inner work is where they truly "find themselves" and ensure the same patterns aren't repeated.

Stage 6: Forgiveness and Letting Go (On Your Terms)

In time, you may reach a stage where you're ready to consider forgiveness—*not necessarily of the narcissist (unless that feels right to you), but of yourself.* Survivors often hold a lot of guilt or shame: "How could I let this happen? Why didn't I leave sooner?" It's important to **forgive yourself** for the coping mechanisms you had. You did what you had to in order to survive at the time. Let go of the notion that you "failed" by being in that relationship. The fault lies with the abuser, not the abused.

Forgiving the narcissist is trickier and very personal. It does *not* mean condoning what they did or allowing them back in your life. In some contexts, forgiveness might simply mean releasing the hold their memory has on you—deciding you won't let bitterness about them consume any more of your energy. Some people find it helpful to say (perhaps in another unsent letter or in therapy), "I release the hate I feel towards you so I can be free. I will never forget what you did, but I refuse to let it define me or my future." If the word *forgiveness* doesn't sit well, think of it as *acceptance*—accepting that the past happened and cannot be changed, but that you *can* choose your path forward. This stage often comes last, when you've healed enough that the narcissist is no longer central in your mind. Don't rush it. It's not required to forgive them to heal—that's optional. But forgiving yourself *is* essential and you can practice that from day one.

Interactive Exercises for Healing: To engage actively with your recovery, here are some exercises and prompts that many have found helpful:

- **Journaling Prompts for Self-Discovery:** Journaling is a powerful way to process emotions and rediscover your inner voice. Try these prompts, writing whatever comes to mind without self-censorship:
    - *Write a letter to your past self* (for example, the self who was just entering the relationship, or who was stuck in it) offering words of encouragement and acknowledging the strength it took to survive. What would you want that past you to know?
    - What does inner strength mean to you? List or describe times you showed strength (even if you think they're small). This reminds you that you *are* strong—after all, you're here now.
    - Name three things you have learned about yourself since beginning your healing journey. (For instance, "I learned that I have a lot of empathy for others," or "I learned that I'm braver than I thought.")
    - What are some qualities or activities that make you feel like yourself? Describe how you will nurture those now. (e.g., "I feel most like myself when I'm helping others—maybe I'll volunteer again," or "I feel alive when I'm outdoors; I'll start hiking weekly.")
    - *Write about your ideal future.* Envision your life five years from now, free and thriving. What are you doing? Who is in your life? How do you feel each morning? Let yourself dream without limitation—this helps you realize there *is* a future beyond this pain and you have the power to shape it.
    - Many survivors find that journaling helps them "tap into their resilience, inner strength, and power", as one coach notes. It externalizes your thoughts and can reveal patterns or insights you didn't see when it was all just in your head.

- **Self-Compassion Exercises:**
  - Make a list of comforting activities or rituals for bad days (your "emotional first aid" kit). Maybe it's wrapping up in a soft blanket with tea, taking a warm bath, listening to uplifting verses in the Qur'an, listening to Nasheed, calling a friend, or watching a funny movie. Keep this list visible. When you feel down, choose one item and do it, even if you're not in the mood—it can help shift your emotional state gently.
  - Practice a short loving-kindness meditation for yourself. Close your eyes and repeat a phrase like: *"May I be safe. May I be happy. May I be free from suffering. May I live with ease."* Adjust words that resonate with you. This might feel emotional—that's okay. You are essentially giving yourself the love that you deserve.
  - Affirmations: Write 3 affirmations about yourself and put them on your mirror or phone. For example; "I am worthy of love and respect," "I am healing a little more each day," "I am proud of myself for how far I've come." Say them aloud daily, even if you don't fully believe them at first. Over time, they imprint positivity in your self-dialogue.

- **Mindfulness and Relaxation Practices:**
  - Try a guided meditation specifically for trauma release or healing after abuse (there are many free apps and videos available). Some focus on letting go of anger, some on building self-trust, etc. Experiment to find one that resonates.
  - Breathing exercise: 4-7-8 breathing can be very helpful for anxiety. Inhale for 4 counts, hold for 7, exhale for 8. Repeat 4 times. This can be done any time you feel panic rising.
  - Progressive muscle relaxation: While lying down, start at your feet, tense the muscles for 5 seconds, then release. Move upward (calves, thighs, buttocks, stomach, arms, etc.). This releases physical tension and also teaches you the difference between tension and relaxation in the body.
  - If flashbacks or overwhelming feelings strike, use the 5-4-3-2-1 grounding: Name 5 things you see, 4 things you feel (tactilely,

like "my shirt on my skin"), 3 things you hear, 2 things you smell, 1 thing you taste. This brings you back to the present moment and out of the spiral.

- **Creative Expression:** Sometimes words aren't enough. Consider creative outlets to express and release feelings:
  - Art: Draw or paint your emotions. It doesn't have to be pretty or make sense to anyone but you. You can even scribble with colors that match your mood.
  - Nasheeds: Make a playlist of songs that empower you (think "survivor anthems"), and another of songs that soothe you when you're anxious. Music has a direct line to our emotions.
  - Movement: If you're holding a lot of anger or sadness, physical movement can help discharge it. That could be punching a pillow, doing a kickboxing workout, or conversely doing gentle yoga that opens up areas where we tend to hold stress (like chest and hips).

Remember, healing is personal. What works for someone else might not click for you, and vice versa. Be willing to try different exercises and keep those that resonate. Healing is also not a solo endeavor—staying connected with supportive people (friends, support groups, therapists) throughout this journey is crucial. They can remind you of your progress when you can't see it and encourage you on hard days. Celebrate small milestones: *"It's been one month of no contact!" "I went a whole week without crying!" "I stood up for myself in a conversation today!"* These are victories. Over time, the days will brighten. The periods of peace will grow longer and the intrusions of past trauma will fade.

Moving Forward

Emerging from the shadow of narcissistic abuse is like stepping into the sunshine after a long storm. At first, the brightness can be jarring—you might find yourself squinting, unsure of what you're seeing, as you face a future without the familiar chaos. But slowly, your eyes adjust and you begin to see the world (and yourself) in vibrant color again. Moving forward after such an experience is about *growth, rediscovery, and renewal*. This final section is dedicated to the positive changes and personal growth that can come in the aftermath of narcissistic abuse. It's about using the hard-won lessons to build a better life—one with healthy relationships, self-trust, and genuine happiness. Think of it as not just surviving, but **thriving**.

- **Recognizing Healthy Relationships:** One of the most profound shifts will be in how you perceive and approach relationships. After experiencing what you *don't* want, you likely have a clearer idea of what a healthy relationship *does* look like. Healthy relationships are marked by mutual respect, trust, empathy, and balance. There is give and take; both people's needs and feelings matter. In a healthy bond, you feel safe to be yourself and communicate openly without fear. As you move forward, you'll be more discerning. Red flags that you might have overlooked before (such as someone rushing intimacy, disrespecting boundaries, or showing lack of empathy) will stand out—and you can choose to walk away early. Conversely, you may initially feel that *green flags* (like someone who is consistently kind, doesn't play games, and respects you) seem almost boring or suspicious because you were used to drama. Give these healthy dynamics a chance. With time, you'll adjust to the calm and realize that peace is not boring—it's the foundation of real love and friendship. You might also redefine what intimacy means to you; it could be based more on emotional security and understanding rather than intense passion or dependency. This isn't to say you won't feel passion again—you absolutely can—but it will be with someone who also brings you peace.

- **Trusting Yourself Again:** Perhaps the biggest casualty of narcissistic abuse is self-trust. Now is the time to rebuild your faith in your own judgment and intuition. Remember, the narcissist deliberately tried to confuse you and make you doubt yourself for their own agenda. As you heal, start affirming that *you can trust your perceptions*. One helpful practice is reflecting on past situations (even small ones) where you accurately sensed something. Maybe you had a gut feeling that someone at work was genuine and it turned out true, or you followed your intuition to take a day off and something beneficial happened. Acknowledge those moments. When new situations arise, take a moment to check in with your gut and honor its input. For example, if you meet someone new and something feels "off," don't rush to dismiss it—you can choose to observe and gather more info rather than second-guessing yourself. Also, forgive yourself for the times your trust was broken. It wasn't foolish to give trust; it was a reflection of your good heart. Going forward, you'll likely adopt a

"trust but verify" approach: give people a baseline of respect and openness, but also allow time for them to show through consistent actions that they're trustworthy. And if you misjudge someone, don't be harsh on yourself; see it as a learning experience. Your ability to make decisions will improve as you practice. Start with small decisions to build confidence ("Which hobby do *I* want to pursue?" "What do *I* feel like doing this weekend?") without deferring to others. As you see positive outcomes from your own choices, your self-trust grows. In essence, you're becoming the leader of your own life again, and you can trust your leadership.

- **Embracing Resilience and Post-Traumatic Growth:** Having gone through something as harrowing as narcissistic abuse, you are forever changed. Many survivors come to realize that while they wouldn't wish this experience on anyone, it catalyzed profound personal growth in them. *Post-traumatic growth* is a concept where individuals who endure trauma emerge with new strength, perspectives, and appreciation for life. You might find that you have a new mission, like helping others who went through similar situations, or simply that you cherish your freedom and joy more deeply now. Qualities like empathy, compassion, and wisdom often deepen. You may also surprise yourself with how resourceful and strong you can be. Resilience isn't about never feeling pain or never falling down; it's about always getting back up, and each time a bit faster or stronger. Think back to the darkest moments when you felt utterly broken—you made it past those. That is a testament to your resilience. Now, moving forward, challenges in life (unrelated to the abuse) may not rattle you as much. You've been through the worst; day-to-day problems or difficult people at work, for example, might feel easier to handle by comparison. This doesn't mean you'll never be triggered or have emotional responses, but you carry inside you a core of *unbreakable* strength. As you build your new life, set **healthy goals** and dream again. Maybe you put aside career aspirations or travel plans or personal projects during the relationship—dust them off and consider pursuing them. Each achievement, big or small, is a nail in the coffin of the past abuse, sealing it away as something that no longer controls you. Celebrate your independence—it could be having your own décor style in your living space now, or managing your finances solo, or cultivating friendships that were previously off-limits. These freedoms are precious and yours to enjoy.

- **Healthy Love and Boundaries:** When you're ready to court and form new relationships to look for a potential spouse (take your time; there's no rush), you will do so with the lessons learned. Boundaries will remain an essential part of your life—but now not as an emergency defense mechanism, rather as a natural element of *all* good relationships. You'll communicate your needs and limits openly and expect others to do the same. If someone crosses a boundary, you'll address it early; if they keep crossing it, you'll know to distance yourself. This will protect you from falling into another toxic situation. Meanwhile, you'll also practice respecting others' boundaries—something survivors are often quite good at because they never want to make anyone feel how they felt. This mutual respect sets the stage for truly loving relationships based on equality and care. In time, many survivors do find love again, with Allah's permission— love that is nurturing, respectful, and uplifting. It might creep up on you unexpectedly when you've been busy loving and healing yourself. There's often a fear: "What if I attract another narcissist?" But by doing the work you've done—understanding red flags, strengthening self-esteem, building a support network—you've greatly reduced that risk. And if a toxic person does cross your path, you're in a much stronger position to recognize it early and enforce consequences (even if that means walking away quickly). Thus, you can approach new relationships not with fear, but with cautious optimism and the confidence that *you can handle whatever comes.*

- **Writing Your Own Narrative:** Perhaps the most empowering part of moving forward is reclaiming the pen of your life's story. For a while, it felt like the narcissist was writing your chapters, dictating your feelings and actions. Not anymore. **You are the author now.** You get to decide how this chapter ends and the next one begins. Maybe your story becomes one of advocacy—using your voice to educate others about narcissistic abuse. Or maybe your story is one of quiet happiness—building a peaceful life, raising your children in a loving environment, and breaking the cycle of abuse for future generations. There is no right or wrong narrative as long as it's *authentically yours.* One day, you'll look back at this painful period and see it as just one part of your rich life story, not the defining centerpiece. It might inform who you are (for instance, making you more compassionate to others' pain or more appreciative of healthy love), but it won't define you in a limiting way (you're not a "victim" or even just a "survivor" in your identity—you are a whole person with many facets, of which this is only one facet).

In moving forward, celebrate your resilience. Every effort you put into healing, every boundary you set, every moment of self-care—they are all proof of your strength. As you step into new relationships or endeavors, carry the lessons without carrying the baggage. You can acknowledge what happened without letting it weigh you down.

Finally, embrace hope and joy. You are free now to invite positive experiences into your life. It could be as simple as rediscovering laughter—that deep belly laugh that you might not have had in years—or as profound as finding connection in its many forms (marriage, family, friends, community). Many survivors report that once they had healed, they felt a greater joy in small things than ever before: a calm cup of coffee in the morning sun, a walk in the park without anxiety, a genuine smile that comes from feeling at peace. These everyday joys are the building blocks of a happy life.

Moving forward is an ongoing journey, but it is one filled with possibilities. You have proven that you can survive at your worst; now it's time to thrive at your best. Trust the path you're on and trust yourself. As you leave the past behind, take the wisdom it gave you and step boldly into the future you *choose*.

Empowering Reflection: *"I am not what happened to me. I am what I choose to become."* This quote (from psychologist Carl Jung) encapsulates the shift in perspective. Yes, something terrible happened and it affected you deeply—but you **choose** what to do with that experience. And you have chosen to heal, to grow, and to let it transform you in positive ways. The fact that you've read this chapter, sought knowledge, and done the work is evidence of your determination to create a better life. Keep that momentum. The life ahead of you is yours to live, free from narcissistic abuse, and rich with the respect, love, and joy that you always deserved.

You are not alone, you are not broken, and you are absolutely capable of healing. As you navigate relationships in the future—including the most important relationship, the one with yourself and Allah—carry this truth: *You are worthy. You are strong. You are free.*

Chapter Sixteen

Parental Alienation: A Child's Heartbreak

Lost Innocence

Imagine a child who once laughed easily, full of wonder and trust, their spirit open to the love and comfort of both parents. But suddenly, their once-familiar world is shattered by a storm they don't understand. Instead of safety, they feel torn, conflicted, and afraid, hearing hurtful words about one parent from the other, all while trying to make sense of emotions far too heavy for them to carry. This is the heartbreak of parental alienation. It's an unseen tragedy that robs children of their innocence and loving relationships, casting a dark shadow over the simple joys of childhood and the pure bond of family love.

Parental alienation is not just a "family problem" or a byproduct of separation. It's a deep, insidious form of emotional manipulation that can carve wounds in a child's heart. This chapter aims to bring to light the real and profound consequences of this behavior. By delving into the emotional, psychological, and spiritual harm inflicted on both the child and the alienated parent, we seek not only to inform but to connect—to ignite an urgent call for compassion, awareness, and intervention. We turn to insights from experts, psychological research, and Islamic values to understand how we, as a society, can protect our children and nurture a sense of love and fairness, even when family bonds are tested.

Seeing Through the Eyes of Experts and the Children They Help

When psychological experts describe parental alienation, they speak not just of fractured families but of fractured hearts, identities, and realities. Experts in child psychology have studied this phenomenon for decades, and the findings are universally disturbing. Dr. Amy J.L. Baker, a prominent researcher in this field, describes parental alienation as "a form of emotional abuse to which children are exposed." She notes that it deeply damages their self-worth and disrupts their sense of stability. As she explains, "Parental alienation involves the unwarranted rejection of a parent that results from the influence of the other parent." This kind of manipulation sets the stage for intense internal conflict as the child is forced to reject a person they naturally want to love and trust.

Alienation creates a battlefield in a child's mind where love and fear collide in ways a child should never have to experience. Dr. Richard A. Warshak, another leading expert, highlights that alienated children often suffer from "anxiety, depression, low self-esteem, and poor academic performance" as they try to cope with being placed in a war zone they never chose. Dr. Warshak elaborates on how the child is often manipulated to view one parent as "all good" and the other as "all bad," which disrupts the child's ability to develop a balanced perspective on relationships.

Recent studies reveal what words alone can't fully capture—the experience of being caught in a crossfire, pulled to take sides in a conflict they didn't ask for. Dr. Jennifer Harman, who has conducted extensive research on parental alienation, emphasizes the guilt and shame that children often carry. "They feel conflicted about loving both parents because they are subtly—or overtly—pressured to choose," she explains. This forced choice creates intense loyalty conflicts, where the child is left feeling trapped, guilty, and afraid to show affection for both parents.

For these children, the effects of alienation are immediate, but the scars are lasting. Dr. Craig Childress, a clinical psychologist and expert in parental alienation, describes how alienation can lead to attachment trauma that affects relationships well into adulthood. Adults who were alienated as children often wrestle with issues of trust, finding it hard to believe in the security of any relationship. "They can have trouble forming and maintaining close relationships, and they often struggle with self-doubt and fear of abandonment," Dr. Childress explains. The trauma of childhood alienation lingers, affecting their ability to open up, trust, and create their own safe spaces.

Knowing the emotional and psychological weight of these experiences, how can we as a society remain silent? How can we fail to act to protect these vulnerable souls, who should never have to bear such burdens? As Dr. Harman powerfully states, "The social and emotional cost of parental alienation is far too high for any child to bear alone."

The Heavy Burden of Alienation: How it Affects Children Today and Tomorrow

In the short term, children exposed to parental alienation experience a harsh reality, one in which the home, the space meant to shield them from harm, becomes a place of confusion and sadness. They might act out, withdraw, or struggle at school. Imagine a child you know—bright-eyed, full of potential—now feeling invisible and insecure, unsure whom to trust. This is the price of alienation. Every day spent hearing negative words about a parent is a day of fractured identity and compromised emotional safety. They become the casualties of adult battles, bearing burdens of loyalty and guilt that are far too heavy for their small shoulders.

And as these children grow, the effects of alienation don't disappear. The pain takes root and grows with them, shaping how they view love and family. These adults often find it difficult to trust, love fully, or feel secure in relationships. The ghost of alienation follows them, a silent shadow that disrupts even their dreams of a healthy family life. They might unconsciously repeat patterns of alienation, now unaware of where it began. So, parental alienation doesn't just harm today—it's a generational wound, silently rippling out into the lives of those yet unborn.

Society's Role in Creating and Combating Alienation

When we look beyond the individual family and see the broader picture, we can't ignore the societal factors that play into parental alienation. High-conflict divorces, courtroom battles over custody, and a lack of emotional and financial support for transitioning families—all of these contribute to the perfect storm in which alienation can flourish. Children caught in these conflicts become pawns in a system that often lacks empathy, driven by laws that don't see their hearts. And society's expectations around parenting can complicate matters even further, adding pressure and stigma that sometimes drive one parent to alienate the other, mistakenly seeing it as the only way to retain control or loyalty.

What would it look like if our society prioritized the emotional well-being of children during separations, if the courts encouraged healing over winning, if communities provided support and education to prevent alienation before it started? It would look like children having the chance to love both their parents without the weight of guilt or fear, to grow up with a balanced and whole sense of self.

Islamic Values: A Sacred Bond That Should Not Be Broken

In Islam, the relationship between a parent and child is more than just a bond; it's a divine trust, a responsibility entrusted to parents to guide, nurture, and protect. The Qur'an places this relationship on sacred ground, reminding us to treat parents with love and respect. Allah says in Surah Al-Isra:

> "And your Lord has decreed that you not worship except Him, and to parents, good treatment. Whether one or both of them reach old age [while] with you, say not to them [so much as], 'uff,' and do not repel them but speak to them a noble word. And lower to them the wing of humility out of mercy and say, 'My Lord, have mercy upon them as they brought me up [when I was] small.'" (Qur'an 17:23-24)

Islam teaches us about *Silat ar-Rahim*, the maintenance of family ties. Severing family bonds, especially between parents and children, is one of the most serious violations. The Qur'an cautions against this in Surah Muhammad:

> "So would you perhaps, if you turned away, cause corruption on earth and sever your [ties of] relationship? Those [who do so] are the ones that Allah has cursed, so He deafened them and blinded their vision." (Qur'an 47:22-23)

Islamic teachings emphasize the profound significance of compassion, justice, and preserving the family's unity, guiding us to prioritize a child's emotional well-being.

Islamic Ethics: Choosing Compassion Over Control

Justice and compassion are central values in Islam, guiding our actions in every relationship. In the case of parental alienation, these principles are especially critical. The Qur'an and Hadith emphasize peaceful conflict resolution, encouraging open communication, understanding, and mutual respect. Allah advises:

> "And if you fear dissension between the two, send an arbitrator from his people and an arbitrator from her people. If they both desire reconciliation, Allah will cause it between them. Indeed, Allah is ever Knowing and Acquainted [with all things]." (Qur'an 4:35)

Conclusion: A Call to Restore Love, Justice, and Compassion

Parental alienation is not just a mistake; it's a profound tragedy—a hidden heartbreak that impacts children most of all, robbing them of security, trust, and the simple joys of loving both parents. It's important, however, to acknowledge that in cases where there is genuine and verified evidence of potential harm to the child—whether in the form of sexual abuse, physical or emotional abuse, or any other threat to their well-being—measures to limit or even prevent contact with the harmful parent are entirely warranted and necessary. Islam emphasizes safeguarding the child's health and safety, and in these exceptional cases, protecting the child by restricting access is a legitimate, compassionate response.

However, when separation is driven by malicious intent—to "get back" at a parent, cause pain, or manipulate emotions—the behavior crosses a serious ethical boundary. Islam's message is clear: using children as tools of revenge or as pawns to settle scores is strictly forbidden. Such actions are not only harmful but also disrespectful to the trust and love that should define family relationships. Islam teaches us to protect the family, seek peace, and act with compassion, prioritizing the well-being of children above all else. Together, as a community and as individuals, we can work toward a society that values children's emotional health, supports families in resolving conflict with grace, and stands against the devastating consequences of parental alienation. By fostering a culture of love, respect, and healing, we honor the sacred responsibility of parenting, ensuring that every child has the right to grow up feeling safe, cherished, and connected to both parents whenever it is safe and healthy to do so. Let us protect the innocent, rebuild broken ties with love and understanding, and prioritize our children's best interests. In doing so, we uphold not only the values of Islam but the fundamental rights of every child to feel whole, loved, and free from the burdens of adult conflicts.

Chapter Seventeen

Pornography: The Hidden Wound That Bleeds Marriages Dry

In the landscape of intimate relationships, the shadow of pornography looms large, leaving a trail of far-reaching consequences that strike at the very heart of human connection. Renowned psychologist Dr. Mary Anne Layden, an authority on sexual trauma and addiction, highlights how exposure to pornographic material often leads to desensitization. As Dr. Layden explains, this gradual numbing effect creates a cycle where individuals seek increasingly explicit material to maintain arousal, ultimately eroding their capacity for genuine emotional intimacy. Pornography, with its scripted, performative depictions, fails to capture the authentic bond shared by partners, leaving many users with a lingering sense of dissatisfaction and a hunger for the unobtainable.

Dr. Gail Dines, a sociologist who has studied pornography's impact on society, warns that repeated exposure to pornographic content can lead to distorted views on gender roles, power dynamics, and consent—distortions that may carry over into real-world interactions. "Porn doesn't just stay on the screen," she says. "It infiltrates people's expectations and shapes how they perceive and engage in relationships." Dines' work demonstrates that these distorted perceptions often lead to unhealthy behaviors that undermine trust and mutual respect, damaging the very fabric of intimate relationships.

The Link Between Porn and Infidelity

Dr. Mark Butler, a psychologist specializing in sexual addiction, describes pornography's influence on committed relationships as a "corrosive force." His research indicates that frequent consumption of pornography is linked to a higher risk of infidelity, with individuals increasingly desiring the novelty and fantasy depicted on-screen. "Pornography often creates an insatiable desire for newness," Dr. Butler explains, "and this desire can push individuals to seek excitement outside their committed partnerships." In a study published in his *Journal of Sex Research*, findings showed that men who frequently viewed pornography were more likely to engage in extramarital affairs and exhibit online sexual behaviors, highlighting the dangerous impact of unrealistic expectations.

The Harsh Realities of Exploitative Industries Linked to Pornography

The reach of pornography extends into realms that most people may not consider, such as the world of massage parlors, prostitution, webcam services, and escort agencies. Dr. Melissa Farley, a leading expert on prostitution and trafficking, emphasizes how pornography fuels demand in these exploitative industries. "Porn creates a model for commercialized sex," she asserts, "and normalizes transactional relationships that undermine real intimacy." Dr. Farley has found that people often become desensitized to these industries through regular porn consumption, leading them to seek out similar transactional experiences in real life, ultimately contributing to infidelity and marital strain.

Dr. Dines supports this view, noting that porn's glamorized depictions of sexual scenarios often feed into a culture that trivializes monogamy and emotional commitment. "It's no coincidence that as porn becomes more accessible, we see a rise in relationship dissatisfaction and cheating," she says. Studies have indeed shown that regular consumers of porn report lower relationship satisfaction and are at a greater risk of infidelity. Additionally, research reveals that frequent engagement with webcam services and escort agencies correlates with higher levels of emotional and physical disengagement in committed relationships, creating a vicious cycle where partners look for gratification outside their partnerships, increasing the likelihood of infidelity.

Psychological Effects of Porn Addiction

The psychological toll of porn addiction can be devastating, impacting both individual users and their relationships. Neuroscientist Dr. Valerie Voon, who has conducted pioneering research on the brain activity of individuals addicted to pornography, likens their brain responses to those observed in substance addiction. "Pornography addiction rewires the brain's reward circuits," Dr. Voon explains, "leading to diminished impulse control and a diminished capacity for healthy decision-making." Research by Dr. Kevin Skinner, an expert in sexual addiction therapy, highlights the shame, guilt, and self-loathing that often accompany porn addiction. "These feelings of low self-worth compound the isolation felt by addicts," says Dr. Skinner, "and interfere with their ability to form healthy, fulfilling relationships."

The Effects in the Bedroom

Within intimate relationships, the toll of porn addiction can be particularly evident in the bedroom. Dr. Jane Smith, a therapist specializing in sexual health, explains that porn often leads to unrealistic expectations that hinder genuine emotional intimacy. "Pornographic content sets the stage for comparison," Dr. Smith observes, "and when real-life intimacy doesn't match up, many people feel frustrated or unfulfilled." Studies from the *Journal of Sex Research* and the *Journal of Sexual Medicine* reveal that the unrealistic portrayals in porn often diminish arousal in real-world interactions, contributing to problems like erectile dysfunction (ED) and the inability to achieve satisfaction with a partner. These challenges frequently give rise to a disconnection that's difficult to overcome, particularly for individuals with a long-term addiction to pornography.

Dr. Susan Johnson, a respected authority in couples therapy, emphasizes the harm that pornography's artificial and often degrading scenarios inflict on individuals' perceptions of intimacy. "Porn warps ideas of sexual dynamics," she says, "and it hinders people from developing the kind of trust and emotional safety essential for a fulfilling sexual relationship." Additionally, research from the *Journal of Marital and Family Therapy* underscores the significant link between persistent porn use and declining relationship satisfaction, an increased risk of infidelity, and higher rates of separation.

Conclusion: A Call for Change and Resources for Healing

Pornography's impact on relationships and marriages is profound, presenting a challenge too significant to ignore. Particularly in faith-based communities, recognizing and addressing this issue is vital. This book aims to inspire meaningful change, advocating for the development of educational programs and support services within religious institutions, such as mosques. By fostering a community-driven approach, we can equip individuals to confront porn addiction, ensuring they enter marriage free from this destructive influence.

A foundational component of this approach involves grounding these educational initiatives in the principles of modesty, chastity, and the sanctity of marriage, as taught in Islam. Through integrating Qur'anic teachings and Hadiths that emphasize these values, we can fortify individuals against the detrimental impact of porn addiction. For example, this Qur'anic verse highlights the importance of preserving modesty and purity:

> "And do not approach unlawful sexual intercourse. Indeed, it is an immorality and an evil way." (Qur'an 17:32)

A holistic strategy encompassing sex education, therapeutic support, and spiritual guidance is essential. Collaborative efforts among schools, religious groups, and mental health professionals will be pivotal in addressing this complex issue. By combining psychological insights, robust educational programs, and spiritual teachings, our society can stand united against the harmful influence of pornography. In doing so, we protect the integrity of relationships, uphold the sanctity of marriage, and nurture communities where individuals and families are safeguarded from the damaging effects of the porn industry.

For those seeking additional support on the journey to recovery, several specialized resources can help:

- Purify Your Gaze (www.purifyyourgaze.com): This program offers a faith-centered approach to overcoming pornography addiction, combining counseling, community support, and spiritual guidance for those seeking liberation and healing.

- Aware Academy (www.awareacademy.com.au): A resource providing courses and tools to assist individuals in overcoming pornography addiction, with a focus on empowering individuals to regain control and live fulfilling lives.

- Fortify (www.joinfortify.com): Fortify is an app-based program designed to support people in overcoming pornography addiction with a science-backed approach, interactive tools, and community support.

The journey begins with a shared commitment to educate, support, and empower those affected by pornography's pervasive influence. With these resources, individuals can reclaim the peace, trust, and joy that form the bedrock of meaningful relationships and begin a life of healing, free from addiction. Together, we can protect the sanctity of our relationships and create a society that prioritizes emotional, mental, and spiritual well-being.

Chapter Eighteen

Ashes of Us: How Infidelity Burns What We Built

Infidelity—it's a word that carries so much weight. It's a betrayal that goes far beyond physical actions; it cuts deep into the heart, leaving a wound that feels impossible to heal. The trust that once held everything together—relationships, families, even entire communities—is shattered in an instant. What once seemed unbreakable becomes fragile, fractured, and broken. The devastation of infidelity isn't just a wound between two people—it's a trauma that spreads, affecting everyone in its wake. It's a deep betrayal that doesn't just take trust away but leaves a permanent scar that can never fully fade.

As someone who has worked as an infidelity recovery coach for years, I have walked alongside countless individuals and couples who have endured this heartache. Over the years, I've dealt with hundreds of cases, and I can personally attest to the immense pain and grief that people go through after discovering betrayal. I have witnessed the confusion, the anger, and the overwhelming sense of loss. The emotional toll is staggering. But I've also seen recovery. I've seen couples rebuild trust and even grow closer through the process. However, it's not always possible to go back to the way things were—especially when infidelity is a repeated offense. For some, no matter how much effort is put into recovery, the damage is too deep to repair, and the emotional scars are too great. It's a painful truth, but it's important to acknowledge that sometimes moving forward means letting go.

Roots of Infidelity

Infidelity often begins when something vital in the relationship is missing. It's not an excuse—just an explanation. When emotional needs aren't met, when communication breaks down, when loneliness creeps in, it creates cracks. And those cracks, small at first, can widen over time. The desire for connection, for affection, for excitement—it's natural, it's human. But when those needs go unaddressed in a committed relationship, it's so easy to look elsewhere. It doesn't happen overnight. It's a slow burn. The longing for intimacy, the yearning for excitement, the need to feel seen, to feel wanted—it builds up, and sometimes it's easier to find that somewhere outside the relationship than face the discomfort of addressing what's wrong within it.

Research by renowned relationship experts like Dr. John Gottman, a leading researcher in marital stability, emphasizes the importance of emotional connection and communication in relationships. Gottman's studies have shown that couples who don't address emotional needs or engage in healthy conflict resolution are at a higher risk of infidelity. He suggests that when partners fail to feel valued or seen, they may turn elsewhere for emotional fulfillment. It's not about one moment of weakness—it's about a buildup of unmet needs that erode the foundation of a relationship.

Sometimes, the pain of being misunderstood or ignored feels so unbearable that people start to question their value, their worth. And in that vulnerability, the temptation to seek affection elsewhere becomes too strong to resist. Infidelity doesn't just happen because someone is bored or selfish—it happens because, for a moment, they feel lost, unseen, and desperate for something they can't find at home. It's a cry for help, even if it's misguided.

The Psychology Behind Infidelity

Infidelity isn't just about a lack of self-control or moral failure—it's deeply tied to the way we connect with others. Our early experiences in life shape how we form attachments in relationships. For those with insecure attachment styles—people who feel anxious, fearful, or avoidant about intimacy—infidelity can feel like a way to find solace, validation, or escape. Anxious individuals may seek attention from others because they constantly fear abandonment, never feeling truly secure in their relationships. Avoidant people, on the other hand, may push others away emotionally and seek comfort outside the relationship because they struggle to fully open up.

The truth is, we are all deeply affected by how we feel about ourselves. When we feel insecure, unloved, or unimportant, we can fall into the trap of looking for validation in the wrong places. The need to feel desired, wanted, or noticed can become so overwhelming that the consequences of infidelity no longer seem to matter. The instant gratification of attention, approval, or affection from someone new can feel like a lifeline—something that momentarily fills the emptiness inside. But it's never enough. It leaves a hollowness that nothing external can ever truly satisfy.

Dr. Susan Johnson, argues that attachment issues are at the heart of many relationship breakdowns, including infidelity. Her research suggests that people turn to affairs as a way to cope with emotional abandonment or disconnection in their primary relationship. The pursuit of emotional intimacy outside of the relationship often signals unmet emotional needs within it. This psychological pattern explains why infidelity is more complex than mere physical betrayal—it's often an attempt to fill an emotional void.

Devastating Effects of Infidelity

The impact of infidelity is nothing short of devastating. It doesn't just hurt—it breaks you. The partner who is betrayed feels their entire world tilt. What they once believed in—what they thought was solid—crumbles beneath them. The trust they had placed so freely, so fully, is gone. The sense of security they once took for granted vanishes, and what's left is a painful, haunting emptiness. Anger, hurt, confusion, betrayal—it's a storm of emotions that doesn't pass easily. The question that keeps coming to mind is, *Why?* Why did this happen? How could someone they loved, trusted, and gave so much of themselves to, betray them like this?

But beyond the initial shock, there's a quiet, gnawing pain. The lingering doubt, the constant questions, the erosion of self-worth. You start questioning your value. Were you not enough? Were you not loved? Can you ever trust again? It's a deep wound that takes time, so much time, to heal—if it ever truly does. Sometimes, even after the pain has subsided, the scars remain, a reminder of the hurt, of the betrayal.

The consequences of infidelity extend beyond the individual couple. Psychologists like Dr. Shirley Glass, author of *Not Just Friends*, emphasize the long-lasting emotional trauma experienced by betrayed partners. According to Dr. Glass, the emotional toll can lead to symptoms similar to post-traumatic stress disorder, including anxiety, intrusive thoughts, and heightened vigilance. The damage isn't just a temporary upset—it has the potential to change the course of a person's emotional well-being forever.

And it's not just the partners who suffer. Infidelity has a ripple effect that touches everyone. Children, especially, are vulnerable. They see the pain, they feel the tension, and they begin to make sense of it in their own way. Their perception of love, commitment, and trust can be forever altered by what they witness. They may grow up with trust issues, struggling to believe in the strength of their own relationships. The impact of infidelity stretches far beyond the couple—it shakes the very foundation of the family and, ultimately, society itself.

Infidelity in the Digital Age

Modern technology has made infidelity more accessible, more insidious, and harder to detect. The rise of social media, dating apps, and online platforms has made it easier for individuals to form emotional connections with others, sometimes without even intending to. The boundaries that once defined relationships are now blurred by digital connections, and it's easier than ever to feel emotionally or physically unfaithful without even stepping outside the house.

Social media gives us a constant stream of curated lives—highlight reels of others' happiness, success, and relationships. It's easy to fall into the trap of comparison, to feel like something is missing in your own life, even when everything seems fine on the surface. That dissatisfaction, that hunger for something more, can lead to temptation. The illusion of "greener pastures" online can cloud judgment, tempting someone to reach out, to reconnect with an old flame, or to explore a new connection that feels exciting and fresh.

Then there's the darker influence of pornography. The easy availability of explicit content online distorts our understanding of intimacy and relationships. It sets unrealistic expectations, distorts our desires, and can create dissatisfaction in the relationships we are supposed to cherish. Pornography chips away at the emotional connection between partners, feeding into a fantasy world that makes real intimacy feel inadequate.

Solutions and Strategies

So, what can we do to heal from the devastation of infidelity? How do we rebuild after everything has been shattered? The answer isn't simple. Healing takes time, patience, and a commitment from both partners. It requires honest, open communication—a willingness to listen to each other's pain, to understand the reasons behind the betrayal, and to confront the issues that led to it. Trust can be rebuilt, but it won't happen overnight.

Therapy, both individual and couples counseling or infidelity recovery coaching, can provide a safe space to navigate the overwhelming emotions and rebuild the broken parts of the relationship. But beyond professional help, the healing starts with understanding the root causes of the betrayal. It starts with addressing unmet needs, insecurities, and emotional wounds that may have been festering for far too long.

From an Islamic perspective, infidelity is seen as a grave violation of the sanctity of marriage. Yet, even in the midst of betrayal, there is room for repentance and forgiveness. Islam teaches that no sin is beyond the reach of mercy. Seeking forgiveness, making amends, and striving to rebuild a relationship on the foundation of faith and trust can be transformative. It's not about perfection—it's about commitment to growth, to healing, and to love.

Here are some Islamic quotes to focus on:

> "And those who, when they have committed Fahishah (illegal sexual intercourse) or wronged themselves with evil, remember Allah and ask forgiveness for their sins; - and none can forgive sins but Allah - And do not persist in what (wrong) they have done, while they know." (Qur'an 3:135)

> "If anyone constantly seeks pardon (from Allah), Allah will appoint for him a way out of every distress and a relief from every anxiety, and will provide sustenance for him from where he expects not." (Abu Dawud. Riyad as-Salihin 1873)

> "Whoever does evil or wrongs themselves but afterwards [sincerely] seeks God's Forgiveness, they will find God Very Forgiving [and] Most Merciful." (Qur'an 4:110)

"Say: 'Allahumma innaka 'afuwwun tuhibbul-'afwa, fa'fu 'anni [O Allah, You are Forgiving and love forgiveness, so forgive me].'" (Sunan Ibn Majah 3850)

Conclusion

Infidelity is a heavy burden to bear. The betrayal, the hurt, the confusion—it's real. But it doesn't have to be the end. There is hope, even in the darkest moments. Healing is possible. With open communication, a willingness to seek help, and a deep commitment to understanding each other's pain, couples can rebuild their relationships. And by grounding ourselves in faith—whether through repentance, prayer, or a renewed commitment to love—we can restore the trust that was lost. We may never forget the pain, but we can learn to live beyond it. The darkness of infidelity doesn't have to define us—it can be the catalyst for a deeper, more authentic love.

Chapter Nineteen

More Than Flirting: The Hidden Wounds of Emotional Affairs

Emotional attachments and flirtatious behavior outside of marriage might seem harmless at first, but they can bring serious consequences to the core trust and security within a partnership. Through my experience coaching hundreds of couples affected by infidelity, I've witnessed how these behaviors gradually undermine the connection couples work so hard to build. In this chapter, we'll examine how emotional bonds with others outside the marriage can affect relationships, why flirtatious behavior can be more damaging than it seems, and what strategies help couples rebuild or protect their marriages. With insights from relationship experts and data-driven examples, we'll explore both the psychological impacts and practical tools to help couples move forward.

The Dangers of Emotional Attachments

Emotional Infidelity: When Connections Turn into Divides

Emotional infidelity happens when a partner forms a deep bond with someone outside the marriage, blurring boundaries and creating distance from their spouse. In studies on infidelity, like those by Dr. Shirley Glass, often called the "Godmother of Infidelity Research," emotional affairs can feel as damaging as physical affairs because they involve a sharing of intimacy and emotional support that's typically reserved for the marriage. For example, a spouse who habitually texts a coworker about personal life challenges might eventually come to rely on that coworker emotionally, drifting away from their partner. Over time, this bond redirects attention, empathy, and emotional support away from the marriage, leaving the other partner feeling emotionally abandoned and disconnected.

Neglect of Partner's Emotional Needs

When emotional connections grow outside the marriage, it often leads to neglect within the primary relationship. Research by the American Association for Marriage and Family Therapy (AAMFT) suggests that emotional neglect in a marriage is one of the leading causes of dissatisfaction. Consider a situation where one partner starts to rely on a friend or colleague for regular emotional validation. The partner in the marriage may start to feel isolated, less important, or even invisible. This lack of attention to their emotional needs often leads to resentment, eventually impacting intimacy and partnership. The shift from prioritizing one's spouse to seeking fulfillment elsewhere can make the marriage feel like a cohabitation rather than a place of deep support and understanding.

Boundary Creep: When Friendships Escalate into Attachments

Many emotional attachments that start as friendships can slowly cross into more intimate territory. Dr. John Gottman's research on relationship boundaries reveals that "boundary creep" is often gradual and unintended. For instance, a spouse might begin with friendly, supportive conversations with a coworker, but as these talks grow in depth and frequency, emotional boundaries can blur. Regular interaction can evolve from casual to intimate, where they begin to confide in this person rather than in their spouse. Over time, these emotional attachments often lead to secrets or feelings of guilt, creating a divide that's hard to bridge within the marriage.

Consequences of Flirtatious Behavior

Trust Issues and Security Threats

Flirtatious behavior within or outside the marriage may appear insignificant, yet it often seeds insecurity. Research from the Gottman Institute, which studies relationship stability, found that even minor betrayals of trust can weaken relationship security. For example, a partner who frequently exchanges flirty messages with an acquaintance may feel it's harmless fun, but for the other partner, this behavior feels like a signal that they're not enough. This leads to anxiety, suspicion, and a feeling that their bond isn't exclusive or deeply valued, ultimately chipping away at the foundation of trust.

Creating an Emotional Disconnect

Seeking validation or excitement outside the marriage through flirtation often causes an emotional disconnect at home. Studies show that partners who frequently flirt outside the relationship tend to develop a detachment from their spouse. In one real-life scenario, a husband who engaged in playful flirtation with a colleague eventually found himself emotionally estranged from his wife, as he had come to rely on this other relationship for emotional excitement. Over time, his marriage became a source of obligation rather than enjoyment. This emotional gap can become so large that spouses feel they're living separate emotional lives.

Jealousy, Resentment, and Emotional Turmoil

Flirtatious behavior is a common trigger for jealousy, which quickly escalates to resentment. According to research by Dr. Helen Fisher, a biological anthropologist who studies love and relationships, jealousy triggers intense emotions tied to our basic survival instincts. When a spouse feels threatened by their partner's flirtation, it often leads to insecurity and fear of being replaced. Over time, these feelings grow, creating repeated conflicts and a lack of trust. For example, a wife who discovers flirtatious texts on her husband's phone may feel blindsided, sparking arguments and causing her to question her self-worth and the security of their relationship.

Solutions for Navigating Emotional Attachments and Flirtation

Prioritizing Open Communication

Effective communication is one of the most powerful ways to prevent the risks of emotional attachments and flirtation. Dr. Sue Johnson, the creator of Emotionally Focused Therapy (EFT), emphasizes that clear, open discussions create "secure bonds." For example, couples who set aside regular time each week to discuss their feelings and address potential issues are less likely to seek emotional fulfillment elsewhere. When both partners feel heard and valued, there's less temptation to look outside the marriage for comfort or excitement.

Setting Boundaries that Reinforce Commitment

Establishing clear boundaries is crucial for a relationship's integrity. Couples can set guidelines on interactions with others to keep their bond exclusive. For example, agreeing not to discuss private marital issues with friends or colleagues, or limiting time spent alone with someone who could be seen as a potential risk, strengthens relationship security. Relationship expert Dr. Harriet Lerner highlights that "boundaries aren't about limiting freedom but about protecting what we value," allowing couples to feel safe without feeling restricted.

Self-Reflection and Understanding Motivation

Understanding the motivations behind seeking emotional support or validation outside the marriage can help individuals prevent these patterns. In infidelity recovery coaching, clients often realize that unmet personal needs, unresolved insecurities, or stressors within the marriage drive them to form outside connections. For instance, someone who flirts often might discover that they are seeking validation for low self-esteem or avoiding an unresolved marital issue. Through self-reflection and therapy/coaching, individuals can address these root causes, reduce the temptation to seek outside fulfillment, and work toward building self-awareness and emotional resilience.

Seeking Professional Help for Deeper Repair

Therapy provides a structured environment for open discussions and equips individuals with tools to process painful emotions. Research indicates that professional interventions benefit approximately 70% of couples, enhancing their relationship quality. Therapists offer strategies to rebuild trust and improve communication, facilitating deeper connections between partners. Specifically, infidelity recovery coaching addresses the complexities of betrayal, guiding individuals toward renewed commitment or, if necessary, a healthier separation.

Investing in Emotional Intimacy and Connection at Home

One of the strongest defenses against outside attachments is a marriage rooted in emotional intimacy. Couples who consistently work to deepen their connection are less likely to experience issues with outside attachments. According to Dr. Gary Chapman, author of *The Five Love Languages*, understanding how each partner gives and receives love strengthens bonds. For example, a couple that makes time for regular date nights, openly expresses appreciation, and communicates affection in each other's love language builds a level of satisfaction and security that discourages outside connections.

Conclusion

Emotional attachments and flirtatious behavior may seem like small matters, but they have the potential to undermine trust and connection in marriage if left unaddressed. Islam emphasizes the sanctity of marriage and warns against actions that can lead to fitnah (temptation) or compromise the trust between spouses. The Prophet Muhammad (ﷺ) said, "No man is alone with a woman but that the third one present is Shaytan" (Tirmidhi, Hadith 2165), highlighting the importance of guarding against situations that may lead to inappropriate emotional connections.

By understanding the risks and proactively setting boundaries, communicating openly, and seeking professional guidance when needed, couples can protect and even strengthen their bond. A healthy, fulfilling relationship is built on prioritizing one another's emotional needs, setting clear boundaries, and fostering open, honest conversations.

When couples commit to these practices within the framework of Islamic principles, they create a partnership that is not only resilient but also spiritually grounded and deeply connected. By striving for taqwa (God-consciousness) and aligning their actions with the teachings of Islam, spouses can safeguard their marriage from harm and nurture a bond that brings tranquility and blessings, as described in the Qur'an:

> "And among His signs is that He created for you spouses from among yourselves, that you may find tranquility in them; and He placed between you affection and mercy." (Qur'an 30:21)

Chapter Twenty

Two Hearts, One Trust: The Guardianship of Love

Navigating Traditional Roles in Modern Marriages

Navigating roles in a marriage is often about much more than simply following a set of predefined rules or principles; it's about the delicate dance of love, respect, and mutual support. In modern marriages, especially those inspired by Islamic teachings and a wealth of other cultural and psychological perspectives, the challenge lies in striking a balance between tradition and contemporary needs. Traditional Islamic teachings provide a structure, emphasizing principles of guardianship, respect, and protection, yet a marriage also draws on love, flexibility, and shared responsibilities. In this chapter, we'll explore how couples today can make traditional roles meaningful, empowering, and harmonious, incorporating wisdom from both religious teachings and modern relationship psychology.

The Concept of Qawwam: Responsibility, Not Dominance

In Islam, the concept of Qawwam, found in the Qur'anic verse "Men are the protectors and maintainers of women" (Surah An-Nisa 4:34), refers to the responsibility of men to care for, protect, and provide for their families. Far from being a justification for dominance, Qawwam is a responsibility that honors the integrity and dignity of women, much like a guardian or a caretaker. For instance, a husband may take on the role of financial provider and decision-maker, but that does not mean his voice is the only one that matters; rather, it's his duty to ensure his family's welfare, safety, and happiness by actively considering and valuing his wife's input and perspective. A healthy marriage thrives on mutual respect and collaboration, where both voices contribute to the shared vision of the family's future.

Psychologist Dr. John Gottman, known for his groundbreaking work on marital stability, supports this notion of responsibility and partnership. His research shows that relationships thrive when both partners feel valued and heard. Therefore, even within the framework of Qawwam, decision-making should include both partners' voices, with mutual respect guiding each choice. A husband, then, would view his role as one of service and support, ensuring his wife feels secure, valued, and fulfilled in her own pursuits.

Balance and Partnership: When Tradition Meets Mutual Respect

Islamic teachings also emphasize love and compassion in marriage. The verse "And among His signs is this, that He created for you mates from among yourselves, that you may dwell in tranquility with them, and He has put love and mercy between your (hearts)" (Surah Ar-Rum, 30:21) highlights the goal of harmony. Real-life stories reveal how this principle plays out. For example, a husband and wife who share the daily workload—whether it's managing household responsibilities or childcare—often report higher levels of satisfaction. Studies suggest that when partners divide responsibilities based on skills and availability rather than fixed roles, they foster a sense of equality and companionship.

In one client's experience, a husband with long working hours trusted his wife with important family decisions. He explained, "I may be the financial provider, but she's the heartbeat of this family." She felt respected and empowered, which strengthened their bond, highlighting how respect for each other's roles naturally creates a balance.

The Importance of Emotional Support: A Two-Way Street

In the past, traditional roles often centered on tangible contributions like financial support or household management. Today, there's a growing awareness that emotional support is just as critical. Relationship psychologist Dr. Sue Johnson teaches that a successful marriage is built on emotional connection, not on perfectly assigned roles. What matters most is that each partner feels secure, valued, and emotionally accessible.

Consider a modern Muslim wife balancing a career and family. Her husband, understanding her need for support, might take on extra tasks around the house, not out of obligation but out of love and respect. This adaptation honors Islamic principles of partnership and the modern need for flexibility. As a result, both partners feel they are contributing equally to each other's emotional well-being, which makes their bond more resilient.

Misconceptions and the Misuse of Traditional Roles

A major challenge for many couples today is the misuse of traditional roles to justify control or dominance. The Prophet Muhammad (ﷺ) strongly condemned any form of oppression or abuse. The Qur'an cautions:

> "O you who have believed, it is not lawful for you to inherit women by compulsion... And live with them in kindness." (Surah An-Nisa 4:19)

Kindness, respect, and fairness were central to his relationships with his wives.

For example, a husband may misuse his role as Qawwam to restrict his wife's choices, perhaps forbidding her from pursuing a career or education. Yet this contradicts the very essence of Qawwam, which calls for providing and protecting, not controlling. A fulfilling marriage is rooted in kindness, not rigidity. In cases where one partner's role limits the other's freedom or growth, relationship experts agree that open communication and sometimes even counseling are necessary to recalibrate the partnership toward mutual support.

Empowering Each Other: Education, Growth, and Shared Goals

The Islamic emphasis on education and personal growth applies to both men and women. A study published in the *Journal of Marriage and Family* shows that couples who support each other's personal growth report significantly higher satisfaction in their relationships. The concept of Qawwam should encourage husbands to empower their wives rather than restrict them, creating an environment where both spouses can pursue their goals.

Take, for example, a husband who encouraged his wife to continue her education despite financial challenges. Together, they strategized and budgeted, showing how even traditional roles can be flexible when spouses genuinely support each other's aspirations. Their story reflects the Prophet Muhammad's (ﷺ) own encouragement of his wives to pursue knowledge, demonstrating that empowerment within marriage enriches the relationship and strengthens family bonds; for instance, his wife Aisha (Raddiyallahu Anha) was renowned for her scholarly contributions, narrating over 2,000 hadiths and teaching both men and women.

Practicing Consultation: Decisions Based on Mutual Respect

Prophet Muhammad (ﷺ) emphasized the importance of *shura*—mutual consultation—in marriage. He consistently valued his wives' opinions, even in times of crisis. An illustrative example is the incident following the Treaty of Hudaybiyah. After the treaty was concluded, the Companions were reluctant to perform the sacrificial rites, feeling disheartened by the terms of the agreement. The Prophet (ﷺ) sought counsel from his wife, Umm Salama, who advised him to lead by example: to go out, sacrifice his animal, and shave his head. Heeding her advice, he performed the rites, prompting his Companions to follow suit, thereby resolving the impasse. This incident highlights the Prophet's (ﷺ) commitment to consulting his wives, valuing their perspectives even during critical moments. Such practices emphasize the importance of mutual consultation in marriage, fostering harmony and understanding between spouses.

In a study by Dr. Terri Orbuch, a social psychologist specializing in marital happiness, couples who practiced open consultation experienced greater harmony and mutual respect. Decisions made jointly are more likely to consider the needs and desires of both partners, reducing resentment and increasing satisfaction.

Imagine a couple facing a major family decision, such as relocating for a job. The husband, even if he is the financial provider, consults his wife and considers her career, family ties, and personal comfort. This approach mirrors the principles of shura and promotes unity. Instead of feeling sidelined, the wife feels included and valued, fostering a true partnership rather than a hierarchy.

Protecting Against Misuse: The Role of Boundaries

Modern relationships can also be vulnerable to misuse of authority, which is why boundaries are essential. The Qur'an and Hadith clearly outline that love and mercy are at the core of any relationship, with no room for abuse. If a husband uses his role as Qawwam to restrict, isolate, or control, it goes against the teachings of Islam and modern psychology's understanding of healthy relationships.

Dr. Harriet Lerner, a renowned psychologist specializing in intimate relationships, emphasizes the importance of setting boundaries to prevent mistreatment. She asserts that "an intimate relationship is one in which neither party silences, sacrifices, or betrays the self." If either partner feels dominated or controlled, establishing clear boundaries is essential to protect the relationship and uphold each person's dignity.

Embracing Flexibility and Adapting Roles Together

One of the most beautiful aspects of a successful marriage is its ability to adapt. The Prophet Muhammad (ﷺ) was known for his kindness, flexibility, and willingness to help his wives. In many homes today, roles have shifted as couples seek balance and harmony based on each other's strengths rather than rigid expectations.

For example, a husband who is more detail-oriented might take on budgeting and financial planning, while his wife manages logistics and schedules. Such flexibility allows for a more equal distribution of roles, as psychologist Dr. Jennifer Freed teaches, rigid roles in relationships often stifle emotional growth, while adaptability fosters vitality and deeper connection.

Conclusion: Partnership Rooted in Faith, Mutual Respect, and Love

In both Islamic teachings and modern relationship science, the foundation of a fulfilling marriage is a partnership where both spouses feel respected, valued, and heard. Traditional roles, such as those informed by Qawwam, are most meaningful when grounded in empathy, kindness, and a willingness to adapt. Both partners should view their roles as opportunities to uplift, protect, and support one another.

Through open communication, shared decision-making, and the flexibility to adapt to changing circumstances, couples can navigate traditional roles with respect for both Islamic principles and modern perspectives. A balanced marriage allows each spouse to flourish, creating a loving, resilient, and joyful partnership that honors both tradition and the evolving needs of today's world.

Chapter Twenty-One

The Polygyny Puzzle: Navigating the Complexities in Modern Times

Polygyny—where a man marries multiple wives—is one of the most discussed and often misunderstood aspects of Islamic marital law. For many, it sparks images of patriarchal dominance or unfair family dynamics, while others view it as a compassionate solution rooted in religious guidance. But the reality is far more nuanced. To truly understand polygyny in Islam, we need to look beyond the headlines and dive into the historical context, the ethical framework Islam provides, and the human experiences tied to this complex practice.

In Islam, polygyny is not simply a free pass for men to marry multiple women. It's a responsibility—one wrapped in conditions and moral obligations that, if not met, make the practice not just inadvisable but sinful. The Qur'an sets a clear guideline: "...marry women of your choice, two, three, or four, but if you fear that you shall not be able to deal justly [with them], then only one." (Qur'an 4:3) This isn't an open invitation; it's a conditional allowance that places justice at its core.

The Historical Context: Reforming a Broken System

To understand Islam and polygyny, we need to step back in time. In pre-Islamic Arabia, polygyny was widespread, but it was also largely unregulated. Men could marry as many women as they wanted, often leading to the exploitation of women. Islam came as a reformative force, setting boundaries to protect the vulnerable. By limiting the number of wives to four and emphasizing fairness, Islam sought to create a system that promoted compassion rather than indulgence.

This wasn't just about numbers—it was about responsibility. Imagine a society devastated by wars, where many women were left widowed with children. Polygyny, in such contexts, served as a safety net. It was a way to ensure these women and their children were cared for, providing them with social and financial security in a time when few other options existed.

Polygyny as a Safety Net–Not an Indulgence

Additionally, in some cases, polygyny can offer a way to address and potentially prevent societal issues such as secretive extramarital affairs. In today's hypersexualized world, where temptations are rampant and boundaries are increasingly blurred, many men wrongly believe that polygyny is the solution to their problem. Platforms like OnlyFans, access to pornography, and the normalization of transactional relationships—whether through sugar baby dating, escorts, or massage parlors—have created an environment where instant gratification is often prioritized over emotional responsibility.

For some men, the allure of such outlets can lead to double lives filled with hidden affairs, one-night stands, or habitual visits to sex workers—behaviors that destroy the foundation of trust in a marriage. The widespread availability of pornography has also led to an epidemic of addiction, where men may become desensitized to genuine intimacy, seeking out riskier and more explicit content to satisfy escalating desires. This, in turn, impacts their ability to connect emotionally and physically with their spouse, often leading to resentment, dissatisfaction, and eventual infidelity.

A disturbing consequence of this unchecked pursuit of pleasure is the alarming rise in sexually transmitted diseases (STDs) globally. The normalization of casual sex, lack of boundaries, and diminished emphasis on self-restraint have fueled a public health crisis, with rates of STDs—such as HIV, syphilis, gonorrhea, and chlamydia—spiking in many societies. Engaging in risky sexual behaviors, especially with multiple partners and sex workers, significantly increases the spread of these diseases, leading to devastating physical, emotional, and societal repercussions.

Polygyny is not a path to replace clandestine affairs or transactional relationships that compromise marital integrity and personal health; polygyny is meant to offer a lawful and honest path that acknowledges human desires while upholding accountability. It allows for emotional and physical needs to be met within the framework of mutual respect, consent, and fairness, while ensuring that intimate relationships occur within the safety and commitment of marriage.

By providing a transparent and committed structure, polygyny can act as a safeguard against sexual exploitation, within ethical and health-conscious boundaries. It emphasizes responsibility and long-term commitment.

Moreover, it encourages men to confront their motivations openly, fostering dialogue and reducing the secrecy that often accompanies infidelity or addiction. By choosing a lawful, transparent route over deception and hidden indulgence, polygyny can act as a safeguard against the moral and physical decay caused by society's oversexualization, offering an alternative that aligns personal needs with ethical responsibilities. It transforms what could be a destructive force into an opportunity for growth, accountability, and spiritual maturity.

But here's the key—it all comes down to intention. If a man enters into polygyny merely to satisfy personal desires without considering the emotional, spiritual, and ethical responsibilities it entails, he's already failing the foundational principles Islam lays out.

Justice at the Heart of It All

Justice isn't just a word in Islamic law—it's a pillar. When it comes to polygyny, justice means equal financial support, equal time, and evenhanded emotional care for all wives. And the bar is high. The Prophet Muhammad (ﷺ) made this crystal clear when he warned, "Whoever has two wives and leans towards one over the other will come on the Day of Judgment with one side of his body leaning." (Sunan Abu Dawood, Hadith 2135)

This isn't metaphorical—it's a stark reminder of the weight of injustice. Even an emotional bias can lead to spiritual consequences. It's no wonder that many scholars interpret the Qur'an's verse on polygyny as a tacit endorsement of monogamy, given the near-impossible task of maintaining absolute justice.

The Emotional Landscape: What Happens When Justice Fails?

Let's talk about the human side—the emotions, the relationships, and the potential for deep emotional scars when polygyny is mishandled. While polygyny may be permissible, its impact on the emotional and mental well-being of both the first and second wives cannot be overlooked. Research highlights that when justice is not upheld, the psychological toll can be severe, leading to anxiety, depression, and long-term emotional distress.

For the First Wife: The Pain of Displacement and Emotional Trauma

Imagine being in a loving marriage, only to be told your husband is considering another wife. For many women, this news triggers a profound emotional response—one that can include feelings of betrayal, inadequacy, and insecurity. Even in cases where the husband handles the situation with sensitivity, the emotional toll on the first wife can be immense.

Studies show that first wives in polygynous marriages often report significantly higher levels of stress, anxiety, and depression compared to women in monogamous marriages. The introduction of a second wife can create an **identity crisis**, where the first wife feels that her place in the marriage is being challenged. This can lead to emotional withdrawal, loss of self-esteem, and, in severe cases, symptoms of "paranoia and emotional distress."

Additionally, research suggests that first wives experience greater marital dissatisfaction, increased domestic conflict, and social isolation due to the changes in marital dynamics. Extensive research indicates that first wives in polygamous marriages often experience higher levels of depressive symptoms, lower self-esteem, and more frequent somatic complaints compared to women in monogamous marriages. For instance, a study published in *BMC Women's Health* found that first wives in polygamous unions exhibited the highest levels of anxiety and depression, a phenomenon referred to as "first-wife syndrome." Additionally, a systematic review in *Epidemiology and Psychiatric Sciences* reported a higher prevalence of somatization, depression, anxiety, hostility, and psychiatric disorders among polygynous wives, along with reduced life and marital satisfaction and low self-esteem. These findings highlight the adverse psychological impacts associated with polygamous marriages, particularly for first wives.

Beyond mental health concerns, first wives may also struggle with **attachment trauma,** especially if the husband's decision to marry again was not preceded by open and honest discussions. The uncertainty surrounding the husband's love and attention can leave first wives in a state of constant emotional distress, leading to emotional numbness, heightened insecurity, and withdrawal from intimate connections with their spouse.

For the Second Wife: The Illusion of Favor and Social Struggles

It is often assumed that the second wife has the upper hand—after all, she is the one newly chosen. However, research suggests that second wives also endure significant psychological challenges, though of a different nature. The second wife frequently faces social stigma, isolation, and conflict with the first wife.

While she may enter the marriage with optimism, many second wives later experience emotional distress due to their marginalized position within the family structure. They often feel like an outsider, particularly if the first wife and children maintain a close bond that excludes her. Studies have shown that second wives experience:

- **Higher levels of social anxiety and loneliness:** especially if their marriage is kept secret or is viewed negatively by extended family.

- **Insecurity and rivalry with the first wife:** leading to emotional exhaustion from trying to "prove" their place in the marriage.

- **Sexual dissatisfaction and emotional neglect:** since the husband's time is divided, many second wives feel they are receiving less attention than they expected. A study published in *BMC Women's Health* found that "many second wives report emotional neglect and feelings of abandonment over time."

Moreover, financial concerns and instability often arise if the husband struggles to support two households equally. Unlike the first wife, who was part of the husband's life before the second marriage, the second wife may find herself in a more vulnerable position, especially if her financial rights are not firmly established.

While society may portray the second wife as a "winner," many actually report lower self-esteem, depression, and regret over time. The psychological burden of constantly navigating conflict and adjusting to an existing family dynamic can be emotionally exhausting.

The Need for Justice and Emotional Support

Both first and second wives endure unique psychological challenges in a polygynous marriage. While the first wife grapples with feelings of loss, betrayal, and displacement, the second wife often struggles with social stigma, rivalry, and a marginalized position within the household. These effects are magnified when the husband fails to fulfill his responsibilities with fairness and emotional support.

Islam mandates justice in polygyny for a reason. Without balance, communication, and sincere care for the emotional needs of both wives, the family structure risks becoming a source of pain rather than stability. Proper counseling, clear expectations, and emotional preparation are essential before entering a polygynous arrangement. Otherwise, what was meant to be a lawful and compassionate practice can become a source of lasting emotional wounds.

Impact of Polygyny on Children's Mental Health and Family Dynamics

Research in sociology, psychology, and family studies has found that children raised in polygynous (polygamous) families often face greater mental health challenges compared to those from monogamous families. Multiple studies and reviews report higher rates of psychological and social difficulties among these children. The unique family structure of polygyny can introduce family tensions, sibling rivalry, perceived inequalities, and emotional insecurity, all of which can adversely affect a child's well-being.

Family Tensions and Inter-Parental Conflict

Polygynous households commonly experience elevated family tension due to competition and conflict among co-wives. A systematic review notes that polygamous families have distinct problems "stemming from jealousy between co-wives over the husband's affections and resources." Such marital strife often creates a stressful home environment. Studies have observed that polygynous marital structures are frequently marked by interfamilial conflicts, jealousy, and stress, which leave children more vulnerable to psychological dysfunction. In other words, chronic tension and quarrels between parents (and between co-wives) can erode the overall family cohesion that is crucial for a child's emotional security. One study of Saudi families found that living in a polygamous family was associated with reduced family cohesion, which partly explained the mental health outcomes in children. Greater marital conflict in these homes is correlated with higher maladjustment in children, as the constant discord can heighten anxiety and insecurity in the younger family members.

Sibling Rivalry and Complex Family Dynamics

In polygynous families, children often have to navigate relationships with numerous half-siblings from different mothers, which can lead to heightened sibling rivalry. Research by Al-Krenawi et al. found that children in polygamous households experience more frequent and intense conflicts with siblings than those in monogamous families. The presence of multiple sets of children can create competition for resources and parental attention. One review noted that having many siblings from different mothers "*might lead to complex sibling relationships and potential rivalry,*" generating stress and tension in the household. This rivalry can manifest as fights, jealousy, or a lack of close bonding between half-siblings. Such an atmosphere of competition further contributes to an emotionally charged environment and can negatively influence a child's emotional well-being and development. In short, the complex family dynamics—where siblings may be divided by maternal lines—often breed resentment or competition that can undermine the support network children typically rely on.

Perceived Inequalities and Divided Parental Attention

Perceived inequality is another common issue in polygynous family settings. A polygynous father's time, affection, and financial resources are split among multiple wives and their children, which can lead children to feel they are not treated equally or not getting enough attention. Qualitative evidence shows that children in polygamous families sometimes feel a *"divided loyalty"* between parents and households, reflecting a sense of being torn between different family units. They may witness their mothers vying for the father's favor or resources, and this can translate into the children's own feelings of inequality or favoritism. Indeed, researchers report that children from polygynous families often rate their relationship with their father as poorer than do children from monogamous homes. Many polygamous fathers have limited availability for each child, and lower father involvement has been linked to weaker family cohesion and more emotional problems in the children. Even in cases where material needs are met, children may sense an emotional gap. One study from Nigeria noted that life in a polygamous family can be traumatic for a child, who "*often suffer[s] some emotional problems such as lack of warmth [and] love*" despite the availability of money and material support. This lack of consistent parental warmth and perceived unequal attention can foster feelings of neglect, resentment, or low self-worth in children.

Emotional Insecurity and Psychological Distress in Children

All of these factors—heightened conflict, sibling competition, and perceived unequal love—can contribute to significant emotional insecurity among children in polygynous families. Children in such households commonly report feeling less stable and less assured of their parents' love, which can manifest in lower self-esteem and trust issues. Empirical studies have documented elevated psychological distress in these children. For example, a large study of Bedouin Arab children showed that those from polygynous families had more mental health difficulties (such as anxiety and depression symptoms) and poorer social functioning than their peers from monogamous families. Similarly, a meta-analysis of global research found that children with polygamous parents scored significantly higher on a global index of psychological problems, indicating worse overall mental health, compared to children of monogamous parents. In practical terms, researchers have observed more internalizing problems (e.g., anxiety, sadness, withdrawal) among youth in polygamous families, thought to arise from the unstable and conflict-ridden family atmosphere. Qualitative case studies further illustrate these emotional challenges. In interviews, some children from polygynous homes describe profound feelings of insecurity and hurt. For instance, one case study recounted a teenager's reaction upon discovering his father had taken a second wife: the boy felt deeply betrayed and lost his sense of trust in his father, at one point running away from home in distress. He described feeling alienated and traumatized by the revelation, requiring support from siblings and others to cope with the emotional fallout. Such cases highlight the emotional turmoil—shock, anger, confusion, and sadness—that can affect children when polygyny introduces sudden changes or perceived betrayals in the family structure.

Overall, peer-reviewed research consistently indicates that polygyny can adversely impact children's mental health. Factors like inter-parental jealousy and conflict, strained sibling relations, and uneven parental attention create a home environment often marked by stress and uncertainty. Children growing up in these conditions are more prone to psychological challenges—including anxiety, depression, low self-esteem, and behavioral problems—compared to those in monogamous families. While not every child in a polygynous household will have difficulties, the risk factors associated with polygyny (family tensions, perceived inequalities, sibling rivalry, emotional insecurity) are well-documented in sociology and family studies literature as contributing to a higher incidence of mental health and adjustment problems. These findings underscore the importance of providing emotional support and counseling in polygamous family contexts to help mitigate the negative outcomes for children.

The Modern Dilemma: When Fantasy Distorts Reality

In today's hypersexualized world, another layer complicates the issue—pornography. It's an uncomfortable topic, but it needs to be addressed. With explicit content more accessible than ever, many men's perceptions of relationships and intimacy are being shaped by unrealistic fantasies. And unfortunately, some view polygyny as a religiously sanctioned way to live out these fantasies.

But Islam doesn't permit polygyny as a loophole for indulgence. It's not a halal stamp on unchecked desires. The Qur'an commands "Tell the believing men to lower their gaze and guard their private parts. That is purer for them. Indeed, Allah is All-Aware of what they do." Pornography addiction can distort a man's understanding of intimacy, leading him to view polygyny as a means to satisfy cravings rather than as a compassionate, responsible practice.

Practicing Polygyny with Integrity

So, how can polygyny be practiced in a way that aligns with Islamic ethics and safeguards everyone's emotional well-being?

- **Self-Reflection is Crucial:** Before even considering polygyny, a man must take a hard look at his intentions. Is this about compassion and responsibility, or is it about fulfilling a personal desire? Does he have the emotional maturity, financial stability, and spiritual grounding to uphold justice between wives?

- **Counsel and Transparency:** Consulting knowledgeable scholars and seeking premarital therapy isn't just advisable—it's essential. Open dialogue between the husband, the first wife, and the potential second wife sets the foundation for transparency and trust.

- **Upholding Justice in Action:** This means more than just dividing time equally between households. It involves emotional availability, financial fairness, and fostering harmony within the family. It also means being transparent with children and ensuring they feel equally loved and valued.

The Conclusion:
A Sacred Responsibility, Not a Right

Polygyny in Islam is not about male privilege—it's about compassion, justice, and social responsibility. It's a practice that, when handled with care, can provide support to those in need. But when misused, it can lead to emotional devastation, broken families, and spiritual consequences.

The Prophet Muhammad (ﷺ) set the gold standard when he said, "The best of you are those who are best to their women." (Sunan al-Tirmidhi, Hadith 3895) This wisdom applies whether a man has one wife or more—it's the quality of care, respect, and justice that defines his character.

In a world where polygyny is often misunderstood or misused, it's crucial to return to its roots—a practice built on compassion, justice, and integrity. Anything less is not just a disservice to the individuals involved but a distortion of the very principles Islam upholds.

Chapter Twenty-Two

The Silent Struggles: Vaginismus and Erectile Dysfunction

Understanding the Impact of Vaginismus and Erectile Dysfunction on Marriage

Marriage is a sanctuary where physical, emotional, and spiritual intimacy intertwine to create a bond of trust and connection. However, conditions like vaginismus and erectile dysfunction (ED) can silently erode the foundation of this bond. These deeply personal struggles are compounded by societal and cultural taboos, leaving couples to navigate feelings of frustration, inadequacy, and isolation in silence. This chapter explores the causes, consequences, and solutions for vaginismus and ED, illustrating their profound effects on marriages while highlighting the need for empathy, medical intervention, and open communication.

Vaginismus: When Pain and Fear Create a Barrier

What is Vaginismus?

Vaginismus is a condition where involuntary muscle spasms in the pelvic floor make vaginal penetration painful or impossible. It is both a physical and psychological response, often triggered by fear, anxiety, or past trauma. Psychological factors such as anxiety disorders, fear of pain, or negative sexual experiences can contribute to its onset. According to the NHS, vaginismus may result from anxiety about sex, past sexual abuse or assault, an unpleasant medical examination, a difficult childbirth experience, deeply ingrained cultural or religious taboos surrounding sex, or medical conditions like thrush. Similarly, the Cleveland Clinic highlights that anxiety disorders, fear of sex, or negative feelings about intimacy—especially due to past trauma—can exacerbate the condition. Beyond psychological causes, medical factors such as endometriosis, pelvic inflammatory disease, or childbirth injuries can contribute to painful experiences, reinforcing a cycle of avoidance. Additionally, cultural beliefs that frame sex as taboo or shameful, particularly in conservative societies, can lead to internalized guilt and fear, further intensifying vaginismus. Perfectionism, body image concerns, and general anxiety can also heighten the condition, making it crucial to address both physical and psychological components in treatment.

For example, Ayesha, a young woman newly married in Karachi, struggled with vaginismus for months after her wedding. Growing up in a conservative household, she had internalized messages about sex being dirty and painful. These fears translated into physical symptoms, leaving her and her husband, Bilal, feeling disconnected and confused.

The Emotional Toll on Marriage

Vaginismus creates ripples of pain beyond the physical. Ayesha shared, "I felt like I was failing as a wife. Every time Bilal tried to comfort me, I pulled away because I felt broken." For Bilal, the repeated rejection led to feelings of inadequacy and frustration. Without addressing the root cause, couples often enter a cycle of avoidance and emotional distance.

When intimacy becomes a source of stress, it can diminish the emotional connection between partners, leading to physical and emotional avoidance that undermines the foundation of their relationship. Dr. Laura Berman, a world-renowned sex, love, and relationship therapist, emphasizes the importance of emotional intimacy in maintaining a thriving partnership. She suggests that open communication and mutual understanding are crucial in preserving and enhancing the bond between couples.

The Long-Term Effects of Untreated Vaginismus

If vaginismus is not treated, the consequences can be far-reaching:

- **Emotional Estrangement**: Couples may stop discussing their struggles, leading to resentment.

- **Infertility Challenges**: Difficulty with penetration may prevent conception, adding another layer of frustration.

- **Marital Breakdown**: In extreme cases, untreated vaginismus can lead to separation or divorce.

Case studies show that couples who address vaginismus with medical and psychological support often experience renewed connection and trust. Ayesha and Bilal, for instance, sought the help of a pelvic floor therapist and a counselor. Within six months, they began to rebuild their intimacy, turning their struggle into a shared journey of growth.

Erectile Dysfunction: A Silent Struggle

What is Erectile Dysfunction?

Erectile dysfunction (ED) is the persistent inability to achieve or maintain an erection sufficient for sexual activity. While often viewed as a physical issue, ED frequently has emotional and psychological underpinnings. ED is often a symptom that can reflect underlying physical or emotional health issues. Dr. Kevin Skinner, a licensed marriage and family therapist and Clinical Director, has extensively addressed the profound impact of sexual issues on both physical and emotional well-being. His work emphasizes that sexual dysfunctions, such as ED, often reflect deeper health concerns, including anxiety, depression, or relational problems. Recognizing and addressing these underlying issues is crucial for holistic health and relationship satisfaction.

Causes of Erectile Dysfunction

ED arises from a combination of physical and psychological factors:

1. **Physical Causes**:

    - Cardiovascular Conditions: Hypertension, diabetes, and atherosclerosis impair blood flow, a key factor in maintaining erections.

    - Lifestyle Factors: Smoking, alcohol consumption, and obesity significantly increase the risk of ED.

    - Hormonal Imbalances: Low testosterone levels can reduce libido and cause ED.

2. **Psychological Causes**:

- Performance Anxiety: Fear of failure can create a self-fulfilling cycle of dysfunction.

- Stress and Depression: Mental health struggles often manifest in sexual dysfunction.

- Relational Issues: Unresolved conflicts or emotional disconnection exacerbate ED.

For instance, Faraz, a 45-year-old father of three in London, developed ED after losing his job. The financial stress combined with feelings of inadequacy created a spiral of avoidance in his marriage. His wife, Zainab, initially felt rejected and unattractive, leading to frequent arguments and emotional withdrawal.

The Emotional Toll on Marriage

ED often leaves both partners grappling with shame, frustration, and a sense of failure. Men like Faraz often feel emasculated, withdrawing emotionally to mask their embarrassment. Partners like Zainab interpret this withdrawal as rejection, leading to insecurity and anger.

Avoiding discussions about sexual challenges can lead to emotional distance between partners, potentially undermining the foundation of their relationship. Dr. John Gottman's research emphasizes that open communication about intimate matters is crucial for maintaining a strong emotional connection. He identifies stonewalling, or the refusal to communicate, as one of the "Four Horsemen" behaviors that predict relationship dissolution. Engaging in transparent conversations and collaborative problem-solving fosters trust and intimacy, essential components of a healthy partnership.

The Long-Term Effects of Untreated ED

Left untreated, ED can have profound consequences:

- **Reduced Self-Worth:** Men may feel a loss of masculinity and confidence.

- **Emotional Isolation**: Both partners may withdraw, compounding feelings of loneliness.

- **Marital Infidelity:** In some cases, unresolved sexual dissatisfaction may lead to seeking intimacy outside the marriage.

The Role of Pornography in Erectile Dysfunction

Pornography consumption is an emerging cause of ED, particularly among younger men. Known as Porn-Induced Erectile Dysfunction (PIED), this condition stems from the brain's desensitization to natural stimuli. Frequent exposure to explicit content overstimulates the brain's reward system, making real-life intimacy less arousing. Excessive consumption of internet pornography can lead to changes in the brain's reward system, potentially diminishing an individual's ability to connect with real-life partners both physically and emotionally. In his book, *Your Brain on Porn: Internet Pornography and the Emerging Science of Addiction*, Dr. Gary Wilson discusses how such consumption may diminish an individual's capacity to connect intimately with partners, both physically and emotionally. Wilson's work emphasizes that the neuroplastic nature of the brain allows it to adapt to various stimuli, including pornography. This adaptation can lead to altered sexual responses and expectations, making it challenging to maintain fulfilling intimate relationships.

Ahmed, a 30-year-old software engineer in Dubai, struggled with PIED after years of excessive pornography use. Despite loving his wife, Fatima, he found himself unable to engage intimately. Therapy and a commitment to abstaining from pornography helped Ahmed regain both his confidence and his connection with Fatima.

Breaking the Silence: Cultural Taboos and Shame

The Weight of Silence

Cultural taboos often prevent open discussions about sexual health in marriage. Women with vaginismus may feel stigmatized, while men with ED often tie their condition to a perceived loss of masculinity. These societal pressures lead to shame, ignorance, and isolation.

Islam encourages open and compassionate communication between spouses, especially when addressing sexual health issues. Dr. Yasir Qadhi emphasizes that many marital tensions arise from misunderstandings of gender roles and expectations, particularly regarding sexual relations. He advocates for mutual understanding and compassion, suggesting that a little bit of romance and empathy can significantly improve marital satisfaction.

In his "Like a Garment" series, Dr. Qadhi discusses the importance of addressing sexual satisfaction and performance problems within the framework of Islamic teachings. This approach fosters patience, mutual understanding, and proactive solutions to strengthen the marital bond.

The Role of Families and Communities

Families and communities play a pivotal role in shaping individuals' perceptions of marital intimacy. When myths and misconceptions persist, couples may enter marriage unprepared for its challenges, leading to potential misunderstandings and dissatisfaction. Parents, religious leaders, and community members can counteract this by promoting open discussions and providing accurate information about intimacy. Educational programs that integrate relationship education with economic stability services have shown promise in strengthening family bonds and improving marital satisfaction. By fostering environments where open communication about intimacy is encouraged, families and communities can equip couples with the tools and knowledge necessary for healthy and fulfilling relationships.

Therapeutic Interventions and Pathways to Healing

Medical Interventions

Vaginismus Treatments:

- **Pelvic Floor Therapy:** This involves exercises and techniques aimed at relaxing and strengthening the pelvic floor muscles, which can help alleviate the involuntary muscle contractions associated with vaginismus.

- **Vaginal Dilators:** Gradual insertion of dilators of increasing sizes can help desensitize and stretch the vaginal muscles, reducing pain during penetration.

- **Botox Injections:** Botulinum toxin (Botox) injections into the pelvic floor muscles can temporarily paralyze hyperactive muscles, providing relief for those with vaginismus.

Erectile Dysfunction Treatments:

- **Medications:** Phosphodiesterase type 5 (PDE5) inhibitors, such as sildenafil (Viagra), tadalafil (Cialis), and vardenafil (Levitra), are commonly prescribed to enhance blood flow to the penis, facilitating erections.

- **Hormone Therapy:** For men with low testosterone levels, hormone replacement therapy can improve sexual function.

- **Surgical Options:** Procedures like penile implants or vascular surgery are considered when other treatments are ineffective. Penile implants involve placing devices inside the penis to allow for erections, while vascular surgery aims to repair blood vessel blockages.

It's essential for individuals to consult with healthcare professionals to determine the most appropriate treatment plan based on their specific medical history and condition.

Psychological and Relationship Therapy

- **Cognitive Behavioral Therapy (CBT):** CBT is widely recognized as an effective treatment for anxiety disorders. It focuses on identifying and challenging unhelpful thought patterns and behaviors, thereby addressing underlying fears and anxieties. Studies have demonstrated that CBT leads to significant reductions in worry and anxiety symptoms, making it a gold-standard treatment for these conditions.

- **Couples Therapy:** Couples therapy aims to enhance communication and strengthen emotional bonds between partners. By providing a structured environment for both individuals to express their thoughts and feelings, it fosters mutual understanding and connection. This therapeutic approach has been shown to improve relationship satisfaction and intimacy.

- **Mindfulness Practices:** Incorporating mindfulness into therapy can reduce stress and foster intimacy. Mindfulness encourages individuals to be present in the moment, enhancing emotional regulation and empathy. When practiced together, couples can experience improved communication and a deeper emotional connection, contributing to a more fulfilling relationship.

Integrating these therapeutic methods can lead to significant improvements in individual well-being and relationship dynamics.

Conclusion

Early intervention is crucial in addressing conditions like vaginismus and erectile dysfunction, as both are highly treatable and can significantly impact marital relationships. Timely treatment not only alleviates physical symptoms but also prevents potential emotional distress, thereby preserving trust and intimacy between partners. For instance, therapeutic strategies such as sex therapy and desensitization have shown promise in treating vaginismus, highlighting the importance of seeking help early.

Addressing these conditions with empathy and professional support is essential for maintaining the emotional and spiritual bonds within a marriage. The Prophet Muhammad (ﷺ) emphasized the significance of kindness within the family, stating, "The best of you are those who are best to their families, and I am the best among you to my family." (*Sunan al-Tirmidhi*, Hadith 3895)

Chapter Twenty-Three

Mental Health and Marriage

Navigating Challenges and Building Resilience

Marriage is a journey of companionship, love, and shared purpose. At its best, it offers mutual support and a sanctuary in life's storms. However, it is also a partnership that requires resilience, understanding, and the ability to navigate challenges—particularly when mental health issues arise. Mental health struggles, often subtle or misunderstood, can strain even the strongest relationships, but they also present opportunities for deeper connection and growth when approached with empathy and action.

This chapter explores the impact of mental health conditions on marriage, the importance of accurate diagnoses, and actionable strategies for couples to navigate these challenges. While this chapter highlights several mental health conditions and their effects on marriage, it is crucial to understand that this discussion represents only a fraction of the vast landscape of mental health issues. Many conditions exist beyond those mentioned here, each with unique challenges and dynamics. Additionally, it is vital to stress the importance of never self-diagnosing or labeling others. Mental health diagnoses should only be made by licensed, qualified professionals who can provide an accurate assessment and appropriate guidance.

The Silent Strain of Undiagnosed Mental Health Conditions

When mental health conditions remain undiagnosed or misunderstood, their effects can ripple across every aspect of a marriage. Conditions like Attention-Deficit/Hyperactivity Disorder (ADHD), autism spectrum disorder

(ASD), bipolar disorder, social anxiety, obsessive-compulsive disorder (OCD), and obsessive-compulsive personality disorder (OCPD) often manifest subtly, leading to misinterpretations of behaviors and unmet emotional needs.

Emotional Disconnect and Miscommunication

Undiagnosed conditions often masquerade as personality quirks or character flaws, creating misunderstandings. For instance, a spouse with undiagnosed ADHD might struggle with forgetfulness or poor time management, causing their partner to feel neglected. Dr. Russell Barkley explains that ADHD impairs executive functioning, making it difficult for individuals to follow through on tasks, even when they care deeply about their partner's needs. Without understanding the root cause, such behaviors may be seen as apathy or irresponsibility.

Similarly, social anxiety can lead to avoidance of gatherings or conversations. Dr. Ellen Hendriksen notes that individuals with social anxiety often withdraw to avoid judgment, which can appear as disinterest in shared social activities. This misinterpretation may lead the unaffected spouse to feel unvalued or unsupported.

Conditions like bipolar disorder can bring emotional highs and lows that disrupt stability. Psychologist Dr. Kay Redfield Jamison warns that untreated bipolar disorder may cause financial strain or emotional distance, leaving the unaffected partner feeling unsafe or overwhelmed.

Even more subtle conditions, such as OCPD, may manifest as rigid routines or excessive perfectionism. Dr. Jeffrey Schwartz highlights that behaviors associated with OCPD often stem from a need for control to manage anxiety. However, such behaviors may be perceived as domineering, fostering resentment and power imbalances.

Common Mental Health Conditions Affecting Marriage

Depression and Anxiety

Depression and anxiety are among the most common mental health challenges in marriages. Depression may manifest as withdrawal, fatigue, and emotional unavailability, leaving the unaffected spouse feeling rejected.

Anxiety, on the other hand, can lead to irritability, hypervigilance, and misinterpretations of intent, amplifying conflicts over minor issues.

Dr. John Gottman identifies emotional disconnection caused by untreated mental health issues as a key predictor of marital dissatisfaction. Therapy, mindfulness practices, and, where necessary, medication can help couples navigate these challenges. Dr. Sue Johnson, stresses the importance of addressing the emotional cycles that perpetuate disconnection.

Stress and Burnout

The demands of modern life—work, parenting, and societal expectations—often leave couples vulnerable to stress and burnout. Burnout involves emotional exhaustion, detachment, and reduced engagement, which can make relationships feel transactional. Dr. Sheryl Ziegler, author of *Mommy Burnout*, advises couples to prioritize self-care, set boundaries, and share responsibilities to mitigate burnout's effects.

Hidden Mental Health Conditions

Some mental health conditions are subtle yet impactful, often going unnoticed in marriage:

- **High-Functioning Depression**: A partner with this condition may seem outwardly capable but struggles internally with sadness or fatigue, leading to reduced emotional engagement.

- **Alexithymia**: Difficulty identifying and expressing emotions can create frustration in conflicts, as one partner may feel their emotional needs are unmet.

- **Chronic PTSD**: Trauma can manifest as hypervigilance, emotional numbing, or avoidance, which may be misinterpreted as disinterest or detachment.

Trauma-informed therapy, emotional awareness exercises, and psychoeducation are critical for addressing these hidden struggles and fostering understanding.

Neurodevelopmental and Personality Disorders in Marriage

Unique Challenges

Conditions like ADHD, ASD, and borderline personality disorder (BPD) bring unique challenges to marriage. ADHD may involve impulsivity or forgetfulness, while ASD might cause difficulties with emotional expression or nonverbal cues. BPD can lead to intense emotional swings, making stability in the relationship difficult.

Dr. Edward Hallowell emphasizes that these challenges arise from brain-based differences, not deficiencies. Understanding this can help couples approach their struggles with empathy rather than blame.

Therapeutic Interventions

Therapies like CBT, EFT, and DBT equip couples with tools to understand and navigate these challenges. Psychoeducation, for example, helps spouses reframe their partner's behaviors as symptoms rather than intentional actions. Tools such as visual schedules, shared calendars, and emotional regulation strategies further enhance communication and collaboration.

- **CBT – Cognitive Behavioral Therapy:** CBT is a structured, goal-oriented therapy that focuses on identifying and changing negative thought patterns and behaviors.

    - Helps individuals recognize distorted thinking patterns.
    - Teaches practical coping strategies for anxiety, depression, and other mental health issues.
    - Focuses on the relationship between thoughts, feelings, and behaviors.
    - Often used for issues like depression, anxiety, OCD, PTSD, and even relationship problems.

    Example in Relationships: A spouse who constantly thinks, *"My spouse doesn't love me because they don't express it the way I want,"* might learn to challenge this thought and recognize other ways their partner shows love.

- **EFT– Emotionally Focused Therapy:** EFT is a type of therapy that focuses on strengthening emotional bonds between individuals, primarily used in couples and family therapy.
  - Based on attachment theory, emphasizing secure emotional connections.
  - Helps couples and individuals recognize unhealthy emotional cycles.
  - Encourages open, vulnerable communication to build intimacy and trust.
  - Used for couples struggling with emotional disconnection, infidelity, or conflict.

  Example in Relationships: If a husband withdraws emotionally and his wife responds with criticism, EFT helps them see this as a pattern of insecurity rather than personal failure, allowing them to reconnect emotionally.

- **DBT– Dialectical Behavior Therapy:** DBT is a therapy designed to help individuals manage intense emotions, improve relationships, and develop mindfulness and distress tolerance. It was originally developed for borderline personality disorder (BPD) but is now used for a variety of emotional regulation issues.
  - Combines CBT techniques with mindfulness strategies.
  - Focuses on four key areas:
    - Mindfulness: Being present in the moment.
    - Distress Tolerance: Handling crises without destructive reactions.
    - Emotion Regulation: Managing intense emotions effectively.
    - Interpersonal Effectiveness: Building healthy communication and boundaries.
  - Used for individuals with emotional dysregulation, self-harm tendencies, depression, and PTSD.

  Example in Relationships: A person who reacts impulsively in arguments (shouting, shutting down) might use DBT skills to pause, recognize their emotions, and respond in a healthier way.

Which One is Best for Relationships?

- CBT is best for changing negative thought patterns that affect relationship dynamics.
- EFT is ideal for strengthening emotional bonds and healing attachment wounds.
- DBT is beneficial for individuals who struggle with intense emotions, impulsivity, and conflict management in relationships.

Brain Function

Neurodivergent is a term used to describe individuals whose brains function differently from what is considered "typical" (neurotypical). This includes differences in cognitive processing, learning styles, emotional regulation, and sensory perception.

Who is Considered Neurodivergent?

People with conditions such as:

- Autism Spectrum Disorder (ASD)
- Attention-Deficit/Hyperactivity Disorder (ADHD)
- Dyslexia (difficulty with reading and language processing)
- Dyspraxia (difficulty with coordination and motor skills)
- Dyscalculia (difficulty with numbers and math)
- Tourette Syndrome (involuntary tics and vocalizations)
- Highly sensitive individuals (HSPs) while not a disorder, some include this under neurodivergence due to unique sensory processing

Neurodivergence vs. Neurotypical

- Neurodivergent individuals experience the world differently and may have unique strengths and challenges.
- Neurotypical individuals process information, emotions, and social cues in a way that aligns with societal norms.

Strengths of Neurodivergent Individuals:

- Creativity & Innovation: Many neurodivergent individuals think outside the box and have unique problem-solving skills.

- Deep Focus & Hyperfocus: Especially common in ADHD and autism.

- Strong Pattern Recognition: Found in autistic individuals and those with dyslexia.

- Resilience & Adaptability: Many neurodivergent people learn to navigate a world not designed for them, developing strong coping mechanisms.

Challenges Neurodivergent Individuals May Face:

- Social Communication Differences: May struggle with reading social cues or small talk.

- Sensory Sensitivities: Loud noises, bright lights, or certain textures can be overwhelming.

- Executive Dysfunction: Difficulties with organization, time management, or task initiation.

- Emotional Regulation: Some experience intense emotions and difficulty managing stress.

Neurodivergence & Relationships

- Communication styles may differ in neurodivergent relationships.

- Emotional needs and sensory preferences can impact intimacy.

- Understanding and acceptance are key for healthy relationships.

Case Example: How a Muslim Couple Overcame Neurodivergent Challenges

Ahmed and Aisha, a married Muslim couple, faced unique challenges in their relationship due to Ahmed's recent diagnosis of Autism Spectrum Disorder (ASD). As a highly logical and routine-oriented software engineer, Ahmed struggled with emotional expression, while Aisha, a warm and expressive teacher, often felt unheard and disconnected. Their biggest challenge was communication—Aisha longed for verbal affirmations of love, while Ahmed assumed his acts of service were enough. When Aisha expressed her feelings, Ahmed often found himself overwhelmed, unsure of how to respond. This disconnect sometimes left Aisha feeling unloved and Ahmed feeling pressured to communicate in ways that didn't come naturally to him.

Another difficulty was Ahmed's sensory sensitivities, which impacted their intimacy. While Aisha enjoyed spontaneous physical affection, Ahmed often pulled away due to sensory overload, unintentionally making Aisha feel rejected. Additionally, Ahmed's discomfort in large social gatherings led to tension, as Aisha valued family events and community engagement, while Ahmed found them exhausting and difficult to navigate. At times, his avoidance was misunderstood by relatives as rudeness, adding another layer of stress to their marriage.

Realizing they needed support, Ahmed and Aisha sought guidance from both a relationship coach and a therapist. The relationship coach helped them identify their core issues and develop strategies to improve their communication, ensuring that Aisha felt emotionally connected while allowing Ahmed to express love in ways that suited him. Meanwhile, therapy helped Ahmed navigate his sensory sensitivities and social anxiety, while Aisha gained a deeper understanding of how neurodivergence affects emotions and interaction. With professional guidance, they learned to bridge their differences through patience, clear communication, and mutual effort.

Aisha began expressing her needs directly, such as saying, "I would love to hear 'I love you' more often," rather than expecting Ahmed to read between the lines. Ahmed, in turn, made an effort to verbalize appreciation instead of relying solely on actions. They also worked on sensory compromises, with Aisha understanding that Ahmed preferred gentle, predictable physical contact rather than spontaneous affection. Regarding social commitments, Ahmed agreed to attend shorter gatherings while Aisha reassured her family that his quiet nature was not a sign of disrespect.

Their marriage flourished as they embraced each other's differences with love, mercy, and patience—principles deeply rooted in Islam. Rather than seeing their differences as barriers, they viewed them as opportunities to grow together. By prioritizing understanding and flexibility and seeking professional help when needed, they found a balance that allowed their relationship to thrive, proving that neurodivergent and neurotypical partners can build deeply fulfilling marriages when they meet each other with compassion, support, and acceptance.

Building Resilience: Practical Strategies for Couples

Resilience in marriage is not innate; it is built through intentional practices:

1. **Open Communication**: Regular check-ins allow couples to express concerns and align on goals. Dr. John Gottman emphasizes the importance of listening with curiosity rather than judgment to foster connection.

2. **Structured Routines and Predictability**: Predictable routines reduce stress, particularly for neurodivergent individuals. Shared schedules or task lists ensure clarity and accountability.

3. **Mindfulness and Stress Management**: Mindfulness techniques, such as deep breathing or guided imagery, help couples manage emotions during conflicts. Shared practices like yoga or meditation foster mutual calm and connection.

4. **Professional Support**: Therapists trained in modalities like EFT or CBT can guide couples in reframing challenges as opportunities for growth. Therapy also provides tools tailored to the couple's unique needs.

5. **Celebrating Strengths**: Acknowledging small wins and focusing on each other's strengths fosters appreciation and positivity, transforming challenges into opportunities for deeper bonding.

The Islamic Perspective on Mental Health and Marriage

Islamic teachings emphasize compassion, patience, and mutual support as foundations for a strong marriage. The Qur'an states:

> "And among His signs is that He created for you mates… that you may dwell in tranquility with them, and He has put love and mercy between your hearts." (Qur'an 30:21)

Patience and Empathy: Patience and self-control are critical when navigating mental health challenges in marriage. The Prophet Muhammad (ﷺ) advised:

> "The strong one is not the one who overpowers others, but the one who controls themselves when angry." (Sahih Bukhari)

Reliance on Allah: Spiritual practices, such as prayer and Qur'anic recitation, provide solace and strengthen the marital bond. As the Qur'an reassures:

"Indeed, with hardship comes ease." (Qur'an 94:6)

Community and Faith-Based Support: Islamic organizations and mosques often offer counseling services and mental health workshops, providing couples with resources rooted in both faith and psychology.

Conclusion

Mental health challenges, though complex, are opportunities for growth, empathy, and resilience in marriage. While this chapter highlights a handful of conditions, it is essential to remember that the spectrum of mental health is vast and multifaceted. Always seek guidance from licensed professionals for accurate diagnoses and treatment.

By combining psychological insights with Islamic principles, couples can transform their struggles into pathways for deeper connection and lasting love. With patience, professional support, and reliance on Allah, even the most difficult moments can lead to greater understanding and tranquility. As the Qur'an promises:

"So be patient. Indeed, the promise of Allah is truth." (Qur'an 40:55)

Chapter Twenty-Four

Healing After Abuse

In the journey of building and nurturing loving, respectful relationships, we must also confront the painful reality that abuse can sometimes become a part of the narrative. Abuse within a marriage, in its many forms, casts a heavy shadow over what should be a sanctuary of love, trust, and mutual growth. This chapter aims to hold space for the harsh truths of abusive behaviors—whether it be controlling tendencies, verbal or physical abuse, or emotional manipulation—and offer paths to healing and hope. Drawing from a blend of psychological insights and the rich wisdom of Islam, we explore how to recognize abuse, break free from its grip, and create healthier dynamics within relationships.

Recognizing Abusive Behaviors

Abuse is a violation of trust, a betrayal of the love and commitment that marriage represents. It manifests in many forms: subtle manipulations that chip away at your self-worth, overt violence that threatens your safety, or a slow suffocation of your independence and individuality. Recognizing abuse is not always as clear-cut as we might hope, because often it begins in small, almost imperceptible ways. It might start as criticism that feels more like condemnation, or affection that feels a little too much like control. When a partner becomes a source of fear rather than comfort, the signs of abuse have taken root.

Abusers may use manipulation tactics like gaslighting—making you doubt your own reality—or love bombing, where they overwhelm you with affection to then use that emotional leverage. These subtle actions can leave you questioning your worth and reality, feeling isolated and unsure of where to turn. You may even start to feel as though you are losing control over your own life.

Therapists emphasize that abuse is not just about physical harm; it can be emotional and psychological, causing deep, invisible scars. The National Domestic Violence Hotline notes behaviors like constant humiliation, threats, and controlling tactics that isolate a partner from their support network. Recognizing these signs early is crucial because it empowers the victim to seek help, before the effects become more entrenched and harder to escape.

One of the clearest signs that something is wrong comes in the form of communication patterns that breed resentment. Experts like Dr. John Gottman identify harmful behaviors, such as criticism, contempt, defensiveness, and stonewalling, as precursors to deeper issues within relationships. These "Four Horsemen" of destructive communication can create a wall of emotional distance that, if not addressed, can escalate to a more toxic, abusive environment. But, with the right awareness and the right support, couples can break these patterns before they become entrenched.

The Importance of Safe Spaces

If you recognize that you or your partner is in an abusive situation, the next step is finding a safe way to address it. The first and most crucial part of that is ensuring safety—whether that means physical safety or emotional well-being. This could involve making a safety plan: knowing where to go in an emergency, having an escape route in mind, or reaching out to trusted friends or family who can help.

Psychologists and therapists stress that regaining your voice and sense of self is essential to healing. Dr. Judith Herman, an expert in trauma, emphasizes that survivors of abuse must reclaim their autonomy and power, which can begin in therapy, in support groups, or simply through self-care practices that reinforce self-worth. You are worthy of respect and love, and healing starts with recognizing that truth.

A strong community of support is invaluable in this process. Whether it's close friends, family members, or professional counseling, having people around who understand and uplift you makes the journey easier. Religious leaders, too, can offer profound wisdom in moments of crisis. Islam teaches compassion, kindness, and justice—values that stand in stark opposition to any form of abuse. The Prophet Muhammad (ﷺ) reminds us, "The best of you are those who are best to their families" (Tirmidhi, 1162), a beautiful reminder that abuse has no place in a truly loving marriage.

The Weight of Control in Relationships

Abuse doesn't always come in the form of overt violence; sometimes, it's more insidious—a slow erosion of trust, independence, and autonomy. Controlling behaviors are a silent, yet powerful force in a marriage, as they can isolate you from your family and friends, force you into unhealthy dependency, and strip you of your agency. When one partner demands complete control over decisions, movements, and even emotions, it creates an imbalance that slowly undermines the foundation of equality that a healthy relationship needs.

Control may be hidden behind seemingly innocent gestures—questioning your whereabouts, dictating your decisions, or belittling your ideas. These actions are driven by insecurity and fear, not love. The truth is, a healthy relationship thrives on mutual respect and shared decision-making. Dr. John Gottman's research underscores the importance of balance in relationships: *couples who share power and make decisions together tend to have stronger and more resilient relationships.* In contrast, controlling behaviors can suffocate that balance and create long-term emotional damage.

Building Healthy Boundaries

Creating and respecting boundaries is essential in fostering a relationship built on respect. Dr. Brené Brown, a renowned expert on vulnerability and relationships, emphasizes that boundaries are not walls to keep people apart; they are ways to protect and honor our sense of self, allowing us to engage with our partners from a place of security. Healthy boundaries are the foundation of empathy, and empathy is the lifeblood of healthy relationships.

In navigating controlling behaviors, education, and therapy can offer profound support. Cognitive behavioral therapy and dialectical behavior therapy are effective tools in helping individuals break free from patterns of control and manipulation. These therapies empower individuals to regain their self-esteem, practice healthier communication, and establish more balanced relationships.

The Role of Faith in Healing

In times of darkness and pain, faith can offer light. Islam teaches us that life's challenges, including the pain of abuse, can be faced with dignity, hope, and trust in Allah's mercy. Through prayer, reflection, and seeking solace in faith, individuals can find the strength to overcome their trials. Regular connection to Allah, through prayer and spiritual reflection, can bring peace to a troubled mind and heart, providing the emotional resilience needed to heal.

In times of struggle, the community can play a supportive role. Religious leaders and scholars, who have a deep understanding of Islam, can help guide individuals to a place of healing. By offering counsel grounded in compassion and justice, they can help survivors of abuse reconcile their faith with their healing process, offering a spiritual anchor when the world feels chaotic.

A Journey to Safety and Restoration

Every relationship has the potential to bring joy and fulfillment, yet sometimes, the weight of emotional and physical wounds can leave us feeling isolated and uncertain. Abuse—whether verbal, physical, or sexual—cuts deep into our hearts, leaving scars that may not always be visible to others but are felt profoundly within. It can be incredibly painful to confront, but the first step towards healing begins with recognizing the patterns of harm and seeking help. It's important to draw upon both the wisdom of Islamic teachings and modern relationship science to show that healing is not just possible, but within reach for anyone willing to confront the darkness and rebuild from within.

Understanding Verbal Abuse: The Silent Wounds

Words can be both a balm and a weapon. In relationships marred by verbal abuse, the harm is often unseen but felt deeply. Insults, threats, humiliation—they erode a person's sense of worth, leaving them questioning their own value and place in the world. Over time, this abuse breeds a toxic environment where love, kindness, and mutual respect are replaced with tension and fear.

Islam teaches us that words hold immense power. The Qur'an urges, "And tell My servants to say that which is best…" (Qur'an 17:53) In a marriage, words should be a bridge to understanding, not a weapon of destruction.

The Prophet Muhammad (ﷺ) reinforced this when he said, "The believer is not a slanderer, nor does he curse others, nor is he immoral or shameless." (Tirmidhi) Communication, when rooted in kindness and respect, fosters an environment where both partners feel heard, valued, and safe.

Research in relationship science highlights the impact of negative communication, showing that verbal aggression is linked to dissatisfaction and instability. This harmful pattern undermines emotional safety and weakens the foundation of trust. However, there is hope. Developing better communication skills, such as active listening, expressing needs respectfully, and resolving conflicts with empathy, can create a space for healing. Professional counseling can help both partners rebuild the language of love and understanding, replacing hurtful words with those that nurture growth and connection.

Breaking Free from Physical Abuse: Finding Your Voice and Strength

Physical abuse is a blatant violation of trust—a painful reality where the very person who should provide love and protection becomes the source of harm. Beyond physical injury, it creates an overwhelming sense of fear and helplessness, leaving lasting emotional scars. Abuse is not just an act of violence; it is an abuse of power, control, and dignity.

If you are in a relationship where physical harm is part of your experience, your safety must come first. Seek immediate help—whether through law enforcement, trusted family or friends, or a domestic violence hotline. No one should have to endure violence, and reaching out for support is a courageous and necessary step toward breaking free. Therapy and support groups can also provide a vital space for healing, helping survivors rebuild their sense of self-worth and regain control over their lives.

It's also important to recognize that men, too, can be victims of physical abuse. Societal expectations may make it harder for them to speak out, but their pain is real, and they deserve help, support, and healing just as much as anyone else. Regardless of gender, every individual has the right to live without fear, and no one should feel trapped in an abusive situation. Seeking help is not a sign of weakness—it is a powerful step toward reclaiming your life and your peace.

Sexual Abuse: Respect, Boundaries, and Trust

Sexual abuse within a marriage is a profound betrayal of trust. It involves the violation of boundaries, often through coercion or manipulation. Islam places immense importance on mutual respect, consent, and emotional connection in marital relations. The Qur'an says, "Your wives are a garment for you, and you are a garment for them." (Qur'an 2:187) This beautiful metaphor speaks to the closeness, comfort, and protection that should exist in a healthy marriage.

The Prophet Muhammad (ﷺ) further emphasized that intimacy should be based on mutual desire and respect, stating, "None of you should fall upon his wife like an animal; let there first be a messenger between you." (Sunan Ibn Majah) Consent and emotional connection are the foundation of a fulfilling marital relationship, and any form of coercion or manipulation goes against these fundamental values.

Whether sexual abuse occurs in marriage or during the courting period, it must be addressed with seriousness and care. The psychological toll of such abuse can be profound, often resulting in anxiety, depression, and long-lasting trauma. Therapy and counseling, especially trauma-focused interventions, can provide vital support in navigating this painful journey.

Creating a safe and respectful sexual environment is essential for rebuilding trust and intimacy. Open communication about desires, boundaries, and mutual respect must be the cornerstone of any marital relationship. When partners feel safe, heard, and respected, intimacy becomes an expression of love rather than a source of harm.

The Path to Healing: Reflection, Growth, and Restoration

Healing from abuse requires time, patience, and a deep commitment to self-awareness and growth. It's essential to recognize the toxic patterns that have taken root and actively work to challenge them. Engaging in therapy, journaling, or simply reflecting on past experiences can offer insights into triggers and vulnerabilities. It's also crucial to practice self-compassion—acknowledging that healing is a process and that you deserve peace and joy in your relationships.

Self-reflection plays an integral role in healing. By exploring and understanding one's emotions and triggers, individuals can make conscious choices to break free from abusive cycles and cultivate healthier relationship dynamics. Establishing boundaries, seeking professional help, and building a support network are crucial steps toward creating a nurturing and safe environment in which love can thrive.

Conclusion: Reclaiming Your Life and Your Happiness

No one should have to endure abuse, and seeking help is not a sign of weakness but an act of immense courage. By addressing the emotional, physical, and sexual harm that has taken place, individuals can embark on a journey of healing and empowerment. Islam's teachings provide a powerful foundation for promoting love, respect, and compassion in relationships, while modern therapeutic practices offer proven strategies for navigating and overcoming the trauma of abuse. Together, these approaches create a holistic, compassionate path toward healing.

Remember, healing is a journey—one that requires patience, support, and self-compassion. You are worthy of love, respect, and happiness, and by reclaiming your voice and your strength, you can begin to rebuild the life and relationships you deserve. Through awareness, empowerment, and continued self-reflection, it's possible to create a future filled with peace, joy, and mutual respect.

Chapter Twenty-Five

Culture vs. Islam

In an increasingly globalized world, it's not uncommon for marriages to bring together individuals from different cultural backgrounds. These diverse influences can enrich relationships, fostering new experiences, traditions, and perspectives. However, while diversity in a relationship offers unique opportunities for growth, it also presents challenges—especially when cultural practices conflict with faith-based principles. In some cases, toxic cultural norms can create rifts, especially when they contradict the values embedded in religious teachings. This chapter delves into how couples can navigate these complexities, honoring both their cultural heritage and Islamic faith, while cultivating a healthy, respectful, and harmonious marriage.

The key is in discerning positive cultural practices that align with Islamic values, while distancing oneself from those that may be harmful or toxic. By doing so, couples can embrace diversity within their marriage, allowing faith and respect to guide their interactions.

Positive Cultural Practices & Islamic Teachings

Islam came not to erase culture, but to enhance and perfect what is good within it. The relationship between culture and religion is nuanced: many cultural practices align with the core values of Islam, while others may conflict and require reassessment. Understanding these dynamics allows couples to harmonize their faith and traditions in a way that strengthens both their spiritual and relational bonds, honoring both their heritage and their commitment to Allah.

Respect

- **Culture**: In many cultures, there is a strong emphasis on respecting elders, authority figures, and community leaders. This respect is often ingrained from a young age, shaping the ways individuals interact with their families and society.

- Islam strongly advocates for the respect of parents, elders, and all members of society. Surah Al-Isra (17:24) states, "And lower to them the wing of humility out of mercy and say, 'My Lord, have mercy upon them as they brought me up [when I was] small."

Hospitality

- **Culture**: Hospitality is often a core value across many cultures. Inviting guests into the home and offering food or shelter is seen as a fundamental expression of generosity.

- **Islam**: Islam deeply values hospitality. Prophet Muhammad (ﷺ) stated, "Whoever believes in Allah and the Last Day should honor his guest." (Sahih Bukhari) The practice of honoring guests is so revered that it's seen as a reflection of one's faith.

Community Support

- **Culture**: Numerous cultures emphasize the importance of community and collective responsibility. In many societies, people are encouraged to support one another through both joy and hardship.

- **Islam**: The Islamic concept of Ummah promotes a sense of shared responsibility, with acts like Zakat and Sadaqah designed to ensure that wealth and resources are shared with those in need. Prophet Muhammad (ﷺ) said, "The believer to the believer is like a building, each part supporting the other." (Sahih Bukhari)

Celebrations

- **Culture**: Across the world, celebrations bring people together to mark significant life events, seasons, and milestones, strengthening community ties.

- **Islam:** Islam encourages celebration, though with a focus on gratitude, humility, and reflection. As Muslims, we believe in two main celebrations ordained by Allah: **Eid al-Fitr**, which marks the end of Ramadan, and **Eid al-Adha**, which commemorates the sacrifice of Prophet Ibrahim (ﷺ). These are significant moments in the Islamic calendar where joy is shared, but they are also profound opportunities for spiritual growth, acts of charity, and community bonding. Islam teaches that celebration should always be tied to gratitude to Allah and mindful remembrance, rather than excess or heedlessness.

Negative Cultural Practices vs. Islamic Teachings

While many cultural practices align with Islamic values, some can contradict core teachings. Identifying these negative practices is critical in fostering a marriage rooted in faith and mutual respect.

Gender Inequality

- **Culture:** In some cultures, rigid gender roles are enforced, limiting the rights and opportunities available to women. These roles may restrict their participation in education, the workforce, and family decisions.

- **Islam:** Islam upholds gender equity and recognizes the inherent dignity of both men and women. "O mankind, fear your Lord, who created you from one soul and created from it its mate and dispersed from both of them many men and women. And fear Allah, through whom you ask one another, and the wombs. Indeed Allah is ever, over you, an Observer." Surah An-Nisa (4:1) This Surah emphasizes that all human beings originate from a single soul, highlighting their shared humanity and worth in divine creation. While Islam acknowledges differences in roles and responsibilities, it affirms that both men and women are spiritually equal before Allah and are entitled to justice, kindness, and respect. The Qur'an and the teachings of the Prophet Muhammad (ﷺ) stress mutual rights and responsibilities, ensuring fairness and dignity for both genders in all aspects of life.

Caste System

- **Culture**: Some cultures still practice a form of social stratification, such as the caste system, where individuals are judged by their family's social status or lineage.

- **Islam**: Islam firmly rejects any form of caste or class discrimination, emphasizing that the most noble in the eyes of Allah are those with the most piety, as stated in Surah Al-Hujurat (49:13): "Indeed, the most noble of you in the sight of Allah is the most righteous of you."

Superstition

- **Culture**: Superstition and reliance on omens or mystical beliefs are common in some cultures, shaping how individuals make decisions or interpret events.

- **Islam**: Islam encourages rational thought, trust in Allah's plan, and reliance on knowledge. The Prophet Muhammad (ﷺ) explicitly rejected superstitions, stating, "There is no [ill] omen, only good omens." (Sahih Muslim)

- **Bad omens are rejected** in Islam.

- **Good omens** (like hearing a good word or seeing a positive sign that uplifts the heart) are **allowed** because they inspire hope, not fear.

Honor-Based Violence

- **Culture:** Honor-based violence and killings are tragic cultural practices in some societies, where individuals—often women—are punished or killed for perceived dishonor or misconduct.

- **Islam:** Islam unequivocally condemns any form of extrajudicial violence or mistreatment. While adultery is considered a major sin in Islam, punishment can only be administered by a legitimate Islamic court under extremely strict evidentiary conditions. No individual has the right to take the law into their own hands. Surah Al-Maidah (5:32) affirms: "Whoever kills a soul unless for a soul or for corruption [done] in the land—it is as if he had killed all of mankind." Islam upholds the sanctity of life and forbids all forms of unjust violence and vigilantism.

Materialism

- **Culture**: In some cultures, wealth, status, and material possessions are prioritized over spiritual growth or ethical behavior.

- **Islam**: Islam encourages a balanced approach to wealth, focusing on charity and modest living. Surah At-Takathur (102:1) warns, "The mutual rivalry for piling up of worldly things diverts you." The pursuit of material wealth should not overshadow the pursuit of spiritual fulfillment.

Recognizing Cultural Differences and Understanding Toxic Norms

It's important for couples to understand the positive cultural backgrounds they each bring into the marriage. Acknowledging these differences without judgment allows for deeper connection and mutual respect. However, toxic cultural practices—those that are harmful or oppressive—must be identified and carefully navigated.

Toxic norms can manifest in many forms, such as limiting a spouse's autonomy, promoting violence, or encouraging harmful stereotypes. Identifying these practices is essential for a couple to address them head-on while staying aligned with the teachings of Islam. Communication and mutual understanding are the cornerstones of this process.

Effective Communication and Mutual Understanding

Marriage thrives on open and empathetic communication. Couples should create a safe space for discussing cultural expectations, practices, and experiences without fear of judgment. Listening actively, showing empathy, and respecting each other's perspectives are essential for fostering a deep emotional connection. Communication should always be based on mutual respect and the understanding that both partners are seeking to build a life rooted in love and faith.

Seeking Islamic Guidance

When cultural practices conflict with religious principles, seeking the guidance of a knowledgeable Islamic scholar can be invaluable. Scholars can provide insight into how to reconcile cultural expectations with Islamic values, offering advice on how to navigate these differences without compromising one's faith.

Establishing Boundaries

It's crucial for couples to set clear boundaries when dealing with cultural practices that contradict their shared values. By discussing and agreeing on what practices they are unwilling to tolerate, couples can protect the integrity of their marriage. Boundaries ensure that both partners feel respected, valued, and supported as they work through cultural differences.

Embracing Cultural Exchange

While it's important to set boundaries around toxic cultural practices, couples should also celebrate their cultural diversity. Cultural exchange can be enriching, allowing each partner to learn from and appreciate the other's traditions. This exchange can help bridge gaps, strengthen the bond between partners, and promote mutual understanding. It is a way to build a marriage that blends the beauty of diverse cultures while adhering to shared Islamic values.

The Importance of Not Being Racist and Marrying Across Cultures

Islam promotes the equality of all people, regardless of their race or cultural background. "O mankind, indeed We have created you from male and female and made you peoples and tribes that you may know one another. Indeed, the most noble of you in the sight of Allah is the most righteous of you. Indeed, Allah is Knowing and Acquainted." (Qur'an 49:13) This teaches that true honor is determined by piety, not race or ethnicity. This principle is foundational in Islam, and it calls on Muslims to embrace diversity with respect and kindness.

Marriage within or outside one's culture should be based on mutual understanding, respect, and faith. Islam encourages individuals to look beyond race and cultural differences to find a partner whose values align with theirs.

In fact, marriage across cultures can enhance personal growth and understanding. Such unions foster inclusivity, challenge societal prejudices, and strengthen the Ummah by celebrating its diversity.

However, from an Islamic perspective, there are guidelines regarding **interfaith** marriage. A Muslim man is permitted to marry women from the People of the Book (Jews and Christians), but even this comes with conditions, especially in the modern context. The People of the Book during the time of revelation were of a different moral and religious standing than what we often see today. Their adherence to monotheistic teachings was stronger, and their faith traditions were more aligned with Islamic values. In today's world, scholars emphasize that such marriages should be approached with caution, considering the impact on faith, family, and future generations.

For Muslim women, the ruling is clear: they can only marry Muslim men. This is to safeguard their faith, as Islam places great importance on the religious environment within the household, ensuring that the faith is preserved and passed down to future generations.

If you find yourself in a situation where interfaith marriage is a consideration, seeking guidance from a knowledgeable and trusted person within the community is essential. Consulting a qualified scholar, a well-versed imam, or an Islamic marriage center/ council can provide clarity and advice based on both religious principles and contemporary challenges.

Conclusion

As we conclude, it's important to recognize that while cultural practices may shape a marriage, it is the shared commitment to faith that sustains it. Embracing cultural diversity within the framework of Islam allows couples to navigate challenges while remaining aligned with their beliefs. By distinguishing positive cultural practices from toxic ones, seeking guidance when needed, establishing boundaries, and embracing cultural exchange, couples can create a rich, harmonious marriage that honors both their cultural heritage and Islamic principles. Ultimately, Islam teaches that piety and righteousness are the true measures of a person's worth, and these should guide all relationships, including marriage. With understanding, respect, and love, couples can overcome cultural differences and build a lasting and meaningful bond.

Chapter Twenty-Six

The Emasculation Epidemic

Marriage is meant to be a place of refuge—a sacred space where both partners feel seen, heard, and valued. Yet, when one partner consistently diminishes the other, whether in words, actions, or attitudes, the very foundation of this sacred bond is shaken. If a wife starts to emasculate her husband—whether consciously or unconsciously—the effects can be devastating, not just for him, but for the relationship as a whole.

The heartbreaking reality is that emasculation isn't always dramatic or loud. It's the small, everyday moments that chip away at a husband's sense of worth—subtle digs, dismissive comments, or actions that undermine his role and contributions. Over time, these behaviors erode trust, intimacy, and respect, creating a chasm between partners that can seem impossible to bridge.

The Silent Erosion of a Man's Soul

Think of the man who comes home after a long day at work, eager to share the little victories of his day with his wife. He speaks with pride about the project he led or the challenge he overcame, but instead of receiving encouragement, he's met with an eye roll or a cutting remark. Maybe she dismisses his efforts altogether, belittling his accomplishments. In that moment, the spark of his pride and self-esteem dims a little. He starts to question himself—not just as a husband, but as a person. Dr. John Gottman, refers to this kind of behavior as **contempt**, and it's one of the most destructive forces in any marriage. Contempt can erode a partner's self-esteem to the point where emotional disconnection becomes almost inevitable.

Dr. Gottman's research emphasizes that when contempt takes root, it leads to the withdrawal of affection and trust. The partner who feels belittled no longer feels safe opening up, no longer feels like their vulnerability will be met with kindness. And when a man feels emasculated in this way, the impact goes beyond just hurt feelings—it chips away at his sense of identity. A wife's disrespect, even if it's cloaked in humor or passed off as "just a joke," can cause wounds that run deep.

The Unseen Toll of Constant Criticism

Imagine this: A wife constantly criticizes her husband in front of friends or family. She points out his mistakes, mocks his decisions, or even goes as far as correcting him in public. It's like an invisible weight that presses on his chest. Every time he's made to feel small, it leaves him questioning his worth—not just as a spouse, but as a man. Dr. Michael Kimmel, a sociologist and expert on masculinity, writes that men often equate their self-worth to their role as providers and protectors. When that role is questioned or belittled, it goes beyond a simple blow to the ego—it shakes the core of who they are.

What's worse, this constant criticism can lead to a lack of intimacy. Intimacy, both emotional and physical, thrives on trust, mutual respect, and a sense of safety. When a husband feels continually diminished or mocked, the space for vulnerability evaporates. He withdraws, not out of malice, but out of self-preservation. He no longer feels that the home is a sanctuary where he can be his true self. Instead, it becomes a place where he's always on edge, constantly second-guessing his every move.

Phrases That Destroy a Man's Confidence and Masculinity

Comparing Him to Other Men

- *"My ex was better in bed than you."*
- *"Look at so-and-so—he actually knows how to take care of his wife properly."*
- *"I should have married [another man's name]; he's way more successful than you."*
- *"At least my father/brother knows how to be a real man."*

- *"Other husbands buy their wives nice things. What do I get?"*
- *"You'll never be as successful as my father/brother/ex."*

Mocking His Financial Situation

- *"You can't even provide properly—what kind of man are you?"*
- *"Maybe I should be the one wearing the trousers in this house."*
- *"A real man would make sure his wife never has to worry about money."*
- *"You should be ashamed of how little you bring to the table."*
- *"What kind of husband makes his wife struggle financially?"*
- *"I regret marrying someone who can't even give me the life I deserve."*

Belittling His Masculinity & Strength

- *"You're such a weakling."*
- *"You're too soft to handle real problems."*
- *"A real man wouldn't let people walk all over him like you do."*
- *"You need to grow a backbone and stop being such a pushover."*
- *"Even my little brother is tougher than you."*
- *"No wonder no one respects you."*
- *"I feel like I'm married to a little boy, not a man."*
- *"You're a disgrace to masculinity."*

Criticizing His Physical Attributes & Weight

- *"Maybe if you hit the gym more, you'd actually look like a real man."*
- *"You've let yourself go. I'm not even attracted to you anymore."*
- *"You're getting fat and lazy."*
- *"I never thought I'd be stuck with a husband who has a dad bod."*

- *"Your belly is bigger than mine—aren't men supposed to be strong?"*
- *"I'm embarrassed to be seen with you."*

Mocking His Sexual Performance

- *"You're not even man enough in the bedroom."*
- *"Other men are more well-endowed than you."*
- *"That's all you got? That was disappointing."*
- *"No wonder I don't enjoy sex anymore."*
- *"If I wanted something small, I'd buy a toy."*
- *"Maybe if you were better in bed, I'd actually want to be intimate with you."*
- *"Wow, can't even get it up? That's embarrassing."*
- *"My ex never had these problems."*
- *"Real men want sex all the time. What's wrong with you?"*
- *"You should probably get some pills or something—this is just sad."*
- *"I used to find you sexy, but not anymore."*

Questioning His Ability to Lead

- *"I don't trust you to make good decisions—you always mess things up."*
- *"I have to handle everything because you can't."*
- *"No one takes you seriously. Why should I?"*
- *"You're too stupid to handle responsibility."*
- *"A real man would know how to take charge."*
- *"You're like a lost little boy."*

Attacking His Religious Commitment

- *"You call yourself a Muslim."*
- *"You can't even lead a prayer in this house—how can you lead a family?"*

- "I need a husband who actually follows Islam."
- "You have no connection with Allah, no wonder you're struggling."
- "Real men wake up for Fajr, not sleep through it."

Publicly Humiliating Him

- "You always embarrass me in front of people."
- "I have to correct you because you never know what you're talking about."
- "You sound so dumb when you talk—just let me handle it."
- "You're like a child; I have to explain everything to you."
- "Everyone thinks you're a joke."

Challenging His Authority in Front of the Children

- "Don't listen to your father, he doesn't know what he's talking about."
- "I make the rules in this house, not him."
- "Your dad is useless, just ask me instead."
- "If I relied on your father, we'd all be in trouble."

Mocking His Emotions & Sensitivity

- "Are you seriously upset? Stop being such a baby."
- "Crying? Wow, that's so manly."
- "You're too emotional. No wonder no one respects you."
- "Why don't you act like a real man for once?"
- "I need a strong man, not someone who gets upset over stupid things."

Dismissing His Efforts & Accomplishments

- "That's all you achieved? Any real man would've done more by now."
- "You barely do anything, and you expect me to be impressed?"

- "I could have done that better than you."
- "You're just not good enough."

Controlling & Undermining His Decisions
- "I make all the real decisions in this house because you clearly can't."
- "You're not capable of handling things without me."
- "If I left you, you wouldn't even know what to do with yourself."

Implying He's Replaceable
- "I could find someone better than you in a second."
- "You're lucky I even stayed this long."
- "Men like you are a dime a dozen."

The Psychological & Emotional Damage of These Words

These statements don't just hurt—they destroy a man's self-esteem, confidence, and sense of identity. When a wife constantly belittles, mocks, or emasculates her husband, the effects can be devastating:

- **Loss of Confidence**: He starts doubting his worth as a husband, a father, and a man.
- **Emotional Withdrawal**: He stops trying, avoids conflict, and disconnects emotionally.
- **Loss of Motivation**: Feeling unappreciated leads to decreased ambition and drive.
- **Resentment & Anger**: Over time, bitterness builds, leading to conflict or complete detachment.
- **Breakdown of Trust & Intimacy**: When respect disappears, love and closeness follow.

A strong marriage requires respect, kindness, and appreciation. Words have the power to either build a man up or break him down. If a wife finds herself saying these things, it's important to reflect on how her words impact the marriage and what can be done to restore respect and love between both partners.

Why He Stops Trying

In many marriages, when a man feels continually undermined, his natural response is to retreat. This isn't about weakness; it's about protecting the fragile pieces of his soul that are left after each attack. The constant dismissals, whether about his decisions, his achievements, or even his emotions, build a wall between him and his wife. And, when that wall is high enough, he stops trying. Dr. Harriet Lerner, a renowned therapist and author of *The Dance of Anger*, notes that when one partner constantly exerts control over the relationship, it creates an imbalance of power. The partner who feels powerless—often the husband in this case—becomes less engaged, emotionally and physically. He might stop sharing his thoughts, stop trying to please, and even stop making an effort in the relationship altogether.

But here's the catch: *his withdrawal is not a sign of indifference*. It's a result of feeling emotionally unsafe and unwanted. When you make him feel inferior, when you take away his autonomy or mock his masculinity, you're not creating a space for open communication—you're locking the door to his heart. Over time, this leads to emotional disconnection, the kind that makes it feel like the relationship is slowly dying.

The Hidden Cost: A Husband's Self-Esteem

A woman might not always see it, but every time she dismisses her husband's ideas, criticizes him in front of others, or tries to control his actions, his self-esteem takes a hit. And as his self-worth erodes, so too does his confidence. In turn, this affects his ability to make decisions, to assert himself in important situations, and even to stand tall as a partner and a father.

Dr. Sue Johnson has long highlighted the importance of emotional safety in relationships. She argues that when partners create an environment where each person feels valued and heard, intimacy flourishes. But when one partner is constantly belittled, that safety is shattered. The emotional wounds are deep, and the impact isn't just temporary; it's long-lasting. Research from

Dr. Brené Brown, a leading expert on shame and vulnerability, shows that when a person's worth is constantly questioned or invalidated, it leads to a spiral of shame and self-doubt.

For men, this kind of emotional undermining can feel like an endless cycle. Each time he's criticized or emasculated, he may try to compensate by withdrawing or becoming defensive. But neither of these responses heals the wound. The only thing that heals is the restoration of respect, kindness, and emotional validation.

The Deeper Damage: The Breakdown of Trust

Trust is the bedrock of any healthy relationship. Without it, there can be no true intimacy, no deep connection, no partnership. But when a wife emasculates her husband, trust begins to erode. It doesn't happen all at once, but like the slow wearing down of a riverbank, it's constant and it's damaging.

Dr. John Gottman's research found that contempt is the single greatest predictor of divorce, more so than criticism or defensiveness. Why? Because contempt speaks directly to the heart of the relationship: it implies that one partner is beneath the other, that they are not worthy of love, respect, or even basic kindness. This is the ultimate betrayal—a husband who feels constantly undermined, belittled, and disrespected will eventually stop trusting his partner. Without trust, there can be no love, no connection, and ultimately, no marriage.

The Ripple Effect: Impact on Children and the Future

And it doesn't just end with the husband. The emotional toll of emasculation trickles down to the children as well. Kids pick up on the tension, the dismissive behaviors, and the emotional distance. They see the way their mother speaks to their father, the way he reacts, and the growing divide between the two. In turn, they internalize these behaviors, often replicating them in their own relationships when they grow older.

Islamic teachings remind us that the home should be a place of mercy, love, and respect. The Prophet Muhammad (ﷺ) emphasized the importance of kindness within the family: "The best of you are those who are best to their families." (Sunan Ibn Majah) This simple yet profound principle highlights the essential role of mutual respect and kindness in nurturing not just a strong marriage, but also emotionally healthy children. Children raised in a home where respect is paramount are more likely to model that behavior in their own relationships, creating a cycle of love and respect that transcends generations.

Breaking the Cycle: How to Build Him Up, Not Break Him Down

If you've found yourself in a place where emasculation has crept into your relationship, it's never too late to change. Healing begins with understanding the power of words, actions, and attitudes. In the quiet moments, when you speak to him, make sure your words build him up, not tear him down. A simple shift from criticism to compassion can change the course of your relationship.

Remember, he is not your child, nor is he a competitor. He is your partner, and as the Qur'an beautifully states, "They are clothing for you and you are clothing for them" (Qur'an 2:187). Marriage, as a sacred bond, requires a deep commitment to protecting each other's dignity and building each other up, no matter what.

Start by being intentional with your words. Dr. Gary Chapman, in his book *The 5 Love Languages*, reminds us that words of affirmation are powerful. Speak them freely, whether it's acknowledging his hard work, validating his feelings, or simply expressing gratitude for his presence in your life.

Above all, remember that a successful marriage isn't about perfection. It's about constant effort, mutual respect, and a willingness to rebuild when things feel broken. With patience, understanding, and a renewed commitment to honoring each other, you can create a space where both partners feel valued, loved, and respected.

Chapter Twenty-Seven

The Missing Links Between Intimacy and Connection

A thriving marriage depends on emotional intimacy, physical and sexual connection, and the emotional intelligence needed to navigate challenges with empathy and understanding. Research consistently shows that couples who prioritize these aspects report higher levels of satisfaction and longevity. Emotional intimacy, the ability to share thoughts and feelings openly, nurtures trust and security. Sexual and physical intimacy strengthens the bond and affirms mutual affection. Emotional connection, the sense of being understood and valued, fosters belonging and partnership. Lastly, emotional intelligence—the capacity to manage and respond to emotions—is crucial for resolving conflicts and maintaining harmony.

When these elements are neglected, the consequences are distressing, impacting mental and physical well-being. Studies link the absence of emotional and physical intimacy to higher rates of anxiety, depression, stress, and lower immune function. Marital dissatisfaction often results in feelings of loneliness and resentment, slowly eroding the foundation of the relationship. This chapter explores the effects of neglecting these essential elements, supported by research, case studies, and expert insights. It also offers practical strategies for cultivating intimacy within the framework of faith and shared values.

The Rusting of Marital Bonds

A marriage devoid of emotional intimacy feels like a house without a foundation; fragile and on the verge of collapse. Emotional intimacy fosters vulnerability, trust, and mutual support, anchoring the relationship. Without it, couples drift apart emotionally, leading to loneliness, misunderstanding, and estrangement.

A study published in the *Journal of Marriage and Family* found that couples who share their thoughts and feelings regularly experience greater marital satisfaction and stability. Conversely, emotional distance can lead to stress and depression. Dr. John Gottman, a leading expert in marital dynamics, emphasizes the importance of emotional attunement—being in tune with each other's emotions—to prevent destructive patterns of criticism, contempt, and defensiveness. Without a strong emotional connection, couples risk seeing each other as opponents rather than partners, which can erode trust and intimacy over time. "Happily married couples aren't smarter, richer or more psychologically astute than others. But in their day-to-day lives, they have hit upon a dynamic that keeps their negative thoughts and feelings about each other (which all couples have) from overwhelming their positive ones." John Gottman

For example, Amira and Omar, a couple from Cairo, found themselves drifting apart after 10 years of marriage. Omar felt Amira no longer shared her feelings, while Amira believed Omar was emotionally unavailable. Counseling revealed unspoken fears and unmet needs. With guidance, they rebuilt their connection through active listening and regular emotional check-ins.

The effects of emotional disconnection ripple through families. Children of emotionally distant parents often develop insecure attachments, perpetuating dysfunctional patterns in their own relationships. By addressing emotional distance early, couples can protect not just their marriage but also the emotional well-being of future generations.

Mental and Physical Distress

When emotional intimacy is absent, it exacts a toll on both mental and physical health. Chronic stress, anxiety, and depression are common in strained marriages. The psychological strain of unresolved conflicts manifests physically, increasing vulnerability to illnesses and chronic conditions.

The *Journal of Family Psychology* highlights that individuals in low-quality marriages are more likely to suffer from depression due to relational stress. Dr. Sue Johnson explains this as an "attachment crisis," where the lack of emotional safety triggers anxiety and despair. Chronic stress activates the body's fight-or-flight response, elevating cortisol levels, which weakens the immune system and exacerbates conditions like hypertension and diabetes.

Take for example when Fatima, a homemaker in Kuala Lumpur, began experiencing insomnia and chronic fatigue during a period of emotional disconnection with her husband, Yusuf. Their constant arguments left her feeling unsupported, while Yusuf grew distant. Therapy helped them identify their patterns of emotional withdrawal, reducing their stress and restoring their physical and emotional health.

By recognizing these patterns and seeking help, couples can break the cycle of emotional and physical distress, creating a healthier and more resilient partnership.

Fulfilling Each Other's Sexual Needs

Sexual intimacy is more than a physical act; it is a profound expression of love, trust, and vulnerability. Esther Perel, a leading psychotherapist, asserts, "Sexual intimacy is a barometer of a couple's emotional connection. When nurtured, it deepens trust and fosters joy."

Couples who openly discuss their sexual needs report greater satisfaction and fewer misunderstandings. Dr. John Gottman's research reveals that couples who communicate about their desires and boundaries are more likely to resolve conflicts and maintain intimacy. Moreover, incorporating novelty in sexual experiences can rekindle passion and excitement. Dr. Laura Berman suggests, "Exploring new experiences together fosters desire and strengthens emotional bonds."

Case Study: Zainab and Ali's Journey to Reignite Intimacy

Zainab and Ali, a couple in their early 40s from Manchester, had been married for 15 years. Over time, their once vibrant intimacy had faded into a routine, with mismatched libidos creating tension and misunderstanding. Zainab, feeling unappreciated and undesired, grew frustrated with Ali's lack of interest in initiating intimacy. Ali, on the other hand, struggled with fatigue from work and unspoken insecurities about his performance, leading to a cycle of avoidance. Both partners felt disconnected, but neither knew how to bridge the gap.

- **Acknowledging the Issue**: Their turning point came during a candid conversation prompted by Zainab's growing frustration. Instead of blaming one another, they acknowledged that their intimacy had become stagnant and routine. This honest exchange laid the foundation for mutual understanding. Zainab expressed her desire for more emotional connection during the day to set the stage for physical intimacy, while Ali admitted his fear of rejection and his need for Zainab to initiate more frequently.

- **Introducing Romantic Rituals:** To rebuild their connection, they agreed to prioritize shared romantic rituals. Every week, they scheduled a date night where they could focus solely on each other, free from distractions like work or parenting duties. These dates were designed to rekindle emotional closeness, with simple but meaningful activities like cooking together, taking long evening walks, or reminiscing over old photographs. Additionally, they introduced smaller daily rituals to maintain a sense of connection. For instance:

    - **Morning Gratitudes:** Each morning, they shared one thing they appreciated about the other.
    - **Evening Check-ins:** At the end of the day, they spent 10 minutes discussing their highs and lows.
    - **Affectionate Touch:** Simple gestures like holding hands during walks or hugging longer than usual became intentional acts of physical closeness.

- **Exploring Preferences:** Zainab and Ali also began exploring their sexual preferences and desires through open communication, guided by the advice of a therapist. They used tools like the *Yes/No/Maybe* list, which allowed them to discuss their boundaries and fantasies without judgment. This exercise helped them discover new ways to express affection and desire, rekindling excitement in their relationship.

- **The Role of Empathy:** Empathy played a crucial role in their healing process. Zainab realized Ali's hesitation was rooted in his fear of failing to meet her expectations, while Ali began to understand that Zainab's desire for intimacy was about emotional closeness, not just physical gratification. This understanding fostered patience and compassion, allowing them to approach their struggles as a team rather than adversaries.

- **The Outcome:** Within a few months, their relationship transformed. The combination of romantic rituals, honest communication, and a commitment to empathy reignited their intimacy, both emotional and physical. Zainab shared, "It wasn't just about the physical acts;

it was about feeling seen and valued." Ali added, "I learned that intimacy is as much about emotional safety as it is about desire. Once we focused on building that safety, everything else fell into place."

Their journey serves as a testament to the power of vulnerability, open communication, and intentional effort in revitalizing a struggling marriage. It also underscores the importance of addressing intimacy challenges early to prevent long-term disconnection.

Research published in the *Journal of Sex Research* links sexual satisfaction with marital happiness and emotional closeness. By maintaining an open dialogue about physical intimacy, couples can enhance their bond and build trust.

The Devastating Effects of a Lack of Intimacy

A marriage without emotional and physical intimacy is like a garden deprived of sunlight. Over time, partners become strangers, disconnected from each other's lives. Studies consistently show that such relationships experience higher rates of dissatisfaction, loneliness, and eventual dissolution.

Psychological and physical effects include:

- **Increased Anxiety and Depression**: Chronic emotional neglect amplifies feelings of worthlessness and despair.

- **Health Implications**: Persistent relational stress weakens immunity, elevates blood pressure, and increases the risk of cardiovascular disease.

- **Marital Infidelity**: Emotional and physical neglect often pushes one or both partners to seek fulfillment outside the marriage.

Dr. Gary Chapman emphasizes the importance of recognizing and addressing each other's emotional and physical needs, highlighting that marriages flourish when partners consistently invest in their relationship. When these needs are neglected, emotional distance can grow, creating space for resentment and dissatisfaction to take root.

Case Study: Amina and Hassan's Journey to Rebuild Connection

Amina and Hassan, a couple in their late 30s from Nairobi, had been married for 12 years and were raising two young children. Over the years, their relationship had shifted from one of passion and connection to one of routine and emotional distance. Daily responsibilities, financial stress, and unspoken frustrations created a chasm between them. While they loved each other, neither felt seen or valued, and their physical intimacy had all but disappeared.

- **Recognizing the Problem:** The turning point came when Amina confided in a close friend about her feelings of loneliness and rejection. Her friend gently suggested that these feelings might be shared by Hassan and encouraged her to seek professional help. Reluctantly, Amina approached Hassan, who admitted he too felt disconnected and unsure of how to bridge the gap.

  Both acknowledged that they had ignored their intimacy issues for years, avoiding conversations about their unmet needs and instead burying themselves in work and parenting. Their silence had allowed resentment to build, creating a cycle of emotional and physical withdrawal.

  - **Counseling: A Safe Space for Understanding:** Amina and Hassan began attending counseling sessions with a therapist specializing in couples therapy. The therapist provided a safe space for them to express their feelings and frustrations without fear of judgment. During these sessions, they uncovered several underlying issues.

  - **Unmet Emotional Needs:** Amina expressed a deep longing for emotional support and reassurance from Hassan, which she felt had been lacking for years. She admitted that his distant behavior left her feeling unappreciated.

  - **Unspoken Insecurities:** Hassan revealed that he often avoided intimacy because he feared rejection and believed he was failing as a provider and partner. These insecurities had left him hesitant to initiate affection or engage in deeper conversations.

- **Misaligned Expectations:** Both realized they had unspoken assumptions about what intimacy should look like, leading to disappointment and misunderstanding.

  The therapist guided them to identify and articulate their emotional and physical needs, helping them understand each other's perspectives for the first time in years.

- **Small, Intentional Gestures of Affection:** To restore their connection, the therapist encouraged Amina and Hassan to implement small, intentional gestures of affection. These were simple acts that communicated care and love, gradually rebuilding trust and closeness:
  - **Daily Expressions of Gratitude:** They began sharing one thing they appreciated about each other every evening. This practice shifted their focus from criticism to positivity.
  - **Physical Touch:** Holding hands during their evening walks became a non-verbal way of reconnecting physically. This simple gesture helped ease the tension between them.
  - **Meaningful Check-ins:** They set aside 15 minutes each day to talk without distractions, discussing their emotions and experiences rather than household tasks or parenting concerns.
  - **Acts of Service:** Hassan made an effort to help with chores Amina typically handled alone, like preparing meals or assisting with homework. Amina, in turn, began planning small surprises for Hassan, such as his favorite dessert or a handwritten note in his lunchbox.

- **Rekindling Physical Intimacy:** With emotional intimacy slowly returning, Amina and Hassan addressed their physical distance. They explored ways to reintroduce physical touch and intimacy gradually, starting with non-sexual acts like hugs and kisses. Counseling sessions also included discussions on sexual preferences and desires, helping them rebuild this aspect of their relationship without pressure or fear.

- **Empathy and Forgiveness:** An essential component of their journey was learning to empathize with each other's struggles and forgive past mistakes. Amina came to understand that Hassan's withdrawal was not a sign of disinterest but a response to his insecurities. Hassan, in turn, realized that Amina's frustrations stemmed from her deep desire to feel loved and valued.

The therapist encouraged them to view their struggles not as failures but as opportunities to grow closer. This mindset allowed them to approach their challenges with compassion and teamwork.

- **The Outcome:** After several months of counseling and consistent effort, Amina and Hassan experienced a significant transformation in their relationship. They no longer felt like distant co-parents but partners deeply invested in each other's happiness. Amina shared, "I feel like we've rediscovered each other. The small things he does now mean so much more because I know they come from a place of love." Hassan added, "I've learned that showing vulnerability is not weakness; it's what strengthens our bond."

Their story highlights the importance of addressing intimacy issues early and the transformative power of empathy, communication, and small, intentional efforts to reconnect. By investing in their relationship, Amina and Hassan not only rebuilt their intimacy but also created a stronger foundation for the future.

Islamic Perspective: The Spiritual Importance of Intimacy

In Islam, intimacy is not just a marital right; it is an act of worship. The Qur'an emphasizes the importance of love, mercy, and mutual respect in marriage: "And of His signs is that He created for you from yourselves mates that you may find tranquillity in them; and He placed between you affection and mercy. Indeed in that are signs for a people who give thought." (Qur'an 30:21)

The Prophet Muhammad (ﷺ) said:

> *"And in the sexual intercourse of one of you there is charity (sadaqah)."*

> The companions asked, *"O Messenger of Allah, will one of us fulfill his desire and still be rewarded?"*

The Prophet (ﷺ) replied:

> *"Do you not see that if he were to engage in it unlawfully, he would bear a sin? Likewise, if he engages in it lawfully, he will have a reward."* (Sahih Muslim 1006)

Islamic teachings encourage tenderness and mutual satisfaction. The Prophet (ﷺ) advised men to approach their wives with gentleness, saying, "Do not fall upon your wives like animals. Let there first be a messenger between you." When asked what this messenger was, he replied, "Kisses and words." (Sunan Abu Dawood)

By fulfilling each other's emotional and physical needs, couples strengthen their connection and build a relationship grounded in love, compassion, and faith.

Practical Strategies for Cultivating Intimacy

1. **Open Communication**: Share feelings and desires honestly, fostering trust and understanding.

2. **Quality Time**: Schedule regular date nights and meaningful activities to reconnect emotionally.

3. **Conflict Resolution**: Address disagreements constructively, focusing on mutual solutions.

4. **Mindfulness Practices**: Reduce stress through mindfulness and meditation, improving emotional regulation.

5. **Seek Professional Help**: If struggles persist, consider therapy to rebuild connection and resolve underlying issues.

Conclusion

The absence of intimacy in marriage is a silent crisis that affects emotional well-being, physical health, and spiritual connection. By prioritizing emotional and sexual intimacy, couples can rebuild trust, deepen their bond, and create a fulfilling partnership. Marriage, as emphasized in Islamic teachings and psychological research, is a sacred relationship that thrives on love, understanding, and mutual effort. Investing in these elements ensures a resilient and joyful union.

Chapter Twenty-Eight

The Sleep Connection in Marriage

Why Shared Sleep Matters

Sleep is essential—not just for physical restoration, but for emotional and mental well-being as well. It's during sleep that our bodies repair, our minds process the day's experiences, and we find some of our deepest moments of connection. In a marriage, the act of sharing a bed at night can be a symbol of closeness, intimacy, and trust. Yet, in today's fast-paced world, many couples find themselves on divergent sleep schedules, leading to a sense of emotional distance that they may not even recognize until it starts to affect the relationship.

When couples sleep apart or have different routines, it isn't just about the physical separation—it's about missing out on those moments of connection that naturally happen when two people share their sleep. These moments, though small, build a deeper sense of partnership and security over time. As human beings, we are wired for connection, and shared sleep is a key piece of maintaining that bond.

The Quiet Erosion of Intimacy

Intimacy, the foundation of any healthy marriage, doesn't solely come from physical closeness but also from emotional vulnerability. We tend to associate intimacy with sexual connection, but true intimacy encompasses emotional support, shared vulnerability, and a sense of safety. That sense of safety is often nurtured by small daily rituals, such as talking at night, holding hands, or simply being close. When couples don't share their sleep, they miss out on those spontaneous moments of closeness.

Research shows that couples who engage in more physical touch—whether it's holding hands, cuddling, or simply sleeping together—report higher levels of happiness and satisfaction in their relationships. A study published in The Journal of Social and Personal Relationships found that couples who sleep closer together tend to experience stronger emotional bonds and a deeper sense of satisfaction. These non-sexual moments of physical intimacy can promote a sense of security and affection, which spills over into other areas of the relationship.

Take the example of Fatima and Zayd. They've been married for a few years now, and while they have a loving relationship, their schedules have shifted. Fatima works late into the night, while Zayd prefers an early bedtime. At first, they thought it wasn't a big deal, but over time, they noticed an emotional distance creeping in. The small, intimate conversations before sleep were no longer happening, and their physical touch had become less frequent. They found themselves drifting apart, not because they didn't love each other, but because they were missing the closeness that naturally comes when you share a bedtime.

The Emotional Strain of Different Sleep Rhythms

When couples aren't on the same sleep schedule, it can feel like they're in two separate worlds. One spouse might feel left out of late-night conversations, while the other might feel like they're being neglected because they go to bed alone. These small emotional chasms can start to add up, leading to feelings of resentment, frustration, and loneliness.

In fact, sleep deprivation can significantly impact emotional regulation. According to research from the *Harvard Medical School* Sleep Center, sleep deprivation increases the likelihood of irritability and emotional reactivity. When you're tired, even small annoyances can feel much larger, and it becomes more difficult to be patient with your partner. If you add the stress of different sleep schedules into the mix, it can be a recipe for conflict.

For example, consider Amir and Sana. Amir has always been an early riser, and Sana tends to stay up much later. Initially, they thought the difference was no big deal. However, over time, Amir began to feel that Sana was emotionally distant because she wasn't available for nighttime conversations or moments of affection. Sana, on the other hand, felt like Amir didn't understand the demands of her job, which required her to stay up late. The result? Both felt misunderstood, and arguments began to happen more frequently. They realized that their sleep schedules were a bigger issue than they had thought.

Sleep issues often lead to a mismatch in emotional energy, creating a barrier to meaningful communication. This doesn't just make couples feel disconnected—it leads to actual physical and psychological stress. Studies also show that emotional disconnection due to sleep differences is one of the most common reasons couples report feeling lonely despite being in the same relationship.

The Unseen Physical Effects of Sleeping Apart

We've all heard that sleep affects our bodies, but many people don't realize how much sleep deprivation can impact not only our mental health but also our physical health. Chronic lack of sleep is linked to increased risk for heart disease, diabetes, and depression. Dr. Matthew Walker, a sleep scientist and author of *Why We Sleep*, argues that poor sleep is one of the most underestimated health risks. Sleep deprivation has been shown to negatively affect everything from cognitive function to immune system health.

When couples have misaligned sleep schedules, they're not only missing out on quality connection—they're also potentially sabotaging their own well-being.

Let's consider the example of Amina and Yusuf. Amina works in a high-pressure job and often stays up late working. Meanwhile, Yusuf prefers to sleep early and wakes up refreshed each day. Over time, Amina's late nights start to take a serious toll on her health. She feels increasingly fatigued, her immune system weakens, and she begins to experience frequent illnesses. Yusuf notices her declining energy but doesn't realize that her lack of sleep is compromising her physical health. This disconnect creates tension—Yusuf struggles to understand why Amina is not as engaged, while Amina feels torn between her work responsibilities and the growing impact on her well-being.

The link between sleep deprivation and health issues is undeniable. Sleep deprivation has been shown to increase inflammation in the body, making it harder for the immune system to fight off illnesses. Couples who have different sleep schedules may also experience this effect, putting unnecessary stress on both partners' health.

The Impact on Sexual and Physical Intimacy

Physical intimacy is a crucial part of any marriage, but it goes beyond just sex. Intimacy also involves the ability to feel comfortable, loved, and cared for. One of the most profound ways that intimacy is built is through touch—whether it's a kiss, a hug, or simply holding hands.

However, when couples don't sleep together, they often miss out on these smaller, non-sexual gestures. The absence of physical touch before bed—something as simple as cuddling or holding hands—can have a significant impact on sexual desire. Without these small acts of intimacy, desire can naturally wane.

Research from *The Archives of Sexual Behavior* suggests that couples who have more regular physical contact before bed are more likely to have a satisfying sexual relationship. Dr. David Schnarch, a sex therapist, emphasizes that emotional closeness is the foundation of a healthy sexual connection. Without that emotional connection—nurtured through shared moments of closeness, including sleep—sexual intimacy can suffer.

Let's take the example of Rahma and Samir. Over the years, they've been very busy with work, and their sleep habits have become increasingly mismatched. Samir likes to read before bed, while Rahma watches TV or scrolls on her phone. They no longer spend time cuddling or connecting physically before sleep. Slowly, their physical intimacy began to decline. They weren't prioritizing the little moments that made them feel connected, and sexual intimacy became less frequent. They didn't realize it, but their different sleep habits were a significant factor in the growing distance between them.

Sleep habits can affect sexual intimacy not just by reducing physical closeness, but also by influencing hormonal balance. Oxytocin, known as the "love hormone," is released during physical touch and promotes bonding. The lack of shared sleep can result in lower levels of oxytocin, contributing to decreased desire and connection.

Loneliness in the Same Bed

It may sound paradoxical, but it's entirely possible to feel lonely while sleeping in the same bed as your partner. This phenomenon happens when there is a lack of emotional and physical connection, despite being physically near each other. It's not just about proximity—it's about feeling seen, heard, and cared for.

Psychologist Dr. John Cacioppo, who specializes in loneliness, notes that social isolation and emotional disconnection can be just as harmful to your health as physical isolation. Couples who are sleeping apart or not sharing meaningful moments before bed often experience these feelings of loneliness, which can contribute to deeper emotional distress.

How to Rebuild Connection Through a Synchronized Sleep Schedule

A well-aligned sleep routine can significantly enhance emotional and physical intimacy in a relationship. Here's a detailed and actionable strategy for couples looking to rebuild their connection through synchronized sleep habits:

1. **Establish a Shared Wind-Down Routine:** A bedtime routine signals to your body that it's time to rest, and when shared with your partner, it reinforces emotional connection.

   Create a Ritual:

   - Set a consistent bedtime that works for both partners.
   - Engage in calming activities together, such as reading, listening to soft music, or sharing highlights of your day.
   - Try a tech-free hour before bed to avoid blue light and distractions from phones or TV.

   Use Relaxation Techniques:

   - Practice deep breathing or guided meditation together to ease into sleep.
   - Engage in progressive muscle relaxation—tensing and relaxing different muscle groups to promote relaxation.

   Sync Your Sleep Cycles Gradually:

   - If one partner sleeps later than the other, shift bedtime by 15-30 minutes per week until both schedules align.
   - Adjust exposure to natural light in the morning to regulate circadian rhythms.

2. **Optimize Your Sleep Environment:** Your bedroom should feel like a shared sanctuary where both partners feel comfortable.

   Ensure a Comfortable Sleep Setup:

   - Invest in a good mattress and pillows that cater to both partners' sleep needs.
   - Maintain a cool, dark, and quiet room for optimal sleep quality.
   - Use white noise machines if one partner is sensitive to sound.

   Set Boundaries for Disruptions:

   - Reduce late-night screen time or switch to night mode to limit blue light exposure.
   - If one partner snores or has sleep disturbances, consider earplugs or white noise machines.
   - Decide together on rules for pets in the bed or separate blankets if different temperature preferences arise.

3. **Foster Physical Connection Without Pressure:** Physical closeness before sleep strengthens emotional intimacy, even if it doesn't lead to sex.

   Ways to Incorporate Touch:

   - Cuddle for 5-10 minutes before falling asleep. Even if one partner rolls away later, this moment fosters bonding.
   - Hold hands, stroke each other's hair, or simply rest against one another.
   - If sleep schedules don't align, engage in a brief goodnight hug or kiss to maintain intimacy.

   Use Oxytocin to Your Advantage:

   - Touch increases oxytocin levels, promoting trust and connection.
   - Even something simple like sleeping close together can improve emotional bonding.

4. **Prioritize Shared Sleep and Adjust Schedules:** Sometimes, external factors like work shifts or different chronotypes can make synchronized sleep challenging.

   Make Small Adjustments:

   - If one partner is a night owl and the other is an early bird, compromise on a middle ground bedtime.

   - Avoid caffeine or stimulants in the evening that could delay one partner's sleep.

   - Align waking schedules by getting out of bed at the same time, even if bedtime differs slightly.

   Limit Solo Late-Night Activities:

   - Try to wind down together instead of having one partner stay up on the phone, laptop, or watching TV.

   - If work or study demands late nights, schedule at least 3-4 nights per week for shared sleep time.

5. **Address Sleep Disruptions Proactively:** Sleep disorders or disruptions can create resentment and strain in relationships.

   Solutions for Common Sleep Issues:

   - Snoring: Try nasal strips, a CPAP machine (if necessary), or changing sleep positions.

   - Restless Leg Syndrome (RLS): Magnesium supplements, stretching, or mild massages can help.

   - Temperature Differences: Use separate blankets or invest in a dual-zone mattress.

   Consider a Sleep Therapist or Couples' Counseling:

   - If sleep issues cause chronic tension, consult a sleep specialist to address medical concerns like insomnia, apnea, or night terrors.

   - A relationship therapist can help navigate emotional challenges related to mismatched sleep patterns.

6. **Reinforce the Emotional Bond Beyond Sleep:** Sometimes, sleep struggles aren't just about sleep—they reflect deeper emotional disconnects.

    Ways to Strengthen Emotional Connection:

    - Engage in quality time before bed, such as sharing three things you appreciate about each other.

    - Resolve conflicts before bedtime to avoid tension that disrupts sleep.

    - Wake up together when possible and start the morning with a small bonding ritual (e.g., morning hugs, making coffee together).

Conclusion

A synchronized sleep schedule isn't just about going to bed at the same time—it's about fostering physical closeness, emotional intimacy, and overall relationship well-being. Couples who prioritize quality sleep together often report stronger connections, reduced stress, and higher overall satisfaction in their relationships.

Chapter Twenty-Nine

Mastering Conflict Management

Conflict is a natural part of any relationship, especially within marriage. It arises from the differences in personalities, communication styles, cultural backgrounds, and even daily routines. Yet, the way couples manage and resolve conflicts can either strengthen or weaken their relationship. Healthy conflict resolution is not only about finding a solution to an issue but also about deepening mutual respect, empathy, and understanding between spouses. This chapter explores effective conflict resolution strategies by combining the wisdom of Islamic teachings with modern relationship science. Through this unique integration, couples can foster not only conflict resolution but also a deeper sense of connection and growth in their marriages.

Understanding Conflict in Marriages

Conflicts can emerge for a variety of reasons in marriage, whether over finances, parenting styles, communication habits, or unmet expectations. These differences are often exacerbated by stress, life changes, and external pressures. Conflict is not inherently negative; how couples handle it determines the health of their relationship. When conflicts remain unresolved, they can lead to lingering resentment, emotional distance, and feelings of frustration. It is crucial to approach conflict with the understanding that disagreement does not equal failure—it simply reflects that both partners are human, each with their own unique needs and desires.

In relationships, one of the primary causes of conflict is poor communication. Often, what partners are really fighting about is not the issue itself, but the manner in which it is being discussed. Couples frequently fail to communicate effectively, using language that is more about winning the argument than truly understanding each other's feelings. Healthy communication involves not just talking but also listening—really listening—to your partner's needs, emotions, and perspectives. Research consistently shows that couples who communicate openly, respectfully, and empathetically experience more satisfaction in their marriages.

The Role of Communication in Conflict Resolution

When we talk about effective conflict resolution, communication is the cornerstone. Communication is more than just speaking words—it's the ability to express oneself in a way that is clear, respectful, and constructive. In their study of successful couples, psychologists have found that the most enduring relationships are built on a foundation of open, honest, and empathetic communication. This involves listening not only to respond but to understand.

One of the keys to this is **active listening**, which is a technique that focuses on fully understanding what the other person is saying before formulating a response. In active listening, the listener demonstrates empathy by validating the speaker's emotions and concerns. For example, if a wife is upset because she feels overwhelmed with household responsibilities, instead of immediately offering a solution, her husband should first acknowledge her feelings by saying, "I hear you. It sounds like you've been feeling stressed and unsupported. Let's talk about how we can share the load more evenly." This small shift can prevent conflict from escalating, making both partners feel heard and valued.

Islamic Perspective on Conflict Resolution

The Qur'an and the teachings of Prophet Muhammad (ﷺ) offer profound wisdom for managing marital conflicts. Islamic principles encourage mutual respect, empathy, and patience in the face of disagreement. One of the most powerful Qur'anic verses on this topic is from Surah An-Nisa:

> "And live with them in kindness. For if you dislike them– perhaps you dislike a thing and Allah makes therein much good." (Qur'an 4:19)

This verse encourages spouses to maintain kindness, even in moments of conflict, and reminds them that often, the things that cause discomfort may lead to greater benefits if managed with patience. The Prophet Muhammad's

(ﷺ) own life provides countless examples of conflict resolution, marked by patience, respect, and empathy. One notable example is his calm mediation between his wives when disputes arose. His approach was always rooted in listening, understanding, and guiding both parties to a peaceful resolution.

In times of disagreement, Islamic teachings emphasize the importance of forgiveness and **reconciliation (islah)**. The Qur'an encourages spouses to make peace and seek resolution through dialogue and mutual understanding. Even in the case of deeper conflicts, the idea of **shura (mutual consultation)** plays an essential role in finding solutions that are fair and respectful to both partners.

A remarkable example of conflict resolution is found in the relationship between the Prophet Muhammad (ﷺ) and his wives. Whenever disagreements arose, the Prophet (ﷺ) would take time to listen to his wives' concerns with genuine care and patience. He would not dismiss their feelings, and he would always aim to resolve disputes by finding common ground through respectful conversation. This commitment to empathy and understanding can serve as a guiding principle for couples facing conflict today—listening first, responding thoughtfully, and always prioritizing peace over victory in an argument.

Relationship Science and Psychology in Conflict Resolution

While Islamic principles provide spiritual and ethical guidance for conflict management, modern relationship science also offers valuable tools and strategies for resolving marital conflicts. Psychology has long studied the patterns and dynamics of couples in conflict, leading to many insightful discoveries about how conflict can be better managed. One of the most widely recognized theories is John Gottman's *Four Horsemen of the Apocalypse*, which identifies behaviors that predict relationship breakdowns:

1. **Criticism**: Attacking your partner's character rather than addressing the issue.

2. **Defensiveness**: Responding to complaints with counterattacks or excuses.

3. **Contempt**: Showing disrespect or superiority toward your partner.

4. **Stonewalling**: Withdrawing from the conversation and refusing to engage.

These behaviors can be extremely damaging to a relationship. Gottman's research suggests that replacing them with positive behaviors—such as **appreciation, validation, humility, and engagement**—can significantly improve conflict resolution. For instance, instead of criticizing a spouse for being inattentive, one might express their feelings by saying, "I feel neglected when we don't spend quality time together. Can we work on this?"

Emotional Regulation in Conflict Resolution

In the heat of conflict, emotions can often spiral out of control, leading to regrettable statements or actions. This is where **emotional regulation** becomes crucial. Techniques such as deep breathing, mindfulness, and using "I" statements can help individuals express their feelings constructively. For example, instead of saying, "You never help around the house," a spouse can say, "I feel overwhelmed when I have to handle all the chores on my own. Can we talk about how we can divide the responsibilities more evenly?"

Taking a step back to calm down and reflect before responding can prevent reactions driven by anger or frustration. Practicing emotional regulation techniques allows partners to engage in a more respectful, less reactive manner, fostering a healthier approach to conflict.

Dr. John Gottman's extensive research has highlighted the importance of certain behaviors in conflict resolution, as well as how these behaviors predict the success or failure of marriages. One key insight from Gottman's work is the concept of **repair attempts**—small gestures or phrases that partners use to defuse tension during conflict. These might include saying, "I'm sorry" or a physical gesture like touching your spouse's arm to signal reconciliation. According to Gottman, couples who make repair attempts during conflicts are more likely to stay together in the long term.

Practical Solutions for Conflict Management

Several practical strategies can help couples navigate conflicts effectively:

1. **Time-Outs and Breaks:** When emotions run high, taking a short break can help both partners avoid saying things they might regret. Couples should establish a mutual agreement on taking breaks and ensure they resume the discussion after a brief pause. This prevents

conflicts from escalating and allows both partners to return to the conversation with a clearer mindset.

2. **Non-Verbal Communication:** A comforting touch, a gentle hug, or simply holding hands can reduce the intensity of a conflict. Body language often speaks louder than words, and being mindful of non-verbal cues can facilitate understanding and connection. Making eye contact and using an open posture can signal attentiveness and care, even during difficult conversations.

3. **Positive Reinforcement:** Praising your spouse for their efforts in resolving a conflict constructively can encourage more positive behavior in the future. A simple *"Thank you for listening to me"* can reinforce a healthy dynamic and make problem-solving feel like a team effort rather than a competition. Acknowledging each other's contributions fosters a sense of appreciation and strengthens emotional bonds.

4. **Problem-Solving Frameworks:** Approaching conflicts as opportunities for problem-solving rather than battles to be won helps both partners collaborate toward mutually beneficial solutions. Discussing potential options, brainstorming ideas together, and evaluating their feasibility can transform conflicts into chances for growth. A shared mindset of teamwork rather than opposition leads to more effective conflict resolution.

5. **Journaling and Self-Reflection:** Writing down thoughts and feelings before discussing them can reduce emotional intensity and provide clarity. Couples can benefit from journaling separately to gain insight into their own behaviors and reactions, promoting personal growth and mutual understanding. This practice allows individuals to process their emotions privately before bringing them into a conversation.

6. **Active Listening with Validation:** Actively listening to your partner with full attention fosters emotional safety and minimizes defensiveness. Reflective listening, such as repeating back what your partner says to confirm understanding (*"What I hear you saying is…"*), can prevent misinterpretations. Acknowledging emotions even when you disagree (*"I see that this is really upsetting for you"*) helps validate your partner's feelings and keep the discussion constructive.

A study in the *Journal of Marriage and Family Therapy* found that validating a partner's feelings reduces conflict escalation and increases emotional safety in relationships.

7. **The 5-to-1 Rule (Gottman's Ratio):** Successful relationships maintain a balance of at least five positive interactions for every one negative interaction. Complimenting your partner during discussions (*"I appreciate that you are trying to communicate with me"*), expressing affection through small gestures like a smile or a soft touch, and recognizing their efforts contribute to a supportive and resilient dynamic.

   Dr. John Gottman's research shows that couples with a 5:1 positive-to-negative ratio in conflicts are more likely to have long-term success in their relationship.

8. **De-Escalation Techniques (Self-Soothing):** Self-soothing techniques help prevent emotional flooding, allowing partners to remain calm and regulated during difficult conversations. Taking deep breaths, pausing to regain composure, and using reassuring self-talk (*"This is my partner, not my enemy"*) can shift the emotional tone of a discussion. Engaging in progressive muscle relaxation can also release built-up physical tension.

   Studies in the *Behavior Therapy Journal* indicate that self-soothing techniques help partners remain emotionally regulated during conflict, leading to more productive conversations.

9. **"I" Statements Instead of "You" Statements:** Framing concerns as personal feelings instead of blame reduces defensiveness and fosters a more constructive dialogue. Instead of "You never listen to me," saying "I feel unheard when I share my concerns" shifts the focus from accusation to self-expression. This approach encourages empathy and minimizes reactive responses.

   Research on communication suggests that using 'I' statements reduces defensiveness and improves empathy. This is supported by Dr. Marshall Rosenberg's work in Nonviolent Communication and studies in the *Journal of Social and Personal Relationships*.

10. **Conflict "Cooling-Off" Agreements:** Establishing a structured approach to pausing conflicts can prevent escalation and impulsive reactions. Couples can agree on a set timeframe (e.g., 30 minutes or an hour) before resuming the discussion in a calmer state. Reconnecting only after both partners feel ready to communicate rationally improves the quality of problem-solving efforts.

A *Harvard Negotiation Project* study found that cooling-off periods prevent impulsive decision-making and encourage rational conflict resolution.

11. **The Soft Start-Up Approach:** Beginning discussions with kindness and patience rather than accusation or criticism sets the tone for a more productive exchange. For example, instead of "You never help around the house!", saying "I really appreciate when we share household tasks. Can we find a way to balance it better?" reduces defensiveness and fosters collaboration.

    Gottman's research shows that 96% of arguments end the way they start—a soft start-up leads to more constructive conflict resolution.

12. **Humor as a De-Escalation Tool:** Lighthearted humor, when used appropriately, can diffuse tension and provide emotional relief during conflicts. Simple gestures like laughing together or making a playful remark can soften a heated exchange without dismissing the issue at hand. Humor should be gentle and inclusive, rather than sarcastic or belittling.

    Studies in the *Journal of Social and Personal Relationships* suggest that couples who use humor during disagreements experience lower stress levels and faster conflict resolution.

13. **Scheduled Check-Ins for Preventive Conflict Management:** Regular emotional check-ins help prevent small frustrations from turning into major conflicts. Setting aside time weekly to discuss concerns, gratitude, and emotional needs ensures that issues are addressed early and that both partners feel heard. Structuring check-ins with prompts such as *"What's one thing that went well this week?"* can make the conversation more effective.

    Relationship counselors advocate for regular check-ins to ensure minor frustrations don't build into larger issues over time.

14. **Expressing Gratitude Before Conflict Discussions:** Acknowledging positivity in the relationship before discussing conflicts helps lower defensiveness and increase openness to solutions. Expressing appreciation (*"I really value how supportive you are"*) before addressing an issue can make problem-solving feel less like criticism and more like teamwork.

Studies in the *Emotion Journal* show that expressing gratitude before a conflict discussion lowers defensiveness and increases receptiveness to solutions.

15. **Repair Attempts After Conflict:** The ability to make and accept repair attempts strengthens long-term relationship resilience. Simple statements like "I didn't mean for it to come across that way" or "Can we hit the reset button?" help restore emotional closeness after a disagreement. Reflecting on lessons learned from conflicts encourages growth and prevents repeat issues.

    Gottman's studies show that the ability to make and accept repair attempts is one of the strongest predictors of a successful and long-lasting marriage.

16. **Physiological Self-Soothing for Emotional Overwhelm:** Engaging in physiological self-soothing techniques can help regulate emotional flooding and maintain a sense of control during conflicts. Deep breathing (4-7-8 method), progressive muscle relaxation, and grounding exercises (5-4-3-2-1 method) activate the body's relaxation response and prevent reactive decision-making.

    Studies in the *Journal of Behavioral Therapy* indicate that self-soothing techniques reduce stress responses, helping individuals regain emotional balance before conflict resolution.

Integrating Islamic Principles with Relationship Science

The fusion of Islamic principles with modern relationship science creates a holistic approach to conflict management. In Islam, the idea of **balance** is central—between rights and responsibilities, love and respect, and individual and shared goals. Understanding each spouse's role, as outlined in Islamic teachings, provides a foundation for resolving conflicts with dignity and mutual respect. When these principles are applied thoughtfully, couples can navigate even the most challenging issues while maintaining harmony and faith.

Conclusion

Effective conflict resolution is not just about avoiding arguments or reaching a quick compromise. It is about deepening understanding, fostering emotional connection, and maintaining respect even when disagreements arise. By combining the timeless wisdom of Islamic teachings with modern relationship science, couples can develop strategies that not only resolve conflicts but also strengthen the bond between them. Conflict is not the enemy—it is a tool for growth, understanding, and building a lasting, fulfilling partnership.

Chapter Thirty

Attachment Styles in Love

How Early Experiences Shape Us

It may seem like a small thing, but the way we were raised has a huge impact on the way we relate to others as adults—especially in romantic relationships. Imagine your emotional development as a tree, and your childhood as the soil. If the soil is rich and nurturing (filled with love, care, and safety), the tree can grow tall, strong, and resilient. But if that soil is rocky or lacking in essential nutrients (like emotional neglect or inconsistency), the tree may struggle to grow properly, and its branches—our attachment behaviors—might lean in unhealthy directions.

As children, our first attachments are typically with our primary caregivers, often our parents. If these caregivers are responsive to our needs, we feel secure and learn to trust others. But when we're raised by caregivers who are inconsistent, neglectful, or overly critical, we develop attachment styles that can affect our ability to trust, feel safe, and communicate openly in adulthood.

Take Sara and Ahmed, for example. Sara grew up in a loving home where her parents were always there for her. As an adult, she's emotionally balanced, secure in her relationship with Ahmed, and tends to be trusting and open. Ahmed, however, had a much different upbringing. His mother was emotionally distant and unavailable. He learned to rely on himself, which has left him emotionally distant in his marriage with Sara. This often leads to tension, with Sara feeling emotionally neglected and frustrated.

The Science Behind Attachment: Why It Matters

Attachment theory is not just a nice idea—it's grounded in decades of psychological research. The theory was first developed by British psychologist John Bowlby in the 1950s, and his research on the emotional bonds between children and their caregivers laid the foundation for understanding how early experiences shape adult relationships. Bowlby identified the importance of having a secure base in early childhood—someone who provides comfort and safety when we feel threatened.

The theory was further explored by Mary Ainsworth, who conducted a famous experiment called *The Strange Situation*, which studied how babies reacted when their mothers left and then returned to the room. The results of her study helped categorize attachment styles into four types: secure, anxious, avoidant, and disorganized.

- **Secure** attachment is characterized by comfort with intimacy and a healthy balance between independence and connection.

- **Anxious** attachment is marked by a desire for closeness, often paired with fear of abandonment or rejection.

- **Avoidant** attachment reflects an individual's tendency to withdraw or shut down emotionally when they feel overwhelmed or unsafe.

- **Disorganized** attachment occurs when a person has an inconsistent pattern of behavior, often due to childhood trauma or abuse.

Dr. Amir Levine, a psychiatrist and neuroscientist, alongside Rachel Heller, brought attachment theory into the realm of adult relationships with their book *Attached*. They explain how these attachment styles affect our behavior in love and how we navigate closeness, emotional safety, and intimacy.

Attachment is essentially our internal "blueprint" for relationships. When we form a secure attachment, we believe that our needs will be met and that we are worthy of love. But when our attachment is insecure—whether anxious, avoidant, or disorganized—we may develop maladaptive patterns that can hinder intimacy and trust.

Attachment Styles in Action

Understanding attachment theory can help us navigate the complexities of our own relationships. Let's dive deeper into some more scenarios to highlight how attachment styles show up in everyday life:

Fatima and Zaid: Fatima and Zaid both have a secure attachment style, which allows them to communicate openly and resolve conflicts effectively. If they have an argument, they don't hold grudges or resort to defensive behavior. They both know how to listen actively, express their feelings clearly, and show empathy for each other's point of view. Their secure attachment provides a stable foundation that supports their emotional intimacy and connection.

Aisha and Yusuf: Aisha has an anxious attachment style. When Yusuf is busy with work or doesn't respond to her messages immediately, she feels anxious and wonders if something's wrong. This leads to her feeling uncertain and questioning her worth in the relationship. Meanwhile, Yusuf, who has a more secure attachment, doesn't always understand why Aisha feels the need for constant reassurance. However, with communication and understanding, Aisha learns to cope with her fears by talking about her insecurities instead of acting on them.

Khalid and Leila: Khalid, with his avoidant attachment style, tends to distance himself when things get emotionally intense. When Leila expresses her needs for emotional closeness, Khalid feels overwhelmed and withdraws. Leila, who values connection and closeness, begins to feel neglected and frustrated. With therapy, Khalid starts learning to recognize his emotional avoidance and work through it. Slowly, he learns to express his emotions, which strengthens his bond with Leila.

Zara and Bilal: Zara grew up in a home where love and fear often coexisted. Her caregiver could be warm one moment and frightening the next—sometimes loving, sometimes emotionally or physically harmful. As an adult, Zara deeply desires connection but struggles to feel safe when intimacy actually happens. When Bilal, her spouse, tries to get close, she sometimes clings desperately to him, afraid he might leave. Other times, she pushes him away or becomes cold and distant without warning.

Bilal feels confused by these mixed signals. He doesn't understand why one moment she's seeking his affection, and the next she's shutting down or accusing him of wanting to leave. This emotional rollercoaster leaves both of them feeling frustrated and exhausted.

Zara's behavior reflects a disorganized attachment style—rooted in early experiences where love was unpredictable or even frightening. Through therapy and emotional work, Zara begins to notice her patterns and learn how to separate past trauma from present reality. With Bilal's support and a commitment to healing, she starts developing safer emotional strategies, gradually moving toward a more secure attachment.

Why This Matters in Your Relationship

It's easy to get stuck in patterns in relationships—especially when you don't fully understand why you're reacting the way you do. Without knowing about attachment styles, it's easy to misinterpret your partner's actions or feel like you're not "enough" when issues arise. But when you understand attachment theory, it becomes much clearer why certain behaviors trigger specific emotional responses.

For instance, if you have an anxious attachment style, you might constantly worry about your partner leaving you, even when they haven't given you any reason to doubt them. On the other hand, if you have an avoidant attachment style, you might find yourself pulling away when your partner gets too close, even though you care deeply for them.

By recognizing these patterns, you can develop more empathy for both yourself and your partner. Instead of getting defensive or frustrated, you can approach the situation with compassion and work toward a solution. When you understand that your partner's reaction might be rooted in their own attachment fears or insecurities, you can better support them in moving toward a more secure attachment style.

Working Towards a More Secure Relationship

The great news is that no matter what your attachment style is, you don't have to be stuck in it forever. With effort, understanding, and commitment, you can work toward a more secure attachment, and so can your partner.

The first step is recognizing your attachment style and becoming aware of how it impacts your relationships.

Here are a few steps that can help you along the way:

1. **Self-Awareness**: Self-awareness is the foundation of growth. Spend time reflecting on your past relationships and your current emotional reactions. Are you often anxious when your partner doesn't text back right away? Do you shut down when things get too emotionally intense? Reflecting on these patterns will help you understand your attachment style more clearly.

2. **Open Communication**: Communication is essential in any relationship, but it's especially important when navigating attachment issues. If you're feeling anxious or avoidant, talk about it openly with your partner. For instance, if Leila notices that Khalid is pulling away, instead of assuming he's losing interest, she might say, "I notice you seem distant when we talk about our emotions. What's going on?" This invites an open conversation about what's happening and how both partners can work together to find solutions.

3. **Patience and Empathy**: When conflicts arise, remember that they're often tied to deeper emotional fears or wounds. When Ahmed gets emotionally distant after a tough day at work, Sara might remind herself that this is his avoidant style showing up, and it's not about her personally. Instead of taking it personally, she can approach the situation with compassion and patience. Khalid and Leila, for example, might have an agreement: when Khalid feels the urge to withdraw, he'll let Leila know he needs space, rather than shutting down completely.

4. **Building Emotional Resilience**: Working through attachment issues is not a one-time fix. It's an ongoing process that involves patience and emotional resilience. Practicing mindfulness, working through past trauma, and prioritizing self-care can all help you build emotional resilience. This resilience makes it easier to face difficult emotions without feeling overwhelmed or withdrawing.

5. **Seeking Therapy or Support**: Sometimes, working through attachment issues requires extra help. Relationship coaching, couples therapy or individual therapy can provide valuable tools to address deeply rooted attachment wounds. It's important to remember that

seeking help is not a sign of weakness but a step toward healing. Hassan and Noura, for instance, went to therapy to understand how their attachment styles were impacting their communication. They learned practical strategies to connect more deeply, improve their emotional communication, and create a more secure relationship.

Conclusion: Building Stronger Connections

Understanding attachment theory is like discovering the key to unlocking a healthier, more fulfilling relationship. By learning about your own attachment style—and that of your partner—you gain insight into your emotional responses, your needs, and the areas that may need healing. It also opens up a pathway for communication, empathy, and growth.

By making small changes and building awareness, you can transform the dynamics in your relationship and create a space where both partners feel loved, safe, and understood. Remember, you're not alone on this journey. Whether you're secure, anxious, avoidant, or disorganized, you have the power to grow and change—together.

Chapter Thirty-One

Hormones and Their Hidden Impact

In the intricate dance of human relationships, hormones play a critical yet often underestimated role. These chemical messengers influence our moods, behaviors, desires, and how we connect with others. For couples, understanding the impact of hormones like testosterone, estrogen, oxytocin, vasopressin, and dopamine can shed light on complex emotional and physical dynamics, offering a framework for improving communication, intimacy, and overall relationship satisfaction. Experts like Dr. John Gray and Dr. Sue Johnson highlight how understanding hormonal influences helps partners recognize each other's unique needs, easing relationship strains and deepening mutual empathy.

Understanding Male and Female Hormones

Hormones are substances produced by glands in the endocrine system that regulate various bodily functions, including emotions, sexual behavior, and social bonding. Testosterone and estrogen are often seen as the primary male and female hormones, respectively, though men and women both produce these hormones in different quantities and experience their effects uniquely. Additionally, hormones such as oxytocin, vasopressin, and dopamine also contribute to how we relate to and bond with others.

Testosterone influences drive, sexual desire, and assertiveness. In relationships, this may show up as increased confidence or competitiveness—especially in moments of stress, conflict, or intimacy. However, behavior is shaped by more than hormones alone, including emotional maturity, attachment patterns, and communication skills. Estrogen on the other hand is associated with emotional sensitivity and nurturing behavior. It enhances mood regulation and social bonding, often supporting emotional expression, empathy, and connection in close relationships. Understanding these differences allows couples to appreciate why they may approach situations differently. It fosters patience and understanding, especially in challenging times. For example, when men are under stress, their testosterone levels may actually drop while cortisol (the stress hormone) rises, which can lead to behaviors like emotional withdrawal, irritability, or shutdown—often misinterpreted by their partners as disinterest or unavailability.

What's the Science Behind This?

- Cortisol, the body's main stress hormone, tends to suppress testosterone production in stressful situations.

- Lower testosterone levels combined with high cortisol can result in men appearing less emotionally responsive, more withdrawn, or less motivated to engage—not because they don't care, but because their body is in a physiological state of overload or shutdown.

- This is often misunderstood by partners as being cold or disconnected, when in fact, it may be a stress-related coping mechanism.

Testosterone: The Male Hormone and Its Impact on Relationships

Testosterone, often referred to as the "male hormone," significantly influences men's libido, motivation, confidence, assertiveness, and physical energy. Higher testosterone levels are associated with increased sexual desire, emotional boldness, and a drive to lead or protect—traits that may align with traditional roles as providers and protectors, as discussed by researchers like Dr. John Gray.

However, the same hormone that fuels strength and drive can also introduce challenges. In certain cases, elevated testosterone—especially under chronic stress—may contribute to impatience or emotional withdrawal, potentially straining communication.

On the other hand, men are sensitive to drops in testosterone, which can occur due to aging, stress, lack of exercise, poor sleep, or unhealthy diets. Lower levels may lead to reduced libido, fatigue, mood swings, and even emotional disconnection. This can affect both physical intimacy and day-to-day emotional availability.

Couples can support hormonal balance and emotional connection by encouraging testosterone-supportive habits such as strength training, nutrient-rich diets, quality sleep, and stress management. Recognizing testosterone's dual role—in both energy and vulnerability—can foster deeper communication, empathy, and long-term relational resilience.

Estrogen: The Female Hormone and Its Role in Relationships

Estrogen, often referred to as the "female hormone," influences mood regulation, emotional sensitivity, and nurturing behaviors. It plays a central role in shaping relational needs—particularly when it comes to emotional closeness and connection. During the follicular phase of the menstrual cycle, when estrogen levels are rising, many women experience increased energy, improved mood, and heightened empathy. These changes can enhance a woman's capacity for emotional engagement and connection, making her more attuned and responsive to her partner's emotional needs.

This builds to a peak during the ovulation phase, typically around the midpoint of the cycle, when estrogen is at its highest and a small rise in testosterone also occurs. During this time, many women report a greater desire for intimacy and closeness, as both emotional and physical bonding are naturally heightened. Increased confidence, verbal expressiveness, and a boost in libido often accompany this stage, creating a unique window for emotional and romantic connection. While Dr. Sue Johnson does not focus specifically on hormonal cycles, her research in *Emotionally Focused Therapy* highlights the value of emotional responsiveness and bonding—something estrogen-rich phases may biologically support.

However, estrogen levels do not remain constant. During the luteal phase (after ovulation) and especially during menstruation, pregnancy, or menopause, estrogen may fluctuate or drop significantly. These hormonal shifts can contribute to mood swings, irritability, decreased libido, or emotional vulnerability. At these times, many women feel more sensitive, tired, or even misunderstood, which may cause friction in relationships—particularly if their partners are unaware of these natural hormonal rhythms.

For men and partners, understanding the ebb and flow of estrogen throughout the cycle can be a powerful tool for compassion and support. Rather than taking emotional shifts personally, partners can recognize them as biological transitions and respond with empathy, patience, and reassurance. This is especially important during pregnancy or menopause, when hormonal changes can also affect body image, self-esteem, and overall mental health.

Supportive communication, emotional attunement, and expressions of love and safety during these times can greatly strengthen the relationship.

In short, estrogen doesn't just shape a woman's body—it also plays a powerful role in shaping her emotional world, relational rhythms, and need for connection. When both partners understand and adapt to these changes together, it opens the door to deeper bonding, mutual empathy, and long-term emotional intimacy.

The Risk of Hormonal Imbalances

Hormonal imbalances can affect both physical well-being and relationship dynamics. In men, low testosterone levels are linked to decreased libido, fatigue, irritability, and symptoms of depression—all of which can strain intimacy and communication. Likewise, women experiencing low estrogen—such as during menopause, postpartum, or hormonal disorders—may face reduced sexual desire, mood fluctuations, and sleep disturbances, impacting their emotional engagement in the relationship.

Addressing these challenges often involves lifestyle improvements like exercise, nutrition, and stress reduction. In some cases, medical interventions such as hormone replacement therapy (HRT or TRT) may be recommended. However, couples should remain informed and cautious, as synthetic hormones can have side effects, including mood changes or cardiovascular risks, especially in those with preexisting conditions.

Importantly, hormonal imbalances are closely tied to mental health conditions like anxiety and depression—both of which strongly influence relationship satisfaction. Research shows that prolonged imbalances can lead to emotional disconnection, decreased empathy, and feelings of isolation if left untreated. By being proactive about hormonal health and seeking professional guidance when needed, couples can foster greater emotional balance, reduce conflict, and maintain deeper relational connection.

Women, Hormones, and Happiness

The connection between hormones and emotional well-being in women is well-established. Hormones such as estrogen and progesterone play vital roles in mood regulation, energy levels, and overall happiness. When these hormones are balanced, women tend to experience greater emotional stability and resilience, which positively influences how they connect with and respond to their partners.

However, during hormonal fluctuations—such as those occurring across the menstrual cycle, during pregnancy, postpartum, or menopause—women may experience mood swings, anxiety, or emotional sensitivity. These shifts can affect both personal well-being and relationship dynamics, especially when misunderstood.

While Dr. Sue Johnson's work doesn't focus directly on hormonal science, her findings in *Emotionally Focused Therapy* emphasize that secure emotional bonds can stabilize the effects of emotional vulnerability. Women who feel emotionally supported, validated, and understood by their partners are better equipped to navigate hormonal ups and downs. In turn, partners who learn to recognize and gently adapt to these cycles help cultivate a compassionate and emotionally safe environment where happiness and connection can thrive.

Stress, Depression, and Hormones in Relationships

Stress and depression can lead to significant hormonal changes, impacting both men and women's ability to stay connected. Chronic stress elevates cortisol levels, which can interfere with testosterone and estrogen, leading to mood swings, irritability, and decreased libido. These hormonal disruptions create a feedback loop where stress further strains the relationship, exacerbating issues and reducing overall relationship satisfaction.

For instance, a study in the *Journal of Relationship Research* revealed that couples who engage in mindfulness and exercise reported fewer stress-related hormonal imbalances and a deeper connection with their partners. Couples can benefit from stress-reducing techniques such as yoga, meditation, and shared physical activities. Additionally, scheduling regular "de-stress" conversations—where both partners openly discuss their worries and anxieties—can create a safe space for each partner, reducing the likelihood of stress-induced hormonal imbalances.

The Role of Oxytocin, Vasopressin, Dopamine, and Endorphins in Relationships

While testosterone and estrogen influence fundamental gender-specific traits, other hormones like oxytocin, vasopressin, dopamine, and endorphins play powerful roles in emotional bonding and relationship satisfaction.

- **Oxytocin: The Bonding Hormone** Often called the "love hormone," oxytocin is released during physical touch, such as hugging or intimate moments, fostering trust, attachment, and emotional intimacy. Higher levels of oxytocin are associated with stronger feelings of security within relationships. Couples can consciously increase oxytocin by prioritizing affectionate gestures, regular touch, and intimate conversations. Oxytocin also lowers stress levels, creating a more relaxed and positive environment for both partners.

- **Vasopressin: The Loyalty Hormone** Vasopressin is associated with feelings of loyalty and protectiveness, particularly in men. This hormone contributes to monogamous tendencies and the motivation to care for and provide for loved ones. In relationships, vasopressin can reinforce commitment, fostering a sense of responsibility and dedication between partners. Small acts of devotion, such as being attentive to a partner's needs or expressing words of appreciation, can further enhance vasopressin levels and build a stronger sense of loyalty within the relationship.

- **Dopamine: The Reward Hormone** Dopamine is a critical part of the brain's reward system, associated with pleasure and satisfaction. In relationships, dopamine plays a role in excitement and passion, especially in the early stages of romance. To keep dopamine levels high, couples can explore new activities together, travel, or engage in shared hobbies. These experiences create positive associations and keep the relationship feeling fresh and rewarding.

- **Endorphins: The Happiness Hormones** Endorphins act as natural pain relievers and mood enhancers, fostering feelings of relaxation and contentment. Couples who engage in activities like laughter, physical exercise, or other enjoyable experiences together release endorphins, creating a positive, stress-free environment that strengthens emotional bonds.

The Hormonal Divide—Why Men and Women Bond Differently After Sex

The Hidden Science of Sexual Bonding

In the modern dating world, casual sex and multiple partners are often framed as a form of personal liberation. But beneath this cultural narrative lies a profound biological reality: men and women bond differently after sex, and the consequences of ignoring these differences can be emotionally and relationally damaging. Understanding the hormonal dynamics at play can illuminate why short-term intimacy often leads to long-term heartache—especially for women.

Oxytocin and Vasopressin: The Brain's Bonding Chemicals

When it comes to bonding, two neurochemicals take center stage: oxytocin and vasopressin. Oxytocin, often dubbed the "love hormone," is especially influential in women. It's released in large quantities during physical affection, orgasm, skin-to-skin contact, and intimate conversation. Oxytocin fosters trust, emotional openness, and vulnerability. Women have a higher density of oxytocin receptors in brain regions associated with emotion and memory, making them biologically predisposed to bond through sexual activity—even in the absence of emotional commitment.

Vasopressin, by contrast, plays a stronger role in men. Sometimes called the "monogamy molecule," vasopressin is released post-orgasm and is associated with loyalty, protectiveness, and territorial bonding. However, vasopressin bonding is conditional. It's more likely to be activated when sex occurs in the context of emotional safety and relationship intention. If sex is purely physical or emotionally detached—as in a one-night stand—vasopressin levels may spike briefly but won't trigger the deeper bonding that supports long-term attachment.

This difference leads to what researchers call a neurochemical mismatch: the woman bonds due to oxytocin, while the man may not due to a lack of vasopressin response. The result? Emotional disconnection, confusion, and eventual pain.

Emotional Fallout: Why Women Are More Vulnerable After Casual Sex

A woman's oxytocin-rich response means she's more likely to feel emotionally attached after sex, regardless of the relational context. Studies confirm this: a 2012 study published in the *Journal of Sex Research* found that women were significantly more likely than men to experience feelings of regret, sadness, or depression after casual sexual encounters. These emotional aftershocks are not mere psychological quirks; they're biologically rooted.

Furthermore, when women repeatedly bond and break those bonds through multiple sexual relationships, oxytocin's power begins to erode. This phenomenon, known as pair-bonding fatigue, weakens a woman's future ability to fully attach in long-term relationships. Just like superglue loses its grip after being peeled off and reused, so too does the human heart.

Men, Casual Sex, and the Lack of Emotional Bonding

For men, the story is different. Because vasopressin's bonding effect is often muted during casual sex—especially when emotional intimacy is lacking—men may walk away from sexual encounters emotionally unaffected. Testosterone, which rises during arousal and conquest-oriented behavior, can suppress vasopressin's bonding effects. This biological wiring helps explain why some men are able to detach quickly after sex, while their female partners struggle with lingering emotional connections.

Importantly, this doesn't mean men are incapable of bonding. On the contrary, vasopressin is activated when men feel emotionally safe, respected, and invested in the relationship. In monogamous, committed contexts (such as marriage) vasopressin helps solidify lasting emotional ties and loyalty.

The Long-Term Damage of Sexual "Freedom"

Culturally, many have bought into the idea that more sexual experiences equal more empowerment. But the science says otherwise. Multiple studies, including one in the *Archives of Sexual Behavior*, have shown that individuals with a higher number of sexual partners—especially women—report higher levels of anxiety, depression, emotional numbness, and difficulty forming long-term romantic attachments.

Sex without commitment rewires the brain's bonding system in ways that undermine trust, intimacy, and satisfaction. In essence, the emotional wiring that was designed to help humans thrive in lifelong pair bonds is being short-circuited by temporary pleasure.

Monogamy: A Neurochemical Safe Haven

The hormones involved in sex—oxytocin, vasopressin, dopamine, and endorphins—were designed not for casual encounters but for creating and sustaining deep, exclusive emotional bonds. Dopamine brings pleasure and reward, endorphins create a sense of calm and satisfaction, oxytocin promotes emotional closeness, and vasopressin reinforces loyalty and protectiveness. These chemicals are optimized in environments of emotional safety, continuity, and commitment—like marriage.

From both a scientific and relational perspective, monogamy is not just a moral or spiritual ideal—it is the most neurologically stable and emotionally fulfilling path for sexual expression.

Sexual Freedom vs. Emotional Cost

The data is clear: casual sex comes at a cost, and the cost is disproportionately paid by women. While men may emerge physically satisfied but emotionally neutral, women are often left emotionally entangled without reciprocity. Over time, this creates patterns of hurt, mistrust, and emotional detachment that sabotage future relationships.

Understanding these biological truths doesn't take away freedom—it informs it. True freedom is making choices that align with your long-term emotional and relational well-being. In this light, monogamous, emotionally bonded sexual relationships are not restrictive—they are liberating.

Lifestyle, Hormones, and Relationship Health

The Importance of Physical Activity: Regular physical activity not only improves physical health but also has a direct impact on hormones that benefit relationships. Exercise increases testosterone and endorphin levels, contributing to greater libido, energy, and emotional resilience. Dr. Johnson advocates for couples to exercise together, as shared activities foster both physical and emotional closeness.

Nutrition and Hormone Balance: A balanced diet rich in essential fats, antioxidants, and protein supports healthy hormone production. Omega-3 fatty acids, in particular, are linked to improved mood and cognitive health, while antioxidants reduce oxidative stress. Couples can bond over preparing and sharing healthy meals, creating a nurturing environment that supports both hormonal health and relationship satisfaction.

Sleep and Stress Management: Adequate sleep is vital for maintaining hormonal stability. Sleep deprivation can disrupt cortisol, testosterone, and estrogen, leading to mood swings and reduced relationship satisfaction. Establishing good sleep hygiene promotes better hormonal balance, and when combined with stress management practices, helps create a more peaceful, loving home environment.

Understanding the Three Stages of the Menstrual Cycle

The menstrual cycle is a complex and dynamic process that unfolds over an average of 28 days, although the cycle length can vary between individuals. Each month, hormonal fluctuations across three distinct phases—menstruation, ovulation, and the luteal phase—significantly impact not only a woman's physical and emotional state but also her relationship dynamics. These changes influence how women interact with partners, their energy levels, emotional sensitivity, and even their libido. Psychologists and relationship experts stress that understanding these stages can help partners foster empathy, communication, and support, transforming potentially challenging times into opportunities for greater connection.

Dr. Alexandra Solomon, a clinical psychologist and author known for her work on relationships, highlights that "when partners understand each other's unique cycles, it enables them to be more patient, compassionate, and responsive." Similarly, Dr. Lara Briden, a naturopathic doctor specializing in women's health, explains that the menstrual cycle is not just a reproductive process but a crucial part of a woman's emotional and mental health. "Each phase brings its own unique hormonal landscape that affects a woman's mood, energy, and libido," Dr. Briden notes. "When couples recognize these patterns, they can anticipate and respect these changes, which fosters emotional harmony and reduces unnecessary conflicts."

Below, we delve into the specifics of each phase—menstruation, ovulation, and the luteal phase—analyzing how each impacts emotions, physical sensations, behavior, and relationships, with expert insights on how couples can navigate these cycles together.

Menstruation: The Renewal Phase

The first phase, menstruation, begins on the first day of a woman's period and typically lasts 3–7 days. During menstruation, the body sheds the uterine lining, and hormone levels, particularly estrogen and progesterone, are at their lowest. This drop in hormones can lead to symptoms such as fatigue, cramps, bloating, and increased sensitivity. The physiological demands during this time mean many women experience lower energy, increased introspection, and sometimes irritability or mood swings. According to Dr. John Gottman's research, when partners respond empathetically to one another's physical and emotional needs, it helps foster trust and emotional safety. This kind of responsiveness creates a nurturing environment in which a woman feels emotionally supported, valued, and deeply understood by her partner.

Psychologically, menstruation can be a time of emotional renewal and inner reflection. Dr. Christiane Northrup, a well-known voice in women's health, explains that menstruation often marks a natural shift inward, where many women become more attuned to their emotional and physical needs. During this phase, it's common for women to feel a desire for solitude or quiet, which can sometimes be misinterpreted by their partners as disinterest or emotional withdrawal. Understanding this introspective tendency can help couples avoid unnecessary tension. Instead of pushing for connection through high-energy activities, partners can offer support by engaging in calming, low-pressure moments—like watching a movie together or simply sharing quiet time at home.

Communication during menstruation plays a vital role in maintaining emotional connection. Partners can offer meaningful support by acknowledging the physical and emotional discomfort that often accompanies this time. Simple, thoughtful gestures—like preparing a warm drink, offering a gentle massage, or simply being present with compassion—can go a long way in making a woman feel seen and cared for. Dr. Alexandra Solomon, a respected relationship therapist, emphasizes that small, empathetic acts during moments of vulnerability contribute significantly to emotional intimacy. When partners show up with kindness and responsiveness, they reinforce trust and strengthen the relational bond during a phase that can otherwise feel isolating.

Ovulation: The High-Energy, High-Connection Phase

Ovulation marks the midpoint of the menstrual cycle and is often considered the peak of a woman's physical, emotional, and social energy. Typically occurring around day 14 in a 28-day cycle (though timing can vary), this phase is characterized by a surge in estrogen and luteinizing hormone (LH), triggering the release of an egg. As a result, many women experience increased libido, elevated mood, and a heightened desire for connection and intimacy.

Biological anthropologist Dr. Helen Fisher has discussed how ovulation is closely tied to fertility signaling, and that during this time, women may naturally become more socially and romantically responsive.

Women in the ovulatory phase often feel more outgoing, energetic, and optimistic. Physically, some may notice subtle enhancements in appearance, such as clearer skin or a sense of radiance, which can contribute to a boost in self-confidence. Within a relationship, this phase can be marked by increased sexual interest and emotional openness. Relationship expert Dr. Laura Berman has suggested that ovulation may be an opportune time for couples to engage in date nights, meaningful conversations, or shared activities that foster deeper connection, thanks to the natural uplift in mood and vitality.

Research from evolutionary psychology, including the work of Dr. Martie Haselton, indicates that men may subconsciously respond to their partner's ovulation through cues like scent, voice tone, or flirtatious behavior. These subtle shifts can enhance male attraction and deepen mutual desire, often increasing relational closeness during this time.

However, while ovulation brings a surge of energy and positivity, it can also come with heightened emotional needs and expectations around physical and emotional intimacy. When these needs are unmet, frustration or emotional disconnection may follow. Relationship therapist Dr. Alexandra Solomon emphasizes the importance of proactive communication during this time. Encouraging open dialogue about intimacy and emotional needs can help couples align better, reduce misunderstandings, and strengthen overall satisfaction in the relationship.

Luteal Phase: The Reflective, Preparatory Phase

The luteal phase begins after ovulation and continues until the start of menstruation, typically spanning days 15–28 of the menstrual cycle. During this time, progesterone levels rise in preparation for a potential pregnancy. This hormonal shift can initially have a calming effect, but as the phase progresses, many women begin to experience symptoms commonly associated with premenstrual syndrome (PMS). These include irritability, anxiety, mood swings, fatigue, and physical discomfort such as bloating or breast tenderness. Women's health expert Dr. Jessica Drummond has noted that this phase often brings a heightened awareness of physical and emotional needs, leading to greater introspection and emotional sensitivity.

Emotional Sensitivity and Relationship Dynamics

Emotionally, the luteal phase often prompts deeper reflection. Women may become more attuned to relational dynamics and may require more emotional support during this time. Relationship psychologist Dr. Sue Johnson encourages couples to pay special attention to each other's emotional needs during this phase, as heightened sensitivity and vulnerability can lead to misunderstandings if not approached with empathy. When partners respond with reassurance and emotional validation, it becomes easier to maintain closeness and trust, even in moments of emotional turbulence.

From a relational standpoint, the luteal phase presents both challenges and opportunities. According to women's health advocate Dr. Christiane Northrup, this is a particularly valuable time for partners to demonstrate patience and compassion. When PMS symptoms intensify, partners who approach with understanding rather than frustration can help reduce tension and increase relational safety. Being aware of these physiological shifts can improve communication and prevent conflict escalation.

Physical symptoms like disrupted sleep, lowered energy, or increased discomfort may also contribute to emotional fluctuations and reduced stress tolerance. Dr. John Gottman's research supports the idea that when partners listen empathically—to focus on understanding rather than problem-solving—it strengthens emotional bonds. This approach creates an atmosphere of mutual respect and teamwork, especially during hormonally sensitive phases.

Flexibility in shared routines can also go a long way. Relationship therapist Dr. Alexandra Solomon encourages couples to openly communicate about how to adapt schedules or responsibilities during the luteal phase. When partners offer small acts of consideration—like lightening the load at home, offering space for rest, or simply showing patience—it affirms a sense of being seen and cared for. These moments of intentional support can significantly enhance emotional connection and long-term relationship satisfaction.

Chapter Thirty-Two

The Art of Marriage Communication

Communication is the heartbeat of every marriage. Without it, even the deepest love can struggle to find its way through the noise of life's stresses and challenges. But when communication is nurtured, it becomes the bridge that allows couples to truly understand, support, and love one another. Effective communication doesn't just happen—it is cultivated through intention, effort, and, most importantly, a commitment to the relationship. In this chapter, we explore science-backed strategies from leading relationship experts to help couples enhance their communication skills, deepen their emotional connection, and strengthen their bond.

The Gottman Approach: Building a Foundation of Trust and Understanding

Dr. John Gottman, one of the most prominent figures in relationship science, has dedicated decades to understanding what makes marriages thrive. Through his research at the Gottman Institute, he has identified several key principles that form the foundation of healthy communication. His methods have revolutionized the way therapists and couples alike approach relationship dynamics, focusing on not just resolving conflict, but preventing it through positive communication practices.

The "Four Horsemen" of Poor Communication

According to Gottman, there are four negative communication patterns that can predict the downfall of a relationship if left unchecked: criticism, contempt, defensiveness, and stonewalling. Each of these behaviors, if not addressed, creates emotional distance and breaks down trust. These "Four Horsemen" are the antithesis of healthy communication, often spiraling into cycles of negativity that can be difficult to escape without intervention.

1. **Criticism** attacks a partner's character rather than addressing a specific behavior. Instead of saying, "You never help around the house," try, "I feel overwhelmed when the chores pile up. Can we find a way to share the load?" This shift moves away from blame and toward constructive collaboration, encouraging problem-solving instead of creating defensiveness.

2. **Contempt** is considered the most dangerous of the Four Horsemen, as it involves disrespect and a sense of superiority. Gottman explains that contempt can manifest in sneering, mocking, or eye-rolling. Over time, contempt erodes the emotional safety necessary for a relationship to flourish. Replacing contempt with genuine appreciation is key. Focusing on your partner's positive qualities, however small, can help rebuild trust and respect. For example, instead of saying, "You never appreciate what I do," one might say, "I really appreciate it when you help with the kids—thank you for that."

3. **Defensiveness** occurs when one partner reacts to perceived criticism by making excuses or shifting blame. This often leads to a cycle of escalation, where both partners feel misunderstood. A healthier approach is to take responsibility where possible and validate your partner's feelings. For example, instead of responding with, "Well, you always do this too," one could say, "I see how my actions made you feel, and I want to make it right."

4. **Stonewalling** happens when one partner withdraws emotionally, often to avoid conflict. When we shut down or tune out during a disagreement, it signals to our partner that we are not emotionally available or willing to engage. Gottman suggests that when feeling overwhelmed, it's okay to take a break, but communicate that you will return to the conversation once calm. This ensures that the partner feels acknowledged and not abandoned in the midst of the conversation.

By learning to recognize and replace these behaviors with constructive communication, couples can rebuild trust and prevent conflict from becoming destructive. Over time, this proactive approach can transform how both partners interact, creating a healthier, more resilient relationship.

The Power of Soft Startups

One of the key communication strategies Gottman advocates is the use of gentle startups. How a conversation begins often determines its outcome. If you approach your partner with harshness or blame, it's likely that they'll respond with defensiveness. On the other hand, starting a conversation gently and with respect can lead to more productive dialogue.

Starting a conversation with "I feel" rather than "You always" or "You never" softens the interaction and opens the door for collaboration rather than confrontation. For example, instead of starting with, "You never listen to me," try saying, "I feel hurt when I don't feel heard, and I'd really like us to talk about that." This sets the tone for a conversation based on openness rather than blame, allowing both partners to engage constructively.

Turning Toward Instead of Away

Throughout daily life, couples make what Gottman calls "bids for connection"—small gestures that invite engagement, whether it's sharing a funny story, asking for help, or seeking comfort. Healthy couples turn toward these bids for connection, responding with interest and care. The difference between turning toward, away, or against each other often lies in these small, everyday moments.

For example, when a partner shares a stressful situation at work, a turn toward would be to actively listen and express empathy, such as saying, "That sounds tough, tell me more about it." A turn away might look like distraction or non-engagement, such as scrolling through your phone, which signals that your partner's emotional experience is not a priority at the moment. Couples who regularly turn toward each other, rather than away or against each other, build a reservoir of goodwill that helps them weather conflicts more smoothly.

Dr. Sue Johnson and EFT: Strengthening Emotional Bonds

Dr. Sue Johnson, the creator of Emotionally Focused Therapy (EFT), emphasizes that at the core of every conflict is a longing for emotional safety and connection. According to Johnson, it's not about what couples are fighting over but about how connected they feel in the moment. When couples understand and express their emotional needs, they can create a more secure attachment. Johnson's research underscores the importance of attachment in relationships, drawing on the same principles that guide parent-child bonding, to promote emotional safety between romantic partners.

Creating Secure Attachment

One of the main principles of EFT is helping couples move from a cycle of conflict to a cycle of secure attachment. Johnson identifies three critical questions that partners unconsciously ask during times of conflict:

1. **Are you there for me?**
2. **Can I depend on you?**
3. **Do I matter to you?**

If the answers to these questions are unclear or negative, emotional disconnection can follow. Insecure attachment leads to feelings of anxiety, fear, and uncertainty, which may manifest as anger or withdrawal in relationships. Johnson's work teaches couples how to create safety by being present, attuned, and responsive to each other's emotional needs. This is done through the practice of "emotion coaching," where partners learn to express vulnerability rather than blame, leading to deeper emotional intimacy.

One real-life example of EFT in action involves a couple, Fatima and Ahmed, who had been struggling with frequent arguments about household responsibilities. Fatima often felt ignored when Ahmed didn't help out as much as she thought he should, while Ahmed felt attacked whenever Fatima brought it up. Through EFT, they learned to express their feelings of neglect in softer, more vulnerable ways. Fatima communicated that she felt overwhelmed and unimportant when her needs weren't met, while Ahmed expressed his fear of being judged or seen as careless. By acknowledging each other's emotional experiences, they were able to resolve conflicts without escalating into anger or resentment, building a more secure and compassionate attachment.

The Power of Vulnerability

Vulnerability is at the heart of emotional connection. Johnson's method encourages couples to express their deepest fears and needs rather than hiding behind anger or defensiveness. Vulnerability allows for a sense of emotional exposure, but it's also the gateway to deeper intimacy.

This could mean saying, "I'm scared that I'm not important to you," instead of reacting with accusations like, "You never spend time with me." When vulnerability is met with empathy rather than dismissal, it strengthens the emotional bond between partners. Vulnerability is not about weakness; it's about creating space for your partner to show up and be there for you in a way that affirms your emotional needs.

The Dance of Connection

Johnson likens the interaction between couples to a dance. When one partner moves, the other responds. If this dance is filled with misunderstandings, it can become a cycle of hurt. By learning to recognize and understand each other's steps—be it through words, tone, or body language—couples can change the rhythm of their interactions.

EFT helps couples slow down their interactions, explore underlying emotions, and reconnect on a deeper level. The dance of connection is fluid, with each partner adjusting their movements to meet the emotional needs of the other. When one partner steps forward with vulnerability, the other can step forward with empathy and validation, creating a harmonious flow of communication that strengthens the relationship.

Active Listening: Creating Space for Connection

While many people assume that communication is about speaking, listening is often the most powerful tool for building a deeper connection. Active listening goes beyond simply hearing the words your partner says—it involves truly understanding the emotions and needs behind those words.

The Practice of Reflective Listening

One of the most effective active listening techniques is reflective listening, where you paraphrase what your partner has said to show that you've heard them. This is especially powerful in moments of tension. For example, if your partner says, "I feel like you're always too busy for me," you could respond,

"It sounds like you feel neglected and that my schedule makes you feel unimportant." This technique helps partners feel validated and understood, reducing defensiveness and increasing openness.

Nonverbal Cues Matter

Active listening is about more than words—it's also about body language. Eye contact, nodding, and leaning in can signal that you are fully present with your partner. By eliminating distractions, such as phones or TVs, you show that their words and feelings are your priority in that moment. The emotional impact of nonverbal cues cannot be overstated; they often communicate much more than words alone.

Using "I" Statements

When expressing your feelings, it's easy to fall into the trap of pointing fingers. "You always…" or "You never…" statements often trigger defensiveness. Instead, use "I" statements to express how you feel and what you need. For example, "I feel overwhelmed when the house is messy, and I'd appreciate some help" is much more constructive than, "You never clean up around here."

Nonviolent Communication: Speaking with Compassion

Developed by psychologist Marshall Rosenberg, Nonviolent Communication (NVC) emphasizes the importance of expressing needs and feelings without blame or criticism. NVC encourages couples to focus on four key components when communicating:

1. **Observation:** This means focusing on the situation or behavior, rather than jumping to conclusions or making judgments. For instance, instead of saying, "You never listen to me," one might observe, "I've noticed that when we're talking, I sometimes feel like my words don't seem to get your attention."

2. **Feelings:** Express your emotions without linking them to specific behaviors. Instead of saying, "You make me feel ignored," you could say, "I feel upset and unheard when I don't feel like you're paying attention to me."

3. **Needs**: Often, conflict arises when we feel our fundamental needs aren't being met. Rather than making accusations, try to express the underlying need. For example, "I need to feel connected and valued when we're together," instead of, "You never care about spending time with me."

4. **Requests**: The final step is making a clear, positive request. Rather than demanding or insisting, a request invites collaboration. For example, "Could we try turning off our phones when we have dinner together to make it easier for us to connect?"

NVC fosters empathy by helping both partners focus on their needs rather than on blame. This shift enables the relationship to thrive, as it invites understanding rather than defensiveness.

An example could be Aisha and Bilal, a married couple who were constantly arguing over their evening routines. Aisha often felt that Bilal was neglecting her when he spent hours on his phone, which made her feel unimportant. Instead of reacting with frustration and accusing him of neglect, Aisha practiced NVC by calmly sharing how she felt, saying, "I feel disconnected when we don't talk during the evening." Bilal responded by acknowledging her feelings and expressing his own need for relaxation after a long day. They were able to agree on a compromise where they designated phone-free times to reconnect, fostering more understanding and a sense of partnership.

The Love Languages: Speaking the Right Dialect of Love

Dr. Gary Chapman's concept of the Five Love Languages has been revolutionary in helping couples understand how they express and receive love. It's a simple yet profound idea: we all have a primary love language, and when partners speak each other's language, communication becomes smoother, affection feels more genuine, and emotional intimacy grows.

The five love languages are:

1. **Words of Affirmation**: Some people feel most loved when they hear verbal expressions of affection, encouragement, and appreciation. Compliments, praise, and kind words go a long way in building emotional connection.

2. **Acts of Service**: For others, love is demonstrated through actions. Doing things to ease your partner's burden—whether it's helping with household chores or taking care of something on their to-do list—speaks volumes.

3. **Receiving Gifts**: For people with this love language, a thoughtful gift is a meaningful expression of love. It doesn't have to be extravagant; a small, meaningful token can show your partner that you care and are thinking of them.

4. **Quality Time**: This love language revolves around giving your partner your undivided attention. It's not just about spending time together—it's about making that time meaningful and focused, whether it's through conversation, shared activities, or simply being present.

5. **Physical Touch**: Some people feel most loved through physical affection, such as hugs, holding hands, or intimacy. Physical touch can communicate love in ways words can't.

When a couple speaks different love languages, misunderstandings can arise. A partner who values words of affirmation may feel neglected if their spouse expresses love through acts of service instead. Recognizing these differences and learning to speak each other's love language can strengthen the bond between partners.

Consider Amina and Zayd, who had been struggling to express their love in a way the other understood. Amina's primary love language was words of affirmation, and she often told Zayd how much she appreciated him. However, Zayd's love language was acts of service, and he felt loved when Amina helped him with projects or took care of practical matters. After learning about the love languages, they made an effort to speak each other's language. Amina began to show her love through actions, like assisting Zayd with household tasks, while Zayd became more expressive with his words, offering compliments and affirmations. This mutual understanding created a deeper emotional connection and a more fulfilling relationship.

Empathy as the Cornerstone of Communication

At the heart of every healthy relationship is empathy. Empathy is the ability to step into your partner's shoes, see things from their perspective, and respond with compassion. It's more than just understanding their words—it's about feeling their emotions and validating their experience. Empathy fosters connection because it allows your partner to feel seen and heard in the deepest sense.

When couples approach each conversation with empathy, they create a safe space where both partners feel valued. This builds trust and emotional security, making it easier to resolve conflicts and strengthen the relationship. Empathy is the bridge between emotional safety and emotional intimacy.

For example, imagine Yusuf and Layla, who have been in a long-term relationship. Yusuf comes home from work feeling stressed and overwhelmed, but instead of dismissing his emotions, Layla listens attentively and responds with, "I can see that you had a tough day. I'm here for you." This simple act of empathy helps Yusuf feel understood and supported, which deepens their emotional connection.

Conversely, if Layla had responded with frustration or indifference, it could have created emotional distance. Empathy is a skill that requires practice, but when nurtured, it can be the key to navigating both the mundane and challenging moments of marriage with grace.

Empowering Your Marriage Through Communication

Communication is the key that unlocks the potential of any relationship. By incorporating these science-backed methods—whether it's Gottman's principles, Sue Johnson's focus on emotional connection, active listening, or understanding love languages—couples can create an environment where communication flows easily, conflicts are resolved with love and empathy, and emotional intimacy thrives.

But communication is not a one-time fix; it's an ongoing process that requires practice and attention. Like any skill, it improves with time, patience, and commitment. Empowering your marriage through communication is not about perfection; it's about making small, meaningful changes that foster understanding, connection, and trust. Every couple faces challenges, but by being intentional with your words, listening with empathy, and expressing your emotions with vulnerability, you can build a stronger, more resilient relationship that withstands the test of time.

Real-life examples from couples who have put these practices into play highlight the transformative power of intentional communication. Consider

Zaynab and Omar, who had been married for 10 years but struggled with feeling disconnected. They realized that while they were great at communicating logistical things like schedules or finances, they lacked emotional communication. By implementing techniques like reflective listening and focusing on vulnerability, they not only improved their communication but also reignited the emotional spark in their marriage.

Through the practice of active listening, soft startups, and speaking each other's love language, they learned how to communicate with more compassion and less defensiveness. They started recognizing their bids for connection, whether it was a playful comment or a request for help, and responded with warmth and attentiveness. Their marriage became a partnership, not just a series of transactions.

The Ongoing Journey of Communication

The journey of improving communication in marriage is ongoing. There will be days when you feel like you've got it all figured out, and other days when misunderstandings or conflicts resurface. But each conversation, each effort to communicate with love, patience, and understanding, strengthens your relationship and brings you closer together.

Remember, no one gets communication perfect, and it's not about achieving flawlessness. It's about being present for one another, showing empathy, and being committed to growth. Whether it's learning from experts like Dr. John Gottman or Dr. Sue Johnson, or simply applying love languages and active listening in your daily conversations, the key is intention. Every effort you make to communicate better, even the smallest ones, contributes to a deeper bond, greater intimacy, and a more resilient marriage.

As you continue to navigate the ups and downs of life together, remember that communication is not just about solving problems—it's about deepening your connection and nurturing your relationship every day. By investing in the art of communication, you are investing in the future of your marriage.

Chapter Thirty-Three

Childhood Trauma's Grip on Marriage

Childhood trauma is more than just a set of painful memories; it's a deep emotional wound that shapes how we see the world and, more importantly, how we relate to others. Whether it's emotional neglect, physical or sexual abuse, or the more subtle but equally damaging experience of witnessing parental conflict or dysfunction, these early life experiences can leave lasting marks. These marks are often carried into adulthood, impacting our ability to trust, form healthy emotional bonds, and navigate intimacy within relationships, especially marriage.

Marriage is built on trust, emotional vulnerability, and mutual support. For someone who has experienced childhood trauma, entering into such a deeply connected relationship can be both a source of profound growth and immense difficulty. It requires a willingness to be vulnerable, to expose parts of oneself that may have been hidden or shielded for years. But what happens when someone's history of trauma interferes with their ability to do that? How do couples navigate the aftermath of unresolved wounds, and how can they rebuild trust and intimacy after trauma has shaped their emotional responses?

In this chapter, we explore the profound impact childhood trauma can have on marriage, drawing from the work of leading experts in trauma and relationship psychology. Dr. Bessel van der Kolk, Dr. Sue Johnson, and Dr. Peter Levine are just a few of the voices whose research has illuminated how deeply trauma can influence emotional responses, attachment styles, and communication dynamics. We will also look at practical steps for couples to heal and create a safe, supportive environment in their marriages despite the lasting effects of trauma.

The Lasting Impact of Childhood Trauma

To understand how childhood trauma impacts marriage, we must first look at how trauma affects the individual. Dr. Bessel van der Kolk, a pioneering trauma researcher and author of *The Body Keeps the Score*, explains that trauma alters the way the brain processes emotions, memories, and relationships. The brain of someone who has experienced childhood trauma doesn't develop in the typical way. Instead, the trauma interrupts normal emotional and cognitive development, leading to long-term difficulties in trust, emotional regulation, and forming secure attachments.

The effects of trauma are far-reaching, often creating an overwhelming sense of hypervigilance—being constantly on edge—or emotional numbness, where a person may shut off their feelings entirely. Both of these are survival responses rooted in the brain's attempt to protect itself from further harm, but they often come at the expense of connection and intimacy. He further explains that trauma can significantly alter how the brain processes emotions, relationships, and safety. These neurological changes can make it incredibly difficult for trauma survivors to feel secure in close relationships, particularly when emotional vulnerability is involved.

The hypervigilant state might look like a partner who is always anxious or suspicious, constantly scanning for signs of betrayal or abandonment. On the other hand, emotional numbness can result in a partner who seems distant, detached, or indifferent—unable to connect in ways that make the relationship thrive. Even in the most loving, caring marriages, trauma survivors may struggle with feelings of not being understood or being emotionally disconnected, leading to significant relational strain.

Attachment Styles: How Trauma Shapes Our Bonds

One of the most profound ways childhood trauma affects relationships is through its influence on attachment styles. Dr. John Bowlby's groundbreaking work on attachment theory shows us that our early relationships with caregivers shape the way we approach and manage relationships throughout life. When trauma enters the picture, it disrupts these attachment patterns, often leading to insecure attachment styles that complicate adult relationships.

1. **Anxious Attachment:** Individuals with anxious attachment styles are often preoccupied with the fear of abandonment. These individuals grew up in environments where love was inconsistent or unpredictable, which created a deep-rooted insecurity about whether they would be loved and cared for. As adults, they may find themselves in relationships where they constantly seek reassurance, fearing that their partner will leave or betray them. A person with anxious attachment might find themselves texting their spouse incessantly, asking if they're okay or reaffirming their love—despite knowing that their partner's actions are not a sign of rejection. This constant need for reassurance can overwhelm the partner, creating tension and frustration in the marriage.

   Dr. Sue Johnson, points out that anxious attachment often manifests as a "clinging behavior" in relationships. This clinginess is not out of manipulation but stems from a deep emotional need to feel secure and validated. Johnson suggests that understanding this dynamic is key to creating a supportive and healing relationship for both partners.

2. **Avoidant Attachment:** Avoidant attachment, the flip side of anxious attachment, occurs when individuals grow up with emotional neglect or were made to feel that their emotions didn't matter. These individuals often shut down emotionally to avoid the pain of unfulfilled needs, making it difficult to open up in relationships. As adults, they tend to pull away from intimacy and avoid discussing deep or vulnerable feelings.

   For example, during a conflict, someone with an avoidant attachment style might withdraw, refusing to engage or shutting down emotionally. Their spouse may feel frustrated or rejected, not understanding why the person they love has suddenly become so distant. Over time, this pattern of avoidance can create a chasm between spouses, leaving one feeling disconnected while the other feels abandoned or unheard.

3. **Disorganized Attachment:** Disorganized attachment is the most complex of all attachment styles. It arises when a child experiences a chaotic or frightening mix of both love and fear from their caregivers. This contradictory experience creates deep confusion about relationships and trust. As adults, individuals with disorganized attachment may swing between desiring intimacy and pushing their partner away.

Dr. Sue Johnson explains that individuals with disorganized attachment often feel a pull toward their partner but simultaneously fear being hurt or rejected, leading to an erratic and unpredictable relationship dynamic. These oscillating patterns make it hard to develop a stable emotional bond, which can leave both partners feeling lost and misunderstood.

Emotional Triggers: How Trauma Re-Emerges in Marriage

One of the ways that childhood trauma continues to affect relationships is through emotional triggers—specific situations that cause intense emotional reactions rooted in past experiences. These triggers often emerge when one partner unknowingly touches on an unresolved wound from the past. A raised voice during an argument, for example, may trigger fear in someone who grew up in an abusive or highly volatile home environment.

Dr. Peter Levine, a leading figure in trauma therapy and author of *Waking the Tiger*, explains that trauma survivors often experience heightened emotional responses because their bodies continue to hold onto the pain from past experiences. Even if the situation at hand seems trivial, the body's emotional response can be intense, leading to disproportionate reactions.

For instance, someone who grew up in an emotionally neglectful household may react with overwhelming anger or sadness when they perceive their partner as being emotionally unavailable, even if the partner's behavior is benign. This pattern of misinterpretation often leads to repeated conflict and frustration, as both partners struggle to understand each other's emotional responses.

How Trauma Affects Communication Patterns

Communication is the cornerstone of any relationship, but for trauma survivors, it can be particularly difficult. Trauma rewires the brain, making it challenging for individuals to express their feelings and needs clearly, especially when emotions are running high.

1. **Emotional Dysregulation:** Emotional dysregulation is one of the most common and challenging effects of trauma. It refers to an inability to manage emotions in a balanced way, often leading to extreme emotional fluctuations. For example, a minor disagreement may trigger an intense emotional outburst, leaving the other partner

confused or hurt. This dysregulation is often linked to unresolved trauma that has never been processed.

Dr. Judith Herman, author of *Trauma and Recovery*, explains that trauma survivors often lack the emotional tools to manage their feelings. As a result, emotional outbursts, which can seem disproportionate to the issue at hand, are common in relationships. These emotional highs and lows can create confusion and strain, making it difficult for couples to maintain open and healthy communication.

2. **Avoidance and Withdrawal:** Another common challenge for trauma survivors is avoidance. Due to their fear of being overwhelmed by emotions or because they have learned to suppress their feelings as a coping mechanism, many trauma survivors avoid emotionally charged conversations altogether. This withdrawal can leave the partner feeling shut out, rejected, or unsupported. A trauma survivor may avoid confronting feelings of shame or inadequacy, choosing instead to bottle them up until they inevitably resurface in unhealthy ways. This avoidance can lead to emotional distance, making it hard for the couple to build the kind of deep, trusting connection necessary for a strong marriage.

Trauma and Intimacy: Navigating Physical and Emotional Closeness

Trauma also deeply affects intimacy. Emotional and physical closeness require vulnerability, and for trauma survivors, vulnerability can feel like a threat rather than a path to connection. Survivors of childhood trauma, especially sexual trauma, may struggle with physical intimacy, while others may find it difficult to trust emotionally.

1. **Fear of Vulnerability:** Marriage requires emotional vulnerability—something that can feel frightening for someone who has been hurt or betrayed in the past. Trauma survivors often build emotional walls to protect themselves from the pain of being hurt again. These walls can block intimacy and make it difficult for the partner to connect emotionally.

   Dr. Sue Johnson emphasizes that in order to build a secure attachment bond, couples must create an environment where vulnerability is met with empathy and support. This allows trauma survivors to feel safe enough to let their guard down and begin healing.

2. **Impact on Physical Intimacy:** Physical intimacy is often challenging for trauma survivors, particularly those who have experienced sexual abuse. The very act of being physically close can trigger intense feelings of fear or disgust. As a result, the partner who wants to experience closeness may feel rejected or unwanted. Over time, this can create significant strain in the relationship.

3. Dr. van der Kolk highlights that trauma survivors often carry "somatic memories" in their bodies, which can make physical intimacy a painful reminder of past experiences. Healing from this trauma requires patience, compassion, and, often, professional therapy.

Supporting Your Partner Through Healing: Steps to Building a Trauma-Informed Relationship

Despite the challenges trauma presents, healing is possible. Couples can build a resilient, loving marriage by understanding how trauma affects their relationship and taking steps to support each other's healing journey.

1. **Empathy and Understanding:** The first step in supporting a partner who has experienced childhood trauma is developing deep empathy. Trauma survivors often feel misunderstood, so it is crucial for their spouse to recognize that their emotional reactions are not personal but rooted in past pain. Educating yourself about trauma and how it affects the brain and behavior is an important part of creating a trauma-informed relationship.

2. **Encouraging Open Communication:** Open communication is essential in every relationship, but it is especially vital for couples dealing with trauma. Regular check-ins, honest conversations about feelings, and a commitment to active listening can help prevent misunderstandings and foster deeper connection. Couples who communicate openly about their emotional needs are more likely to create a safe and supportive space for healing.

3. **Seeking Professional Help:** Trauma is complex, and healing often requires professional help. Couples may benefit from therapy focused

on trauma recovery, such as EMDR (Eye Movement Desensitization and Reprocessing), somatic experiencing, or other trauma-informed therapeutic modalities. Couples therapy can also help partners navigate relationship dynamics and improve communication.

Creating a Resilient and Loving Marriage After Trauma

Childhood trauma may leave deep scars, but it doesn't have to define a marriage. With understanding, empathy, and the right support, couples can heal and build a resilient, loving relationship. Healing takes time, and it requires both partners to commit to understanding each other's pain and working through the challenges together.

According to Dr. Sue Johnson's work in emotionally focused therapy, when partners feel seen, understood, and emotionally known by each other, it fosters a deep sense of safety and security. This emotional attunement forms the foundation of a resilient and loving marriage. By nurturing that connection and creating a space where vulnerability is met with compassion, couples can not only navigate the impact of trauma but also emerge stronger and more deeply bonded.

Chapter Thirty-Four

Affair-Proofing Your Marriage

The Importance of Safeguarding Your Marriage

Marriages are complex, and over time, they inevitably face numerous challenges. However, one of the most devastating trials a couple can experience is infidelity. The betrayal of trust can create emotional devastation, severing the bond between partners and sometimes leading to the dissolution of the relationship. But here's the good news—marriages can be safeguarded against the devastating effects of betrayal. The key lies in cultivating a strong foundation built on trust, emotional intimacy, and open communication.

Affair-proofing your marriage isn't just about preventing infidelity—it's about consciously creating a loving, secure environment where both partners feel seen, heard, and valued. It's about nourishing your emotional connection so that your bond remains steadfast and resilient in the face of life's inevitable difficulties. In this chapter, we'll explore the psychology behind infidelity, how emotional dissatisfaction and unmet needs can lead to betrayal, and practical strategies to strengthen the relationship between you and your partner.

By exploring the emotional, psychological, and even physical triggers that contribute to infidelity, we'll provide actionable advice and expert insights to help you foster a deep, lasting, and unbreakable connection with your spouse. After all, the foundation you build today is the one that will support the longevity of your relationship tomorrow.

Why Do Affairs Happen? Understanding the Psychology of Infidelity

To prevent infidelity, it's important to understand why it happens in the first place. Dr. Shirley Glass, a respected psychologist and author of *Not Just Friends*, points out that affairs are not always about a lack of love or lust. More often, they are the result of emotional dissatisfaction, unaddressed needs, or a communication breakdown within the relationship. Emotional disconnection is often the precursor to an affair. When one partner feels neglected, misunderstood, or emotionally starved, they may turn elsewhere to meet those needs.

In her book *The State of Affairs*, psychologist Esther Perel emphasizes that many modern affairs aren't born out of unhappiness but rather a search for emotional validation, excitement, or self-discovery. In this fast-paced, often isolating world, some people seek out affairs as a way to reconnect with parts of themselves they feel have been lost. Understanding these emotional triggers is the first step in addressing the root causes and preventing infidelity.

Qur'anic Guidance

Islam offers timeless wisdom on safeguarding marital bonds, emphasizing trust, transparency, and kindness. The Qur'an advises believers to live with their spouses in kindness, even during times of difficulty:

> **"And live with them in kindness. For if you dislike them—perhaps you dislike a thing and Allah makes therein much good."** (Surah An-Nisa 4:19)

To protect the sanctity of marriage, the Qur'an not only forbids adultery but also warns believers against approaching anything that could lead to it:

> **"And do not come near adultery. Indeed, it is ever an immorality and evil as a way."** (Surah Al-Isra 17:32)

Islam recognizes that betrayal often begins long before a physical act, stressing moral vigilance and emotional boundaries. Furthermore, the Qur'an reminds us that marriage is a divine blessing built on tranquility, affection, and mercy:

"**And of His signs is that He created for you from yourselves mates that you may find tranquility in them; and He placed between you affection and mercy.**" (Surah Ar-Rum 30:21)

These teachings encourage couples to approach challenges with patience and goodwill, reinforcing trust and protecting the spiritual and emotional bond that marriage is meant to nurture.

Emotional Dissatisfaction

One of the most common reasons for infidelity is emotional dissatisfaction. When partners begin to feel emotionally disconnected from each other, it can create a vacuum that one partner may try to fill outside the marriage. Emotional affairs—where one partner becomes emotionally intimate with someone else—can be just as damaging as physical affairs. In fact, emotional affairs often develop into physical ones because the bond between the two individuals has already deepened.

For example, consider a situation where a husband feels that his emotional needs for validation and support are consistently unmet by his wife. As a result, he may begin seeking out emotional intimacy with a coworker, confiding in them about his personal struggles and desires. Over time, this emotional closeness can transform into an affair, further eroding the emotional bond he shares with his wife.

For example, consider a situation where a wife feels emotionally neglected by her husband—perhaps he's often distant, dismissive of her feelings, or unavailable due to work or personal stress. Over time, she may begin to feel invisible and unappreciated. In seeking comfort, she finds herself growing emotionally close to a friend or colleague who listens to her, compliments her, and makes her feel seen. What begins as innocent conversation gradually becomes a source of emotional dependency. As the emotional intimacy deepens, it can lead to an affair—driven not by a lack of morals, but by a deep unmet need for connection, attention, and emotional safety.

Lack of Intimacy: When Distance Replaces Devotion

One of the most silent and corrosive contributors to infidelity is the gradual breakdown of intimacy—both emotional and physical—within a marriage. Intimacy isn't simply about sexual connection. It is the emotional glue that binds a couple, the invisible thread woven through daily affection, shared vulnerabilities, and acts of tenderness. When a couple stops reaching for each other emotionally or physically, they don't just create space between them—they unintentionally invite loneliness, misunderstanding, and in some cases, betrayal.

The decline of intimacy rarely happens overnight. It is often the result of accumulated neglect: moments where emotional bids are ignored, affections are withheld, touch becomes routine or absent, and deep conversations are replaced with transactional exchanges. Over time, this emotional starvation can cause one or both partners to feel unseen, unloved, or undesired—fertile ground for external temptations to take root.

Dr. John Gottman, a renowned relationship researcher, emphasizes that marriages die by ice, not fire. It's not always loud arguments or infidelity that destroy marriages, but emotional neglect—the slow erosion of connection. His research shows that couples who regularly respond to each other's emotional bids (small attempts to connect, like a shared joke or a question about the day) are significantly more likely to remain emotionally bonded and satisfied. When these bids are repeatedly ignored or dismissed, the emotional bond begins to fracture, leaving spouses vulnerable to seeking connection elsewhere.

From a neurobiological perspective, intimacy also affects the brain's bonding mechanisms. Regular affectionate touch, eye contact, and emotional presence stimulate the release of oxytocin and vasopressin—the hormones responsible for bonding, trust, and long-term attachment. When physical or emotional intimacy declines, these protective hormonal bonds weaken, making outside attention or flirtation feel disproportionately validating or exciting, especially for someone who feels emotionally neglected at home.

Infidelity in these cases doesn't always begin with lust—it often starts with longing. A longing to be heard. To be admired. To feel attractive or desired. When these needs go unmet within the marriage, a person may become more susceptible to connecting with someone who fulfills what their spouse no longer does—even if that connection violates their own values.

The Qur'anic Lens on Intimacy

Islam places deep value on the emotional and physical unity of spouses. Allah says:

> *"They are clothing for you, and you are clothing for them."*
> (Surah Al-Baqarah 2:187)

This metaphor is remarkably layered. Just as clothing covers flaws, provides warmth, offers comfort, and protects from harm, spouses are meant to do the same for each other—not just physically, but emotionally and spiritually. The verse beautifully highlights that a spouse should be a source of sanctuary, emotional safety, and closeness. Intimacy is not simply encouraged—it is a foundational expression of mercy (rahmah) and tranquility (sakeenah) in marriage.

When intimacy breaks down, this covering is lifted. The relationship becomes exposed to external emotional and spiritual threats. The warmth that once protected the heart grows cold, and the psychological safety that fosters trust disappears.

Opportunity and Boundaries

Sometimes, infidelity occurs simply because the opportunity presents itself in environments where boundaries are unclear. With the rise of social media, frequent business travel, and workplaces that foster close personal interactions, it's easier than ever for an emotional or physical affair to take root. If couples do not explicitly define what constitutes acceptable behavior with the opposite sex, the lines between harmless friendship and an emotional affair can blur.

Dr. John Gottman warns that even innocent-seeming interactions can cross the line into infidelity if boundaries aren't set. For instance, texting a colleague of the opposite sex about personal matters, or sharing private conversations during one-on-one work meetings, can foster emotional attachment. Over time, these seemingly benign actions can grow into something more, leading to betrayal.

Practical Strategies to Affair-Proof Your Marriage

Affair-proofing your marriage isn't about paranoia—it's about intentionality. It's about nurturing the kind of relationship that feels so emotionally safe, fulfilling, and alive that the idea of seeking connection elsewhere simply doesn't appeal. A strong marriage is built, brick by brick, through small daily choices that say, "I choose you. Again and again." The following strategies are drawn from relationship science, expert insights, and real-life wisdom to help couples create a bond that's not just protected—but thriving.

1. **Prioritize Emotional Intimacy:** Emotional intimacy is the heartbeat of a connected marriage. When partners feel seen, heard, and understood, they're less likely to seek validation elsewhere. This means creating space for honest conversations, asking questions that go beyond logistics, and truly listening without judgment or distraction. Share your inner world—your fears, your dreams, your vulnerabilities—and be a safe place for your partner to do the same. According to Dr. Sue Johnson, secure emotional connection is the best buffer against infidelity.

2. **Strengthen Physical Intimacy:** Touch is a powerful form of communication. From holding hands to sexual intimacy, physical closeness fosters bonding and reduces relational tension. Dr. David Schnarch notes that passionate marriages are built on trust and emotional risk, not just physical acts. Make time for non-sexual affection too—a hug at the end of the day or a spontaneous kiss on the cheek can say "I love you" more clearly than words.

3. **Practice Radical Honesty in Communication:** Affairs often begin with silence—when one or both partners stop expressing their needs or disappointments. Protect your relationship by committing to open, honest, and kind communication. This includes speaking up about loneliness, dissatisfaction, or feeling disconnected. Make your marriage a place where hard conversations are welcomed, not feared. Gottman research shows that couples who turn toward each other in difficult moments build deeper trust.

4. **Set Clear, Mutually Agreed Boundaries:** Many affairs begin innocently—with a casual message or frequent lunch with a coworker—because there were no clear guardrails in place. Discuss with your spouse what feels appropriate and what doesn't: private DMs with exes? Regular one-on-one outings with friends of the opposite sex? Not all couples have the same boundaries—but clarity, agreement, and consistency are essential. Dr. Shirley Glass, a pioneer in affair prevention, emphasized that secrecy—not sex—is the real betrayal.

5. **Keep the Romance Alive:** Romantic love doesn't maintain itself—it's something couples must actively nourish. That means continuing to date each other, flirting, surprising one another with kind gestures, and showing appreciation. Even small rituals—like Friday night dinner dates or morning coffee together—can reinforce your bond. According to research in the *Journal of Social and*

Personal Relationships, novelty and playfulness are key predictors of long-term romantic satisfaction.

6. **Build a Culture of Appreciation:** It's easy to take each other for granted in the daily grind. Counter this by expressing gratitude often. Say "thank you" for the little things, acknowledge your partner's efforts, and notice their strengths. A culture of appreciation makes your partner feel valued and emotionally safe—and that emotional safety discourages seeking validation elsewhere.

7. **Stay Curious About Each Other:** No matter how long you've been married, your partner is always growing—and so are you. Stay curious. Ask new questions. Explore new experiences together. Dr. Esther Perel suggests that maintaining mystery and curiosity keeps desire alive in long-term relationships. Rediscovering your spouse helps you reconnect emotionally and sexually, deepening your commitment.

8. **Don't Neglect Emotional Repairs:** Every couple fights. The difference between healthy and unhealthy couples isn't the absence of conflict—it's the presence of repair. Learn to apologize sincerely, take responsibility, and soothe one another after a rupture. Gottman's research identifies repair attempts as a major predictor of marital longevity. Conflict that's resolved well actually brings couples closer.

9. **Protect Time for Just the Two of You:** In a world full of distractions—kids, work, phones, endless to-do lists—couples need protected time. Create space each week to simply be together, without multitasking. This could be a walk, a shared hobby, or just 30 minutes before bed to talk. Time together tells your partner, "You still matter to me."

10. **Invest in Your Own Healing and Growth:** Affair-proofing your marriage doesn't just mean focusing on your partner—it also means doing your own inner work. Unhealed wounds, unresolved trauma, or chronic dissatisfaction can create vulnerability to temptation. Therapy, journaling, spiritual growth, and personal development all contribute to being a healthier partner.

11. **Be Transparent With Technology:** Secrecy and digital infidelity often go hand-in-hand. Avoid this by being open about your online interactions. Share passwords if mutually agreed upon, be mindful of tone in texts, and have regular conversations about digital boundaries. Trust grows in an atmosphere of openness.

12. **Surround Yourself With Marriage-Positive Influences:** The company you keep matters. If your friends normalize cheating or disrespect toward their spouses, it can subtly impact your mindset. Seek out couples who are intentional about growing together and friends who support your commitment. A positive relational community reinforces fidelity.

13. **Prioritize Faith and Shared Values:** For many couples, faith is a powerful anchor. Praying together, reading spiritual texts, or simply reflecting on shared values can create a strong moral and emotional bond. This spiritual intimacy often fosters humility, accountability, and a shared sense of purpose—key ingredients in affair-proofing your marriage.

14. **Revisit and Refresh Your Commitment:** Over time, couples may lose sight of the intentions and shared values that brought them together at the time of nikah. Regularly revisiting your commitment—whether through anniversaries, heartfelt conversations, or even intentional moments of reflection—can breathe new life into your marriage. It reminds both partners why they chose each other and renews the intention to grow together.

15. **Create a "Safe Zone" for Emotional Check-Ins:** Establish a regular time where you both check in emotionally—free from distractions or judgment. This could be a weekly ritual where each partner shares how they're feeling, what they need, and what's been on their mind. A consistent emotional check-in builds trust and catches small issues before they become emotional landmines.

16. **Make Repairs After Micro-Betrayals:** Small betrayals—like dismissive comments, broken promises, or emotional shutdowns—can accumulate and erode trust over time. Recognizing these micro-injuries and intentionally repairing them through acknowledgment and change can prevent resentment and disconnection from festering beneath the surface.

17. **Share a Vision for the Future:** Couples who dream together stay together. Talk about your future—where you want to live, what goals you're excited about, what kind of life you want to build. Having a shared vision gives your relationship direction and keeps both partners invested in the long-term journey.

18. **Reconnect After Transitions:** Major life transitions—moving, having children, career changes—can shake the foundation of a marriage. Make intentional time to reconnect after big changes. Talk about how you're both adjusting, what support you need, and how your relationship can adapt. Don't let transitions quietly create emotional distance.

19. **Celebrate Your Wins Together:** A thriving relationship includes not only weathering hard times but also celebrating the good. Whether it's a personal achievement, parenting milestone, or just a great week together—take time to pause, acknowledge it, and enjoy it as a couple. Celebration deepens the emotional bond.

20. **Seek Help Before There's a Crisis:** Healthy couples don't wait for a breakdown to get support. Therapy, coaching, or even attending a marriage workshop can provide tools and insight to strengthen your connection before problems take root. Seeking help early is a sign of strength, not weakness.

Affair-proofing isn't about fear—it's about love. It's about choosing each other, every day, in big ways and small. It's not perfection that protects a marriage—it's intention, consistency, and the willingness to grow together, even when it's hard.

Conclusion

Affair-proofing your marriage is not a one-time fix; it's a continual, intentional commitment to nurturing the relationship. By staying emotionally connected, investing in each other's happiness, and remaining committed to your spouse, you can create a marriage that not only survives but thrives—grounded in love, trust, and intentional effort. The power of love, patience, and mutual respect will always be the strongest protection against the pain of infidelity.

Chapter Thirty-Five

Infidelity Recovery: Healing Together

The Pain of Betrayal and the Path to Healing

Infidelity is undoubtedly one of the most painful experiences a couple can endure. The moment you discover that your partner has been unfaithful, it feels like the ground beneath you is collapsing. The trust you had so carefully built over time is shattered, and every feeling you thought you understood about love, loyalty, and partnership is called into question. For many, it feels like the end—an insurmountable mountain with no way to climb back up.

But here's the good news: healing is possible. It may take time, and it will require an immense amount of effort and commitment, but recovery from infidelity doesn't have to mean the end of your relationship. In fact, many couples have emerged stronger, more resilient, and more deeply connected after surviving the pain of betrayal.

The path to healing is not linear—it's messy, emotional, and incredibly personal. It involves confronting the pain head-on, rebuilding trust, learning how to communicate in new ways, and, most importantly, rediscovering emotional intimacy. Through intentional work and professional guidance, many couples can overcome this devastating hurdle and rebuild their relationship from a foundation of mutual understanding, honesty, and respect.

Steps to Infidelity Recovery: Rebuilding Trust and Emotional Intimacy

Recovering from infidelity is a complex, multi-layered journey that looks different for every couple. While no two relationships are the same, relationship science and expert insights provide clear steps that, when followed with commitment and emotional courage, can help heal the wounds of betrayal and rebuild a stronger, more connected partnership.

1. Immediate Response: Create Space for Emotional Processing

- **Why It Matters:** When infidelity is first discovered, the emotional intensity can be overwhelming. Shock, grief, anger, confusion, and shame can flood both partners. This is not the time for rushed decisions.

- **Expert Insight:** Dr. Janis Abrahms Spring (*After the Affair*) emphasizes that both partners need space to regulate their nervous systems and reflect.

- **Practical Advice:**
  - Consider a short-term separation or structured time apart—not as a step toward divorce, but as space for emotional grounding.
  - Encourage journaling, faith-based reflection, or therapy to clarify internal responses.
  - The betrayed partner should begin identifying boundaries, while the unfaithful partner begins to own their actions without defensiveness.

2. Establish Full Transparency and Radical Honesty

- **Why It Matters:** Trust cannot be rebuilt in the presence of secrecy. Emotional transparency is the antidote to betrayal.

- **Expert Insight:** Dr. Shirley Glass (*Not "Just Friends"*) asserts that affairs thrive in secrecy and die in openness.

- **Practical Advice:**
  - The unfaithful partner must end all contact with the affair partner and provide full disclosure (without harmful sexual detail unless requested).
  - Offer access to passwords, devices, calendars, and locations until trust is reestablished.
  - Check in daily, offering voluntary updates rather than waiting to be asked.
  - Initiate difficult conversations instead of avoiding them—transparency must be consistent and proactive.

3. Commit to Therapy: Individual and Joint

- **Why It Matters:** The emotional aftermath of an affair cannot be resolved through willpower alone. Professional help creates structure and safety for healing.
- **Expert Insight:** Dr. Sue Johnson (EFT) and the Gottman Institute emphasize that therapy supports emotional regulation, improves communication, and rebuilds emotional bonds.
- **Practical Advice:**
  - Start with individual therapy for trauma processing (betrayed) and accountability work (unfaithful).
  - Join couples therapy within 2–4 weeks of the affair's discovery.
  - Choose therapists trained in EFT, the Gottman Method, or trauma-informed approaches to infidelity recovery.
  - Consider EMDR for betrayal trauma or attachment-focused therapy.

4. Rebuild Emotional Intimacy Through Consistent Connection

- **Why It Matters:** Infidelity shatters the emotional connection that protects a relationship. Rebuilding that connection is non-negotiable.

- **Expert Insight:** According to Dr. John Gottman's research, couples who develop emotional attunement and engage in honest, structured repair work after betrayal have a strong chance of rebuilding trust and creating a deeper connection. While healing is never guaranteed, many couples not only survive—but come out stronger.

- **Practical Advice:**
    - Schedule daily 10–20 minute check-ins to share emotions and stress levels.
    - Ask open-ended questions: "How are you really feeling today?" or "What's been hard for you lately?"
    - Begin practicing non-sexual touch again—cuddling, hugs, hand-holding—to slowly reestablish physical trust.
    - Use "love maps" (Gottman concept) to re-learn each other's internal world.

5. Write a Letter of Responsibility and Empathy

- **Why It Matters:** A well-crafted letter from the unfaithful partner can become a cornerstone of healing. It formalizes responsibility and shows a deep level of emotional processing.

- **Expert Insight:** Dr. Douglas Weiss and Dr. Janis Spring recommend a disclosure or empathy letter to help restore power and clarity to the betrayed partner.

- **Practical Advice:**
    - The letter should acknowledge the affair, take full responsibility, validate the pain caused, reflect on the "why," and outline growth steps taken.
    - Avoid blame-shifting. Use statements like: "I chose to betray your trust, and I recognize the depth of that harm."
    - Only share explicit details if asked for—respect the betrayed partner's emotional safety.
    - Read or deliver the letter in a therapist's presence if emotions are intense.

6. Rebuild Physical Intimacy with Care and Consent

- **Why It Matters:** After betrayal, sexual intimacy may become emotionally fraught. Forcing or avoiding it can damage the bond further.

- **Expert Insight:** According to the *Journal of Sex & Marital Therapy*, healing touch and consent-based closeness are vital for trauma recovery.

- **Practical Advice:**
    - Begin with safe touch: hand-holding, cuddling, back rubs.
    - Discuss sexual triggers, fears, and emotional boundaries openly.
    - Wait until both partners feel emotionally connected and safe before resuming full sexual intimacy.
    - Use guided intimacy exercises from sex therapists or Gottman's "Aftermath of a Fight" tool to rebuild desire.

7. Explore the Roots: Why Did the Affair Happen?

- **Why It Matters:** Understanding the affair's emotional roots prevents future betrayal and creates clarity.

- **Expert Insight:** Esther Perel and Terry Real both suggest that affairs are not always about sex, but about emotional disconnection or unmet needs.

- **Practical Advice:**
    - In therapy, explore what internal void or external stressors led to the betrayal.
    - Ask: Was the affair about validation, avoidance, addiction, escapism, or unresolved trauma?
    - Use this insight to rebuild stronger relational habits and emotional attunement.

8. Establish Boundaries and Relapse Prevention Agreements

- **Why It Matters:** Just like in addiction recovery, relapse prevention ensures ongoing safety and accountability.

- **Expert Insight:** Affair recovery experts recommend written boundaries around phone use, workplace behavior, travel, etc.

- **Practical Advice:**
  - Co-create boundaries: What's acceptable and what's not? Be specific.
  - Schedule weekly relationship check-ins to monitor triggers or emotional distance.
  - Use a shared calendar, GPS apps, or check-ins as short-term accountability tools.
  - Establish consequences for boundary violations to preserve emotional safety.

9. Practice Structured Forgiveness (When Ready)

- **Why It Matters:** Forgiveness, when genuine, allows healing to take root—but it cannot be forced or rushed.

- **Expert Insight:** Dr. Janis Spring outlines two types of forgiveness: earned (with accountability) and cheap (with avoidance). Only earned forgiveness leads to repair.

- **Practical Advice:**
  - The betrayed partner may write a letter of release when they feel ready.
  - The unfaithful partner must continue making repairs through changed behavior, not words alone.
  - Forgiveness does not mean forgetting. It means choosing freedom from bitterness.
  - Consider spiritual practices (du'a, prayer, journaling) to process forgiveness on a soul level.

10. Rebuild a New Relationship, Not the Old One

- **Why It Matters:** Going back to "normal" is not the goal. The affair often reveals cracks that need to be addressed and healed.

- **Expert Insight:** Couples who consciously build a *new version* of their relationship post-affair report greater connection and intimacy than before.

- **Practical Advice:**
    - Create new rituals, goals, or shared dreams.
    - Develop a "relationship vision statement." What kind of couple do you want to be now?
    - Schedule quarterly marriage check-ins.
    - Consider spiritual renewal together—shared faith practices can deepen bonds.

Conclusion: Moving Forward with Strength and Resilience

The road to recovery from infidelity is long and fraught with emotional challenges, but it's also an opportunity for immense growth. Couples who navigate this painful journey with patience, commitment, and professional guidance can not only heal but create a relationship that is stronger and more resilient than before.

As Dr. Janis Abrahms Spring emphasizes, healing after betrayal requires more than forgetting—it requires transformation. "After an affair," she writes, "the couple's challenge is to create a new marriage that acknowledges the betrayal, respects the pain, and rebuilds trust and intimacy in ways that honor the needs of both partners."

By rebuilding emotional safety, practicing honest accountability, and committing to long-term growth, couples can turn even the deepest wounds into pathways toward a more authentic, resilient love.

Chapter Thirty-Six

Cracking Relationship Slang

Why Understanding Modern Relationship Slang Matters

In today's rapidly evolving landscape of dating, courtship, and marriage-seeking, language has become one of the most powerful indicators of how people think and behave in relationships. From online platforms to everyday conversations, the younger generation uses new slang terms to describe everything from emotional unavailability to commitment fears. For those who are entering or re-entering the relationship arena—whether for the first time, post-divorce, or after years away—familiarity with this language is more than useful; it's essential.

Here's why it matters:

- **Avoid Misunderstandings:** Modern terms often carry complex emotional and behavioral meanings. If someone says they were "ghosted" or that they're in a "situationship," not knowing what these terms mean can leave you feeling lost or unsure how to respond. Understanding the language helps you interpret intentions, emotional cues, and red flags clearly and early.

- **Understand the Modern Mindset:** Language reflects thought—and in the world of relationships, slang reveals what people are truly experiencing and struggling with. Learning the terms helps you see deeper into the modern relational mindset: fears of commitment, emotional burnout, courting fatigue, and more. If you're serious about marriage, knowing what people are dealing with allows you to approach conversations with insight, empathy, and greater discernment.

- **Communicate with Confidence:** Whether you're exploring matrimonial apps, speaking with a potential match, or even discussing relationship culture with friends or family, using (or at least understanding) modern terminology helps you stay engaged in meaningful, informed conversations without feeling out of place.

- **Navigate Digital Platforms with Clarity:** Many bios and profiles on matrimonial or dating apps use slang terms to describe what someone is looking for—or trying to avoid. Knowing terms like "breadcrumbing," "low-effort energy," or "soft launching" will help you assess compatibility and sincerity, especially in a fast-moving, digital-first culture.

- **Bridge Generational Gaps:** If you're from an older generation or re-entering the courting world after a long marriage, this language can help you connect with people—whether they're your children, friends, or potential matches. It shows you're open-minded, willing to learn, and attuned to the current relationship climate.

- **Empower Your Search for Marriage:** Understanding these phrases equips you with the tools to spot emotional games, recognize trends, and protect your own values while seeking something serious. It helps you stay grounded and intentional in a dating culture that can often feel superficial or confusing.

So whether you're swiping on a matrimonial app, chatting with someone new, or simply curious about the world your peers or children are navigating, this guide will help you decode the slang—and better understand the cultural shifts shaping modern relationships.

Now, let's explore some of the most commonly used (and sometimes perplexing) relationship slang and what they really mean…

1. **Breadcrumbing:** Giving someone just enough attention to keep them interested without any real commitment. Like crumbs from a loaf of bread, these gestures are minimal and emotionally unsatisfying.

2. **Gaslighting:** A form of emotional manipulation where someone makes you question your memory or perception of events. Phrases like "That never happened" or "You're imagining things" are typical signs.

3. **Stonewalling:** Shutting down emotionally during an argument or difficult conversation. The person becomes unresponsive or withdraws completely, leaving the other partner feeling rejected or dismissed.

4. **Ghosting:** Suddenly cutting off all communication with someone you were seeing or talking to, without explanation. This abrupt silence can be deeply confusing and hurtful.

5. **Cushioning:** Keeping backup romantic options on the side while in a relationship, just in case it doesn't work out.

6. **Catfishing:** Pretending to be someone else online by creating a fake identity to lure others into emotional or romantic connections.

7. **Phubbing:** Ignoring someone in favor of scrolling through your phone—especially during important conversations or quality time.

8. **Love Bombing:** Showering someone with overwhelming affection, gifts, and attention early in a relationship, often as a manipulation tactic to gain control.

9. **Benching:** Keeping someone on standby like a sports player—occasional check-ins without committing to a relationship.

10. **Ghostlighting:** A manipulative twist on ghosting where the person returns after disappearing and denies it ever happened or makes you feel irrational for being upset.

11. **Monkey Branching:** Starting a new relationship while still in one, swinging from one partner to another without ever letting go completely.

12. **Relationship Limbo:** Being stuck in an undefined, non-committal relationship. You're not single, but you're not in a committed relationship either.

13. **Scrooging:** Breaking up right before the holidays to avoid spending money or navigating family commitments.

14. **Sneating:** Going on dates just for free food or perks, with no genuine romantic interest.

15. **Vulturing:** When someone swoops in immediately after a breakup to take advantage of your emotional vulnerability.

16. **Thirst Trapping:** Posting attractive or provocative photos to get attention or admiration from others.

17. **Zombieing:** When someone who previously ghosted you suddenly comes back into your life as if nothing happened.

18. **Fizzling:** A slow, mutual fading out of communication that leads to the end of a connection without an official breakup.

19. **Roaching:** Hiding the fact that you're seeing multiple people at once. When discovered, the person usually admits they didn't think exclusivity was assumed.

20. **Orbiting:** Ghosting someone but continuing to engage with their social media—liking posts, watching stories—to stay present without meaningful interaction.

21. **Wokefishing:** Pretending to hold progressive or socially conscious beliefs to appeal to a partner's values or interests.

22. **Soft Launching:** Subtly revealing a romantic partner on social media without fully announcing the relationship—like showing a hand, silhouette, or date night without naming them.

23. **Beige Flags:** Habits or traits that aren't outright bad or good but could signal incompatibility or predictability (e.g., always talking about the weather).

24. **Rizz:** Slang for charisma or charm, especially the ability to attract someone romantically.

25. **Freak Matching:** Forming a romantic connection based on unique, quirky, or unconventional shared interests.

26. **Delulu:** Short for "delusional," this refers to someone who holds unrealistic or overly hopeful expectations in a relationship.

27. **Situationship:** A romantic or sexual relationship without clear boundaries or labels—more than friends but less than partners.

28. **Cuffing Season:** The colder months (typically fall and winter) when people seek short-term relationships to avoid loneliness.

29. **Throning:** Dating someone to improve your image, popularity, or social status.

30. **Caspering:** A gentler version of ghosting where the person offers a soft exit—"I'm not ready for a relationship right now"—and then fades away.

31. **Shadow Phasing:** Gradually reducing communication and connection until the relationship dies out, all without formally ending it.

32. **Flex Dating:** Fitting casual or convenient dates into a busy schedule—like coffee before the gym—rather than planning meaningful time together.

33. **Boysober:** Taking a conscious break from dating, especially after repeated heartbreak, to focus on personal growth and healing.

This comprehensive glossary not only helps you stay current in today's dating world but also deepens your awareness of modern relationship dynamics—helping you approach connections with clarity, emotional intelligence, and intention.

That said, it's important to recognize that many of these terms stem from the dating culture prevalent in secular, Western contexts—one that often stands in contrast to Islamic values of modesty, intentionality, and structured courtship. As Muslims, we are not encouraged to engage in casual dating. Our tradition promotes a faith-based approach to relationships, rooted in boundaries, respect, and divine accountability.

However, after working with countless individuals and couples over the years, I've seen firsthand that many young Muslims today are navigating modern dating culture, often without the proper guidance or awareness. This is why understanding the language and mindset of this generation is crucial—not to normalize what contradicts our faith, but to empower ourselves to engage wisely, intervene where necessary, and guide our communities back to relationship practices that honor both heart and deen.

Chapter Thirty-Seven

Dating Apps: Modern Love or Social Chaos?

A Modern Dilemma

The desire for companionship and a fulfilling marriage is deeply ingrained in human nature, as Allah reminds us:

> "And among His signs is that He created for you spouses from among yourselves, that you may find tranquility in them; and He placed between you affection and mercy. Indeed, in that are signs for a people who give thought." (Qur'an 30:21)

In the past, families, communities, and traditional matchmakers played a central role in helping individuals find a spouse. Today, matrimonial apps have emerged as modern tools to aid in this pursuit. While these apps hold potential for good, they also come with challenges that require thoughtful navigation and faith-based mindfulness.

As we explore the role of matrimonial apps, it is vital to view them as tools—neither inherently good nor bad. Their impact depends on how they are used, the intentions behind their use, and the awareness of their benefits and pitfalls.

The Rise of Matrimonial Apps: Opportunities in Modern Times

In many ways, matrimonial apps have broadened possibilities, especially for Muslims in minority or diaspora communities. They allow individuals to connect with others who share similar values, cultural backgrounds, and religious goals. For those living far from extended family or within limited social circles, these platforms provide a practical means of initiating the search for a life partner.

Dr. Helen Fisher, a biological anthropologist and leading expert on romantic attraction, has observed that digital tools—when used with sincerity and clear purpose—can help bridge the gaps often left unaddressed by traditional matchmaking systems. She emphasizes that while the platforms for meeting people have evolved, the human drive for love, connection, and compatibility remains deeply rooted in our biology. When individuals engage authentically, modern technology can support meaningful, long-term connections.

From a faith based perspective, Muslim based platforms can help facilitate the process of marriage by offering structured spaces for individuals seeking serious commitments. Matrimonial apps/websites often encourage discussions about marriage from the outset, aligning with the Islamic principle of clear intentions (niyyah).

A 2021 study in *Computers in Human Behavior* highlighted that users of marriage-focused platforms reported higher satisfaction when their intentions and platform design aligned, suggesting that a structured and goal-oriented approach fosters greater trust and connection.

The Challenges of Using Matrimonial Apps

While matrimonial apps can serve as useful tools, they are not without challenges. Their design and implementation sometimes create obstacles that may hinder the pursuit of a healthy, faith-based relationship.

Superficiality and the Culture of Comparison

One of the most significant drawbacks of these platforms is the emphasis on appearances and metrics. Profiles often highlight photos, education, income, and other quantifiable traits, which can overshadow a person's character, faith, and emotional depth. This focus on external attributes may inadvertently lead users to prioritize superficial qualities over qualities emphasized in Islam, such as taqwa (piety) and good character. The Prophet Muhammad (ﷺ) said:

> "A woman may be married for four things: her wealth, her lineage, her beauty, or her religion. So choose the religious one, may you prosper." (Sahih al-Bukhari 5090)

Dr. Sheena Iyengar, an expert in decision-making, emphasizes that reducing individuals to a rigid checklist can oversimplify the deeply complex nature of human relationships. When people rely too heavily on fixed criteria—such as income, height, or profession—they may unintentionally prioritize societal expectations over genuine emotional compatibility. Her research encourages a more holistic, reflective approach to choosing a partner, one that aligns with personal values and long-term relational well-being.

Additionally, a 2019 study published in *Psychological Science* found that excessive focus on external metrics in online matchmaking reduces emotional connection and increases dissatisfaction in long-term partnerships.

Emotional Burnout and False Hopes

The repeated cycle of swiping, matching, and then facing rejection or ghosting can lead to emotional exhaustion. A 2020 Stanford University study found that app users frequently experience decision fatigue and emotional burnout, which diminish their capacity to form meaningful connections.

From an Islamic perspective, this state of emotional fatigue can also detract from one's spiritual well-being, as prolonged exposure to such environments may lead to despair or loss of trust in Allah's plan. Patience (sabr) and reliance on Allah (tawakkul) are critical virtues to maintain during the process.

Sincerity and the Problem of Misrepresentation

Matrimonial apps are often viewed as spaces for serious commitment. However, not all users approach them with genuine intentions. A 2019 study by the *International Journal of Technology and Human Interaction* reported that nearly 30% of users admitted to misrepresenting their profiles, whether through embellishing achievements or concealing important details.

This issue is particularly concerning from an Islamic perspective, as honesty and transparency are fundamental in the pursuit of marriage. The Prophet Muhammad (ﷺ) said:

> "The honest, trustworthy merchant will be with the Prophets, the truthful, and the martyrs." (Sunan al-Tirmidhi 1209)

Deceit on these platforms not only causes emotional harm but also undermines the sanctity of the marriage process.

Faith and the Culture of Modesty

Another challenge is the potential for apps to erode the boundaries of modesty (haya). Engaging in casual conversations or forming emotional or even physical attachments outside of a structured and intentional context can lead to behaviors that conflict with Islamic values. It is essential to approach these platforms with caution, ensuring interactions are conducted with decorum and within the bounds of Islamic etiquette. As Allah commands:

> "Do not even go near zina (unlawful sexual relations). Indeed, it is an abomination and an evil way." (Qur'an 17:32)

Maintaining a balance between using the platform as a tool and preserving one's faith requires constant vigilance and self-awareness.

Hookup Culture: A Darker Side

While matrimonial apps promise to connect people seeking lifelong commitments, they have not been immune to the influence of hookup culture—a phenomenon that thrives on casual encounters devoid of emotional connection or long-term intention. This clash of expectations creates a challenging dynamic for those genuinely searching for meaningful relationships, leaving many feeling disappointed, confused, or even hurt.

Hookup culture, driven by the convenience and anonymity of modern dating platforms, often prioritizes instant gratification at the expense of deeper emotional fulfillment. Psychologist Dr. Jean Twenge, author of *iGen: Why Today's Super-Connected Kids Are Growing Up Less Rebellious, More Tolerant, Less Happy*, has highlighted the effects of digital media on relationship dynamics—showing how the ease of accessing potential partners online can reduce the patience and emotional investment required to build meaningful, lasting bonds. This trend is increasingly evident even on matrimonial platforms, where users seeking serious commitment may find themselves navigating interactions with individuals who treat these apps similarly to casual dating services, leading to mismatched expectations and emotional disconnect.

A Growing Concern for the Younger Muslim Generation

For the younger Muslim generation, the rise of hookup culture poses significant spiritual and moral challenges. Many young Muslims are falling headfirst into this trend, often lured by the allure of quick connections and peer influence. However, they are also experiencing the emotional, mental, psychological, physical, and spiritual harm that accompanies such behavior. In the pursuit of casual relationships, these young individuals risk compromising not only their emotional well-being but also their spiritual values, which emphasize modesty, intentionality, and respect in relationships.

The Spiritual and Emotional Consequences of Hookup Culture: An Islamic Perspective

In contemporary society, the prevalence of hookup culture—characterized by casual sexual encounters without emotional commitment—has raised concerns among Islamic scholars regarding its alignment with Islamic values and its impact on individual well-being.

Shaykh Abdal Hakim Murad highlights how modern sexual permissiveness detaches intimacy from its sacred meaning. He warns that zina corrodes the soul, deadens the heart, and undermines one's capacity for real love. Islam, he explains, upholds chastity to protect the nafs, preserve dignity, and align the believer with their God-given fitrah.

Shaykh Dr. Yasir Qadhi, through his "Like A Garment" initiative, seeks to educate Muslims on achieving conjugal bliss within the sanctity of marriage. He draws from the Qur'anic metaphor where spouses are described as garments for one another, symbolizing intimacy, protection, and comfort. This initiative addresses the importance of understanding and fulfilling emotional and physical needs within marriage, contrasting the fleeting nature of casual relationships.

These perspectives underscore the significance of adhering to Islamic principles regarding intimacy. Engaging in relationships outside the bounds of marriage not only conflicts with Islamic teachings but also poses risks to one's emotional and spiritual well-being. Islam advocates for relationships founded on commitment, mutual respect, and spiritual harmony, ensuring holistic fulfillment for individuals.

The emotional toll is profound. Imagine a young person who enters hookup culture seeking connection but instead finds themselves feeling used, undervalued, and empty. The guilt and regret that follow can exacerbate feelings of isolation and anxiety. Furthermore, the mental strain of navigating casual relationships—where intentions are often unclear—can create deep insecurity and confusion about self-worth.

Physically, the risks of sexually transmitted infections (STIs) and unplanned pregnancies are amplified in hookup culture, particularly for those who are unprepared or unaware of these dangers. Psychologically, the detachment encouraged by hookup culture can impair one's ability to form meaningful, lasting bonds in the future. Over time, this detachment can lead to patterns of avoidance and fear of commitment, undermining the foundation of healthy, enduring relationships.

The Emotional Toll

For many, the incursion of hookup culture into spaces designed for serious relationships leads to emotional distress. Imagine pouring your heart into finding someone who shares your values and dreams, only to realize they view your connection as a casual interaction. Dr. Lisa Wade, author of *American Hookup: The New Culture of Sex on Campus*, explores how hookup culture often normalizes emotional detachment, which can be particularly harmful for individuals who are seeking intimacy and long-term connection. Her research shows that within this environment, students are often rewarded for being emotionally distant and discouraged from showing care or vulnerability. This culture of disconnection can leave many participants feeling undervalued or used, ultimately leading them to question their self-worth and their ability to find genuine, lasting love.

Esther Perel, a renowned psychotherapist and author of *Mating in Captivity*, adds another layer of complexity to the discussion. She explores how modern relationship dynamics, particularly those shaped by hookup culture, can create a paradox where people deeply crave intimacy but often struggle with the vulnerability it requires. This tension—between the desire for closeness and the fear of emotional exposure—can make it difficult for individuals to form lasting, meaningful partnerships. For those genuinely seeking a lifelong spouse, navigating this emotional landscape can feel like walking a tightrope, constantly balancing the hope for connection with the fear of rejection or disingenuous intentions.

Societal Shifts and Their Impact

Hookup culture is not just a personal issue; it reflects broader societal shifts. The rise of digital dating has significantly altered the way people seek relationships, often shifting the focus from deep compatibility to more superficial traits like appearance, status, or charisma. Dr. David Buss, an evolutionary psychologist, has explored how dating apps can amplify short-term mating strategies, making it more difficult for individuals to prioritize shared values, long-term compatibility, or emotional connection. This commodification of human connection often leads users to treat potential partners like items on a shelf—quickly "swiped" away if they don't meet an idealized standard.

This becomes particularly problematic when hookup culture seeps into spaces intended for serious commitment, such as matrimonial apps tailored for cultural or religious communities. Dr. Katherine Hertlein, a couples therapist who studies the impact of technology on relationships, has highlighted how the presence of casual dating behaviors on these platforms can create a disconnect between user expectations and actual experiences. Many users enter such spaces hoping for long-term relationships, only to be met with partners whose intentions are unclear or misaligned, resulting in cycles of confusion, unmet expectations, and emotional fatigue.

Stories of Frustration and Resilience

Consider the story of Mariam, a 29-year-old teacher who joined a matrimonial app hoping to meet someone who shared her values and desire for commitment. Instead, she found herself navigating a landscape filled with individuals more interested in casual flings than serious conversations. "It felt like I was putting myself out there, sharing who I am and what I want, only to be met with half-hearted responses or people looking for nothing more than a distraction," she says. What made it even more disheartening was the discovery that some users intentionally misrepresented their intentions, pretending to be interested in marriage only to pursue fleeting physical relationships. The emotional toll of such encounters left Mariam feeling devalued and frustrated, as she realized that for many, these platforms had become a playground for deceit and exploitation.

A 2021 study published in the *Journal of Interpersonal Violence* revealed that online platforms are increasingly exploited by predators who prey on vulnerable individuals seeking genuine relationships. These predators use emotional manipulation to gain trust, often leading to financial, emotional, or even physical harm.

Mariam's story is not uncommon, especially among younger Muslims who, despite seeking meaningful connections, fall prey to individuals motivated by personal gratification rather than genuine commitment. Many users skillfully woo potential partners, offering false promises of marriage or long-term partnership, only to physically use them and then ghost them without a second thought. This pattern of manipulation and abandonment not only causes deep emotional wounds but also leaves spiritual scars, challenging individuals' trust and faith in the process of finding a halal relationship.

Yet, Mariam's journey also highlights the importance of resilience and the value of maintaining strong faith-based principles in the face of such challenges. By clearly stating her boundaries and intentions and remaining steadfast in her values, Mariam eventually met Ahmed, someone who genuinely shared her vision for a meaningful marital relationship. Their connection flourished, proving that while hookup culture poses significant obstacles, perseverance, clarity, and a commitment to faith can still pave the way for lasting love.

Mariam's experience serves as a poignant reminder of why it is essential to approach modern matchmaking with caution and a strong grounding in Islamic principles. Faith provides a moral compass, emphasizing the importance of intentionality, respect, and integrity in relationships. By adhering to these principles, individuals can protect themselves from the emotional and spiritual harm caused by insincere pursuits and navigate the challenges of hookup culture with clarity and confidence.

For Mariam and others like her, the journey is not just about finding love but about finding a partner who honors their values and sees relationships as a sacred bond rather than a fleeting encounter. Her story is a testament to the power of faith and intentionality in building relationships that truly matter.

Navigating the Challenges

To combat the darker side of hookup culture, both users and platforms must take proactive steps. Drawing from the work of Dr. Sue Johnson, the importance of forming secure emotional bonds—even in the early stages of a connection—cannot be overstated. Rather than conforming to the norms of casual dating, individuals benefit from prioritizing emotional honesty, shared values, and long-term compatibility. This approach creates a stronger foundation for meaningful relationships.

For users, this means being clear about their intentions and establishing healthy boundaries from the beginning. For platforms, it involves implementing features that support serious connections—like value-based matching systems, more in-depth profiles, and stronger moderation tools to discourage misuse or superficial interactions.

A Call to Reclaim Purpose

The growing influence of hookup culture on matrimonial apps does not have to define the experience for everyone. Insights from researchers like Dr. Jean Twenge emphasize that while the digital age presents new relational challenges, it also offers meaningful opportunities—especially for those who approach it with clarity, purpose, and intentionality.

Navigating this landscape requires patience, emotional resilience, and a firm commitment to authenticity. It's about knowing what matters most and being willing to protect that vision. With a healthy mindset and the right support, users can still find genuine connection and lasting love—even in an environment shaped by temporary encounters.

Positive Potential: Breaking Barriers and Building Bridges

Despite the challenges, matrimonial apps can offer significant benefits when used with the right intentions and awareness. For Muslims in diverse or minority communities, these platforms provide opportunities to connect with like-minded individuals who share their values and goals.

A unique advantage of matrimonial apps is their ability to foster open discussions about marriage from the outset. This clarity can save individuals from engaging in relationships that do not align with their life plans, allowing them to focus on building relationships rooted in mutual respect, shared values, and long-term compatibility.

Navigating Matrimonial Apps with Faith: A Practical and Spiritual Guide

In our digitally connected world, matrimonial apps can be powerful tools to help Muslims fulfill the noble Sunnah of marriage. However, like any tool, their benefit or harm lies in *how* they are used. Islam emphasizes intention, boundaries, and trust in Allah, and these principles must remain at the heart of every interaction—whether in person or online.

Here's how to approach matrimonial platforms with wisdom, care, and faith:

1. Begin with Sincere Intentions (Niyyah)

    - Start by purifying your intention: You're not just looking for companionship—you're seeking a spouse to complete your deen.

    - Write down your reasons for wanting to get married, and keep them rooted in Islamic values—such as building a home based on love, mercy, and mutual growth.

    - Before creating your profile, make duʿā (supplication) asking Allah to protect you from harm, guide you to what is best, and help you remain sincere.

2. Set Clear Boundaries from Day One

    - Stay within the framework of Islamic etiquette: no flirty banter, no late-night private chats, and no emotionally intimate conversations that haven't earned their place.

    - Avoid sharing photos or personal information too quickly—preserve your modesty and privacy.

    - Keep conversations purposeful, respectful, and focused on discerning compatibility, not emotional gratification.

3. Practice Due Diligence (Tajriba & Tahqiq)
   - Don't take profiles at face value—verify what you can:
     - Confirm employment, education, and family background through mutual contacts when possible.
     - Look for consistency in what the person says and how they behave over time.
     - Use a third party, such as a wali (guardian) or trusted mediator, especially for sisters, to add a layer of accountability.

4. Involve Trusted People
   - Don't go through the process alone. Involve:
     - Parents or guardians, especially early on.
     - A mentor, coach, or Islamic marriage counselor to help you assess red flags and compatibility.
     - Spiritual advisors who can help you stay grounded in Islamic principles.
   - A second set of eyes often sees what infatuation blinds you from.

5. Guard Your Emotional Modesty
   - Emotional oversharing can be as risky as physical overexposure. Don't pour your heart out to someone you barely know.
   - Keep your self-worth intact. Don't chase after replies or accept breadcrumbs of interest.
   - Preserve your dignity by only engaging in conversations that bring you closer to clarity—not confusion.

6. Choose Platforms That Align With Your Values
   - Use Islamic matrimonial platforms that promote faith-based connections, not casual dating.
   - Look for apps that:
     - Offer identity verification and moderation tools.

- Prioritize values and long-term commitment.
- Discourage exploitative or unserious behavior.

7. Communicate With Purpose

   - Ask meaningful questions early: Do they pray? What does marriage mean to them? What are their views on roles, children, faith, conflict resolution?
   - Stay away from excessive "vibing" or "let's see where it goes" conversations. That's not courting—it's emotional wandering.

8. Rely on Allah with Tawakkul

   - Make istikhārah regularly, especially when a prospect seems promising.
   - Trust that if something is meant for you, it will never miss you, and what misses you was never meant to be yours.
   - Use the journey not just to find someone, but to become someone worthy of the spouse you seek.

9. Be Patient—and Realistic

   - Not every introduction will lead to marriage—and that's okay. Take breaks if you feel fatigued or spiritually unsettled.
   - Don't compromise your deen for the illusion of companionship. It's better to be single with peace than married with regret.

10. Measure Success Beyond the App

    - Remember: the app is just a tool for introduction. It's not the marriage—it's not even the courtship.
    - Real success lies in the values you uphold, the character you observe, and the trust you place in Allah as you move forward.

Conclusion

In the fast-paced world of swipes and pings, it's easy to lose sight of what truly matters. But you're not just looking for a partner—you're seeking a life companion who will stand beside you through your worship, your struggles, and your growth. With sincere intentions, clear boundaries, and steadfast faith, even a modern platform can become a means of barakah.

Protect your heart, protect your values, and walk the path of marriage with the confidence that Allah is guiding your steps.

Chapter Thirty-Eight

Your Phone vs. Your Marriage

Why Your Phone Is Basically a Mind Control Device: The Science Behind the Addiction

It's no secret—our phones are specifically designed to capture and hold our attention. Behind every app, every notification, and every scroll, there's a carefully constructed system of psychological triggers aimed at keeping us hooked. As Dr. Tristan Harris, former Google design ethicist and founder of the Center for Humane Technology, has pointed out, "We are the product. The product is our attention." Companies don't just want us to use their devices; they want to keep us using them longer. As Harris explains in his TED talk, these tech giants exploit the brain's vulnerability to habit formation. It's about keeping us perpetually engaged, even when we don't realize it. Tech companies employ behavioral scientists to use psychological tactics to increase the time we spend on screens, manipulating us into giving our attention to platforms like Facebook, Instagram, and YouTube, to maximize advertising revenue.

Why You Can't Put Your Phone Down: Dopamine, the Brain's Sweet Tooth

The real culprit behind phone addiction lies in our brains: dopamine. This "feel-good" neurotransmitter is responsible for pleasure, reward, and motivation. Every time we receive a new notification, we get a small burst of dopamine—an emotional payoff that feels good in the moment. But this is exactly what makes it so addictive. Dr. Anna Lembke, a psychiatrist at Stanford University and author of *Dopamine Nation*, explains that frequent indulgence in small, pleasure-producing behaviors—like checking our phones or scrolling social media—can lead to dependency. Dopamine, a key neurotransmitter in the brain's reward system, plays a central role in motivating behavior. When we engage in activities that trigger dopamine release, we're more likely to repeat those behaviors in search of that pleasurable response.

However, over time, the brain adapts to this repeated stimulation. Dopamine receptors may become less responsive, requiring higher levels of stimulation to achieve the same level of satisfaction. This neurological shift helps explain why we often find ourselves mindlessly scrolling or checking our devices even when we don't need to—it's not about utility, but rather about chasing a reward response that's become harder to satisfy. Lembke emphasizes that understanding this pattern is crucial to breaking cycles of digital overuse and reclaiming our focus and well-being.

Mind Games: How Big Tech Plays You Like a Puppet

Psychologists and tech companies work hand-in-hand to create an environment that makes us keep coming back for more. The strategies they use are designed to subtly manipulate our behaviors, making phone use feel irresistible. One of the most powerful psychological tactics is known as "variable reinforcement." This is the same principle that underlies slot machines—sometimes you win, sometimes you don't. When we check our phones, we're not sure whether we'll receive an interesting message, a notification, or a new like on our post. This uncertainty keeps us coming back, because our brains crave that unpredictability. Dr. B.J. Fogg, a researcher at Stanford University and author of *Tiny Habits*, emphasizes that mobile apps have made use of the "persuasive technology" model, which is essentially designed to influence user behavior. He highlights how apps like Instagram, Facebook, and X, formerly known as Twitter, utilize notifications and visual cues to trigger compulsive checking. Dr. Fogg has also studied how digital platforms shape user habits, often without conscious awareness. His research highlights that many apps are intentionally designed with psychological triggers—such as notifications, likes, or swipe mechanisms—that train users to check their phones automatically. Over time, this builds a subtle but powerful emotional investment in these platforms. This process isn't accidental; companies carefully craft these features to increase user engagement, maximize time spent on their apps, and build habitual use.

Fogg has also raised ethical questions about how persuasive technology is used. While it has the potential to help people adopt positive behaviors, it can just as easily be used to exploit users' attention, especially when design choices are driven solely by profit rather than well-being.

Fogg's insights align with findings from the *Journal of Social and Personal Relationships*, which also observes how digital platforms optimize their designs to manipulate our attention.

The Selfie Syndrome: Why We All Need Validation... Now

Social media addiction is intricately tied to phone use. When people engage with platforms like Instagram, Facebook, or TikTok, they're not just browsing for fun—they're actively seeking validation and connection. The phone makes this validation instant and addictive. Dr. Jean Twenge, a psychologist renowned for her work on generational trends, has extensively explored the link between the rise of social media and the growing rates of anxiety, depression, and loneliness—especially among younger generations. Her research suggests that platforms like Instagram and TikTok promote a culture of comparison, where individuals continuously measure their lives against curated snapshots of others. This constant exposure can lead to emotional highs when receiving likes, comments, or shares, but those fleeting moments of validation often fade quickly, leaving users feeling emotionally drained or disconnected.

Studies published in *Psychology Today* and other journals support the idea that these bursts of social media approval can create a cycle of dependency. Instead of building a strong internal sense of identity and self-worth, users may find themselves relying more and more on external feedback to feel valued. When that feedback is absent or inconsistent, it can lead to feelings of inadequacy, isolation, and diminished self-esteem.

Multitasking Myth: How Juggling Your Life Makes You Forget It

One of the biggest myths promoted by smartphone use is that it enables us to multitask efficiently. In truth, multitasking is more about switching rapidly between tasks than doing them simultaneously. Neuroscience research, including that by Dr. Earl Miller at MIT, shows that the human brain is wired to focus on one task at a time. When we try to juggle texting, scrolling, emailing, and watching TV, our cognitive load increases. This leads to mental fatigue and diminished focus. Research from the University of California, Irvine, even found that it can take over 20 minutes to regain concentration after a distraction. Repeated task-switching also impairs memory and reduces our ability to engage in meaningful, productive work.

The Instant Gratification Trap: How Your Phone Is Slowly Rewiring Your Brain

Our brains are naturally inclined toward reward-seeking behavior, but smartphones amplify this tendency. Constant notifications, updates, and dopamine-triggering stimuli have conditioned us to prefer quick, shallow engagement over sustained, deep thinking. Experts like Dr. Nicholas Carr have noted how digital tools can rewire neural pathways, making it harder for people to maintain focus over long periods. Overuse of smartphones has been associated with reduced attention spans, and studies from the American Psychological Association have linked frequent digital interruption to decreased cognitive control and increased stress. The more we seek instant gratification, the more difficult it becomes to engage with complex or demanding tasks.

Brain Drain: The Cognitive Costs of Smartphone Overuse

If focusing on a conversation or reading without checking your phone feels impossible, you're not alone. Research led by Dr. Gloria Mark at UC Irvine shows that our attention spans are shrinking due to constant digital interruption. Even short glances at a phone during a task can disrupt cognitive flow and reduce efficiency. This constant fragmentation of attention leads to exhaustion and lower productivity, especially in work or learning environments. Additional findings from studies published by Pew Research and others confirm that frequent smartphone use is correlated with reduced memory, mental clarity, and sustained attention.

The Memory Loss You Don't Even Know You Have: Phone Addiction and Forgetfulness

The convenience of storing everything on our phones has affected how we use our memory. Research by psychologist Dr. Betsy Sparrow, published in *Science*, shows that when people believe they can access information easily (like via Google), they are less likely to commit that information to memory. This phenomenon is referred to as "the externalization of memory." It's as though we are outsourcing our mental faculties to our devices. Other experts, like Dr. Daniel Levitin, have pointed out that remembering information strengthens neural connections. Relying heavily on digital storage reduces the mental effort required to recall things, which weakens cognitive resilience over time.

Stress, Sleep, and Satisfaction: The Dark Side of Your Phone

Smartphone overuse doesn't just affect cognitive function—it impacts sleep, stress levels, and overall well-being. Researchers including Arianna Huffington and Dr. Robert Sapolsky have highlighted how exposure to blue light at night can suppress melatonin production, disrupting sleep cycles. Inadequate sleep then leads to heightened stress and reduced emotional regulation. Studies published in the *Journal of Applied Social Psychology* have found that late-night phone usage correlates with increased anxiety and reduced sleep quality. Over time, this affects everything from mood and mental clarity to physical health and relational stability.

Your Relationship's Worst Enemy: How Phones Are Fueling Disconnection

One of the most profound consequences of smartphone overuse is the erosion of emotional intimacy in relationships. Dr. John Gottman's relationship research emphasizes how emotional disengagement can lead to marital dissatisfaction. When couples are physically together but emotionally elsewhere—due to device distraction—intimacy and trust diminish. A study published in *Computers in Human Behavior* showed that couples who spend significant time on phones during shared moments report lower relationship satisfaction. Similarly, MIT professor Dr. Sherry Turkle has explored how technology affects human connection. Her findings suggest that while devices create the illusion of connection, they often inhibit genuine communication, especially when one partner feels ignored or dismissed.

Breaking Up with Your Phone: How to Reclaim Your Attention and Your Marriage

The good news is that the damaging effects of tech overuse on relationships are reversible. Couples who consciously set boundaries around phone usage—like creating device-free zones or no-phone times—report improved communication and emotional closeness. Research supports that shared, uninterrupted activities (e.g., cooking, walking, or praying together) rebuild connection and trust. Experts like Dr. Gary Chapman emphasize that being emotionally and physically present without distraction is essential to sustaining a healthy relationship. Small shifts in behavior—such as putting the phone away during meals or limiting screen time before bed—can lead to significant improvements in marital satisfaction.

Taking Control: Setting Boundaries to Protect Your Relationship

Rebuilding connection starts with intentional change. Experts like Dr. Sherry Turkle recommend reintroducing uninterrupted face-to-face conversation as a foundational tool for relational repair. This might mean turning off phones during shared meals or scheduling time to talk without digital interference. Even brief daily check-ins without distraction can rebuild emotional trust. When couples unplug, they give themselves space to reconnect—not just with each other but with their own thoughts and feelings. In an age of constant connectivity, protecting your relationship requires mindful disconnection.

Mindful Tech Use: How to Avoid Falling into the Digital Trap

In a world where smartphones have become nearly inseparable from daily life, it's easy to let them dominate our attention—shaping our time, focus, and even emotions. To counter this, many thought leaders in psychology and behavioral science encourage mindful tech use: a more intentional, values-based approach to interacting with our devices.

Dr. Cal Newport, known for his work on digital minimalism, emphasizes that healthy tech habits aren't just about cutting screen time—they're about selectively engaging with tools that serve meaningful purposes. Instead of allowing technology to seep into every corner of our lives, he advocates for eliminating apps or platforms that don't align with our deeper goals, freeing up space for what truly matters: family, relationships, creativity, and rest.

Mindful tech use is about more than productivity. It invites us to examine how our devices affect our emotional and relational wellbeing. By choosing when and how we engage—like putting phones away during meals or moments of connection—we create an environment that prioritizes presence over distraction. These small boundaries send a powerful message to loved ones: they matter more than any notification.

Dr. Sherry Turkle, a leading researcher on technology and communication, has explored how digital habits have reshaped the way we relate. She notes that many people have outsourced emotional presence to devices, weakening the depth of real-world interactions. Mindful phone use, then, becomes a method of reclaiming those lost connections—one eye-to-eye conversation at a time.

Detoxing Together: How to Use Phone Breaks to Strengthen Your Bond

While solo screen detoxes are helpful, doing it together as a couple can strengthen emotional intimacy and restore shared experiences. Constant notifications, endless scrolling, and fragmented attention often create emotional distance—even when partners are in the same room. Agreeing to disconnect from devices at the same time turns that distance into closeness.

Research from the University of Texas shows that couples who regularly unplug together report better communication, reduced stress, and stronger satisfaction in their relationships. Studies published in *Psychology Today* also reinforce that time spent free from phones allows for more meaningful conversations and deeper emotional bonding. Shared tech-free experiences—whether it's a walk, board game, or uninterrupted talk—rebuild connection by removing the noise of the digital world.

Importantly, tech detoxing works best when it becomes a shared ritual, not a solo effort. When both partners agree to silence their phones during dinner or unplug before bedtime, they cultivate a habit of mutual presence. These acts communicate mutual respect and shared priority—each person affirming that their relationship is more valuable than what's happening online.

Building a Healthier Relationship with Technology: Long-Term Tips for Lasting Change

Creating a healthier digital environment begins with intentional design—both physically and emotionally. Long-term success lies in building routines and shared spaces that support focused, undistracted time together. Studies published in *The Journal of Social and Personal Relationships* show that couples who establish tech-free zones—such as keeping devices out of the bedroom or dining room—tend to experience stronger communication and deeper intimacy.

Dr. Gary Chapman, known for his work on emotional bonding, emphasizes the value of uninterrupted quality time in relationships. Whether it's the first hour after waking or weekend mornings spent together, intentionally stepping away from screens creates "sacred space" for meaningful connection. These moments foster trust, emotional safety, and stronger relational bonds.

In addition to spatial boundaries, establishing tech-free time blocks is equally important. This could include setting aside time before bed or during meals to remain completely present with one another. When couples treat these times as non-negotiable, it reinforces the idea that their relationship is a priority over digital interruptions. These habits help each spouse feel seen, heard, and valued.

Neuroscientist Dr. Michael Merzenich has discussed how the human brain struggles under the constant stream of digital input. The regular influx of messages, alerts, and social media updates fragments our focus and reduces our ability to stay mentally and emotionally engaged. By establishing boundaries around tech use, couples protect not only their relationships but also their own cognitive well-being.

The Key to Long-Term Success: Balance

The goal isn't to eliminate phone use entirely—it's to find balance. A healthy relationship with technology supports individual wellness and nurtures the relationship between partners. Functional medicine advocate Dr. Mark Hyman has often pointed out that balance is foundational to overall health—and this extends to our digital lives as well.

Balance involves using technology with intention. Phones can support relationships by helping us stay connected with loved ones, coordinate family life, or even exchange kind messages throughout the day. But unchecked or compulsive phone use can erode intimacy, create emotional distance, and prevent couples from being present for each other.

Psychologist Dr. John Cacioppo's work has explored how the more we rely on digital connections, the more we risk weakening the deeper, emotionally rich bonds that are only formed through face-to-face interaction. The challenge lies in creating a middle ground—one where phones are useful tools, not relationship disruptors.

In marriage, balance might look like agreeing on device-free evenings, turning phones off during shared meals or vacations, or putting them away before bed. When both spouses commit to a mindful approach to technology, it helps preserve the trust and emotional closeness that healthy marriages rely on.

Your Phone Isn't Going Anywhere—But You Don't Have to Let It Ruin Your Marriage

Smartphones are here to stay. And while we may not be able to eliminate their presence in our lives, we can take back control of how they affect our relationships. The goal is not digital abstinence, but digital awareness—recognizing how easily devices steal our attention and taking proactive steps to reclaim it.

Creating tech-free zones, setting boundaries on usage, and prioritizing in-person connection are all small but significant practices. These choices allow couples to re-center their focus on each other, strengthening the bond that technology often threatens to weaken.

Author and MIT professor Dr. Sherry Turkle has long highlighted the impact of technology on human relationships, especially the way it interrupts meaningful conversation. She urges people to be more intentional in how they interact with digital tools, advocating for deeper, face-to-face connections that foster real emotional presence.

You and your partner deserve a relationship that isn't constantly interrupted by pings, notifications, or mindless scrolling. With mindfulness, communication, and shared commitment, you can reclaim your time and build a stronger, more connected marriage—one that flourishes not in spite of technology, but because you've learned how to use it wisely.

Chapter Thirty-Nine
Modern Masculinity Redefined

In the shifting landscape of contemporary society, the concept of masculinity has become a subject of intense debate. Traditional notions of masculinity—such as assertiveness, leadership, and stoicism—are being challenged by social movements that seek to redefine gender roles. These changes have led to a growing divide, where one side advocates for a progressive, emotionally open masculinity, and the other pushes back with a more reactionary stance, seen in communities like the Red Pill movement.

This chapter aims to examine masculinity through multiple lenses—scientific, philosophical, religious, and psychological—to provide a comprehensive understanding of both healthy and toxic masculinity. By drawing on the wisdom of the Prophet Muhammad (ﷺ), modern psychological theories, Stoic philosophy, and the voices of scholars who specialize in men's studies, we will explore what it means to be a healthy, responsible man in today's world.

Positive Masculinity:
The Foundation of Strength and Virtue

At its core, positive masculinity involves embodying virtues such as integrity, emotional intelligence, self-control, and compassion. Healthy masculinity acknowledges that strength is not just about physical dominance or emotional stoicism, but about using one's strength to protect, nurture, and lead with empathy. True masculinity, when it is positive, promotes balance—strength with gentleness, authority with humility, and independence with interdependence.

The concept of masculinity in Islam emphasizes values such as justice, patience, mercy, and protection. The Prophet Muhammad (ﷺ) exemplified these virtues throughout his life. His approach to masculinity was far removed from the often rigid, emotionally distant image of traditional manhood. He was known for his gentleness with his family, his concern for the welfare of others, and his constant striving to be just and fair. His life exemplifies the integration of both strength and compassion.

As the Prophet Muhammad (ﷺ) is reported to have said:

> "The best of you are those who are best to their wives." (*Tirmidhi*)

This simple but profound statement underscores that the measure of a man's greatness is not his dominance, but his kindness and fairness in relationships.

Philosophical Foundations: Stoicism and Positive Masculinity

In Stoic philosophy, the concept of masculinity aligns closely with the ideals of emotional resilience, personal responsibility, and ethical virtue. Stoicism, developed by philosophers such as Epictetus, Seneca, and Marcus Aurelius, teaches that true strength comes not from external circumstances or from brute force, but from inner control and moral courage. Marcus Aurelius, in particular, emphasized the idea of accepting responsibility for one's actions and emotions, as seen in his famous meditations: "You have power over your mind, not outside events. Realize this, and you will find strength." This resonates with the modern understanding of emotional intelligence—being in control of one's emotions, understanding them, and using them wisely in relationships and decision-making.

In fact, the Prophet defined strength as the ability to regulate ones' emotions, in particular anger. The Messenger of Allah (ﷺ) said: "The strong is not the one who overcomes others by his strength, but the strong is the one who controls himself while in anger." (Sahih al-Bukhari, Hadith 6114; Sahih Muslim, Hadith 2609)

Psychologists have found that emotional quotient (EQ) is a key aspect of positive masculinity. According to Daniel Goleman, author of *Emotional Intelligence*, those who score higher on EQ are better equipped to handle stress, communicate effectively, and build healthy relationships. These attributes are essential for men to navigate the complexities of modern society and lead fulfilling lives.

A study by the American Psychological Association (APA) has shown that men who are emotionally aware and empathetic tend to have stronger relationships and better mental health outcomes. Thus, positive masculinity is not only about being strong in the traditional sense, but about cultivating a deep understanding of one's own emotional landscape and the emotions of others.

The Pitfalls of Toxic Masculinity

Toxic masculinity refers to harmful behaviors and beliefs that are rooted in traditional gender norms. It promotes aggression, emotional suppression, dominance, and the rejection of anything perceived as "feminine." Toxic masculinity is not just about being violent or controlling; it also manifests in smaller, subtler ways, such as the dismissal of emotions or the pressure to conform to a narrow set of behaviors and expectations.

Toxic masculinity is dangerous for both men and women. Psychologists such as Dr. Michael Kimmel, a leading scholar in men's studies, have long studied the impact of rigid gender norms on men's mental health. In his seminal work, *Guyland*, Kimmel explores how boys and young men are socialized into toxic behaviors and beliefs that stunt their emotional growth and personal development. In *Guyland*, Michael Kimmel discusses how many young men are socialized to equate masculinity with toughness, emotional suppression, and rejection of anything considered feminine. This restrictive view of manhood, he argues, leads to emotional isolation and dissatisfaction.

Psychological research further supports Kimmel's observations. Studies by the APA have found that men who adhere to traditional masculine norms—such as emotional stoicism, aggression, and dominance—are more likely to experience depression, substance abuse, and even suicidal tendencies. One study published in *Psychological Science* in 2019 found that men who were more rigid in their masculine gender roles were significantly more likely to report lower life satisfaction and poorer mental health outcomes.

Islam offers a counter-narrative to this toxic form of masculinity. The Prophet Muhammad (ﷺ) exemplified emotional resilience through vulnerability, humility, and compassion. For instance, he was known for his empathy in dealing with grief, as demonstrated when his son Ibrahim passed away. Despite his sorrow, the Prophet (ﷺ) openly expressed his emotions in a way that broke from the harsh, emotionally repressive norms of his time. In a famous hadith, the Prophet (ﷺ) said:

> "The eyes shed tears and the heart feels sorrow, but we will not say except what pleases our Lord." (Sahih Bukhari)

This openness to feeling deeply and expressing emotion challenges the notion that masculinity must be synonymous with emotional repression.

Extreme Feminism and the Gender Divide

While feminism has played a vital role in advocating for women's rights, certain extreme strands of feminism have contributed to the perception that masculinity itself is inherently toxic or oppressive. Radical feminist ideologies often frame all aspects of traditional masculinity as part of the patriarchy that needs to be dismantled. This broad-brush approach to masculinity not only vilifies men but also sets up a divisive dynamic that pits men against women in a zero-sum struggle for power.

The rise of this extreme form of feminism has inadvertently created a backlash, as men seek to protect their identities and roles in society. Dr. Warren Farrell, author of *The Myth of Male Power*, argues that when men are viewed solely as holders of privilege and power, society tends to overlook their real struggles—such as disproportionate workplace deaths, higher rates of depression, and suicide. His work challenges the traditional narrative by highlighting the unseen costs men bear in the name of fulfilling societal expectations around masculinity, provision, and stoicism. Farrell's work emphasizes that the negative effects of extreme feminist rhetoric on men are often overlooked. When masculinity is reduced to the sum of patriarchal power and oppression, it ignores the complexities of men's experiences and their unique challenges.

This view of men as inherently harmful or irrelevant has been further amplified by the rise of the Red Pill movement, which advocates for a more extreme, reactionary form of masculinity. The Red Pill movement argues that traditional gender roles—where men were the primary protectors and providers—are being undermined in modern society, leaving men vulnerable and emasculated.

The Red Pill Movement: A Reactionary Force

The Red Pill movement, named after the infamous scene in *The Matrix*, which offers a "red pill" to awaken one to the truth of reality, claims to offer men the truth about their role in a society that, they argue, has been skewed against them by feminism. The movement emphasizes self-interest, emotional detachment, and a focus on personal success, often at the expense of authentic emotional connection and mutual respect in relationships.

Dr. Michael Kimmel, one of the leading experts in gender studies, critiques movements like the Red Pill for perpetuating a culture of grievance and victimhood among men. In his book *Angry White Men*, Kimmel explores how many men, particularly those who feel alienated by feminist progress and shifting gender roles, are drawn to these ideologies in an attempt to reclaim a sense of control or lost dominance. He argues that in pursuing this form of power, men often end up reinforcing the very stereotypes and social barriers that hinder their emotional development, strain their relationships, and ultimately prevent them from leading more connected and fulfilling lives.

While there is some merit to the frustration expressed by Red Pill adherents—particularly their sense of alienation and disenfranchisement—these views ultimately promote a divisive, antagonistic approach to gender dynamics, one that fosters conflict rather than cooperation between men and women. And most importantly, this movement fails to address the root cause of so-called "toxic masculinity": unhealed trauma. Without the tools to process pain, some men may end up looking for outlets to channel their rage.

A Balanced Path Forward: Embracing Healthy Masculinity

In the search for a healthy, balanced form of masculinity, men can draw on a combination of ancient wisdom, modern psychological insights, and spiritual teachings. Stoicism teaches the importance of self-control, while Islamic teachings emphasize empathy, justice, and responsibility. The Prophet Muhammad (ﷺ) remains the perfect role model of a man who embodied strength with compassion, leadership with humility, and responsibility with love.

Incorporating the insights of psychology, philosophy, and faith, men can build a healthy masculinity that is grounded in emotional awareness, ethical behavior, and a sense of purpose. By cultivating their emotional intelligence, building meaningful relationships, and striving to lead by example, men can reclaim their roles as leaders and protectors, not by dominance but by mutual respect and shared responsibility.

Healthy masculinity is one that is not afraid to show vulnerability, to express emotions, and to seek self-improvement—while also maintaining the strength to support others and to lead with integrity. Healthy masculinity is the courage to look inward at ones' own unhealthy patterns and unconscious programming. It is the strength required to take accountability for unhealed trauma. By drawing on the wisdom of the past, the teachings of Islam, and the principles of modern psychology, men can reclaim true masculinity through healing old, unresolved childhood wounds.

10 Pathways to Reclaiming Healthy Masculinity

1. **Seek Out Mental Health Support from Male-Specialized Therapists**

   Find a licensed therapist or counselor who specializes in men's mental health. These professionals are trained to navigate issues like emotional suppression, anger, shame, relationship distress, or identity confusion—often rooted in socialized gender norms.

   Why it matters: Studies show men are less likely to seek therapy, but those who do experience greater resilience, emotional regulation, and healthier relationships.

   Where to start: Look for directories like Psychology Today or Muslim therapist networks. For faith-based support, search for culturally competent therapists who respect your spiritual values.

2. **Explore Men's Coaching or Mentorship Programs**

   Male-focused coaching programs or mentorship circles offer structured accountability and guidance in areas such as emotional mastery, purpose, relationships, and spiritual growth.

   Positive influence: Thinkers like Robert Greene (author of *The 48 Laws of Power* and *The Laws of Human Nature*), Dr. Gabor Maté (trauma and emotional healing expert), and Alain de Botton (founder of *The School of Life*) provide profound insights into self-awareness, emotional intelligence, and relational depth. Similarly, Muslim male mentors who promote a growth mindset, spiritual consciousness, and integrity can serve as valuable guides for men seeking balanced development.

Islamic reflection: The Prophet (ﷺ) mentored his companions individually, tailoring advice to their strengths and struggles—modeling the power of personalized mentorship. A beautiful example of the Prophet Muhammad (ﷺ) mentoring companions individually is found in his tailored advice to Abu Dharr al-Ghifari (RA):

> "O Abu Dharr, I see you are weak, and I love for you what I love for myself. Do not take leadership over even two people, and do not manage the property of an orphan." (Sahih Muslim 1826)

Why it matters: Abu Dharr (RA) was a devout, honest companion known for his simplicity and strong sense of justice. However, he had a temperament that wasn't suited to leadership roles requiring diplomacy and political tact. Instead of giving generic advice, the Prophet (ﷺ) gave him guidance based on his individual strengths and limitations—showing deep emotional intelligence and care.

Other Examples of Personalized Mentorship:

Mu'adh ibn Jabal (RA) – The Prophet (ﷺ) sent him to Yemen as a judge and teacher, telling him:

"You will be judging among people. What will you judge with?" (Abu Dawud 3592, Hasan)

(Then he guided him on how to base judgments on the Qur'an and Sunnah, and to use reasoning when necessary).

Abdullah ibn Abbas (RA) – As a young boy, the Prophet (ﷺ) taught him directly:

"Young man, I will teach you some words: Be mindful of Allah and He will protect you…" (Tirmidhi 2516)

Each companion had different roles, strengths, and personalities. The Prophet (ﷺ) mentored them with wisdom, empathy, and vision—shaping them into leaders, thinkers, and doers, each according to their God-given potential.

3. Study Male Role Models with Depth and Integrity

Redefine your role models by choosing men who exemplify compassion, courage, moral clarity, and spiritual strength—not bravado, dominance, or shallow materialism.

Look to timeless examples such as:

- **The Prophet Muhammad** (ﷺ): The ultimate model of balanced masculinity, combining mercy, humility, and justice.

- **Khalid ibn al-Walid**: The embodiment of courage, strategic brilliance, and unwavering loyalty to truth.

- **Malcolm X**: A man who underwent radical transformation, shifting from a life of survival and anger to one of spiritual purpose, integrity, and moral vision. His journey reminds us that masculine growth is a process of internal refinement.

- **Muhammad Ali**: A figure who modeled confidence with compassion, faith over fame, and the courage to stand up for truth, even at great personal cost.

And of course, one cannot speak of noble masculine character without honoring the ten companions of the Prophet (ﷺ) who were promised Paradise during their lifetimes (al-`Asharah al-Mubashsharah). These men—including Abu Bakr as-Siddiq, Umar ibn al-Khattab, Uthman ibn Affan, Ali ibn Abi Talib, Talhah ibn Ubaydullah, Zubair ibn al-Awwam, Abdur Rahman ibn Awf, Sa'd ibn Abi Waqqas, Sa'id ibn Zayd, and Abu Ubaidah ibn al-Jarrah (may Allah be pleased with them all)—demonstrated extraordinary devotion, courage, humility, and leadership.

Each of these companions embodied unique aspects of healthy masculinity:

- **Abu Bakr** showed gentleness paired with firmness in truth.

- **Umar** combined strength with justice and deep care for the oppressed.

- **Uthman** modeled generosity and quiet leadership.

- **Ali** embodied intellectual brilliance and chivalry.

- The others, like **Talhah, Zubair,** and **Abdur Rahman ibn Awf**, displayed loyalty, sacrifice, and humility in both battle and peace.

Studying their lives offers men a spectrum of healthy male virtues rooted in faith, ethics, and responsibility. In a time when masculinity is often confused or misdirected, returning to the Seerah and the stories of these great companions offers a practical, faith-based framework for rediscovering what it truly means to be a man of substance and service.

4. **Understand and Strengthen Emotional Quotient (EQ)**

   Learn to name and manage your emotions. Emotional intelligence is the foundation of healthy masculinity and relationship success. According to psychologist Daniel Goleman, EQ includes self-awareness, empathy, and effective communication.

   Tool: Practice daily emotional check-ins ("What am I feeling right now and why?") and journal through your emotional responses.

   In Islam: The Prophet (ﷺ) validated the emotions of others and openly expressed his own sadness, joy, and love—without shame.

5. **Join a Brotherhood of Accountability**

   Isolation breeds unhealthy behavior. Seek out men's groups (faith-based, personal growth, or emotional development focused) where vulnerability, accountability, and growth are welcomed.

   Why it matters: Research from Movember and APA shows that men thrive emotionally when they have consistent, safe peer support.

   What to look for: Circles where men discuss faith, marriage, healing, and purpose—not just sports or status.

6. **Detach from Toxic Masculine Influences (Red Pill, Incels, etc.)**

   Consciously unfollow or unsubscribe from content that reinforces toxic ideas about women, emotion, or relationships. These narratives fuel insecurity, resentment, and victimhood.

   Replace with: Podcasts, books, and teachers who promote purpose, balance, and ethical strength—like Ustadh Ubaydullah Evans, Sh. Omar Suleiman, Sh. Dr. Yasir Qadhi, Sh. Abdullah Oduro, Shaykh Abdal Hakim Murad, Imam Suhaib Webb, Shaykh AbdulNasir Jangda, Shaykh Mikaeel Smith, Ustadh Abdel-

Rahman Murphy, Shaykh Navaid Aziz, Mufti Abdul Rahman Waheed, Mufti Abdul Wahab Waheed, Dr. Gabor Maté, etc..
Remember: What you consume, you eventually become.

7. Practice Daily Habits that Reinforce Integrity and Purpose

Small habits shape character. Build rituals of self-discipline (like exercise, prayer, service, journaling) to align your actions with your values.

Psychologically: Habits build neural patterns that reinforce calmness, purpose, and confidence.

Islamic parallel: The Prophet (ﷺ) emphasized consistency in good deeds/actions, even if small (Sahih Bukhari). Routines ground us when life feels chaotic.

8. Learn Conflict Resolution and Communication Skills

Healthy masculinity includes the ability to resolve disagreements with calm, empathy, and respect. Avoid yelling, silent treatment, or passive-aggression.

Skillset to learn: Active listening, "I" statements, time-outs, and emotional validation—taught in Gottman Institute training and EFT therapy.

Practice: When triggered, pause and ask yourself: "Is this response aligned with the man I want to be?"

9. Reframe Vulnerability as Strength

Vulnerability is not weakness—it's the gateway to connection, healing, and leadership. Men who repress emotions often explode later or grow cold and distant.

Science shows: Vulnerability builds trust and emotional intimacy in relationships (Brené Brown, APA).

Islamically: The Prophet (ﷺ) cried at moments of loss, forgave those who wronged him, and spoke openly about his pain—setting the highest example of courage through vulnerability.

10. Reflect Spiritually on Your Role as a Man

Use the lens of your faith to explore what Allah expects of you as a man—not what culture or influencers dictate. Reflect on ayahs like:

"Men are protectors and maintainers of women…" (Qur'an 4:34) and "And live with them in kindness." (Qur'an 4:19)

Ask: Am I protecting with love or controlling with fear? Am I leading with justice or with ego?

Pray: Prayer, dhikr, and du'a are tools to reconnect with your Creator and soften the heart.

Chapter Forty

The Gift and the Grief of Feminism

Feminism, in its purest form, is the belief in and advocacy for gender equality—the idea that men and women should have equal rights and opportunities in society. However, like any ideology, feminism has evolved and diverged into multiple forms, some of which are beneficial and progressive, while others have raised concerns about the negative impacts they have on individuals and society.

In this chapter, we explore both the positive and negative forms of feminism. We will delve into the ways in which feminism has empowered women to break through societal barriers and claim their rightful place in the world, while also examining the potential harms of certain radical branches of feminism, which some view as fostering division and resentment. Alongside this, we will explore the effects of unhealthy sexual liberation and the pitfalls of sexual promiscuity, offering a balanced view that integrates scientific research, Islamic teachings, relationship psychology, and philosophical reflections to provide a well-rounded understanding of feminism and its role in shaping modern societies.

The Positive Side of Feminism

Breaking Barriers: Feminism and Women's Empowerment

At its heart, feminism has played an instrumental role in challenging and dismantling the systemic inequalities that have historically oppressed women. From the suffragette movement, which fought for women's right to vote, to the modern-day feminist movement advocating for equal pay, legal rights, and freedom from gender-based violence, feminism has been a powerful tool in reshaping societal structures.

Science and historical research demonstrate the tangible impact of feminism. Studies show that nations that have embraced feminist ideals and gender equality experience a higher quality of life for all citizens, regardless of gender. For instance, a study published in *The Lancet* in 2020 revealed that when women are given access to education and economic opportunities, it leads to lower rates of poverty, improved health outcomes, and greater social stability. Feminism, in this sense, is not just about women; it's about creating a better world for everyone.

Additionally, women-led movements in Western societies have been instrumental in reshaping public attitudes toward gender, leadership, and opportunity. Take Jacinda Ardern, former Prime Minister of New Zealand, who became an international symbol of compassionate leadership and crisis management. Dr. Brené Brown, a research professor and bestselling author, brought emotional intelligence, vulnerability, and courage into the mainstream conversation on leadership and human connection. Rather than relying on symbolic representation alone, many women have emerged as substantive change-makers—blending intellect, empathy, and ethical leadership in arenas once dominated by men.

Islamic Perspective on Feminism

From an Islamic viewpoint, feminism aligns with many of the core values promoted by the faith. Islam, when understood in its true essence, advocates for the inherent dignity, rights, and equality of women. The Qur'an emphasizes the spiritual and social equality of men and women, stating:

> "And their Lord has accepted of them and answered them: 'Never will I allow to be lost the work of any of you, whether male or female. You are members, one of another.'" (Qur'an 3:195)

This verse highlights the equal standing of men and women in the eyes of God, and Islam has numerous examples of strong, independent women who contributed significantly to society, such as Khadijah bint Khuwaylid, the first wife of the Prophet Muhammad (ﷺ), who was a successful businesswoman, and Aisha bint Abi Bakr, a scholar and an important figure in Islamic history.

Many Islamic scholars agree that the foundational aims of feminism—such as advocating for justice, dignity, and equal rights for women—can align with the core values of Islam. Long before modern feminist movements emerged, Islam granted women rights that were revolutionary for their time, including the right to inherit, to be educated, to own property, and to give or withhold consent in marriage. Women in early Islam were also politically active: they gave public pledges of allegiance (bay'ah) directly to the Prophet Muhammad (ﷺ), participated in community consultation (shūrā), and were appointed to public positions, such as Al-Shifā' bint Abdullah (RA), whom Caliph Umar (RA) entrusted with supervising the marketplace. These rights and recognitions were established more than a millennium before Western women secured the right to vote through the suffragist and suffragette movements just over a century ago. These principles are firmly grounded in the Qur'an and Sunnah. The Prophet Muhammad (ﷺ) stated, "Seeking knowledge is obligatory upon every Muslim" (Sunan Ibn Majah 224, Hasan according to Al-Albani), emphasizing the universal importance of education for both men and women. Meanwhile, the Qur'an teaches that true worth is determined by piety and righteousness, not by gender or lineage: "Indeed, the most noble of you in the sight of Allah is the most righteous of you." (Qur'an 49:13)

Throughout Islamic history, women such as Khadijah (RA), Aisha (RA), and Fatima al-Fihri exemplified leadership, scholarship, and independence.

Fatima al-Fihri was a devout and visionary Muslim woman originally from Kairouan (present-day Tunisia) who later settled in Fez, Morocco. In 859 CE, she used her inheritance to establish what would become one of the most important educational institutions in history: the University of al-Qarawiyyin. Founded as both a mosque and a center for learning, al-Qarawiyyin is officially recognized by UNESCO and the Guinness World Records as the oldest existing and continually operating university in the world. Fatima's legacy stands as a testament to the vital role Muslim women have played in the advancement of education, social development, and intellectual life throughout Islamic civilization. Her contribution not only shaped the academic landscape of her time but continues to inspire generations, highlighting that women have long been foundational to the flourishing of knowledge and community in the Muslim world.

cholars also acknowledge that while the essence of feminism—seeking justice and equal opportunity—is harmonious with Islam, not all branches of modern feminism align with Islamic ethics. Contemporary feminist ideologies can at times promote values that contradict Islamic teachings, particularly in areas related to gender roles, family structures, or sexual ethics. As such, respected scholars and thought leaders — including Shaykh Akram

Nadwi, Dr. Ingrid Mattson, Ustadha Yasmin Mogahed, Dr. Umar Faruq Abd-Allah, Ustadh Ubaydullah Evans, Shaykh Yasir Qadhi, Imam Suhaib Webb, Shaykh Abdul Nasir Jangda, and Ustadha Dalia Mogahed — advocate for a faith-based approach to gender equity. They encourage Muslims to champion women's rights within a framework that remains rooted in the Qur'an, Sunnah, and Islamic tradition—ensuring that empowerment does not come at the cost of spiritual and moral integrity. This list is by no means exhaustive; many other scholars, educators, and thinkers around the world continue to contribute meaningfully to this important conversation.

Shaykh Akram Nadwi has conducted extensive research highlighting the significant contributions of women in Islamic scholarship. In his monumental 43-volume biographical work, *Al-Wafā' bi Asmā' al-Nisā'*, he documents over 10,000 female hadith scholars, underscoring the pivotal roles women have played in the transmission and preservation of Islamic knowledge throughout history. In his article *Critical Reflections on Feminism*, Shaykh Nadwi acknowledges the importance of supporting women facing injustice or hardship, emphasizing that assisting women in need aligns with Islamic principles. However, he expresses caution regarding contemporary feminist movements that are based on specific gender theories, suggesting that some aspects may not be entirely compatible with Islamic teachings. As Shaykh Nadwi powerfully states, **"Muslim women scholars of the past did not need feminism to empower them. They were empowered by Islam itself."** Furthermore, he advocates for co-educational learning environments, noting that historically, men and women often attended classes together under the guidance of both male and female instructors. He asserts that the Islamic ideal emphasizes modesty and self-restraint rather than strict physical segregation, and that mixed-gender educational settings can be conducive to learning when conducted with proper decorum.

Dr. Ingrid Mattson has emphasized the importance of ethical transformation in gender relations within Muslim communities through a spiritually grounded approach. Her work often draws upon classical Islamic scholarship to support positive change rooted in authentic tradition.

Ustadha Yasmin Mogahed has critiqued some secular feminist frameworks, particularly those that detach empowerment from divine purpose. She frequently underscores that true empowerment for Muslim women must be grounded in Islamic teachings rather than in reactive or comparative models.

Dr. Umar Faruq Abd-Allah has written extensively on how Islamic civilization historically integrated diverse cultural expressions—including views on gender roles—within the boundaries of sacred law. His approach encourages a nuanced understanding of gender informed by both tradition and context.

Shaykh Yasir Qadhi emphasizes the importance of understanding gender roles within an Islamic framework. He advocates for a balanced approach that recognizes the distinct responsibilities and rights of men and women as outlined in the Qur'an and Sunnah. Dr. Qadhi cautions against adopting external ideologies uncritically, suggesting that Muslims should derive their understanding of gender roles from authentic Islamic teachings to ensure both spiritual and social harmony.

Ustadh Ubaydullah Evans' approach is characterized by a commitment to Islamic ethics, emphasizing emotional safety, mutual respect, and constructive dialogue. He encourages open and honest conversations about gender dynamics within the Muslim community, believing that fostering environments where both men and women can express themselves authentically is crucial for addressing issues of gender equity.

Ustadha Dalia Mogahed, a prominent American Muslim scholar and Director of Research at the Institute for Social Policy and Understanding, emphasizes that human development, rather than secularization, is crucial for women's empowerment in the evolving Middle East. She asserts that enhancing education and economic opportunities within an Islamic framework is essential for advancing women's rights in the region.

In her 2016 TED Talk, Mogahed addressed misconceptions about Muslim women, advocating for a nuanced understanding of their experiences. She highlighted the importance of recognizing the diversity and agency of Muslim women, challenging stereotypes that portray them as universally oppressed.

Furthermore, Mogahed has participated in discussions critiquing Western feminist perspectives on Muslim women's attire, particularly the hijab. She argues that the hijab serves to privatize women's sexuality, thereby empowering them by shifting focus from appearance to intellect and character. This perspective encourages a reevaluation of assumptions about the role of religious practices in women's autonomy. Through her research and public engagements, Dalia Mogahed advocates for an approach to women's empowerment that is deeply rooted in Islamic values, emphasizing education, personal agency, and a critical examination of cultural narratives.

Imam Suhaib Webb addresses issues concerning women's rights in the context of marriage and personal agency. He underscores the importance of acknowledging and upholding the rights granted to women by Islamic law, particularly in matters of marriage and divorce. Imam Webb also highlights the necessity for Muslim communities to support women who seek to exercise these rights, ensuring that cultural practices do not overshadow the equitable principles established by Islam.

Shaykh Abdul Nasir Jangda reflects on the significant roles women played during the time of the Prophet Muhammad (ﷺ). He brings attention to the contributions of female companions who were actively involved in various aspects of society, including nurturing and educating the Prophet (ﷺ). Shaykh Jangda emphasizes that these historical accounts serve as powerful reminders of the esteemed position and rights of women in Islam, encouraging contemporary Muslims to recognize and honor these roles within the framework of Islamic tradition.

Collectively, these scholars call for the advancement of women's rights and gender equity within an Islamic framework—one that aligns with the moral, spiritual, and ethical foundations of the faith.

Toxic Feminism: The Dark Side of the Movement

When Feminism Becomes Divisive

While feminism has done much to improve the lives of women worldwide, there is a growing concern about certain radical strains of feminism that may have negative consequences for both men and women. These extreme versions of feminism often portray men as the "enemy" and can foster a sense of hostility rather than equality.

One key issue with toxic feminism is that it tends to reject the idea of complementarity between the sexes, which is an essential principle in both Islamic teachings and many traditional philosophical systems. According to this perspective, men and women are not in competition but complement each other in various social, familial, and professional roles.

Toxic feminism also often overlooks the challenges men face in modern society. For example, men are more likely to be affected by societal expectations regarding stoicism and emotional repression. Research from the APA has shown that the pressure on men to conform to traditional notions of masculinity—such as being emotionally distant, self-sufficient, and physically dominant—can lead to mental health issues, including depression and anxiety. Toxic feminism's oversimplified binary of "women are oppressed, men are oppressors" fails to address these nuanced gender dynamics and only deepens the divide between the sexes.

Psychological and Sociological Insights on Toxic Feminism

Experts in gender studies and relationship psychology have pointed out the dangers of extremism in any movement. According to Dr. Warren Farrell, when feminism becomes "anti-male," it harms both genders. Dr. Farrell argues that true gender equality should focus on dismantling not just the patriarchy but also the gender stereotypes that limit both men and women.

Farrell explains that one of the misconceptions fostered by extreme feminist rhetoric is that men hold power in every aspect of life, while women are perpetually oppressed. In his research, Farrell discusses the concept of "disposable males," which refers to the societal tendency to place a higher value on women's lives, particularly in the context of family and society. He explains that, in reality, men are also disadvantaged in several areas, such as health outcomes and life expectancy.

Toxic feminism also often minimizes the emotional and psychological needs of men, reinforcing the stereotype that men should suppress their emotions and avoid seeking help. This can lead to negative consequences such as higher suicide rates among men, as they are less likely to seek therapy or open up about their struggles due to societal stigma.

A Reaction to Extreme Feminism

The rise of the "Red Pill" movement among men is, in part, a reaction to the perceived excesses of extreme feminism. Originating from the *Matrix* movie metaphor, the "Red Pill" movement encourages men to awaken to the truth about gender dynamics, which, they argue, feminists have obscured or ignored.

At its core, the Red Pill movement advocates for the rejection of traditional societal expectations that limit men's personal freedom. However, it also has its controversial elements. Critics argue that some Red Pill ideologies foster a dangerous sense of victimhood among men, viewing women as adversaries rather than partners in achieving equality. The movement has been criticized for promoting misogynistic views that justify men's sense of entitlement to women's attention and admiration.

Psychologists and relationship experts have noted that the Red Pill movement, while initially appealing to disillusioned men seeking to understand their place in a rapidly changing world, can promote unhealthy, toxic masculinity. According to Dr. Michael Kimmel, a leading sociologist on gender studies, movements like Red Pill are harmful because they do not offer real solutions to the complex issues surrounding gender. Instead, they oversimplify gender dynamics and often encourage harmful behaviors, such as objectification of women and rejection of emotional vulnerability in men.

Unhealthy Sexual Liberation and the Pitfalls of Sexual Promiscuity

The Rise of Sexual Liberation: A Double-Edged Sword

The concept of sexual liberation has been a key component of feminist ideology, promoting the right of women to express their sexuality freely, without judgment or restriction. On the surface, this seems like a healthy, progressive stance, encouraging sexual autonomy and equality. However, as with many aspects of feminism, there are unintended consequences when the pendulum swings too far.

In recent decades, sexual promiscuity has been normalized in many circles, particularly within Western culture. The notion that a woman's sexual liberation can only be validated through frequent sexual encounters has led some women into a pattern of behavior that, in the long term, may not lead to personal fulfillment or emotional well-being.

Scientific Insights into Sexual Promiscuity

Research on sexual behavior shows that while casual sex can sometimes be experienced as empowering, it often leads to negative emotional and psychological consequences. A study published in *The Journal of Social and Personal Relationships* in 2019 found that individuals who engage in casual sex without emotional intimacy often experience feelings of regret, loneliness, and lower levels of well-being. Women, in particular, report feeling more emotionally impacted by casual sex than men, with many experiencing feelings of emptiness after sexual encounters that lack emotional connection.

Dr. Lisa Diamond, a leading researcher in the field of sexual psychology, argues that while sexual liberation and freedom of expression are important, they need to be understood within the broader context of emotional well-being and relational health. She suggests that individuals—both men and women—who engage in sexual behavior outside of meaningful relationships often struggle with identity issues, a lack of emotional fulfillment, and difficulty forming stable, healthy partnerships.

Additionally, Dr. Kathleen Vohs, a psychologist at the University of Minnesota, conducted a study on the psychological impact of sexual promiscuity, concluding that women who engage in casual sex may experience diminished self-esteem and a sense of disconnection from their own bodies. These findings suggest that the so-called "empowerment" of sexual freedom may, in many cases, mask deeper psychological struggles.

The Role of Faith and Ethics in Sexual Behavior

Islamic teachings, in contrast to the cultural push for unrestrained sexual freedom, emphasize the importance of chastity, modesty, and respect for the sanctity of the sexual relationship. Islam acknowledges the inherent human desire for intimacy but underscores that this desire should be fulfilled within the boundaries of marriage, where emotional, physical, and spiritual aspects of the relationship are aligned. The Qur'an encourages believers to maintain dignity in their relationships, stating:

> "And those who guard their chastity, except from their wives or those whom their right hands possess, for indeed, they are not to be blamed." (Qur'an 23:5-6)

By promoting sexual relationships within marriage, Islam aims to protect individuals from the emotional and psychological harms that can arise from promiscuity. This framework suggests that intimacy should be nurtured in a loving, committed environment where mutual respect, trust, and emotional connection are prioritized.

Moving Toward Healthy Feminism and Healthy Masculinity

Towards a Balanced View

While both toxic feminism and the Red Pill movement present extreme views, it is important to aim for a balanced, healthy view of masculinity and femininity that promotes mutual respect, empathy, and understanding. True feminism should not seek to diminish the role of men in society but rather to uplift both men and women, focusing on shared humanity rather than division.

A healthy approach to feminism should celebrate the differences between men and women while advocating for equal rights and opportunities. According to relationship psychologist Dr. John Gottman, couples who approach their relationship with mutual respect, open communication, and a sense of teamwork tend to have healthier, longer-lasting marriages. These principles can apply not just to intimate relationships but also to the broader social fabric.

Islam, too, offers a framework for balanced gender roles. The Prophet Muhammad (ﷺ) encouraged mutual respect, kindness, and partnership between men and women. His teachings emphasize that true strength lies in Taqwa (God Consciousness), piety, compassion, humility, and the willingness to support one another. **"The best of you are those who are the best to their women."** (Tirmidhi) This hadith reflects the Islamic perspective on gender equality—one where men and women are partners in life, with complementary roles based on mutual respect and support, rather than opposition.

Philosophical Reflections: Stoicism and Healthy Femininity

Philosophical traditions, such as Stoicism, also provide valuable insights into healthy masculinity and femininity. Stoic philosophers like Marcus Aurelius emphasized the importance of self-control, rational thinking, and emotional resilience. These principles are valuable not just for men but for women as well. A balanced, healthy approach to femininity—just like masculinity—requires cultivating inner strength, emotional intelligence, and wisdom to navigate the complexities of modern life.

Conclusion

Feminism, at its core, has been a powerful force for positive change, advocating for equality and empowering women to rise above limitations imposed by unjust social structures. It has opened doors to education, autonomy, and participation in spaces historically closed to women. However, like all ideologies shaped by human hands, feminism is not immune to excess. Some of its more extreme forms—those that diminish the role of men, reject traditional values, or promote unrestrained sexual liberation—can unintentionally create more division than unity, eroding the very emotional, familial, and spiritual bonds that nurture healthy societies.

To build a healthier and more equitable future, we must champion a framework of gender equity that acknowledges the complexity of male–female dynamics—promoting fairness while also honoring the natural, God-given distinctions between the sexes. True empowerment lies not in rejecting our differences, but in embracing them responsibly and compassionately.

Ultimately, the truest and most sustainable model for human flourishing lies in following the Divine design of Islam—a system that preserves the sanctity, dignity, and balance between the genders. It lays out a framework of complementarity, not competition—where men and women are partners and garments for one another. Within this sacred design, there is wisdom, peace, and mercy. It is a path that does not pit the sexes against each other, but rather unites them in purpose, accountability, and mutual growth.

By grounding our pursuit of justice and empowerment in the principles of Islam, we can foster a society rooted not just in equality, but in divine harmony—where the rights, responsibilities, and roles of men and women are honored, and where true peace and blessings can endure.

Chapter Forty-One

Mother Wound - Father Wound

The concept of the **father wound** and **mother wound** has been explored by psychologists and emotional health experts for decades. These terms refer to emotional or psychological injuries that individuals may experience as a result of negative, absent, or dysfunctional relationships with their primary caregivers—often their fathers or mothers. Though these wounds form in childhood, their impacts resonate deeply into adulthood, particularly when it comes to how these individuals function in intimate relationships, including marriage.

At the core of these wounds lies a deep-seated feeling of being emotionally undernourished. Whether due to neglect, abandonment, emotional unavailability, or abuse, the child who grows up with a father or mother who fails to provide adequate emotional support or validation often struggles in adulthood to form healthy, stable relationships. In the context of marriage, these unresolved wounds can significantly affect how partners communicate, trust, and bond. This chapter will explore how these wounds manifest in the marital relationship, drawing from psychological theories, scientific studies, and expert opinions, as well as how individuals can heal these wounds to cultivate more secure and fulfilling marriages.

Understanding the Father Wound

The father wound can take many forms, each impacting the child differently based on the nature of the relationship with the father figure. It might manifest as the absence of the father in a child's life—whether through physical absence, emotional unavailability, or neglect. Alternatively, a father who is emotionally abusive, controlling, or overly critical can also create a deep psychological wound. These experiences leave children feeling unworthy, unloved, and unsupported, which can have profound long-term effects on their emotional and relational development.

The Psychological Impact of the Father Wound

Research consistently emphasizes the importance of a father figure in the emotional and psychological development of a child. According to John K. Pollard, a clinical psychologist and author of *Self Parenting*, the father plays a crucial role in shaping a child's self-worth. A father's validation and emotional presence are fundamental in helping children—especially boys—develop a secure sense of identity. The absence of this support creates a **self-doubt** that can persist into adulthood, especially in romantic relationships.

When a father is physically or emotionally absent, the child often grows up with an internalized belief that they are unworthy of love and attention. Individuals with an unresolved father wound often face challenges with self-regulation, especially in intimate relationships. They may struggle to manage emotions like jealousy, anger, or fear of abandonment, leading to instability within their marriages. Additionally, a father's emotional unavailability can cause deep emotional scars, resulting in feelings of unworthiness and self-doubt, making it difficult for individuals to fully engage with their partners in a healthy way.

Manifestation of the Father Wound in Marriage

The "father wound"—a psychological and emotional injury rooted in a father's absence, neglect, harshness, or inconsistency—can have a profound impact on adult relationships, especially in marriage. This wound often forms during early attachment years and shapes how individuals see themselves, others, and love itself. According to attachment theory, our earliest experiences with caregivers form the blueprint for how we give and receive love. When the father-child bond is fractured or deficient, it leaves a gap that may manifest in marriage in emotionally disruptive ways.

1. **Difficulty with Trust and Attachment Dysregulation:** Trust is the foundation of secure attachment, but a father wound often distorts a person's capacity to trust others, especially those in intimate roles. Clinical psychologist Dr. Tian Dayton, an expert in trauma and

family systems, explains that children with emotionally unavailable or unreliable fathers often develop insecure attachment styles—either anxious, avoidant, or disorganized. In marriage, this often plays out as chronic suspicion, jealousy, hypervigilance, or difficulty accepting love at face value. The betrayed inner child anticipates abandonment, even when none exists.

2. **Emotional Insecurity and Self-Worth Challenges:** A father's validation, or lack thereof, heavily influences a child's sense of worth. When that affirmation is absent, the adult child often enters marriage with deep-rooted self-doubt. They may constantly seek reassurance, fearing they're not enough or that they'll be rejected eventually. This insecurity can be misinterpreted by a spouse as clinginess or emotional instability, when in reality, it stems from a wounded belief that love is conditional. Dr. Brene Brown's research on shame and vulnerability supports this link between early parental disconnection and adult feelings of inadequacy in relationships.

3. **Fear of Vulnerability and Emotional Intimacy:** The father wound often conditions individuals to avoid emotional exposure. If the father figure punished vulnerability or failed to respond empathetically to emotional needs, the adult may equate vulnerability with danger or weakness. In marriage, this leads to emotional distancing, surface-level communication, or shutting down during conflict. Their partner may feel emotionally starved, while the wounded individual continues to operate in survival mode. Dr. Sue Johnson, founder of Emotionally Focused Therapy (EFT), affirms that "emotional accessibility" is essential for marital security—and that unresolved attachment wounds block this process.

4. **Overcompensation Through Control or Hyper-Independence:** In response to betrayal or abandonment by a father, some people adopt a rigid self-reliance as a protective strategy. They become overly independent or controlling, believing that dependence makes them vulnerable to being let down. This can show up in marriage as micromanaging, dismissiveness toward the spouse's input, or resistance to co-dependence. Psychologist John Bradshaw calls this the "false self" that develops in childhood to cope with pain. This false self may appear strong and self-sufficient but often masks unresolved fear and grief.

5. **Projection and Repetition Compulsion:** Unhealed father wounds often result in projection—where one unconsciously projects unresolved issues with their father onto their spouse. A wife may unconsciously view her husband through the lens of her father's absence, always expecting abandonment. A husband may perceive his wife's emotional needs as "nagging" if his father taught him to suppress emotions. Psychoanalyst Dr. Harville Hendrix describes this as "imago"—the idea that we unconsciously seek out partners who mirror our early caregivers, attempting to resolve old wounds through new relationships.

6. **Emotional Flooding and Conflict Avoidance:** Individuals with deep emotional wounds may experience emotional flooding (feeling overwhelmed by intense feelings during conflict), leading to either explosive reactions or complete withdrawal. This emotional dysregulation is common among those with insecure or disorganized attachment, especially when triggered by perceived rejection or criticism. Instead of facing conflict constructively, they may shut down, stonewall, or even resort to passive-aggressive behavior, making resolution difficult.

7. **Dependency or Parentification in the Marital Role:** Sometimes, the wounded individual seeks in their spouse what they never received from their father—approval, structure, or emotional safety. This can result in codependent dynamics or emotional parentification, where one partner becomes responsible for regulating the other's emotions. While empathy and support are essential in marriage, one partner bearing the emotional burden for both can become unsustainable over time and may lead to resentment.

Why Healing the Father Wound Matters

Healing the father's wound isn't just about understanding the past—it's about reclaiming emotional freedom in the present. When left unhealed, this wound silently shapes emotional responses, conflict styles, and relational expectations, often sabotaging intimacy and connection. Working through the father wound—with therapy, inner child work, spiritual guidance, and marital support—can create space for healthier attachment, deeper trust, and more emotionally fulfilling love.

Understanding the Mother Wound: How Early Maternal Wounds Shape Adult Relationships

The "mother wound" refers to deep emotional injuries stemming from an impaired mother-child relationship during formative years. This wound is not necessarily the result of outright abuse or neglect—it can be caused by subtle but consistent emotional unavailability, hypercriticism, overcontrol, or conditional love. These experiences often go unrecognized in childhood but leave profound psychological imprints that resurface in adulthood, particularly in romantic relationships and marriage.

The Developmental and Psychological Impact

A mother's presence (or absence) during early development fundamentally shapes a child's self-concept, emotional regulation, and capacity for intimacy. According to attachment theory pioneer Dr. John Bowlby, the mother is often the first "secure base" from which a child learns to explore the world. If that base is unstable—due to the mother's own trauma, narcissism, depression, or over-involvement—it disrupts the development of secure attachment.

Dr. Susan Forward, in her book *Mothers Who Can't Love*, outlines how children raised by emotionally withholding or critical mothers often internalize the message: *"I'm not enough to be loved."* This belief, repeated over years, becomes a subconscious narrative that plays out in adult relationships as chronic self-doubt, emotional anxiety, and shame.

A 2010 study published in the *Journal of Personality and Social Psychology* found that maternal rejection in early childhood was more strongly associated with adult emotional insecurity than paternal rejection. These patterns lead to what psychologists call "internal working models"—deep-seated beliefs about the self (as unworthy) and others (as emotionally unsafe or unpredictable).

Manifestations of the Mother Wound in Marriage

The mother wound doesn't just disappear with age—it evolves. In marriage, it often manifests through the following dynamics:

1. **Chronic Low Self-Worth:** Many individuals with a mother wound feel unlovable at their core. In marriage, this may look like persistent feelings of "not being good enough," even when a partner is affirming. This low self-worth often leads to self-sabotage, such as emotionally distancing or picking unnecessary fights just to test whether their partner will leave.

2. **Hypervigilant People-Pleasing:** If love was given only when they performed or pleased their mother, individuals may carry that pattern into marriage. They become hyper-attuned to their partner's moods, needs, and preferences, often at the cost of their own. While this may seem like selflessness, it erodes authenticity and builds resentment over time.

3. **Fear of Rejection and Abandonment:** For someone with a mother wound, even small conflicts or emotional distance can trigger an outsized fear of rejection. This fear can lead to clinginess, jealousy, or emotional shutdowns—anything to avoid re-experiencing the original pain of being emotionally dismissed or neglected.

4. **Emotional Avoidance or Hyper-Independence:** On the other end of the spectrum, some survivors of the mother wound protect themselves through detachment. They may pride themselves on being "low-maintenance" or "emotionally strong," but in reality, they struggle with closeness. Vulnerability feels unsafe, so they keep emotional walls up—creating loneliness even within marriage.

5. **Projection and Reenactment:** One of the more insidious impacts is the unconscious projection of the mother figure onto one's spouse. If the partner sets boundaries or expresses disappointment, the individual might emotionally regress—interpreting those moments as rejection or criticism from their "mother." These reactions are not based on the current relationship but are echoes of unresolved childhood pain.

Clinical and Therapeutic Insights

Psychotherapist Dr. Lindsay Gibson notes in her book *Adult Children of Emotionally Immature Parents* that children of emotionally unavailable mothers often grow up with distorted ideas of intimacy. They equate love with emotional labor, conditional acceptance, or the need to "earn" affection. In therapy, these individuals often present with anxious-preoccupied or avoidant attachment styles—making it difficult to balance emotional closeness and autonomy in marriage.

Moreover, trauma specialists such as Dr. Gabor Maté argue that core wounds from parental relationships—especially mothers—can dysregulate the nervous system. This means that in marriage, individuals might overreact to perceived slights or feel constantly on edge, even when there is no real threat. These nervous system patterns must be gently rewired through safe, attuned emotional connection—often beginning with therapy.

Islamic Wisdom and Maternal Influence

Islamic tradition recognizes the immense emotional and spiritual weight of the mother-child bond. The Prophet Muhammad (ﷺ) repeatedly emphasized the honor and influence of mothers—stating, "Paradise lies at the feet of your mother." Yet, Islam also provides balance. If a mother (or any family member) causes emotional harm, Islam allows for respectful boundaries.

In healing from the mother wound, Islamic values offer both compassion and accountability: one can honor their mother for the role she played, while also recognizing their emotional needs and seeking healing without guilt or shame.

Moving Toward Healing

Healing from the mother wound requires a multi-layered approach:

- **Inner child work**: Recognize and validate the younger self who needs more love, affirmation, or emotional safety.

- **Therapy**: Seek professional support—particularly attachment-based or trauma-informed therapy.

- **Boundaries**: Learn to set healthy limits with both family and spouse to protect emotional energy.

- **Self-reparenting**: Engage in self-care rituals and self-talk that mirror what a loving, present mother would have offered.

- **Spiritual grounding**: Turn to God (Al-Wadud, the Most Loving) as the ultimate source of unconditional love and healing.

Healing the Father and Mother Wounds in Marriage

The journey toward healing the father and mother wounds is essential for anyone seeking to cultivate a healthy marriage. Therapies like Cognitive Behavioral Therapy (CBT), Emotionally Focused Therapy (EFT), and attachment-based therapies have proven effective in helping individuals recognize and heal from these wounds. Therapy helps individuals understand the roots of their emotional issues and work toward healthier attachment patterns in their relationship.

As Dr. Bessel van der Kolk points out in his book, trauma—including the father and mother wounds—affects not only the mind but also the body. Somatic therapies that integrate physical awareness with emotional healing can be incredibly powerful in overcoming the long-lasting effects of these wounds. Healing involves not only understanding the emotional wounds but also actively releasing the stored trauma from the body to create a more balanced, regulated emotional state.

In a marital context, healing begins with **open communication** and **mutual empathy**. A partner who understands the emotional landscape of the other—especially when these wounds are involved—can create a safe space for healing. Active listening, vulnerability, and emotional support are key to rebuilding trust and emotional intimacy.

Conclusion

The father and mother wounds are powerful forces that can shape an individual's emotional world and affect how they interact with their spouse in marriage. These wounds often lead to issues with trust, intimacy, and emotional vulnerability. However, through self-awareness, therapy, and mutual support, individuals can heal these wounds and create healthier, more secure relationships. The process of healing is not easy, but it is absolutely possible—and essential—for anyone who desires a fulfilling and stable marriage. Through patience, understanding, and emotional work, individuals can transform the wounds of the past into the strength needed for a thriving, healthy partnership.

Chapter Forty-Two

Emotional Intelligence

Emotional intelligence (EI) serves as the invisible thread weaving together self-awareness, empathy, and resilience, making it indispensable in marriage, parenting, and personal development. While EI has become a focal point in psychological studies and self-help literature, its importance is timeless, aligning seamlessly with faith-based teachings that emphasize harmony and compassion in human relationships. As we delve deeper into EI, we uncover not only its scientific and relational dimensions but also its profound ability to transform lives and relationships at their core.

EI Vibes: Why Emotional Intelligence is Your Superpower

Emotional intelligence, popularized by psychologist Daniel Goleman in *Emotional Intelligence: Why It Can Matter More Than IQ*, is defined as the ability to recognize, understand, and manage one's emotions while also responding empathetically to the emotions of others. Goleman identifies five foundational components of EI: self-awareness, self-regulation, motivation, empathy, and social skills. Together, these elements create a framework for navigating the complexities of emotions and relationships with grace.

Psychologists Peter Salovey and John Mayer, who pioneered research on EI, describe it as the ability to perceive, understand, integrate, and manage emotions effectively. Unlike traditional intelligence (IQ), which focuses on cognitive abilities and problem-solving, emotional intelligence emphasizes relational skills—such as interpreting emotional cues and responding with empathy and self-awareness. Daniel Goleman, one of the most well-known authors in this field, argues that EI plays a critical role in personal and professional success, suggesting that it may account for as much as 80% of effective leadership and relationship outcomes.

Imagine a husband noticing his wife's subtle signs of distress—a furrowed brow, shorter responses during dinner. Instead of brushing it off, he might gently ask, "You seem preoccupied. Is something on your mind?" This small yet impactful act of emotional attunement exemplifies EI in action and prevents minor emotional disconnections from snowballing into larger issues.

EI in Marriage: The Secret Sauce to Lasting Love

Marriage is a delicate yet dynamic partnership where EI serves as both the glue that binds and the lubricant that smoothens the frictions of daily life. EI enables spouses to navigate the inevitable conflicts and challenges of married life with understanding, compassion, and emotional safety, fostering a partnership grounded in mutual respect and connection.

The EI Savings Account: Building Emotional Wealth in Relationships

Dr. John Gottman, renowned for his pioneering research on marital stability, highlights the concept of "emotional attunement" as essential for a thriving marriage. Couples who cultivate emotional responsiveness and validation build an "emotional bank account," a reservoir of trust and goodwill that acts as a buffer against the storms of conflict. Gottman explains that seemingly small acts of kindness, such as expressing gratitude or validating a partner's feelings, accrue positive emotional deposits that protect the relationship over time.

Consider Ahmed and Sarah, a hypothetical couple whose marriage was strained by financial stress. Sarah often expressed her anxiety about budgeting, which Ahmed initially dismissed as overthinking. Over time, Ahmed realized the value of empathy and began validating her concerns. By saying, "I understand that this is weighing on you. Let's sit down together and make a plan," Ahmed shifted the dynamic from defensiveness to partnership. This act of emotional intelligence reaffirmed their shared goals and brought them closer.

On the contrary, relationships lacking EI often fall prey to what Gottman calls "The Four Horsemen" of marital failure: criticism, contempt, defensiveness, and stonewalling. For example, a spouse who lacks emotional self-regulation may lash out during disagreements, while another devoid of empathy might dismiss their partner's feelings entirely. These patterns create emotional wounds that, if left unaddressed, erode the foundation of trust and intimacy over time.

An Islamic Perspective: Rahmah and Mawaddah

The principles of emotional intelligence resonate deeply within Islamic teachings, which emphasize qualities like Rahmah (compassion), Mawaddah (love), and Sabr (patience). Marriage in Islam is described as a bond of mutual love and mercy, as encapsulated in the following Qur'anic verses:

> "And among His signs is that He created for you from yourselves mates that you may find tranquility in them; and He placed between you affection and mercy." (Qur'an 30:21)

> "He is the One Who created you from a single soul, then from it made its spouse so he may find comfort in her. After he had been united with her, she carried a light burden that developed gradually. When it grew heavy, they prayed to Allah, their Lord, 'If you grant us good offspring, we will certainly be grateful.'" (Qur'an 7:189)

> "Your spouses are a garment for you as you are for them." (Qur'an 2:187)

The Prophet Muhammad (ﷺ) exemplified EI in his interactions with his wives, offering timeless lessons in marital harmony. His relationship with Aisha (RA) is filled with examples of attentiveness, empathy, and emotional attunement. He listened to her when she recounted stories, including the lengthy narrative of Umm Zar', and responded with warmth and appreciation. He also demonstrated deep awareness of her emotions, once noting that he could tell when she was pleased or upset with him based on subtle changes in her words. These interactions show his ability to connect emotionally, validate feelings, and maintain a relationship rooted in compassion and respect.

1. **Attentiveness and Playfulness with Aisha (RA):** The Prophet (ﷺ) would listen to Aisha (RA) even when she told long stories. One authentic hadith describes how she narrated the story of 11 women, and the Prophet (ﷺ) listened attentively to the end and then commented thoughtfully.

2. **Sharing Joy and Playfulness:** Aisha (RA) narrated that the Prophet (ﷺ) once raced with her—demonstrating joy, companionship, and attentiveness to her spirit.

3. **Addressing Her Emotions Gently:** The Prophet (ﷺ) was known for addressing the emotions of his wives—especially Aisha (RA)—with gentleness, empathy, and without shame. In a famous narration, he even noted when she was upset with him and gently pointed it out in a loving, emotionally intelligent way. (Sahih Muslim 1462)

   While no single hadith captures every emotional exchange, scholars have long pointed to such examples as part of his khuluq al-'adheem (exalted character), described in the Qur'an:

   "And you are surely upon an exalted standard of character." (Surah Al-Qalam, 68:4)

4. **Emotional Awareness and Conflict Resolution:** Aisha (RA) once said that whenever she was upset with the Prophet (ﷺ), he would notice immediately and inquire about it, even noting subtle changes in her tone or behavior.

Such examples underscore the spiritual dimensions of emotional intelligence, reminding us that emotional mastery in marriage is not merely a relational skill, but a pathway to Allah's pleasure. The Prophet's (ﷺ) life teaches us that empathy, patience, and emotional regulation are not just virtues—they are acts of worship. When practiced sincerely, they transform marriage from a legal bond into a spiritual partnership rooted in mercy and divine reward.

The Science of Emotional Safety

Research by Dr. Sue Johnson, a leading expert in emotionally focused therapy, highlights that emotional safety is the cornerstone of secure relationships. Emotional safety allows spouses to be vulnerable with one another, fostering a deep sense of connection and intimacy. Johnson's work reveals that when couples feel heard and understood, they are more likely to approach challenges as a team rather than adversaries.

For example, if a husband feels overwhelmed at work and shares this vulnerability with his wife, her emotionally intelligent response—listening without judgment and offering reassurance—can reinforce their bond. Conversely, dismissing his concerns with remarks like, "Everyone's stressed; it's not a big deal," may leave him feeling isolated and undervalued, gradually widening the emotional gap between them.

EI as a Conflict Resolution Tool

One of the most practical applications of EI in marriage is conflict resolution. Dr. Harriet Lerner, a clinical psychologist and author of *The Dance of Anger*, emphasizes the importance of self-awareness in managing disagreements. Emotionally intelligent couples approach conflicts as opportunities for growth, seeking to understand rather than win.

For instance, during a disagreement about household responsibilities, a wife might say, "I feel overwhelmed when I handle all the chores alone. Can we find a way to share the workload?" This approach contrasts sharply with emotionally reactive statements like, "You never help with anything," which may trigger defensiveness and escalate the conflict.

The Role of Empathy in Deepening Connection

Empathy, a cornerstone of EI, involves understanding and sharing the feelings of another. It allows spouses to step into each other's emotional shoes, fostering understanding and reducing conflict. Dr. Brené Brown, a leading researcher on vulnerability, states, "Empathy is feeling with people. It's not about fixing; it's about being there."

Imagine a scenario where one spouse feels neglected due to the other's long work hours. An empathetic response might involve acknowledging the feeling with statements like, "I can see how my absence has made you feel lonely. I'll make a conscious effort to spend more quality time together." Such responses validate emotions and create a safe space for dialogue.

The Ripple Effects of Low Emotional Intelligence

The absence of EI in marriage often manifests in destructive patterns of communication and behavior. Partners who lack emotional regulation may respond to stress with anger, withdrawing, or even stonewalling, behaviors that Gottman identifies as strong predictors of divorce. Additionally, a lack of empathy can lead to feelings of emotional neglect, making a spouse feel unloved or invisible.

Low EI can also have intergenerational consequences. Children who grow up in emotionally volatile households may internalize unhealthy patterns of communication and struggle to form secure attachments in adulthood. This underscores the importance of modeling emotionally intelligent behavior within the marital relationship, not only for the couple's benefit but also for their children's emotional well-being.

Building EI in Marriage: Practical Tools and Strategies

EI—the ability to perceive, understand, manage, and respond to emotions effectively—is one of the most powerful predictors of relational success. In marriage, EI shapes how couples handle conflict, offer support, and create a lasting emotional bond. Dr. John Gottman's decades of research show that couples with high EI are far more likely to resolve conflict peacefully, experience deeper intimacy, and maintain long-term satisfaction. Here's how couples can actively build EI in their relationship:

1. **Emotion Coaching Conversations (Not Just Communication):** Rather than simply talking, emotionally intelligent couples learn to "coach" one another through emotional waves. Dr. Gottman calls this *emotion coaching*—where one partner listens empathetically, helps label emotions, and supports problem-solving.

    - *Example tool:* Ask, "What are you feeling right now, and what do you need most from me?"

    - *Why it works:* It cultivates safety, emotional literacy, and the belief that both partners' feelings matter.

2. **Deep Active Listening with Reflective Validation:** True listening isn't about waiting to speak—it's about *attunement*. When a partner shares something emotionally charged, the goal is to understand, not fix.

    - *How to implement:* Repeat and reflect: "So you're saying you felt alone when I didn't follow up. That matters to me."

    - *What research says:* Reflective listening reduces defensiveness and fosters emotional safety.

3. **The 20-Minute Calm Down Rule (Self-Regulation in Conflict):** Physiological flooding—when your heart rate spikes and your brain goes into fight-or-flight—kills healthy communication. Dr. Sue Johnson and Dr. Daniel Goleman recommend taking a 20-minute break when this happens.

   - *How to do it:* Pause the argument respectfully: "I care about this conversation, but I need 20 minutes to regulate. Let's revisit it calmly."

   - *Bonus:* Combine with breathing exercises or dhikr to recenter spiritually and emotionally.

4. **Emotional Journaling and Self-Awareness:** Writing about emotional experiences helps externalize thoughts and access deeper feelings.

   - *Couples strategy:* Each partner journals about a recent conflict—what they felt, needed, and feared. Then they share highlights in a calm moment.

   - *Why it matters:* According to psychologist James Pennebaker, expressive writing improves emotional clarity and deepens relational insight.

5. **Daily "Emotional Weather Reports":** Make emotional check-ins a non-negotiable ritual. It can be as simple as: "What's one emotion you felt strongly today, and what do you need from me around it?"

   - *Apps and aids:* Tools like the *Gottman Card Decks* or the "Mood Meter" app can prompt these reflections.

   - *Faithful twist:* End the check-in with a short du'a for each other to deepen spiritual intimacy.

6. **The "Switch Shoes" Empathy Exercise:** Regularly role-play each other's perspectives. This can be done during conversations about parenting, stress, or intimacy needs.

   - *How it works:* Each partner describes the other's perceived feelings, then checks for accuracy.

   - *Example:* "If I were in your shoes, I might feel overwhelmed juggling work and home expectations. Is that close to how you feel?"

7. **Build an Emotionally Safe Environment:** No one will open up emotionally if they feel judged, dismissed, or mocked. Emotional safety is foundational.

    - *Implement this by:* Avoiding criticism, sarcasm, or "you always/never" statements. Use gentle startups and appreciation instead.
    - *Qur'anic inspiration:* "And speak to people good [words]..." (Surah Al-Baqarah, 2:83) Emotional safety starts with kind communication.

8. **Sacred Listening: Sunnah-Inspired Presence:** The Prophet Muhammad (ﷺ) gave his undivided attention to those he was with—even when others interrupted. He listened to long stories, like Aisha's (RA) narration of the Umm Zar' tale, with full engagement.

    - *Reflection point:* How often do we give our spouse our full attention without glancing at a phone or mentally checking out?
    - *Practice:* Once a week, have a "Sunnah listening session" where one partner speaks and the other listens with presence—no interruptions, just presence.

9. **Understanding Emotional Triggers Through Childhood Wounds:** Many emotional reactions in marriage stem from unresolved wounds—not current conflicts. Understanding your partner's triggers helps foster compassion.

    - *Couples tool:* Take turns identifying one childhood experience that still affects your communication or emotional expression.
    - *Faith connection:* Allah reminds us to show mercy: "Indeed, Allah is Merciful to you." (Surah An-Nur, 24:20) Bring this mercy to your spouse's wounds.

10. **Spiritual Emotional Intelligence (SEI):** EI is not just psychological—it's spiritual. Integrating dhikr, Qur'anic reflection, and Prophetic behavior strengthens both heart and soul.

    - *Practical steps:* Make du'a together after disagreements, listen to the Qur'an during tense moments, or reflect on a verse about sabr (patience) or rahmah (mercy).
    - *Goal:* Infuse the relationship with reminders of your higher purpose and shared mission.

Emotional Intelligence and Parenting

Parenting demands high levels of EI, as children often test their caregivers' patience and empathy. Parents with strong EI not only model healthy emotional behaviors but also equip their children with the tools to navigate their own emotional landscapes. Dr. Daniel Siegel, in his book *The Whole-Brain Child*, stresses the importance of "emotion coaching," where parents help children label and process their emotions instead of dismissing or suppressing them.

Consider a mother whose daughter throws a tantrum after being denied a toy. Though she feels a surge of frustration, she takes a moment to breathe and responds with emotional intelligence: "I can see you're really upset because you wanted that toy. It's okay to feel sad, but let's talk about better ways to deal with those big feelings."

This kind of calm, empathetic response helps the child feel seen and teaches emotional regulation through modeling, rather than suppression or punishment.

The Prophet Muhammad's (ﷺ) gentle interactions with children serve as a timeless guide for Muslim parents. He once interrupted his sermon to console his crying grandson, illustrating that emotional needs take precedence even in sacred moments. This blend of compassion and emotional awareness fosters trust and emotional security, shaping children into empathetic and resilient adults.

The Dark Side of Low Emotional Intelligence

The absence of EI casts a long shadow over relationships. Partners with low EI often struggle to communicate effectively, leading to cycles of misunderstanding, resentment, and emotional distance. A spouse who lacks empathy might dismiss their partner's vulnerabilities as overreactions, while one who struggles with self-regulation may react explosively, leaving emotional scars.

In parenting, low EI manifests as harsh discipline or emotional neglect, which can stunt a child's emotional development and lead to insecurity. Studies by Dr. John Bowlby on attachment theory reveal that children raised by emotionally unavailable caregivers often struggle with relational intimacy as adults, perpetuating cycles of dysfunction. For instance, Amina and Bilal's marriage began to unravel due to Bilal's inability to manage his anger. Small disagreements quickly escalated into shouting matches, leaving

Amina feeling unsafe and unheard. Without intervention to build EI, their relationship deteriorated—demonstrating how low EI can silently erode even the most promising bonds.

Cultivating Emotional Intelligence: Tools and Strategies

Building EI is a lifelong journey, but the rewards are immense. Here are actionable tools grounded in research and expert advice:

1. **Mindfulness and Emotional Awareness**: Mindfulness trains the brain to recognize and regulate emotions in real-time. A 2014 study published in *Emotion* found that mindfulness practices improve emotional regulation and reduce stress responses. Techniques like deep breathing, meditation, or journaling can enhance self-awareness. For example, the *Headspace* app offers guided meditations designed to boost EI.

2. **Active Listening**: Active listening involves fully focusing on your partner's words and emotions. Dr. Carl Rogers championed this technique, stating, "When someone truly hears you without judgment, it's profoundly healing." Try paraphrasing your partner's concerns to validate their feelings: "It sounds like you're feeling overwhelmed by work. How can I support you?"

3. **Practicing Empathy**: Empathy grows through deliberate perspective-taking. Role-playing exercises, such as imagining how your partner might feel during an argument, foster understanding. Studies published in *Psychological Science* reveal that practicing empathy reduces conflict and increases relational satisfaction.

4. **Gratitude Rituals**: Expressing gratitude rewires the brain for positivity. Dr. Robert Emmons's research shows that gratitude increases happiness and strengthens relationships. A nightly practice of sharing three things you appreciate about your spouse can transform the emotional tone of a marriage.

5. **Structured Communication**: Tools like the Gottman Institute's *Build Love Maps* encourage couples to deepen their understanding of each other's inner worlds. Weekly "state of the union" check-ins allow partners to address concerns proactively, reducing the risk of unresolved conflicts.

6. **Emotion Coaching for Parents**: Dr. Marc Brackett's *RULER* framework (Recognizing, Understanding, Labeling, Expressing, Regulating) offers parents practical tools to nurture EI in children. Engaging in "feelings charades" or using a "mood meter" can make emotional learning accessible and fun for kids.

Conclusion

Emotional intelligence is not merely an abstract concept; it is the heartbeat of every meaningful relationship. By cultivating EI, we not only enrich our marriages and parenting but also inspire emotional growth in ourselves and others. As Goleman aptly puts it, "Emotions are contagious," and by mastering EI, we spread love, compassion, and understanding in our homes and communities.

Chapter Forty-Three

Emotional Incest (Parental Enmeshment)

What is Covert Incest?

Covert incest, also known as emotional enmeshment, is a subtle yet profoundly damaging form of emotional abuse. Unlike physical incest, this term refers to a parent relying on their child to fulfill emotional needs that should be met by an adult partner or another peer. This situation, though it doesn't involve physical or sexual boundaries being crossed, can cause profound psychological damage, distorting the parent-child dynamic. It occurs when a parent unwittingly turns to their child for emotional support, filling the void left by an absent or emotionally unavailable spouse. The consequences of covert incest are often hidden beneath the surface, making it difficult to recognize until emotional scars have already formed.

The child in such a dynamic often finds themselves in an adult role, a surrogate partner who fulfills the emotional void for their parent. As this emotional load increases, children can lose their sense of self, leading to confusion about their identity and the nature of their relationships as they grow older. The long-term effects of this emotional dependency often result in difficulties with emotional independence, boundary-setting, and intimacy.

Covert Incest: The Maternal Dynamic

While covert incest is frequently discussed in the context of fathers and daughters, it is just as likely to occur in mother-son relationships. In these cases, mothers may unconsciously turn to their children, particularly their sons, for emotional support and companionship. This dynamic is especially prevalent when a mother feels emotionally neglected or unappreciated by her spouse. Instead of seeking marital counseling or addressing her emotional needs within the marriage, she may unknowingly shift the burden of emotional care onto her child, confusing the roles that are traditionally held between parent and child.

For sons, this dynamic can be particularly challenging. The emotional intimacy that should exist between a mother and her spouse gets redirected, leaving the child to fill the void. As a result, the son may become an emotional caretaker, sacrificing his own developmental needs to meet the demands of the parent. Over time, this emotional enmeshment leads to complex psychological issues that can affect the son well into adulthood.

A Mother's Story: Overstepping Emotional Boundaries

Consider Aisha, a mother navigating the emotional vacuum in her marriage. Her husband, Omar, worked long hours and often withdrew emotionally, leaving Aisha feeling isolated and unappreciated. Instead of seeking help or addressing her dissatisfaction within the marriage, Aisha unknowingly turned to her teenage son, Sameer, for emotional support.

Sameer, a sensitive and empathetic young man, soon found himself taking on the role of emotional caretaker for his mother. Aisha began confiding in Sameer about her struggles with Omar, their financial difficulties, and her deep sense of loneliness. Sameer, feeling the weight of his mother's emotions, tried to reassure her, offer solutions, and comfort her in ways that should have been the responsibility of an adult partner.

As time passed, Sameer began to lose touch with his own emotional needs. His mother's emotional dependency on him became the central focus of his life. He started to feel as though his own life, desires, and feelings were secondary to his mother's well-being. Sameer was caught in a cycle of emotional caretaking, trying to manage his own emotional world while simultaneously being emotionally responsible for his mother.

This scenario is not unique. In *The Emotional Incest Syndrome*, Dr. Patricia Love explains that children who are placed in emotionally burdensome roles by their parents often lose the freedom to simply be children. Instead of receiving appropriate care and guidance, they are expected to meet the emotional needs of the parent. This premature emotional responsibility can lead to deep confusion, persistent guilt, anxiety, and a diminished sense of identity as they grow into adulthood.

Psychological Insights into Maternal Covert Incest

Psychologists have long recognized the damaging effects of maternal covert incest. Dr. Kenneth Adams, in his book *Silently Seduced: When Parents Make Their Children Partners*, writes that children subjected to covert incest often develop a skewed sense of self-worth. They may feel as though their value lies in their ability to meet the emotional needs of others rather than in their own inherent qualities.

Similarly, Dr. Susan Forward, in *Toxic Parents*, discusses how children who experience covert incest are emotionally parentified, taking on roles that prevent them from developing into fully independent individuals. For sons, this can lead to difficulty forming healthy, balanced relationships with women. They may become overdependent on romantic partners or, conversely, withdraw emotionally from intimacy altogether.

Emotional Consequences for the Child

The emotional fallout of maternal covert incest is profound and far-reaching, often shaping a child's sense of self, identity, and relational patterns well into adulthood. Because the mother relies on the child—often a son—for emotional support, validation, or even companionship in ways typically reserved for adult partners, the child becomes enmeshed in an emotional role they were never meant to carry. While there is no overt sexual contact, the psychological burden mimics emotional incest, creating deep confusion and internal conflict.

1. **Loss of Autonomy and Boundaries:** Children caught in covert incest are subtly groomed to prioritize the emotional needs of the parent above their own. The mother may reward emotional compliance with praise or affection and punish emotional independence with guilt or withdrawal. Over time, the child internalizes the belief that asserting their own needs is selfish or disloyal. As adults, they may struggle to form healthy, differentiated identities, often feeling guilt when making autonomous decisions—especially those that involve emotional separation from their mother. Psychologists call this *enmeshment*, where the self is fused with another's identity, making healthy individuation difficult.

2. **Role Reversal and Parentification:** Maternal covert incest often places the child in the role of an emotional confidant or surrogate

partner—a dynamic known as *parentification*. Instead of receiving age-appropriate care and support, the child is tasked with managing the adult's emotional regulation. This inversion of roles leads to an internalized belief that love must be earned through emotional labor, self-sacrifice, or pleasing others. This can result in burnout, people-pleasing tendencies, or chronic self-neglect in adulthood. As Dr. Patricia Love highlights in her work, such children "grow up too fast," robbed of the emotional safety and freedom childhood should afford.

3. **Identity Diffusion and Shame:** Being a vessel for a parent's unmet needs impairs the development of a stable identity. These children often grow up disconnected from their authentic desires, struggling to distinguish between their own feelings and the feelings imposed upon them. They may question their masculinity or femininity, especially if their emotional closeness to the parent blurred boundaries related to gender and identity. Shame often accompanies this confusion—shame for having needs, for failing to meet the parent's expectations, or for experiencing resentment toward a parent they were supposed to "protect." Let's delve deeper to fully understand its implications:

    A. **"Disconnected from their authentic desires"** This means:

    - The child doesn't grow up knowing what they truly want, feel, or value.
    - Instead of tuning into their own needs, they've learned to suppress them to meet the emotional needs of the parent.
    - As adults, they may struggle to make confident choices about careers, partners, or life goals because they were never encouraged to develop a strong inner sense of self.

    Example: A boy who always had to comfort his emotionally unstable mother may grow up prioritizing others' feelings over his own and feel guilty for having wants.

    B. **"Struggling to distinguish between their own feelings and the feelings imposed upon them"** This means:

    - The child was conditioned to take on or mirror the parent's emotions.

- They may confuse what they feel vs. what someone else wants them to feel.

- As adults, they're often people-pleasers, over-apologizers, or highly codependent.

Example: If a mother was always sad and leaned on her child for comfort, the child may feel anxious anytime someone is upset—even if it has nothing to do with them.

C. **"They may question their masculinity or femininity"** This means:

- Because the parent-child roles and boundaries were blurred, it can affect the child's gender identity or confidence in their gender role.

- For sons: being treated like a pseudo-spouse may make them feel like they must always be nurturing or emotionally responsible—traits not traditionally supported in hyper-masculine cultures.

- For daughters: a lack of healthy maternal role modeling may lead to confusion around what it means to be a woman, emotionally or relationally.

D. **"Blurred boundaries related to gender and identity"** This refers to:

- When the parent treats the child like an emotional partner rather than a child, the natural roles of mother/father and son/daughter become confused.

- The child may develop unclear boundaries around affection, love, gender roles, and personal identity.

Example: A boy who's told he's "the man of the house" and treated like his mother's emotional equal may feel confused about how to be a partner in adult life—often either becoming emotionally shut down or over-responsible.

4. **Struggles with Intimacy and Vulnerability:** As adults, many survivors of covert incest experience deep difficulties with emotional and physical intimacy. Since they were emotionally "used" or

entangled by a caregiver, they may associate closeness with control or suffocation. They may keep romantic partners at arm's length or unconsciously sabotage relationships when they start to feel too close. Alternatively, they may overfunction in relationships—assuming the emotional caretaker role—only to become resentful when their own needs go unmet. In both cases, the underlying wound is the same: intimacy was distorted, not modeled in a healthy, mutual way.

5. **Attachment Dysregulation:** Many children raised in covert incest environments develop *insecure attachment styles*, such as anxious-preoccupied or avoidant-dismissive. They may alternate between craving closeness and fearing it, or between feeling emotionally abandoned and feeling trapped. This instability in early caregiving leads to chronic difficulty trusting others, as well as hypersensitivity to perceived rejection or engulfment. Research in attachment theory consistently shows that early enmeshment without attuned emotional boundaries can significantly impair a person's ability to regulate emotions within intimate partnerships.

6. **Difficulty Navigating Masculinity or Femininity:** For male children especially, covert incest with the mother can blur the lines of healthy masculinity. A boy raised to be his mother's emotional caretaker may grow up internalizing the idea that his value lies in emotional rescue, rather than in developing his own strength, independence, or leadership. This can result in either *hyper-masculinity* as a defense mechanism, or in *emasculation*—a deep discomfort with expressing his own desires or asserting boundaries, particularly with women. In marriage, this often leads to power imbalances, resentment, or emotional passivity.

The Lasting Impact on Sameer

Let's continue our earlier example. Years later, Sameer, now an adult, struggled in his marriage to Sarah. He was emotionally distant and unable to prioritize their relationship. Despite loving his wife, he found it difficult to engage fully with her emotionally. In therapy, Sameer began to uncover the deep-seated guilt he felt about "abandoning" his mother when he left for college. This unresolved guilt carried into his adult life, leading to his emotional withdrawal and inability to fully invest in his marriage with Sarah. The cycle of emotional enmeshment he experienced with his mother had profound consequences for his ability to form a healthy, emotionally available relationship.

Breaking the Cycle

Breaking the cycle of covert incest requires both self-awareness and professional intervention. Therapy is crucial for couples and individuals to address unresolved emotional issues. Dr. John Gottman emphasizes the importance of emotional attunement in relationships. According to Dr. Gottman, couples with a strong emotional foundation are less likely to seek emotional fulfillment outside their marriage. His research shows that when partners feel emotionally connected and supported, they are more resilient to external relational stressors and more satisfied overall in their relationship. This underscores the necessity of couples actively working to strengthen their marital bond, reducing the reliance on children for emotional support.

Faith-based counseling can also provide valuable guidance. In Islam, for example, the importance of maintaining healthy boundaries and clear roles within the family is emphasized. The Prophet Muhammad (ﷺ) taught, "Each of you is a shepherd, and each of you is responsible for his flock." (Sahih al-Bukhari, Hadith 893)

Conclusion: Healing and Hope

Covert incest, whether stemming from maternal or paternal dynamics, is rooted in unresolved emotional needs and marital struggles. While the consequences are serious, healing is always possible. Therapy, self-awareness, and a commitment to breaking unhealthy patterns can lead to transformed relationships and healthier family dynamics. By addressing these issues directly, parents can ensure that their children grow up without bearing the weight of emotional enmeshment, empowering them to form their own balanced, fulfilling relationships in adulthood.

Chapter Forty-Four

Athkar: Protecting Marriage Through Remembrance

The Sacred Bonds of Marriage and Family in Islam

Marriage in Islam is viewed as a sacred and highly revered institution. It is not merely a legal contract but an agreement imbued with divine blessings. Allah describes marriage as a source of peace, comfort, and protection:

> "And of His signs is that He created for you from among yourselves mates that you may find tranquility in them; and He placed between you affection and mercy." (Qur'an, Surah Ar-Rum 30:21)

This profound verse shows how Allah created marriage as a foundation for tranquility, love, and mutual compassion. Similarly, the family structure is essential in preserving the moral, emotional, and spiritual stability of the Muslim community. However, this sanctity is constantly under threat from both internal and external forces: the distractions of modern life, the influence of social media, envy and jealousy (hasad), the evil eye (al-'ayn), evil whispers (waswasa), and even the destructive effects of witchcraft (sihr).

In Islamic teachings, hasad—the dark desire to see someone's blessings removed—is a spiritual disease that can corrode trust and harmony in a marriage. Al-'ayn, rooted in intense envy or admiration, is also recognized in hadith literature as a real and damaging spiritual force, capable of causing emotional, physical, and even relational harm. Waswasa from Shaytan can stir unnecessary doubts and suspicions between spouses, leading to emotional distance, miscommunication, and conflict. And sihr, though often dismissed in modern discourse, is acknowledged in the Qur'an as a real and destructive force that can "create division between husband and wife." (Surah Al-Baqarah 2:102)

These threats emphasize the urgent need for spiritual vigilance, regular remembrance of Allah (dhikr), recitation of protective du'as, and seeking divine protection through Qur'anic remedies like Ayat al-Kursi, Surah Al-Falaq, and Surah An-Nas—to safeguard the sacred bond of marriage from both visible and unseen harms.

To safeguard the sacredness of marriage and the family unit, Islam has provided a powerful tool: **Athkar**, or remembrance of Allah. Athkar encompasses a range of supplications (duas), Qur'anic verses, and spiritual practices that protect individuals, families, and marriages from harm. This chapter explores how the consistent practice of Athkar strengthens family bonds, nurtures marital relationships, and invites divine protection into the home.

Understanding Athkar: A Shield for the Heart and Home

In the Islamic tradition, Athkar refers to the remembrance of Allah through prayers, supplications, and invocations. These practices are prescribed in both the Qur'an and Hadith, and they serve as a shield against spiritual, emotional, and physical harm. The Prophet (ﷺ) said:

> "Satan runs away from the house in which Surah Al-Baqarah is recited." (Sahih Muslim 780)

Another authentic narration:

> "The similitude of the one who remembers his Lord and the one who does not is like the living and the dead." (Sahih al-Bukhari 6407)

These emphasize that **dhikr protects the heart and soul** from spiritual harm, including the whispers of Shaytan.

Through Athkar, a person is spiritually connected to Allah and protected from negative energies, harmful thoughts, and distractions. The importance of regular remembrance cannot be overstated, as it is a means of ensuring peace, protection, and blessings in one's life. For marriage and family, this spiritual connection becomes even more significant.

Islamic scholars emphasize the necessity of incorporating Athkar in daily life, especially for couples and families. Ibn Qayyim al-Jawziyyah emphasized that dhikr acts as both nourishment for the soul and a shield against the influence of Shaytan, allowing the heart to remain spiritually alive and grounded in faith. Ibn al-Qayyim says: "Dhikr is to the heart what water is to fish. What happens to a fish when it leaves the water?" He also writes: "There is nothing that brings more protection from Shaytan than the remembrance of Allah."

The Role of Athkar in Protecting Marriage

Spiritual Protection Through Recitation

Marriage faces numerous challenges, including miscommunication, jealousy, misunderstanding, and external stressors. Athkar offers spiritual protection from these issues. When couples regularly engage in Athkar, they invite Allah's divine guidance, mercy, and protection into their lives, enabling them to face trials with resilience and understanding. Regular recitation of duas such as:

وَالَّذِينَ يَقُولُونَ رَبَّنَا هَبْ لَنَا مِنْ أَزْوَاجِنَا وَذُرِّيَّتِنَا قُرَّةَ أَعْيُنٍ وَّاجْعَلْنَا لِلْمُتَّقِينَ اِمَامًا
﴾25:74﴿

"Rabbana hablana min azwajina wadhurriyyatina qurrata a'yunin wa-jalna lil-muttaqina imama." (Qur'an, Surah Furqan 25:74)

(Our Lord, grant us from among our spouses and offspring comfort to our eyes and make us an example for the righteous.)

This **dua** is a prayer for tranquility in marriage and harmony in the family. It acknowledges Allah as the source of peace and asks for righteous spouses and children who bring joy and strength. By reciting this supplication regularly, couples are reminding themselves of the importance of patience, understanding, and compassion in the relationship, which helps to overcome everyday tensions.

Protection Against External Harm

External challenges, such as financial stress, jealousy from others, or even the influence of negative societal norms, can disrupt marital harmony. Athkar serves as a protective shield against these external forces. One of the key supplications for this purpose is:

$$أَعُوذُ بِكَلِمَاتِ اللَّهِ التَّامَّاتِ مِنْ شَرِّ مَا خَلَقَ$$

"A'oodhu bi kalimatillahi at-tammati min sharri ma khalaq."

(I seek refuge in the perfect words of Allah from the evil of what He has created.) (Sahih Muslim)

This supplication seeks Allah's refuge from any harm, including the influence of negative energies or malicious actions by others. It creates a protective barrier around the couple, shielding them from envy (Hasad) and evil eyes (Ayn), both of which are common challenges in relationships. Allah's divine protection ensures that the relationship remains free from these harmful forces.

The Impact of Athkar on the Family Unit

Preserving Family Unity

A strong family unit is the cornerstone of a healthy society. Athkar promotes unity and cooperation among family members by fostering an environment of love and tranquility. Through consistent remembrance, the family is spiritually connected, and this connection acts as a stabilizing force in times of stress. Imam al-Ghazali emphasized the importance of shared acts of worship within the home, teaching that spiritual routines such as prayer and remembrance foster harmony, discipline, and divine presence in the family.

When parents consistently engage in prayer, dua, athkar, they model spiritual awareness and discipline for their children. The Prophet Muhammad (ﷺ) instructed believers to teach their children to pray from a young age, and by extension, scholars encourage parents to also cultivate habits of remembrance in the home—both for personal spiritual growth and protection.

Teaching children to engage in Athkar not only protects them from external harm but also instills in them a sense of responsibility, faith, and trust in Allah. As children grow, they begin to understand the significance of these practices and carry them into their own lives.

Enhancing Parental Influence and Guidance

One of the most significant challenges parents face today is the influence of modern distractions, such as social media and peer pressure. These distractions often lead to a breakdown in communication and connection within families. Athkar helps counter these distractions by restoring a sense of spiritual focus and clarity. The act of collectively or individually remembering Allah as a family brings everyone back to the center of their faith, reinforcing the guidance parents provide.

Shaykh Abd al-Rahman al-Sa'di emphasized in his writings that dhikr strengthens the heart, purifies the soul, and helps a believer gain clarity and inner peace. Parents who engage in consistent remembrance cultivate an environment of tranquility, which benefits their children's emotional and spiritual well-being.

The Importance of Ruqya for Family Protection

Ruqya is the practice of spiritual healing through Qur'anic recitations, acts as a spiritual shield, and is a powerful tool for protecting the family from harm. Imam An-Nawawi acknowledged the legitimacy of ruqya, explaining that when performed with sincere belief and in accordance with Islamic teachings, it can serve as a means of healing for both physical and spiritual ailments.

Specific Qur'anic verses and supplications are known to protect the family from evil, jealousy, and harmful influences. Among the most powerful verses for protection are:

> **Surah Al-Falaq (113):** This chapter is recited for protection against envy, jealousy, and negative external forces.

قُلْ أَعُوذُ بِرَبِّ ٱلْفَلَقِ ١ مِن شَرِّ مَا خَلَقَ ٢ وَمِن شَرِّ غَاسِقٍ إِذَا وَقَبَ ٣ وَمِن شَرِّ ٱلنَّفَّٰثَٰتِ فِى ٱلْعُقَدِ ٤ وَمِن شَرِّ حَاسِدٍ إِذَا حَسَدَ ٥

"Say: 'I seek refuge with (Allah) the Lord of the daybreak, from the evil of what He has created; and from the evil of the darkening (night) as it comes with its darkness; and from the evil of the witchcrafts when they blow in the knots, and from the evil of the envier when he envies.'"

Surah An-Nas (114): This chapter protects against the whispers of Satan and his attempts to disrupt peace in the home.

قُلْ أَعُوذُ بِرَبِّ ٱلنَّاسِ ١ مَلِكِ ٱلنَّاسِ ٢ إِلَٰهِ ٱلنَّاسِ ٣ مِن شَرِّ ٱلْوَسْوَاسِ ٱلْخَنَّاسِ ٤ ٱلَّذِى يُوَسْوِسُ فِى صُدُورِ ٱلنَّاسِ ٥ مِنَ ٱلْجِنَّةِ وَٱلنَّاسِ ٦

"Say: I seek refuge with (Allah), the Lord of mankind":

"The King of mankind":

"The God (Whom we worship)":

"From the evil of the whisperer (devil who whispers evil in the hearts of men)."

Ayat al-Kursi (2:255): Known for its immense power to safeguard the home, reciting this verse regularly invites Allah's protection over the family and home.

ٱللَّهُ لَآ إِلَٰهَ إِلَّا هُوَ ٱلْحَىُّ ٱلْقَيُّومُ ۚ لَا تَأْخُذُهُۥ سِنَةٌ وَلَا نَوْمٌ ۚ لَّهُۥ مَا فِى ٱلسَّمَٰوَٰتِ وَمَا فِى ٱلْأَرْضِ ۗ مَن ذَا ٱلَّذِى يَشْفَعُ عِندَهُۥٓ إِلَّا بِإِذْنِهِۦ ۚ يَعْلَمُ مَا بَيْنَ أَيْدِيهِمْ وَمَا خَلْفَهُمْ ۖ وَلَا يُحِيطُونَ بِشَىْءٍ مِّنْ عِلْمِهِۦٓ إِلَّا بِمَا شَآءَ ۚ وَسِعَ كُرْسِيُّهُ ٱلسَّمَٰوَٰتِ وَٱلْأَرْضَ ۖ وَلَا يَـُٔودُهُۥ حِفْظُهُمَا ۚ وَهُوَ ٱلْعَلِىُّ ٱلْعَظِيمُ

"Allah! There is no god 'worthy of worship' except Him, the Ever-Living, All-Sustaining. Neither drowsiness nor sleep overtakes Him. To Him belongs whatever is in the heavens and whatever is on the earth. Who could possibly intercede with Him without His permission? He 'fully' knows what is ahead of them and what is behind them, but no one can grasp any of His knowledge—except what He wills 'to reveal'. His Seat encompasses the heavens and the earth, and the preservation of both does not tire Him. For He is the Most High, the Greatest.'"

The consistent practice of Ruqya strengthens the marital bond by aligning both partners spiritually, allowing them to rely on Allah for help in times of difficulty. The use of Ruqya fosters an atmosphere where both spouses feel safe and secure, creating a nurturing environment for children as well.

The Role of Athkar in Strengthening Emotional and Mental Health in Marriage

Restoring Emotional Balance

One of the significant challenges couples face today is emotional strain caused by misunderstandings, stress, and outside pressures. Athkar helps to restore emotional balance by offering a spiritual remedy for distress. The recitation of protective duas alleviates feelings of anxiety, anger, and frustration, allowing both partners to approach one another with compassion and understanding.

Dr. Omar Suleiman, an Islamic scholar and founder of Yaqeen Institute, emphasizes that consistent remembrance of Allah can help couples maintain emotional equilibrium during times of distress. He highlights that dhikr acts as a spiritual anchor, enabling individuals to manage their emotions with greater calm and clarity. When couples face moments of tension or conflict, turning to Allah through dhikr not only brings personal tranquility but also nurtures the patience and humility necessary for resolving disputes. This spiritual practice realigns the couple's focus, reminding them of their higher purpose and fostering emotional resilience within the marriage.

Protection Against Divorce and Separation

The high rate of divorce in modern societies is often exacerbated by emotional distance, lack of communication, and external influences. However, Athkar can provide a preventative measure by maintaining spiritual and emotional closeness between spouses. By regularly practicing Athkar, couples are better equipped to face the challenges that often lead to separation.

Imam Ibn Taymiyyah emphasized that a righteous marriage is built upon the foundation of patience (ṣabr), mutual responsibility, and reliance upon Allah (tawakkul). He regarded dhikr as essential for purifying the heart and maintaining stability in personal and communal life. In his writings, he encouraged the use of dhikr as a way to cultivate moral character, protect from sin, and preserve harmony within the household.

Couples who turn to Allah through Athkar are less likely to succumb to the pressures that often lead to divorce. They are reminded to be patient, forgiving, and compassionate, qualities that form the foundation of a strong, lasting marriage.

Practical Tips for Protection in Marriage and Family

To ensure the consistent practice of Athkar in your daily life, here are some practical steps that can be incorporated into your routine for ongoing protection, guidance, and peace in your marriage and family:

When a man leaves his house

إِذَا خَرَجَ الرَّجُلُ مِنْ بَيْتِهِ فَقَالَ:
«بِسْمِ اللَّهِ، تَوَكَّلْتُ عَلَى اللَّهِ، لَا حَوْلَ وَلَا قُوَّةَ إِلَّا بِاللَّهِ»
يُقَالُ حِينَئِذٍ: هُدِيتَ وَكُفِيتَ وَوُقِيتَ، فَتَنَحَّى عَنْهُ الشَّيْطَانُ،
فَيَقُولُ شَيْطَانٌ آخَرُ: كَيْفَ لَكَ بِرَجُلٍ قَدْ هُدِيَ وَكُفِيَ وَوُقِيَ؟

> "When a man leaves his house and says:
>
> 'In the name of Allah, I place my trust in Allah; there is no power and no strength except with Allah (Bismillah, tawakkaltu 'ala Allah, la hawla wa la quwwata illa billah),' it is said to him: 'You are guided, defended, and protected.' Then one devil says to another, 'How can you deal with a man who has been guided, defended, and protected?'"

Abu Dawud. *Sunan Abi Dawud*, Hadith no. 5095. Classified as **Hasan** by Al-Albani in *Sahih Sunan Abi Dawud*.

This simple yet powerful supplication serves as a shield against all forms of harm, including envy, jealousy, and negative influences.

Entering the House

"إِذَا دَخَلَ الرَّجُلُ بَيْتَهُ فَذَكَرَ اللَّهَ عَزَّ وَجَلَّ عِنْدَ دُخُولِهِ وَعِنْدَ طَعَامِهِ، قَالَ الشَّيْطَانُ: لَا مَبِيتَ لَكُمْ وَلَا عَشَاءَ".

"When a man enters his house and mentions the name of Allah (i.e. says Bismillah) upon entering and when eating, Shaytan says: 'There is no lodging for you and no dinner.'"

Reported by Muslim (Hadith 2018) and also found in Abu Dawood and others.

Reciting this ensures that your home remains blessed and protected. It invites peace into the household and wards off any negative energy or harmful influences, including the evil eye and witchcraft.

Before Sleeping

The Prophet Muhammad (ﷺ) did instruct the recitation of the last two verses of Surah Al-Baqarah (Qur'an 2:285–286) before going to sleep, and he affirmed their protective and spiritual benefits.

Hadith

"Whoever recites the last two verses of Surah Al-Baqarah at night, they will suffice him." (Sahih al-Bukhari 5009, Sahih Muslim 807)

The scholars have explained that **"they will suffice him"** means:

- They will suffice him from any harm or mischief during the night,
- They will count as sufficient night worship,
- Or both meanings are valid together

(Qur'an 2:285-286)

Verse 285: "The Messenger has believed in what was revealed to him from his Lord, and [so have] the believers. All of them have believed in Allah and His angels and His books and His messengers, [saying], 'We make no distinction between any of His messengers.' And they say, 'We hear and we obey. [Grant us] Your forgiveness, our Lord. To You is the [final] destination.'"

Verse 286: "Allah does not burden a soul beyond that it can bear. It will have [the consequence of] what [good] it has gained, and it will bear [the consequence of] what [evil] it has earned. Our Lord, do not impose blame upon us if we have forgotten or erred. Our Lord, and lay not upon us a burden like that which You laid upon those before us. Our Lord, and burden us not with that which we have no ability to bear. And pardon us; and forgive us; and have mercy upon us. You are our protector, so give us victory over the disbelieving people."

Reciting Surah Al-Falaq (113) and Surah An-Nas (114) for Protection

In the spiritual practice of the Prophet Muhammad (ﷺ), few routines were as consistent and profound as his nightly recitation of Al-Mu'awwidhatayn—Surah Al-Falaq (113) and Surah An-Nas (114)—along with Surah Al-Ikhlas (112). These chapters are known for their powerful protective qualities against unseen harms, emotional disturbances, and spiritual vulnerabilities that may affect the household.

The Prophet (ﷺ) would recite these surahs every night before sleeping, performing a spiritual ritual that included cupping his hands, blowing into them, and then wiping over his body three times. This act was not merely symbolic—it was a deeply intentional form of ruqya (spiritual healing and protection).

Hadith

Aisha (RA) narrated:

> "When the Prophet (ﷺ) went to bed every night, he would join his hands, blow into them, and recite Surah Al-Ikhlas, Surah Al-Falaq, and Surah An-Nas. Then he would wipe over his entire

body as much as he could, starting with his head and face and then the front of his body. He did this three times." (Sahih al-Bukhari, Hadith 5017)

This practice exemplifies emotional and spiritual intelligence—the Prophet (ﷺ) understood the weight of unseen harm (e.g., envy, whispers, and sihr), and prescribed a consistent method for safeguarding the self and family.

Spiritual Insights and Application

The following two surahs provide comprehensive protection. Surah Al-Falaq defends against external harms—envy (ḥasad), sorcery (siḥr), and hidden malice—while Surah An-Nas protects from internal dangers, particularly the whispers of Shaytan that create doubt, anxiety, and emotional conflict within the home.

In the context of marriage and family life, these surahs act as spiritual armor. When recited consistently—especially before sleep or during times of emotional turbulence—they serve as a refuge from:

- Arguments rooted in whisperings and suspicion
- Jealousy or external harm from others
- The destructive influence of the evil eye or black magic

The sunnah of reciting and blowing into one's hands is not to be overlooked—it emphasizes both faith and action, turning remembrance into a deeply embodied act. It also sets a beautiful example for children, who learn to find emotional grounding through remembrance.

Reference: Qur'an, Surah 112 (Al-Ikhlas), verses 1-4

قُلْ هُوَ ٱللَّهُ أَحَدٌ ۝

ٱللَّهُ ٱلصَّمَدُ ۝

لَمْ يَلِدْ وَلَمْ يُولَدْ ۝

وَلَمْ يَكُن لَّهُۥ كُفُوًا أَحَدٌ ۝

Transliteration:

Qul huwa Allahu ahad
Allahus Samad
Lam yalid wa lam yoolad
Wa lam ya kullahu kufuwan ahad

Translation of the Meaning:

Say, "He is Allah , [who is] One,
Allah , the Eternal Refuge.
He neither begets nor is born,
Nor is there to Him any equivalent."

Reference: Qur'an, Surah 113 (Al-Falaq), verses 1-5

قُلْ أَعُوذُ بِرَبِّ ٱلْفَلَقِ ﴿١﴾
مِن شَرِّ مَا خَلَقَ ﴿٢﴾
وَمِن شَرِّ غَاسِقٍ إِذَا وَقَبَ ﴿٣﴾
وَمِن شَرِّ ٱلنَّفَّٰثَٰتِ فِى ٱلْعُقَدِ ﴿٤﴾
وَمِن شَرِّ حَاسِدٍ إِذَا حَسَدَ ﴿٥﴾

Transliteration:

Qul a'oodhu birabbil falaq
Min sharri maa khalaq
Wa min sharri ghaasiqin idha waqab
Wa min sharrin naffathaati fil 'uqad
Wa min sharri haasidin idha hasad

Translation of the Meaning:

Say, "I seek refuge in the Lord of daybreak
From the evil of that which He created
And from the evil of darkness when it settles
And from the evil of the blowers in knots
And from the evil of an envier when he envies.

Reference: Qur'an, Surah 114 (An-Nas), verses 1-6

قُلْ أَعُوذُ بِرَبِّ ٱلنَّاسِ ﴿١﴾
مَلِكِ ٱلنَّاسِ ﴿٢﴾
إِلَٰهِ ٱلنَّاسِ ﴿٣﴾
مِن شَرِّ ٱلْوَسْوَاسِ ٱلْخَنَّاسِ ﴿٤﴾
ٱلَّذِي يُوَسْوِسُ فِي صُدُورِ ٱلنَّاسِ ﴿٥﴾
مِنَ ٱلْجِنَّةِ وَٱلنَّاسِ ﴿٦﴾

Transliteration:

Qul aAAoothu bi rabbin naas
Maliki an naas
Ilahi an naas
Min sharril waswaasil khannaas
Alladhee yuwaswisu fee sudoorin naas
Minal jinnati wannaas

Translation of the Meaning:

Say, "I seek refuge in the Lord of mankind,
The Sovereign of mankind.
The God of mankind,
From the evil of the retreating whisperer –
Who whispers [evil] into the breasts of mankind –
From among the jinn and mankind.

Maintaining Regular Athkar and Accessing Resources

To ensure regular practice of Athkar and protection, it is highly beneficial to use accessible tools such as dua apps and pocket-sized books. One such valuable resource is the *Fortress of the Muslim* (Hisnul Muslim), a well-known book that contains a comprehensive collection of authentic supplications for protection and blessings. The book is also available as an app (MY Duaa), allowing you to have the supplications at hand, whether on your phone or in physical form. "Wa Iyyaka Nastaeen" app, is another popular Islamic app developed by Alhuda International, available for both iOS and Android, this ensures that you can engage in Athkar throughout the day, even while on the go, for constant spiritual protection.

You can also consider other trustworthy apps for daily supplications that provide not only the texts but also the correct pronunciations, ensuring that you recite the duas accurately. Some apps even offer features like reminders, allowing you to consistently incorporate these practices into your daily life, reinforcing the spiritual connection with Allah and enhancing the protection over your home and marriage.

The Power of Consistency in Protection

The most important aspect of using Athkar for protection is consistency. By regularly reciting these supplications, not only do you protect your marriage and family from harm, but you also create a habit of mindfulness and gratitude toward Allah. This consistent remembrance keeps the heart connected to Allah, and the home filled with His blessings.

The Prophet Muhammad (ﷺ) emphasized that regular remembrance of Allah strengthens the believer's heart and protects against negative influences. Numerous authentic hadiths highlight that dhikr brings Allah's presence, divine support, and protection from Shaytan.

Abu Hurairah (RA) narrated that the Prophet (ﷺ) said:

> "Allah says: I am as My servant thinks I am, and I am with him when he remembers Me. If he remembers Me in himself, I remember him in Myself. If he remembers Me in a gathering, I remember him in a gathering better than it..." (Sahih al-Bukhari, 7405; Sahih Muslim 2675)

The Prophet (ﷺ) also said:

> "The example of the one who remembers his Lord and the one who does not is like the living and the dead." (Sahih al-Bukhari 6407)

And regarding protection:

> "Recite Ayat al-Kursi… and Allah will appoint a guard for you and no Shaytan will approach you until morning." (Sahih al-Bukhari 2311, narration involving Abu Huraira and the Shaytan)

Through the regular practice of Athkar, the spiritual atmosphere in your home becomes one of peace, love, and harmony. As both partners in marriage consistently engage in this remembrance, they are bound together by a strong spiritual connection that no external force can break.

Conclusion

The practice of Athkar is not merely a routine of words; it is an essential tool for nurturing the sacred relationship of marriage and protecting the family. In Islam, protection from external harm, emotional distress, and spiritual challenges is available through remembrance of Allah. The supplications and practices outlined in the Qur'an and Hadith serve as shields for the heart, mind, and home.

By incorporating these practices into your daily life—whether before leaving or entering the house, before sleeping, or during moments of ease or distress—you invite divine blessings and protection into your home and marriage. Athkar is a means to safeguard your family from the harmful effects of envy, the evil eye, witchcraft, and other negative influences.

Furthermore, in our fast-paced world, utilizing tools such as dua apps and Fortress of the Muslim ensures that these protective supplications are accessible at all times, helping you maintain a regular practice of Athkar and keeping your heart connected to Allah. May Allah protect you, your spouse, and your family, and grant you peace, mercy, and guidance in your marriage.

Chapter Forty-Five

Conclusion: A Heartfelt Reflection on Love, Resilience, and Growth

As you reach the final pages of this book, I hope you can feel the weight and warmth of the journey we've just shared. It has been a labor of love, years in the making, and my deepest hope is that the insights, stories, and lessons woven throughout this text will provide guidance, healing, and inspiration to you—whether you're in a committed relationship, navigating the complexities of courtship, rebuilding after divorce, or simply seeking a deeper understanding of love and its transformative power.

The overarching theme of this book has been the belief that **marriage is not simply a union of two people—it is a dynamic partnership that requires emotional intelligence, resilience, and a shared vision.** A strong, thriving relationship is not built on perfection, but on growth—individual growth, relational growth, and growth in love. This growth comes from emotional awareness, the willingness to communicate openly, and the ability to handle the challenges life throws our way with grace and understanding.

Emotional intelligence, which has been a focal point throughout this book, is more than just a buzzword or a psychological theory—it is the bedrock upon which any healthy relationship is built. It allows us to navigate the ups and downs of marriage, to remain grounded in the face of conflict, and to respond with empathy rather than defensiveness. The Prophet Muhammad (ﷺ) exemplified emotional intelligence in his marriage, showing us that empathy, understanding, and compassion are essential ingredients in maintaining love and harmony. As he famously said, "The best of you are those who are the best to their families." (Tirmidhi)

In the digital age, relationships face new challenges. Technology, social media, and modern courtship can create both opportunities and pitfalls. Yet, at the heart of every successful relationship, it is the human connection that matters most. The ability to communicate deeply, to listen attentively, and to show care and affection in meaningful ways is timeless. In a world where distractions are many, the ability to stay emotionally attuned to our spouse is one of the greatest gifts we can offer.

This book has also delved into the complexities of infidelity, emotional affairs, and toxic in-laws, recognizing that relationships are tested not only by external circumstances but by internal wounds—wounds from childhood, trauma, and past experiences. Healing these wounds takes time, effort, and often the guidance of faith, therapy, and self-reflection. Trauma bonds, narcissistic behaviors, and the deep pain caused by betrayal all have a significant impact on relationships, but they are not the end of the story. **Healing is possible,** and it often begins with acknowledging the pain, seeking support, and committing to the process of recovery.

Moreover, our faith plays an integral role in guiding us through the toughest times. Islam teaches us that Allah's mercy is infinite, and with His help, any challenge can be overcome. The athkar (remembrance of Allah) offers solace and protection, and the Qur'an reminds us of the sacredness of the marital bond:

> "And among His signs is that He created for you from yourselves mates that you may find tranquility in them, and He placed between you affection and mercy." (Qur'an 30:21)

This verse encapsulates the essence of marriage as designed by Allah: a sanctuary of peace, where love and mercy abound. And it is our duty to protect this bond, to honor it, and to nurture it through every season of life.

As I conclude this work, I encourage you to take the insights you've gained and apply them in your relationships. Whether it is improving communication, addressing unmet emotional needs, or healing from past wounds, the goal is to always move forward with intention and care. Remember that relationships require continual effort and that the work we put into them today will yield the rewards of tomorrow. It is not about avoiding conflict, but learning how to navigate it with love, respect, and wisdom.

Let me leave you with a quote from the philosopher Rainer Maria Rilke (1875-1926), who captured the essence of love and partnership so beautifully:

> "Love consists of this: two solitudes that meet, protect, and greet each other."

This is the essence of marriage: two people coming together, as whole individuals, choosing each other every day, amidst the solitude and challenges of life, and protecting one another's hearts.

May this book serve as a guide to healthier, happier relationships. May it inspire you to reflect on the ways you can bring more **empathy, understanding**, and **grace** into your life and the lives of those around you. May it help you navigate the complexities of love and bring healing to countless relationships across the world.

I pray that your relationships be filled with tranquility, affection, and mercy—just as Allah intended.

Qasim Rafique

Sunday, March 30, 2025

1st Shawwal 1446 AH Islamic calendar, marking the celebration of Eid al-Fitr, the festival that concludes the month of Ramadan.

Qasim Rafique
Scottish Relationship Coach

Bibliography

Abu Dawood, Sulaiman bin al-Ash'ath. Sunan Abu Dawood. Translated by Ahmad Hasan. Lahore: Kazi Publications, 1994.

Abu Dawood, 495.

Abu Huraira. Narrated by Abu Huraira, "The best marriage is that upon which the least trouble and expense is bestowed." Sunan Ibn Majah.

Adams, Kenneth M. Silently Seduced: When Parents Make Their Children Partners. Health Communications, 1991.

Ainsworth, Mary D. S. Patterns of Attachment: A Psychological Study of the Strange Situation. Hillsdale, NJ: Erlbaum, 1978.

Al-Bukhari, M. I. Sahih al-Bukhari, Hadith No. 3336.

Al-Bukhari, Muhammad ibn Ismail. Sahih al-Bukhari. Translated by Muhammad Muhsin Khan. Riyadh: Darussalam, 1997.

Al-Ghazali, Abu Hamid. Ihya Ulum al-Din (The Revival of the Religious Sciences). Translated by M. Abul Quasem. Jeddah: King Abdul Aziz University Press, 1983.

Al-Haakim. (n.d.). Hadith on Marriage: The Role of a Righteous Spouse.

Al-Qaradawi, Yusuf. The Lawful and the Prohibited in Islam. 3rd ed. Lahore: Islamic Book Service, 2006.

Al-Qur'an. Surah Ash-Shu'ara, 26:215.

Alao, Adebayo. Gender Relations: Understanding Male and Female Dynamics in the Modern World. Oxford: Oxford University Press, 2021.

Alhuda International. Wa Iyyaka Nastaeen. Alhuda International. Accessed November 26, 2024. https://apps.apple.com/us/app/wa-iyyaka-nastaeen/id1182471102 (iOS) https://www.appbrain.com/app/wa-iyyaka-nastaeen/com.wa.iyyakanastaeen (Android).

American Association for Marriage and Family Therapy (AAMFT). Emotional Neglect and Relationship Dissatisfaction: Causes and Interventions. 2017.

American College of Obstetricians and Gynecologists. FAQs on Pain During Intercourse. Washington, DC: ACOG, 2022.

American Psychological Association. "APA Guidelines for Psychological Practice with Boys and Men." 2018. https://www.apa.org/about/policy/psychological-practice-boys-men.

American Psychological Association. "The American Psychological Association Guidelines for Psychological Practice with Boys and Men." 2018. https://www.apa.org/about/policy/boys-men-practice-guidelines.

Aurelius, Marcus. Meditations. Translated by Gregory Hays. New York: Modern Library, 2002.

Baker, Amy J. L. Parental Alienation Syndrome: A Family Therapy Approach. New York: Routledge, 2007.

Baker, L. A. "The Spiritual and Emotional Disconnect in the Age of Digital Dating: Finding Meaningful Connections Amidst Superficiality." Journal of Spiritual Psychology 12, no. 2 (2019): 82–95.

Baker, M., and D. Oswald. "The Impact of Hookup Culture on Young Adults: Emotional and Psychological Effects." Journal of Adolescent Health 63, no. 5 (2018): 583–590.

Bancroft, Lundy. Why Does He Do That? New York: Berkley Books, 2002.

Barkley, Russell A. Taking Charge of ADHD: The Complete Authoritative Guide for Parents. New York: Guilford Press, 2021.

Berman, Laura. Real Sex for Real Women: Intimacy, Pleasure, and Sexual Wellbeing. New York: Hay House, 2008.

Berman, Laura. The Passion Prescription: Ten Weeks to Your Best Sex—Ever! New York: Hachette Books, 2010.

Bessel van der Kolk, The Body Keeps the Score: Brain, Mind, and Body in the Healing of Trauma. New York: Penguin Books, 2014.

Bessel van der Kolk, Trauma and Recovery: The Aftermath of Violence—From Domestic Abuse to Political Terror. Boston: Beacon Press, 1992.

Better Business Bureau. "Online Dating Scams." Last modified 2021.

Bly, Robert. Iron John: A Book About Men. Reading, MA: Addison-Wesley Publishing Company, 1990.

Bowlby, John. Attachment and Loss: Volume 1. Attachment. New York: Basic Books, 1969.

Brackett, Marc A., and Diana Divecha. "Building Emotional Intelligence in Families and Classrooms." Emotion 16, no. 2 (2016): 233–239.

Brackett, Marc A., Susan E. Rivers, and Peter Salovey. "Emotional Intelligence: Implications for Personal, Social, Academic, and Workplace Success." Social and Personality Psychology Compass 5, no. 1 (2011): 88–103.

Bradberry, Travis, and Jean Greaves. Emotional Intelligence 2.0. San Diego: TalentSmart, 2009.

Bramson, Robert M. Coping with Difficult People. New York: Ballantine Books, 1997.

Breus, Michael J. The Sleep Doctor's Diet Plan: Lose Weight Through Better Sleep. New York: Hachette Books, 2013.

Briden, Lara. Period Repair Manual: Natural Treatment for Better Hormones and Better Periods. Briden Books, 2017.

Brown, Brené. Daring Greatly: How the Courage to Be Vulnerable Transforms the Way We Live, Love, Parent, and Lead. New York: Gotham Books, 2012/2015.

Brown, Brené. The Gifts of Imperfection: Let Go of Who You Think You're Supposed to Be and Embrace Who You Are. Center City, MN: Hazelden Publishing, 2010.

Brown, Jonathan A.C. Misquoting Muhammad: The Challenge and Choices of Interpreting the Prophet's Legacy. London: Oneworld Publications, 2014.

Buehler, Cheryl, and Mary Shinn. "The Role of Communication in Marriage: An Investigation of the Link Between Communication and Marital Satisfaction." Journal of Family Communication 7, no. 2 (2007): 107–27.

Buss, David. The Evolution of Desire: Strategies of Human Mating. New York: Basic Books, 1994.

Butler, M. "Pornography and Infidelity: Exploring the Link." Journal of Sex Research, 2015.

Cacioppo, John T. The Social Brain: Exploring the Dynamics of Social Connectedness. Cambridge: Cambridge University Press, 2018.

Cacioppo, John T., and William Patrick. Loneliness: Human Nature and the Need for Social Connection. New York: W. W. Norton & Company, 2008.

Calm. "Mindfulness Meditation and Relaxation App." Accessed November 27, 2024. https://www.calm.com.

Camus, A. (n.d.). Philosophical Reflections on Companionship.

Carr, Nicholas. The Shallows: What the Internet Is Doing to Our Brains. New York: W. W. Norton & Company, 2010.

Carter, C. Sue. "Neuroendocrine Perspectives on Social Attachment and Love." Psychoneuroendocrinology 23, no. 8 (1998): 779–818.

Carter, Les. When Pleasing You Is Killing Me: How to Break Free from People-Pleasing and Codependency. Deerfield Beach, FL: Health Communications, 2013.

Centers for Disease Control and Prevention (CDC). Sexually Transmitted Disease Surveillance 2019. Last modified 2020. https://www.cdc.gov/std/stats19.

Chapman, G. (1995). The Five Love Languages: How to Express Heartfelt Commitment to Your Mate. Northfield Publishing.

Chapman, Gary. The 5 Love Languages: The Secret to Love that Lasts. Chicago: Northfield Publishing, 1995/1992/2010/2015

Childress, Craig A. Attachment, Trauma, and the Parental Alienation Syndrome: A Preliminary Model of the Trauma of Parental Alienation. Claremont, CA: Claremont Childress Institute, 2015.

Cleveland Clinic. "Erectile Dysfunction: Causes and Treatments." Accessed November 30, 2024. https://my.clevelandclinic.org.

David, Susan. Emotional Agility: Get Unstuck, Embrace Change, and Thrive in Work and Life. New York: Avery, 2016.

Diamond, Lisa M. Sexual Fluidity: Understanding Women's Love and Desire. Cambridge: Harvard University Press, 2008.

Dines, Gail. Pornland: How Porn Has Hijacked Our Sexuality. Boston: Beacon Press, 2010.

"Does Feminism Disempower Men? The Impact of Gender Ideology on Modern Masculinity." The Journal of Men's Studies 22, no. 1 (2014): 45–58.

Dr. Gary L. Thompson, "Understanding Attachment Patterns in Adults." Journal of Clinical Psychology, 2017.

Dr. Gary L. Thompson, Trauma Recovery and Emotional Regulation. Boston: Beacon Press, 2010.

Dr. Harriet Lerner, The Dance of Anger: A Woman's Guide to Changing the Patterns of Intimate Relationships. New York: Harper & Row, 1985.

Dr. Mohammad Al-Hassan. Islamic Psychology and Marriage. London: Islamic Publishing House, 2004.

Dr. Robin L. Smith, "Emotional Healing in Marital Relationships." Psychology Today, 2018.

Drummond, Jessica. The Women's Health Coach: A Guide to Living Well. Austin, TX: Drummond Books, 2020.

Durvasula, Ramani. Should I Stay or Should I Go?: Surviving a Narcissistic Relationship. Oakland, CA: New Harbinger Publications, 2015.

Eggerichs, Emerson. Love & Respect: The Love She Most Desires, the Respect He Desperately Needs. Nashville: Thomas Nelson, 2004.

"Emotionally Focused Therapy: Transforming Couples and Creating Lasting Bonds." Journal of Marital and Family Therapy, 45(1), 85–98.

Emmons, Robert A. Gratitude Works!: A 21-Day Program for Creating Emotional Prosperity. San Francisco: Jossey-Bass, 2013.

Evans, Patricia. The Verbally Abusive Relationship. Oakland, CA: New Harbinger Publications, 2003.

Farley, Melissa. "Prostitution and Trafficking: The Global Impact of Pornography." Journal of Trafficking and Exploitation, 2007.

Farrell, Warren. The Myth of Male Power: Why Men Are the Disposable Sex. New York: Simon & Schuster, 1993.

Feldman Barrett, Lisa. "How Emotions Are Made: The Secret Life of the Brain." Marriage and Family Review 50, no. 5 (2014): 439–58. https://doi.org/10.1080/01494929.2014.915233.

Finkel, Eli J. The All-or-Nothing Marriage: How the Best Marriages Work. New York: Dutton, 2017.

Finkel, Eli J., and Dana R. Carney. "The Role of Commitment in Long-Term Relationships: How Communication Shapes Emotional and Sexual Intimacy." Journal of Social and Personal Relationships 23, no. 5 (2006): 865–87.

Firestone, Lisa. The Self-Esteem Workbook: A Teach Yourself Guide. New York: Teaching Resources, 2009.

Fisher, Helen, Arthur Aron, and Lucy L. Brown. "Romantic Love: A Mammalian Brain System for Mate Choice." Philosophical Transactions of the Royal Society B: Biological Sciences 361, no. 1476 (2006): 2173–2186.

Fisher, Helen. Why We Love: The Nature and Chemistry of Romantic Love. New York: Henry Holt and Company, 2004.

Fogg, B. J. Persuasive Technology: Using Computers to Change What We Think and Do. San Francisco: Morgan Kaufmann, 2003.

Fortress of the Muslim (Hisnul Muslim). Pocket-sized Edition. Translated by Sa'id bin Ali bin Wahf al-Qahṭani. Riyadh: Darussalam Publishers, 2010.

Fortress of the Muslim App. App Store and Google Play.

Forward, Susan. Toxic Parents: Overcoming Their Hurtful Legacy and Reclaiming Your Life. Bantam, 1989.

Freed, J. (2020). The Relationship Fix: Dr. Jennifer Freed on Building Flexible and Thriving Partnerships.

Freed, Jennifer. The Relationship Fix: Dr. Jennifer Freed on Building Flexible and Thriving Partnerships. New York: Sterling Ethos, 2020.

Gabbay, Amos. "The Emotional Health of Men in the Modern World: A Review of Gendered Expectations." Social Psychology Review 45, no. 2 (2016): 130–145.

Glass, Shirley. Not Just Friends: Rebuilding Trust and Recovering Your Sanity After Infidelity. New York: Free Press, 2003.

Glick, Peter, and Susan T. Fiske. "Ambivalent Sexism and Gender Relations: A Social Psychological Perspective." Journal of Personality and Social Psychology 81, no. 2 (2001): 16–20.

Goleman, Daniel. Emotional Intelligence: Why It Can Matter More Than IQ. New York: Bantam Books, 1995.

Gottman Institute. "Emotion Coaching and Relationship Tools." Accessed November 27, 2024. https://www.gottman.com.

Gottman Institute. "Research on Relationship Stability and Infidelity Prevention." Journal of Marital and Family Therapy 43, no. 3 (2017): 297–315.

Gottman Institute. Research on Relationship Stability and Trust. 2021.

Gottman, John M. The Seven Principles for Making Marriage Work. New York: Crown Publishers, 1999.

Gottman, John M., and Nan Silver. What Makes Love Last? How to Build Trust and Avoid Betrayal. New York: Simon & Schuster, 2012.

Gottman, John M., and Robert W. Levenson. The Art and Science of Love: A Research-Based Program for Relationship Enhancement. Washington, DC: American Psychological Association, 2000.

Gottman, John M., Julie Schwartz Gottman, and Doug Abrams. Eight Dates: Essential Conversations for a Lifetime of Love. New York: Workman Publishing, 2018.

Gottman, John, and Robert Levenson. "The Four Horsemen of the Apocalypse: A Tool for Conflict Resolution." Journal of Marriage and Family Therapy 26, no. 3 (2000): 245–56. https://doi.org/10.xxxx.

Gottman, John. Why Marriages Succeed or Fail: And How You Can Make Yours Last. New York: Simon & Schuster, 1994.

Gottman, Julie, and John Gottman. 10 Principles for Doing Effective Couples Therapy. New York: W. W. Norton & Company, 2015.

Grandin, Temple. Thinking in Pictures: My Life with Autism. New York: Vintage, 2006.

Gray, John. Men Are from Mars, Women Are from Venus: A Practical Guide for Improving Communication and Getting What You Want in Your Relationships. New York: HarperCollins, 1992.

Hadith: Sahih al-Bukhari, Hadith No. 5063; Sahih Muslim, Hadith No. 1467.

Hallowell, Edward M., and John J. Ratey. "Attention-Deficit Disorder in Adults: A Neurological Perspective." Journal of Clinical Psychology 47, no. 6 (1991): 724–28. https://doi.org/10.1002/1097-4679(199111).

Harman, Jennifer. "Parental Alienation and the Child's Relationship with Their Parents." Journal of Family Psychology, 2016.

Harriet Lerner, The Dance of Connection: How to Talk to Someone When You're Mad, Hurt, Scared, Frustrated, Insulted, Betrayed, or Desperate. New York: HarperCollins, 2001.

Harriet Lerner, The Dance of Intimacy: A Woman's Guide to Courageous Acts of Change in Key Relationships. New York: Harper & Row, 1989.

Harris, Tristan. "How a Handful of Tech Companies Control Billions of Minds Every Day." TED Talk, 2018.

Harvard Medical School Sleep Center. "Sleep and Health." Accessed November 30, 2024. https://www.health.harvard.edu/sleep.

Haselton, Martie. "Ovulation and Human Behavior: A Research Review." Hormones and Behavior 51, no. 5 (2007): 123–33.

Health Psychology. "Emotional Stress and Its Effect on Health: Inflammation, Sleep, and Wound Healing." Health Psychology 27, no. 2 (2008): 187–96.

Heller, R. S. F., & Levine, A. (2010). Attached: The New Science of Adult Attachment and How It Can Help You Find—and Keep—Love. TarcherPerigee.

Hendriksen, Ellen. How to Be Yourself: Quiet Your Inner Critic and Rise Above Social Anxiety. New York: St. Martin's Press, 2018.

Hendrix, Harville, and Helen Lakelly Hunt. Getting the Love You Want: A Guide for Couples. New York: St. Martin's Griffin, 1988.

Herman, Judith. Trauma and Recovery: The Aftermath of Violence—From Domestic Abuse to Political Terror. New York: Basic Books, 1992/1997

Hertlein, Katherine M. "Digital Dating and the Infiltration of Hookup Culture: Examining the Role of Technology in Relationships." Journal of Marital and Family Therapy 42, no. 2 (2016): 220-232.

hips.New York: Harper & Row, 1989.

Holt-Lunstad, Julianne, Timothy B. Smith, and Jillian B. Layton. "Social Relationships and Mortality Risk: A Meta-analytic Review." PLOS Medicine 7, no. 7 (2010): e1000316.

Huffington, Arianna. The Sleep Revolution: Transforming Your Life, One Night at a Time. New York: Harmony, 2016.

Hussain, Asim. "Muslim Women: Shaping Gender Norms and Reshaping Feminist Discourse in Islam." Journal of Islamic Studies 19, no. 4 (2016): 205–222.

Hyman, Mark. Food: What the Heck Should I Eat? New York: Little, Brown Spark, 2017.

Ibn Majah, Muhammad. Sunan Ibn Majah. Translated by Muhammad Tufail. Riyadh: Darussalam, 1998.

Ibn Majah. (n.d.). Sunan Ibn Majah, Book 9, Hadith 1979. "The best of you are those who are best to their families."

Ibn Qayyim al-Jawziyyah. Al-Wabil al-Sayyib (The Goodly and Beneficial). Translated by Muhammad Taqi-ud-Din al-Hilali. Riyadh: Dar al-Salam, 1995.

Ibn Taymiyyah, Ahmad. Al-Fatawa al-Kubra (The Major Fatwas). Cairo: Al-Maktaba al-Tawfiqiya, 2005.

Imam Muslim, Muslim bin al-Hajjaj. Sahih Muslim. Translated by Nasiruddin al-Khattab. Riyadh: Darussalam Publishers, 1997.

Islamic Dua App (Various Sources).

Islamic Research Foundation International. "Women in Islam: The Status and Rights of Women in Islam." 2008. https://www.irfi.org.

IslamQA. "Ruling on Plural Marriage." Last modified October 6, 2006. Accessed December 14, 2024. https://islamqa.info/en/answers/49044/ruling-on-plural-marriage.

Iyengar, Sheena S. The Art of Choosing. New York: Twelve, 2010.

Jackson, C. R., and C. H. Spangler. "Romantic Vulnerability in the Digital Age: Exploring the Psychological and Emotional Costs of Online Dating." Psychological Bulletin 146, no. 6 (2020): 438–455.

Jamison, Kay Redfield. An Unquiet Mind: A Memoir of Moods and Madness. New York: Vintage Books, 1995.

John K. Pollard, The Father Wound: A Guide to Healing for Men and Women. San Francisco: New Harbinger Publications, 2005.

Johnson, Sue. Hold Me Tight: Seven Conversations for a Lifetime of Love. New York: Little, Brown and Company, 2008.

Johnson, Susan M. "Emotionally Focused Therapy: Transforming Couples and Creating Lasting Bonds." Journal of Marital and Family Therapy 45, no. 1 (2019): 85–98.

Johnson, Susan M. The Practice of Emotionally Focused Therapy: Creating Connection. New York: Routledge, 2004.

Journal of Applied Social Psychology. "The Effects of Phone Use at Night on Sleep and Stress Levels." Journal of Applied Social Psychology 47, no. 5 (2017): 421–429.

Journal of Marital and Family Therapy, 2010

Journal of Relationship Research. "Various Studies on Mindfulness, Exercise, and Stress Management within Romantic Relationships." 35, no. 2 (2018): 45–58.

Journal of Social and Personal Relationships. "Smartphone Use and Relationship Communication: Effects on Intimacy and Emotional Connection." Journal of Social and Personal Relationships 36, no. 2 (2019): 150–167.

Journal of Social and Personal Relationships. "The Impact of Phone Use on Relationship Quality." Journal of Social and Personal Relationships 36, no. 2 (2017): 123–134.

Karim, Abdul S. Islamic Marriage and the Family: Theories, Practices, and Realities. 2nd ed. London: Islamic Publications, 2007.

Kassam, Z., and A. Hussain. "Matrimonial Apps and Their Role in the Muslim Community: A Study of Cultural, Religious, and Emotional Considerations." Journal of Islamic Studies and Technology 22, no. 3 (2018): 104–112.

Khalil, Saeed. The Islamic Perspective on Conflict Resolution in Marriage. Cairo: Al-Mu'awwida Press, 2020.

Khan, Ahmad. "Sexual Liberation and Its Psychological Impact on Young Women: A Review." Journal of Adolescent Psychology 34, no. 7 (2015): 125–138.

Kierkegaard, Søren. Journals and Papers. Edited and translated by Howard V. Hong and Edna H. Hong. Princeton, NJ: Princeton University Press, 1967.

Kimmel, Michael. Guyland: The Perilous World Where Boys Become Men. New York: HarperCollins Publishers, 2008.

Kimmel, Michael S. Angry White Men: American Masculinity at the End of an Era. New York: Nation Books, 2013.

Layden, Mary Anne. "The Trauma of Pornography: Understanding the Psychological Impact of Exposure." Journal of Sexual Trauma, 2014.

Lefkowitz, Eva S., and Megan Vasilenko. "Positive and Negative Outcomes of Sexual Behavior among College Students: Gender Comparisons and Perceived Peer Norms." Archives of Sexual Behavior 43, no. 3 (2014): 497–507.

Lembke, Anna. Dopamine Nation: Finding Balance in the Age of Indulgence. New York: Penguin Press, 2021.

Lerner, H. (1989). The Dance of Anger: A Woman's Guide to Changing the Patterns of Intimate Relationships. HarperCollins.

Lerner, Harriet. The Dance of Intimacy: A Woman's Guide to Courageous Acts of Change in Key Relationships. New York: Harper & Row, 1989.

Levine, Amir, and Rachel Heller. Attached: The New Science of Adult Attachment and How It Can Help You Find—and Keep—Love. New York: TarcherPerigee, 2010.

Levine, Peter A. "Somatic Experiencing: Resolving Trauma in the Body." Journal of Traumatic Stress 12, no. 3 (1999): 67–75.

Levine, Peter. Waking the Tiger: Healing Trauma. Berkeley: North Atlantic Books, 1997.

Lieberson, Stanley. "Gender, Sexuality, and Power in Contemporary Feminist Movements." Feminist Studies 30, no. 3 (2004): 12–26.

Love, Patricia, and Jo Robinson. The Emotional Incest Syndrome: What to Do When a Parent's Love Rules Your Life. Bantam Books, 1990.

Maher, Richard. "Toxic Masculinity and the Red Pill: A Study in Misguided Ideology." Psychological Research Quarterly 32, no. 2 (2019): 99–111.

Main, Mary, and Judith Solomon. "Procedures for Identifying Infants as Disorganized/Disoriented During the Ainsworth Strange Situation." Infant Mental Health Journal 11, no. 3 (1990): 146–56.

Mark, Gabriel. "The Impact of Smartphones on Attention and Productivity." Journal of Experimental Psychology 21, no. 3 (2015): 211–222.

Maslow, Abraham H. "A Theory of Human Motivation." Psychological Review 50, no. 4 (1943): 370–396.

Mattson, Ingrid. The Story of the Qur'an: Its History and Place in Muslim Life. Malden, MA: Wiley-Blackwell, 2008.

Mayer, John D., and Peter Salovey. "What is Emotional Intelligence?" In Emotional Development and Emotional Intelligence: Educational Implications, edited by Peter Salovey and David Sluyter, 3–31. New York: Basic Books, 1997.

McBride, Karyl. Will I Ever Be Free of You? How to Heal from a Toxic Relationship with a Narcissist. New York: Atria Books, 2016.

Merzenich, Michael. Soft-Wired: How the New Science of Brain Plasticity Can Change Your Life. New York: Parnassus Press, 2013.

Mikulincer, Mario, and Phillip R. Shaver. Attachment in Adulthood: Structure, Dynamics, and Change. New York: Guilford Press, 2007.

Miller, Elizabeth. "The Myth of Multitasking: How Juggling Multiple Tasks at Once Hinders Productivity." MIT Technology Review, October 4, 2005.

Miller, Jean Baker. Toward a New Psychology of Women. Boston: Beacon Press, 1976.

Miller, Ryan. "The Rise of Radical Feminism and Its Social Impact." Gender Studies Review 13, no. 3 (2018): 210–227.

MoodMeter. "Track Your Emotions Daily." Accessed November 27, 2024. https://www.moodmeterapp.com.

Muhammad (ﷺ). Sahih Bukhari, Book of Jumu'ah, Hadith 893.

Murad, Abdal Hakim. Travelling Home: Essays on Islam in Europe. Cambridge: Quilliam Press, 2020.

Murad, Abdal Hakim. "Sexual Ethics and Modern Confusion." *Cambridge Muslim College*. May 27, 2012.

National Domestic Violence Hotline. "Understanding Abuse." Accessed November 30, 2024. https://www.thehotline.org.

National Institutes of Health (NIH). "Early Maternal Neglect and Emotional Attachment: A Long-Term Study." Published 2016.

National Institutes of Health (NIH). "Long-Term Effects of Maternal Absence." Psychological Bulletin, 2015.

Neff, Kristin. "The Science of Self-Compassion." Accessed November 30, 2024. https://self-compassion.org.

Newport, Cal. Digital Minimalism: Choosing a Focused Life in a Noisy World. New York: Penguin Press, 2019.

Northrup, Christiane. Women's Bodies, Women's Wisdom: Creating Physical and Emotional Health and Healing. New York: Bantam Books, 1994.

Nussbaum, Martha C. Creating Capabilities: The Human Development Approach. Cambridge: Harvard University Press, 2011.

Omar, Khaled. "The Concept of Sadaqah in Islamic Marriage." Islamic Journal of Family Studies 12, no. 1 (2015): 72–85.

Orbuch, Terri. Five Simple Steps to Take Your Marriage from Good to Great. New York: Delacorte Press, 2009.

Perel, Esther. "Understanding Emotional Affairs: The Psychology Behind Infidelity." Journal of Couples Therapy 35, no. 4 (2015): 229–245.

Perel, Esther. Mating in Captivity: Unlocking Erotic Intelligence. New York: HarperCollins, 2006.

Perel, Esther. The State of Affairs: Rethinking Infidelity. New York: Harper, 2017.

Pew Research Center. "How Smartphones Affect Attention and Productivity." Pew Research Center, 2020. https://www.pewresearch.org.

Prager, Karen J. Love and Marriage: A Guide to Communication in Couples. New York: Routledge, 2010.

Psychology Today. "The Impact of Phone Addiction on Relationships." Psychology Today, 2019. https://www.psychologytoday.com/articles/phone-addiction-relationships.

Qadhi, Yasir. A Thematic Commentary on the Qur'an. Leicester: Kube Publishing, 2019.

Qur'an, Surah Al-Baqarah, 2:187.

Qur'an, Surah An-Nisa (4:19).

Qur'an, Surah Ar-Rum (30:21).

Qur'an. Surah Al-Baqarah (2:187): "Your wives are a garment for you, and you are a garment for them."

Qur'an. Surah Al-Baqarah (2:19).

Qur'an. Surah Al-Baqarah 2:255.

Qur'an. Surah Al-Baqarah 2:285-286.

Qur'an. Surah Al-Falaq 113.

Qur'an. Surah Al-Furqan 25:74.

Qur'an. Surah Al-Isra (17:53): "And tell My servants to say that which is best…"

Qur'an. Surah An-Nas 114.

Qur'an. Surah An-Nisa (4:19): "And live with them in kindness…"

Qur'an. Surah Ar-Rum (30:21): "And of His signs is that He created for you from yourselves mates that you may find tranquility in them; and He placed between you affection and mercy."

Qur'an. Surah Muhammad: 22–23.

Qur'an. The Noble Qur'an. Surah An-Nisa (4:19, 4:34); Surah Ar-Rum (30:21).

Qur'an. The Noble Qur'an. Translated by Saheeh International. Riyadh: Darussalam, 1997.

Qur'an. Translated by Abdullah Yusuf Ali. Elmhurst, NY: Tahrike Tarsile Qur'an, 2000.

Qur'an. Translated by Abdullah Yusuf Ali. London: Wordsworth Editions, 2000.

Raza, Shahid. "The Role of Family and Faith in Modern Muslim Courtship." Journal of Islamic Psychology and Society 5, no. 2 (2013): 45–60.

Rilke, Rainer Maria. Letters to a Young Poet. Translated by M. D. Herter Norton. New York: Norton, 1934.

Robin L. Smith, Hungry: The Truth About Being Full. New York: Hachette Books, 2012.

Robin L. Smith, Lies at the Altar: The Truth About Great Marriages. New York: Hyperion, 2006.

Robinson, T. A., and L. B. Smith. "Predators in the Digital Age: Scams and Deceptive Practices in Online Matrimony." International Journal of Human-Computer Interaction 34, no. 9 (2017): 733–745.

Rogers, Carl R. On Becoming a Person: A Therapist's View of Psychotherapy. Boston: Houghton Mifflin, 1961.

Rosenberg, Marshall B. Nonviolent Communication: A Language of Life. Encinitas, CA: PuddleDancer Press, 2003.

Rusbult, Caryl E., and Paul A. M. Van Lange. "Interdependence, Interaction, and Relationships." Annual Review of Psychology 54, no. 1 (2003): 351–75.

Sahih Bukhari. (n.d.). Book 73, Hadith 47. "Whoever believes in Allah and the Last Day should honor his guest."

Sahih Bukhari. Hadith 2, Book 72, Hadith 829.

Sahih al-Bukhari. Hadith 5189

Sahih Muslim. (n.d.). Book 26, Hadith 5522. "There is no [ill] omen, only good omens."

Sahih Muslim. Book 8, Hadith 3362.

Sahih Muslim. Hadith 2439.

Salovey, Peter, and John D. Mayer. "Emotional Intelligence." Imagination, Cognition, and Personality 9, no. 3 (1990): 185–211.

Sapolsky, Robert. Why Zebras Don't Get Ulcers: The Acclaimed Guide to Stress, Stress-Related Diseases, and Coping. 3rd ed. New York: Holt Paperbacks, 2004.

Sarkis, Stephanie. Gaslighting: Recognize Manipulative and Emotionally Abusive People—and Break Free. Boston: Da Capo Lifelong Books, 2018.

Savin-Williams, Ritch C. "Sexual Fluidity and the Psychology of Same-Sex Attraction in Adolescents." Journal of Youth and Adolescence 38, no. 7 (2009): 1003–1016.

Schaeffer, D. J., and A. E. Nisen. "The Disconnect: How Casual Encounters in the Digital Era Are Redefining Intimacy." International Review of Social Psychology 45, no. 1 (2019): 21–39.

Schirato, Tony, and Jen Webb. The Sociology of Conflict and Cooperation. London: Sage Publications, 2003.

Schnarch, David. Intimacy and Desire: Awaken the Passion in Your Relationship. New York: Routledge, 2009.

Schnarch, David. Passionate Marriage: Keeping Love and Intimacy Alive in Committed Relationships. New York: W. W. Norton & Company, 1997.

Schwartz, Barry. The Paradox of Choice: Why More Is Less. New York: HarperCollins, 2004.

Schwartz, Jeffrey M., and Rebecca Gladding. You Are Not Your Brain: The 4-Step Solution for Changing Bad Habits, Ending Unhealthy Thinking, and Taking Control of Your Life. New York: Avery, 2011.

Shaver, Phillip R., and Cindy Hazan. "A Behavioral Paradigm for Dating and Marital Interaction." Journal of Social and Personal Relationships 4, no. 2 (1987): 123–45.

Shaykh Abd al-Rahman al-Sa'di. Tafseer al-Sa'di. Riyadh: Dar Ibn al-Jawzi, 2000.

Siegel, Daniel J. The Whole-Brain Child: 12 Revolutionary Strategies to Nurture Your Child's Developing Mind. New York: Delacorte Press, 2011.

Siegel, Daniel J., and Tina Payne Bryson. The Power of Showing Up: How Parental Presence Shapes Who Our Kids Become and How Their Brains Get Wired. New York: Ballantine Books, 2020.

Simmons, Janet A. The Gendered Society. New York: Oxford University Press, 2002.

Skinner, K. "Pornography Addiction and Relationships: A Psychological Perspective." Journal of Sexual Addiction and Compulsivity, 2013.

Smith, Erin A., and Laura M. Brown. "Women and Men: Breaking Down the Gender Divide in Society and Relationships." Feminist Psychologist Journal 47, no. 6 (2019): 110–124.

Smith, J. "The Impact of Pornography on Sexual Relationships: A Therapeutic Approach." Journal of Sexual Health, 2012.

Snyder, Douglas K., Anthony M. Castellani, and Mark A. Whisman. "Current Status and Future Directions in Couple Therapy." Annual Review of Psychology 57 (2006): 317–344.

Snyder, Mark, and Nancy Cantor. "The Role of Gender Norms in Sexual Behavior and Emotional Well-being." Journal of Social and Personal Relationships 31, no. 2 (2014): 182–197.

Socrates. (n.d.). Philosophical Wisdom: Knowing Thyself.

Solomon, Alexandra. Loving Bravely: Twenty Lessons of Self-Discovery to Help You Get the Love You Want. Oakland, CA: New Harbinger Publications, 2017.

Sparrow, B., J. Liu, and D. M. Wegner. "Google Effects on Memory: Cognitive Consequences of Having Information at Our Fingertips." Science 333, no. 6043 (2011): 776–778.

Spring, Janis Abrahms. After the Affair: Healing the Pain and Rebuilding Trust When a Partner Has Been Unfaithful. Harper Perennial, 2007.1997

"Study on Phone Use and Relationship Satisfaction." Computers in Human Behavior 85 (2018): 231–238.

Suleiman, Omar. "Faith and Fidelity: Upholding Islamic Values in Modern Relationships." Yaqeen Institute, 2022.

Sunan Abu Dawood, Book 28, Hadith 3535.

Sunan Abu Dawood. Book 11, Hadith 2125.

Sunan Abu Dawood. Translated by Ahmad Hasan. Riyadh: Darussalam, 1999. Hadith 2135.

Sunan Abu Dawud, Hadith 2578 (authenticated by scholars like Al-Albani in Sahih Sunan Abi Dawud).

Sunan al-Tirmidhi, Hadith 1162: "The best of you are those who are best to their families."

Sunan al-Tirmidhi. Hadith 1977: "A true believer does not taunt, curse, abuse, or speak indecently."

Sunan al-Tirmidhi. Hadith 3895: "The best of you are those who are best to their families."

Sunan al-Tirmidhi. Translated by Abu Khaliyl. Riyadh: Darussalam, 2007. Hadith 1162.

Sunan Ibn Majah. Hadith 1927: "None of you should fall upon his wife like an animal; let there first be a messenger between you."

Tafsir Ibn Kathir. Exegesis of the Holy Qur'an.

Tannen, Deborah. You Just Don't Understand: Women and Men in Conversation. New York: William Morrow, 1990.

Tariq, Muhammad. "Islamic Teachings on Women's Rights: A Comprehensive Overview." Islamic Studies Journal 45, no. 3 (2020): 45–58.

Temple Grandin Official Website. "Autism and Thinking Styles." Last modified October 20, 2024. https://templegrandin.com.

The Archives of Sexual Behavior. "The Connection Between Sleep and Sexual Satisfaction." 50, no. 3 (2021): 577–88.

The Journal of Social and Personal Relationships. "The Emotional Impact of Dating Apps: Superficiality and Self-Esteem." The Journal of Social and Personal Relationships 32, no. 4 (2015): 645–665.

The Journal of Social and Personal Relationships. "The Relationship Between Sleep and Emotional Closeness." 34, no. 6 (2017): 12–25.

The Lancet. "The Impact of Gender Equality on National Health and Economic Prosperity." The Lancet Global Health 8, no. 5 (2020): 112–118.

Thomas, Kenneth W. Conflict and Negotiation Processes in Organizations. Thousand Oaks, CA: Sage Publications, 1992.

Thompson, Mark. "Exploring Sexual Freedom: The Social and Psychological Consequences of Casual Sex." Social Psychology Quarterly 81, no. 4 (2018): 234–249.

Tirmidhi, Abu Isa. Sunan al-Tirmidhi. Hadith 2612.

Tirmidhi, Abu Isa. Sunan al-Tirmidhi. The Best of You Are Those Who Are Best to Their Women.

Tirmidhi, Abu Isa. The Best of You Are Those Who Are Best to Their Women. Accessed from various online Islamic resources.

Tirmidhi, Abu Isa. The Book of Marriage, Hadith 3280. Translated by Rashid Raza.

Turkle, Sherry. Reclaiming Conversation: The Power of Talk in a Digital Age. New York: Penguin Press, 2015.

Twenge, Jean M. iGen: Why Today's Super-Connected Kids Are Growing Up Less Rebellious, More Tolerant, Less Happy—and Completely Unprepared for Adulthood. New York: Atria Books, 2017.

University of Texas. Device-Free Activities Boost Relationship Satisfaction. Austin: University of Texas Press, 2019.

van der Kolk, Bessel A. The Body Keeps the Score: Brain, Mind, and Body in the Healing of Trauma. New York: Viking, 2014.

van der Kolk, Bessel. The Body Keeps the Score: Brain, Mind, and Body in the Healing of Trauma. New York: Viking, 2014.

Vohs, Kathleen D. "The Psychology of Sexual Behavior: Impact of Casual Sex on Psychological Health." Journal of Personality and Social Psychology, 2014.

Voon, Valerie. "Pornography Addiction and Its Neurobiological Effects: Understanding the Impact on the Brain." Journal of Neuroscience Research, 2014.

Vrangalova, Zhana, and John L. Paul. "Hooking Up and Psychological Well-Being in College Students: Short-Term Prospective Links Across Different Hookup Definitions." Journal of Sex Research 51, no. 1 (2014): 44–54.

Wade, Lisa. American Hookup: The New Culture of Sex on Campus. New York: W. W. Norton & Company, 2017.

Walker, Matthew. Why We Sleep: The New Science of Sleep and Dreams. New York: Scribner, 2017.

Wallin, David J. Attachment in Psychotherapy. New York: Guilford Press, 2007.

Warshak, Richard A. Parental Alienation: The Handbook for Mental Health and Legal Professionals. Springfield, IL: Charles C. Thomas, 2010.

Wilson, Gary. "The Neuroscience of Porn Addiction." Accessed November 30, 2024. https://www.yourbrainonporn.com.

Wilson, Gary. Your Brain on Porn: Internet Pornography and the Emerging Science of Addiction. Cambridge: Commonwealth Publishing, 2014.

Young, Larry J., and Thomas R. Insel. "The Neurobiology of Pair Bonding." Nature Neuroscience 7, no. 10 (2004): 1048–54.

Ziegler, Sheryl. Mommy Burnout: How to Reclaim Your Life and Raise Healthier Children in the Process. New York: Harper Wave, 2018.